Social Geographies

Social Geographies

An Introduction

THE NEWCASTLE SOCIAL GEOGRAPHIES COLLECTIVE

ROWMAN & LITTLEFIELD

Lanham • Boulder • New York • London

Published by Rowman & Littlefield
An imprint of The Rowman & Littlefield Publishing Group, Inc.
4501 Forbes Boulevard, Suite 200, Lanham, Maryland 20706
www.rowman.com

6 Tinworth Street, London SE11 5AL, United Kingdom

Copyright © 2021 by The Newcastle Social Geographies Collective

British Library Cataloguing in Publication Information Available

ISBN: HB: 978-1-78661-229-8
       PB: 978-1-78661-230-4

Library of Congress Cataloging-in-Publication Data
Names: Newcastle Social Geographies Collective, author.
Title: Social geographies : an introduction / The Newcastle Social
  Geographies Collective.
Description: Lanham, Maryland : Rowman & Littlefield, 2020. | Includes
  bibliographical references and index. | Summary: 'This book provides a
  round-up of the state of the sub-discipline of social geography, capture
  recent themes and directions, and chart new questions and challenges for
  theory, politics and practice'— Provided by publisher.
Identifiers: LCCN 2020026531 (print) | LCCN 2020026532 (ebook) | ISBN
  9781786612298 (cloth) | ISBN 9781786612304 (paperback) | ISBN
  9781786612311 (epub)
Subjects: LCSH: Human geography.
Classification: LCC GF41 .N49 2020 (print) | LCC GF41 (ebook) | DDC
  304.2—dc23
LC record available at https://lccn.loc.gov/2020026531
LC ebook record available at https://lccn.loc.gov/2020026532

*We dedicate this book to all who study social geographies,
past, present and future.*

CONTENTS

ACKNOWLEDGEMENTS

WE WOULD LIKE TO ACKNOWLEDGE all of those who have enabled this book to reach publication. All of the contributors are members of the Newcastle Social Geographies Collective, with most either affiliated with the Geographies of Social Change Research Cluster within Geography or based in neighbouring subject areas within Newcastle University. Our approach has been deliberately inclusive, and doctoral students, early career researchers and established academics have contributed to the collection. Some have moved on to new positions at other universities but remain affiliated with the collective.

One of the largest and most dynamic group of social geographers in the world, we are committed to agenda-setting research that addresses spatial and social inequalities, explores the geographies of justice and illuminates the spaces of everyday life. Our work highlights disparities in wealth, health, violence, living conditions and life chances. It engages and analyses the many sites, scales and dimensions of disadvantage and discrimination that undermine the social and ethical fabric on which human well-being depends.

We thank all of the contributors who took the time to write and to review each other's chapters, especially in the face of other pressing demands of teaching, administration, writing and research. Rachel Pain and Peter Hopkins edited the overall collection.

We are also very grateful to Alison Williamson for her outstanding proofreading skills and to Gurdeep Mattu for his encouragement and support.

INTRODUCTIONS

CHAPTER — 1

Creating More Social Geographies

Newcastle Social Geographies Collective

THE RELEVANCE OF SOCIAL GEOGRAPHIES

We write this book as a collective of forty staff, postgraduates and undergraduates at Newcastle University in the United Kingdom. Most of us work in geography at Newcastle and are affiliated with the Geographies of Social Change Research Cluster, whereas some contributors are in sociology, planning and health research. For those of us in these last three disciplines, it is sometimes clearer to the general public what it is that we research – saying that you are a geographer still raises eyebrows and assumptions about naming capital cities and colouring in land-use maps. Yet, for all of us, social geographies is an area of study with enormous relevance to current-day events; we see this every day in the world outside our offices, on the news and in our fieldwork, our activism and our daily lives.

Put most simply, social geographies is the study of the inter-relationships between society and space. 'Space' is not simply a territory to be portioned up and mapped, nor a container of people and processes, nor the backdrop to more interesting things happening in society. Space does not have a set of fixed characteristics, and neither do the diverse groups of people who inhabit space. Instead, both spaces and social categories are fluid, their meanings continually shifting and being contested and remade. Today in social geography, society and space are considered to have a co-constitutive relationship, meaning that each is continually producing and changing the other (Little, 2014; Valentine, 2001).

Social geographers are interested in how this is manifested in large-scale processes, as well as in how it plays out in particular sites. We often refer to these sites as 'places', as opposed to 'space', which describes wider and more abstract dimensions, areas, positions and relations (Gieseking & Mangold, 2014). However, by the late twentieth century, geographers no longer viewed places as separate, distinct or bounded (Massey, 1995). Rather, both space and place involve shifting, stretching and mobile sets of relations, processes and interactions (see Text Box 1.1).

TEXT BOX 1.1 | Doreen Massey

Doreen Massey was a professor at the Open University in the United Kingdom. Her work on conceptualising space and place was hugely influential in human geography. In suggesting the idea of 'a global sense of place', her work identified that processes and relations operating at a range of spatial scales come together in diverse ways to create experiences of place. Places are both subjective (they can be experienced very differently by individuals) and the result of uneven 'power geometries' (there are common processes that create material inequalities between and within places) (Massey, 1991a).

Take one example from Rachel's recent research on social housing (Pain, 2019). Working in collaboration with local residents and artists, her team researched the auction of over 150 social housing properties on just a few streets in a former coal-mining village in County Durham, North East England. This housing had been available to families on low incomes at below-market rents for decades. But recent changes to national housing policy, and the removal of regulations and protections for those in most housing need in favour of 'market solutions', led to a situation where these properties were suddenly put up for auction. All were purchased by private owners, some then to be rented privately at market rates but many to remain unoccupied. This took place at a time when homelessness in England had been rising rapidly and hundreds of thousands of people were on local authority waiting lists for a dwindling supply of social housing. Rachel's research analysed how the particular place within which these streets of housing sit – in terms of the built environment, community, economic and social history, sense of place, and emotional and intergenerational attachments – intersects with the changing national and global processes that are shaping spatial housing patterns in the United Kingdom (Pain, 2019).

FIGURE 1.1
Social housing home in County Durham. (Credit: Carl Joyce; see carljoyce.com)

Another example comes from Peter's work with ethnic and religious minority young people on their everyday negotiations of place, politics and identity (e.g., Hopkins et al., 2017). The work took place in Scotland during the 2014 Scottish independence referendum (Botterill et al., 2016); this spatial context is important in and of itself, but also because the vote was opened to include sixteen- and seventeen-year-olds (Hopkins, 2015). The team conducted focus groups and interviews with 382 young people from a diverse range of ethnic and religious minority backgrounds, including Muslims, South Asian non-Muslims (e.g., Sikhs and Hindus), refugees and asylum seekers, international students, Central and Eastern European migrants, and White Scottish young people. A key finding was about young people's experiences of misrecognition, particularly their experiences of being mistaken for being Muslim, which led young people from diverse ethnic and religious backgrounds to become targets for Islamophobia. These incidences of misrecognition tended to take place at school, in taxis, at airports and in public spaces. Geopolitical issues and their coverage in the media, stereotypes about the 'Asian' community and the lack of visibility offered to non-Muslim ethnic and religious minority groups all worked to construct the participants as Muslim. Young people responded in diverse ways, such as through using humour, clarifying their religious faith, ignoring the situation or withdrawing from social interactions. The research shows how racism and religious intolerance work to marginalise people in this particular context and how addressing misrecognition requires institutional changes to ensure full participation in society.

FIGURE 1.2

Scottish Muslims. (Credit: Mohammed Hussain, c/o Alwaleed Centre, www.alwaleed. ed.ac.uk)

To summarise, the most important premise of social geographies is that understanding space is fundamental to understanding society (and vice versa). While this is, of course, a common feature of human geography more generally, social geographers focus on the implications of this relationship for social identities, social reproduction, social inequalities and social justice. While there are various theoretical approaches (Chapter 2) and methodological strategies (Chapter 3) by which we might undertake this exploration, if there is one thing we want you to take from this book, it is that social geographies is not an academic subfield that spends its time secluded in an ivory tower. It is an area of study that is relevant, useful and timely, helping us to ask questions and to understand yet also to engage with and contribute to changing the world around us. As we write this book, events going on around the world highlight the continuing relevance of the topics that the book touches upon – from the social ramifications of Brexit for the United Kingdom to the further exclusion of people through damaging welfare reforms, freedom protests in Hong Kong, the water crisis in India, protests about climate change and environmental degradation, increasing levels of hate crime and the escalating stigmatisation of refugees seeking safety in Europe, the everyday impacts of border politics in the United States, and the harshly unequal impacts of COVID-19. And social geographies is expanding its fields of analysis – the range of topics in this book far exceeds that of earlier texts.

WHAT IS SOCIAL GEOGRAPHIES?

Social, Plus . . .

Encompassing a rich, diverse and dynamic set of topics, social geographies is a large branch or subdiscipline of human geography. While it has some distinctive features, it is not a neatly bounded set of approaches or subject matter. It also differs around the world, from textbook to textbook, from university to university and from lecturer to lecturer, as we shall see a bit later in this chapter.

Traditionally, human geography has been divided up into a number of subdisciplines, some of which have endured for over a century. It may be the case that your own geography degree is parcelled up into these distinct strands. In the United Kingdom, where we write from, these most commonly include social, economic and political geography, and what is often called development geography, and then additional options such as cultural geography, environmental geography, historical geography and so on. However, it is increasingly the case that this method of portioning up the discipline to teach it no longer accurately reflects the research that geographers do. For example, the work of Linda McDowell (Text Box 1.2) demonstrates the co-constitution and codependence of social and economic processes. Equally, ideas, topics and methods once considered the territory of social geographies have seeped out into political geography, and vice versa. For example, political geographers' recent interest in the everyday as a scale and subject of analysis has long been a central tenet in social geographies (see Chapter 5 on scale). However, participatory research methods have moved from their early use in development geographies into social geographies, where they have become a popular mode of research with communities in the Global North to better understand the problems they face (see Chapter 3 on researching social geographies).

The boundaries of our conventional subdisciplines may often be the most productive places to do research, and exciting and innovative work is taking place across the margins of social, political, economic, development, environmental and physical geographies.

TEXT BOX 1.2 | Linda McDowell

Linda McDowell is an emeritus professor at the University of Oxford in the United Kingdom. She is an economic and social geographer who has worked extensively on the intersections of class and gender in labour markets and processes. Her book *Capital Culture* exposed the common everyday discriminatory practices based on sexism, racism and class privilege that govern who works in the finance sector in the City of London and what their workplace experiences are (McDowell, 1997).

This is especially the case as geographers focus on the largest and most complex issues facing human societies, such as climate change, energy and migration. We are sure that you can think of other issues that require social/economic, social/political, social/development or social/environmental analysis, or multiple combinations of these. In Smith et al.'s (2010) *Handbook of Social Geographies*, these connections provided a central focus. And the contents of our own book are far more wide-ranging than social geographies textbooks from even a decade ago. These hybrid social geographies are reflected in many of our chapters and provide a key focus in particular for those on nation and nationalism (Chapter 9), social reproduction (Chapter 28), sustainability (Chapter 32), environmental justice (Chapter 33) and food (Chapter 34); these topics have been drawn in to become central concerns in social geographies. The very idea that topics, ideas, theories and methods can be identified as first 'belonging' to particular subdisciplines is a shaky one, given the speed with which they have always been shared and developed not only within human geography but also outside it. Thus, the best way to view subdisciplines is – as always – as mobile and dynamic, and the field is the better for it.

However, all this is not to say that we are *post*–social geographies. For us, there is a body of work brought together under the umbrella of social geographies that has coherence, and there is value in doing this. Social geographies is more than a handy organisational category, filing system or device purely for the purposes of analysis. As we go on to outline in this introduction, social geographies is expansive, eclectic and not exclusive – nonetheless, its subject matter has some important common features. These include a commitment to certain principles and themes, epistemological approaches and methodological innovation, and often to maintaining the relevance of our research to action on social issues in the 'real' world (Pain et al., 2001). None of these features is exclusive to social geographies, but we would argue that social geographies is where they are most often found.

Another reason for highlighting the importance of social geographies is that, as Linda Peake has put it, 'There has been an almost implicit understanding that the social is defined by lack; it is the soft underbelly left over when the state, the economic and the political have been claimed and correspondingly carved off for specialist subdisciplinary study' (Peake, 2010: 56). In other words, a problem with some perspectives in human geography has been that the social (and to some extent the cultural) has been seen as the residue that is left over after more important political and economic analyses have been made of spatial phenomena. How much analytical power does 'the social' have in offering significant explanations? An example is the subfield of emotional geographies, which first arose within social geographies in the very early years of the twenty-first century (Anderson & Smith, 2001). We remember the idea that emotions were worthy of study being ridiculed by some geographers at that time, emotions being seen as soft and inconsequential to the things that really matter. The fact that it was largely feminist geographers writing about emotional geographies partly explains this initial response from other parts of the discipline. However, as two decades of research have shown, and as is now much more widely accepted across human geography, emotional life has a formative and foundational role in society, politics and the economy (Blazek & Kraftl, 2015; Davidson, Bondi & Smith, 2005; see Chapter 12).

Such knowledge hierarchies, which are implicit in questions about which aspects of life are most pivotal, may be explained by the fact that 'the social' tends to be (at least at first glance) concerned with everyday, intimate and quite banal phenomena and processes. These may appear to be less important and impactful than 'big', 'global', spectacular and thus more exciting ones (see the section on the global/intimate towards the end of this chapter). As we show in many of the chapters in this book, however, events and processes at different scales are so intertwined as to make a nonsense of the idea that these scales are separate (Pratt & Rosner, 2012).

Defining Social Geographies

Looking back at previous textbooks from the English-speaking world, our predecessors have defined social geographies quite consistently. Social geographies is

> concerned with the ways in which social relations, social identities and social inequalities are produced, their spatial variation, and the role of space in constructing them. (Pain et al., 2001: 1)

> best summed up as 'the study of social relations and the spatial structures that underpin those relations' (Johnston et al., 2000: 73). (Valentine, 2001: 1)

> the differences that separate us, and the ways in which we may live and think across and beyond those differences as we negotiate questions of identity, power and social action. (Panelli, 2004: xiv)

> a constellation of theoretical and methodological approaches that converge and diverge in an attempt to understand the spatial organization of what we could broadly think of as difference and inequality. (Del Casino, 2009: 15)

> the way space mediates the production and reproduction of key social divides. (Smith et al., 2010: 1)

What these definitions have in common is that they point to the study of the interrelationships between society, space and place, asking how the nature and activity of societies are geographically constituted (created or changed by spatial patterns and processes) and geographically expressed (manifested in spatial patterns and processes). Social geographers are most interested in the study of social relations – in other words, the relationships and interactions between people at different scales (individuals, groups, communities or institutions, for example). To put it another way, social geographers' interest is in the ways we are social beings and the contexts in which this is formed and plays out. These social relations are not random happenings but are governed by particular rules, codes and norms; very different ways of being social exist that may be historically, culturally and politically rooted, yet are also always changing and being remade. Crucially, of course, for social geographers it is the spatial contexts of social relations that are of interest – the geographical variations in ways of being social, the immediate places in which it occurs and the many complex and intersecting spaces that provide its setting (see Text Box 1.3).

TEXT BOX 1.3 | Susan J. Smith

Susan Smith is a professor at the University of Cambridge in the United Kingdom. She is a social geographer who has conducted influential work on fear, health, racism, housing and finance. Her first book, *Crime, Space and Society* (Smith, 1986), was an innovative ethnographic study of crime in Birmingham. As the first geographer to identify the wider social importance of the impacts of crime on its victims, she argued that patterns of crime, fear and policing reflected the distribution of power, and especially structural issues of race and class within the city.

The relations between society and space are not fixed but fluid and changing. This means that there are numerous factors, processes and influences that intervene to give rise to the specific forms of social relations that are the focus of our research. Some of these mediating factors are fairly generic – so, in Rachel's research, outlined at the start of this chapter, the changes to government housing policy create particular housing outcomes for those on low incomes – and some are specific to certain localities – so former coal-mining villages in North East England experience a particular set of additional resources and challenges that are historically embedded and reshaped in the present day.

Susan Smith (1999) offers a useful summary of the changing perspectives on the relationships between society and space in Table 1.1. Within this broad framing, certain themes are frequently of interest to social geographers. One fundamental premise is that social relations are uneven across space in a number of ways, shaped by Massey's (1991a) power geometries (see Text Box 1.1) and forged through struggles within specific places, producing unequal outcomes between different social groups in different places. Indeed, some of the earliest work in social geography in the 1970s identified acute spatial inequalities in resources such as income, health, education and so on (e.g., Ley, 1983; Jones & Eyles, 1977). David Smith's

TABLE 1.1	Changing Perspectives on the Relationships between Society and Space (Smith, 1999: 14)

From Society to Space	The Spatial Construction of Society	Thirdspace
Spaces are scientific and geometric, filled with an accumulation of social facts, providing an accurate but simplified representation of a more complex 'real' world.	Spaces have a material reality and a symbolic significance and can take on a life of their own. Spatial patterns express, but also shape, social relations.	Spaces that those marginalised by racism, patriarchy, capitalism, colonialism and other oppressions choose as a speaking position.
Geographies that are concrete, quantifiable and mappable.	Geographies are negotiated and struggled over.	Geographies that were made for one purpose are appropriate for another, redefined and occupied as a strategic (real or symbolic) location.
An explanatory framework that regards spatial patterns as an index and an outcome of social and political processes.	An explanatory framework that regards social patterns as informing and interacting with socioeconomic processes.	This is about being rather than explaining – an approach that is emancipatory rather than predictive or interpretive.
Social categories and social identities are given. The social distances between groups are expressed in spatial separation; social interaction is signalled by spatial integration.	Social categories and social identities are constructed through spatially discriminatory material practices (markets, institutions, systems of resource allocation) and cultural politics (struggles to control the imagination).	Social categories are resisted by those they are imposed on. Spaces on the margin provide a position from which to build open and flexible identities. Here, commonalities are emphasised and differences tolerated.

(1974) question 'who gets what, where and how?' began to reorient social geography with a concern for human welfare and uncovering the processes that underpinned social inequalities, as well as simply their patterns. Today, social geographers are still conducting vitally important work on mapping inequality (see Text Box 1.4). This mainstay of spatial inequality gives rise to a number of key themes, including identity, difference, justice, community, relationality and social action, which we explore in more detail in the last part of the chapter.

TEXT BOX 1.4	Danny Dorling

Danny Dorling is a professor at the University of Oxford. He conducts research on inequalities of housing, health, employment, education, wealth and poverty in the United Kingdom. Using statistical and mapping techniques, his work is important both for identifying the fine-grained spatial patterning of inequality and for conveying his findings to the wider public. His recent work has helped to expose increasing social and economic inequalities in the United Kingdom (Dorling, 2018).

All this, so far, we suspect many social geographers would agree on. The two broad concepts of social relations and space help define our wide subject matter and point us to use theories and methodologies in certain ways (see Chapters 2 and 3). However, social geographies has more in common than this. A key feature of the subdiscipline is the way that it has critiqued and responded to our troubled positioning as academics and students, asking why, how and from what standpoint we create knowledge. This question was first posed by feminist and postcolonial critiques of mainstream Western academic research, and these have been very influential in shaping social geographies over the past four decades. These are not simply critiques of the formation of knowledge in the past but, importantly, offer new concepts, methods and fields of knowledge in an effort to address the shortcomings identified (see Chapter 8 on Indigeneity, Chapter 13 on race and Chapter 16 on gender; Kobayashi & Peake, 2000 [see Text Box 1.5]; Women and Geography Study Group, 1984; McKittrick, 2011 [see Text Box 1.7]). We examine these issues in more detail in a later section of this chapter.

TEXT BOX 1.5	Audrey Kobayashi

Audrey Kobayashi is a professor at Queen's University in Canada. She conducts research about the social inequalities negotiated by marginalised groups such as women migrants and about issues of racism, racialisation and multiculturalism. Some of her influential work raises important questions about the Whiteness of the discipline of geography, the role of racism within it and the marginalisation of women within the discipline. She has also published widely on the intersections of gender and race and their relevance to conducting research in the field (Kobayashi, 1994).

This is not to pretend that significant knowledge biases born of sexism, racism and empire are a thing of the past in human geography; many recent interventions show how far we have to go, in both geographical research and professional practices (e.g., Mahtani, 2014; Noxolo, 2017). But social geographies generally involves an orientation to challenging injustice in our own academic practices, as well as in the wider world that we study. Indeed, certain ethical and political commitments (such as working together to promote social change) tend to underpin a particular understanding of what 'the social' and 'being social' are (Pain, 2003; Panelli, 2008).

BEING SOCIAL GEOGRAPHERS: WHAT DO WE MEAN BY 'SOCIAL'?

The Oxford English Dictionary defines 'social' as an adjective used in two ways that are of relevance here. First, social means 'relating to society or its organization', which, as we have discussed above, centrally describes the content of social geographies. Second, social also means 'needing companionship and therefore best suited to living in communities'. This idea of togetherness is also part of the subject matter of social geographies – studying social relations implies that we are interested in how people live and interact (see Chapter 27 on encounter).

Equally, given the knowledge critiques that we began to raise above, this second use of 'social' can be applied to us, as social geographers producing knowledge – how do we work together, not only as colleagues but also in our interactions with the wider world through research and teaching? Are collective rather than individualist approaches possible when it comes to studying and researching the social world? What are the social relations between researchers and the lives of the people we research, and how are these particular relations constituted historically, culturally, economically, politically and emotionally? How do we undertake research when we are often part of the societies, and sometimes part of the communities, that we are focusing on, or may be members of the dominant social groups that we are critiquing? These questions relate to the critiques of knowledge mentioned above, and biases of racial, gender and other differences have been the subject of much reflection and changing practices in doing social geographies (see Chapter 3).

While 'social' is generally used as an adjective, not a verb, these ideas about doing together are fundamentally intertwined with social geographers' considerations of the social world, social life and social processes. Being social, sociality and togetherness are all terms that point to more collective ways of organising life, and this is the approach that we espouse in this book. Our ontological perspective on the external world becomes an epistemology of practice – a way of working together, with each other as colleagues, with our undergraduate and postgraduate students, and with others outside the academy who are dealing directly with the social issues under examination. Another writing collective that Rachel belongs to, mrs c. kinpaisby-hill (2011), has argued for this notion of 'more fully social geographies', where the pursuit of knowledge is undertaken collectively in a more connected way to other people and their concerns. The Autonomous Geographies Collective (2010) argues for similar relationships and alliances in research, describing 'anarchist and libertarian socialist interpretations of collectivism . . . the belief that society will be bettered through the achievement of collective goals rather than individual aspirations'.

This interest among social geographers reflects events outside the universities where we mostly work. Since the 1980s, many Western societies have moved away from ideas of collective benefit and responsibility to pursue more individualistic goals, characteristic of neoliberalism. It is notable that two previous social geography textbooks identify this shift as their starting points. So Margaret Thatcher, the UK prime minister, stated in 1987 that 'there is no such thing as society' (Pain et al., 2001), while President George Bush in the United States declared the creation of an 'ownership society', which prioritised individual control (Del Casino, 2009). Fast-forward to the writing of this current book, and a plethora of research studies have shown that such ideologies have tended to entrench unequal outcomes between different social groups and that this is accelerating.

The idea of being social/doing together underpins the way we have written this textbook. The usual format for writing textbooks is to have less than a handful of editors to write the introduction, coordinate the submission of chapters by other contributors and deliver the final manuscript to the publishers. The editors also pocket the pitiful royalties that the book earns towards their largely unpaid labour – chapter contributors usually get nothing. We have worked as a collective on planning and writing this book; forty contributors have written chapters, but, instead of submitting chapters to someone else's book, we are all doing it together – feeding back on other contributors' drafts, commenting on early drafts of this introductory chapter and so on. Any royalties will come back to the collective to support the research and teaching that we are responsible for together here at Newcastle University. This process mirrors the ways many social geographers approach their research: less as a lone scholar, more collaborative and engaged.

Being a more fully social geographer – doing geographical research and study in more *fully social* ways – is therefore also about an ethical commitment to the world and the social problems that we study. Increasingly, social geography academics and students are choosing to become involved in action on the problems we study, whether through the impacts that our research has on society, on policy or practice, through activism or through engagements with people at the sharp end of these problems in everyday life (see Chapter 3). These efforts take place at different scales and in different ways, but emphasise a focus on collective well-being and the belief that our working practices as well as what we work on should reflect this (Askins, 2009; see Text Box 1.6).

Finally, for us, being a more fully social geographer means making our work accessible. We have tried to write this book in a way that is clear, in both the language that we use and the devices with

TEXT BOX 1.6	Caitlin Cahill

Caitlin Cahill is an associate professor at the Pratt Institute, City University of New York, United States. Her work examines young people's experiences of urban space and restructuring. Using participatory action research principles and practices, Caitlin has worked alongside young people as coresearchers, including the Fed Up Honeys, the Mestizo Arts & Activism Collective and the Bushwick Action Research Collective. Seeking to change the injustices that young people identify, Caitlin coauthors reports, articles and other outputs with them (see Cahill et al., 2019).

which we present and illustrate ideas and examples. We also commit to making chapters available on our personal web pages, for those whose libraries cannot or will not buy the final book (or who do not have access to libraries). Like academic journals that are fully open-access (such as the critical geographies journal *ACME*), these are efforts to democratise knowledge, allowing a wider range of readers to read, engage with and critique our work. We hope that this represents a small step in rectifying the seriously inequitable practices that characterise academic working and publishing.

SITUATED KNOWLEDGES AND SOCIAL GEOGRAPHIES

So 'social' indicates something about togetherness and an interest in collective modes of being, living and working. However, this should not be mistaken for a universalist perspective. Our expositions on social geographies in this book are situated – in other words, they come from a particular place. There are social geographies of social geographies, in that our study and creation of knowledge are always socially and geographically specific – different locations, subject positions and histories influence the ways that social geographies has developed in varied contexts. Haraway's (1988) influential idea of situated knowledge tells us that we can only ever offer a partial perspective on the world, which is always heavily shaped by our own position in it. Many academics have pretended otherwise, which Haraway called a 'god trick' of 'seeing everything from nowhere'. What Nayak and Jeffrey (2011) call 'the imperial tradition' has had perhaps an especially strong sway on the discipline of geography, given its early deployment as a science of and for the Western colonial project.

This is a book from somewhere. When we conceived this book, we were all living, working or studying in the North East of England at Newcastle University in the United Kingdom in the Global North, with English as our everyday language. Most of us have been trained in particular traditions in geography in universities in the Global North that are part of the Anglo-American tradition. We occupy a normative global position and are relatively privileged. Of course, there are important differences between us in terms of career stage, job security, income, social class, nationality, gender, age, ethnicity, disability, sexuality and so on, which all come into play at different times and in different spaces and affect the ways we analyse the world. And these positionalities are not static but processual and reflexive, being continually remade through our encounters with the world (Nagar & Geiger, 2007). Some chapters deal with issues outside the Global North, and some of us do our research locally to where we were born, live or work. In compiling the contents, we have been keen to include key areas of 'Western' social geographies, while being mindful that critiques of 'Western geography' from other places and perspectives have had profound impacts. So the book is inflected by antiracist, Indigenous and postcolonial critiques of Western situated knowledges. And, as we discussed above, there are subdisciplinary crossovers; some examples given in this book might easily be labelled 'development' geography in another book, not because it is not 'social' geography but because it focuses on a different part of the world. (For us, development is something that happens everywhere, including to ourselves as we learn about other places.)

One quite stark example of the situated nature of geographical knowledge that we noticed, browsing recent textbooks in human geography while writing this chapter, is how many are edited by groups of senior White men, with no women editors on the team (e.g., Cloke et al., 2012; Cloke, Crang & Goodwin, 2014; Daniels et al., 2016). This is despite growing representation of women in the discipline (although women are still in a minority, and non-White geographers are few and far between) and the prominence of feminist critiques of geographical knowledge. It seems that it is easy to pay lip service to these critiques, as issues of gender and race equality are referred to as topics for study in all of these textbooks, yet much harder to shift the power geometries of the discipline.

A further example is that of citation practices (that is, the practices of referencing specific authors and their research in published books and papers and not citing others). Mott and Cockayne (2017) note that citational practices in geography tend to reproduce 'White heteromasculinity'. They argue that geographers should be aware of citation practices and how these can reinforce social inequalities and exclusions. We are mindful of this situation in writing this book, referring to the work of scholars with a diversity of genders, sexualities and ethnicities. We are also a relatively diverse collective, although conscious, too, that social geographies has much work to do in terms of equality and diversity.

What does this mean for the shape of knowledge, or what we, as social geographers, think we know? Situated knowledges in social geography reflect what has been called the 'Anglo-American hegemony' of geographical knowledge (e.g., Berg, 2013; Garcia-Ramon, 2003; Timar, 2004), a kind of core–periphery model of knowledge production where control – through journal editing, book publishing, funding bodies, peer review and quality audit systems – reflects and reinforces powerful players within academic disciplines located in certain countries. These entrenched patterns result in certain types of knowledge being produced and valourised, inevitably also inflected by gender, race and so on. However, as Berg (2013) argues, the Anglo-American hegemony, while undoubtedly very powerful in human geography, is rather more binary a framing than accurately reflecting more complex assemblages of 'emplaced' geographical knowledges. Berg gives the example of theories and methods originating in the Global South that have often been borrowed without acknowledgement and rebadged as Northern inventions.

Understandings of 'the social' are challenged and changed by research arising from particular communities and contexts. Panelli (2008) argues that concepts and approaches in Indigenous and

TEXT BOX 1.7	Katherine McKittrick

Katherine McKittrick is a professor at Queens University in Canada. Her work has brought Black studies into dialogue with geography. A hallmark of 'Black geographies' is moving beyond simply positioning Black people in terms of suffering (as research predominantly by White scholars has tended to do). Instead, her work focuses on Black people's own knowledges, establishing an agenda for distinct Black experiences and explanations of the structural constitution of space (McKittrick, 2011).

'more-than-White' geographies pose a major challenge to Anglo-American social geographies in their more integrative understandings of the social, for example, encompassing nature for many Indigenous groups. Likewise, the important interventions of Black geographies radically changed the conversation that social geographers had been having about race for decades (see Text Box 1.7).

A BRIEF HISTORIOGRAPHY OF SOCIAL GEOGRAPHIES

It is not surprising, then, that there are wide variations in the type of social geographical work being carried out in places around the world. You may or may not be taught something called 'social geography', depending on where you live and study. Geographical variations reflect different academic historical traditions, as well as the structure of higher education institutions and their programmes (Kitchin, 2007). The long-standing series of commissioned country reviews in the journal *Social & Cultural Geography* highlights this diversity, partly instigated to encourage geographers in various contexts to appreciate and draw upon related work conducted elsewhere. As Kitchin makes clear, barriers are created not just because of distance and language but also because of the power geometries shaping academic knowledge production that we refer to above.

In Text Box 1.8, we identify some key phases of the histories of social geographies (as a Western project). This is just one highly situated history of the subdiscipline in a nutshell, which simplifies what have been complex and overlapping shifts; there have been many other influences and trends. But, together, we consider these the key influences shaping what we now view as Western social geographies.

In the United Kingdom, where we are based, social geographies is now more present and popular in undergraduate degrees and postgraduate research than ever. Still, its fortunes can be seen as mixed; some reject it as concerned in a formulaic way with policy or practice, while others believe that it is outdated and rather passé (Hopkins, 2011), reflecting some parts of academia's obsession

TEXT BOX 1.8 | **Key Phases in the Development of Social Geographies**

The roots of the discipline are usually traced back to Élisée Reclus, who is credited with coining the term 'social geography' in 1895 (Smith et al., 2010). Along with Petr Kropotkin, an anarchist geographer writing at the turn of the nineteenth century, Reclus laid the foundations for critical and radical thought in social geography. Reclus and Kropotkin rejected the imperial tradition in geography and its preoccupation with describing and cataloguing peoples and places in ways that served the interests of colonialism, which were frequently racist and which entrenched class privilege. Instead, they argued for a social geographical imagination oriented to recognising social inequality and its structural causes (Nayak & Jeffrey, 2011), principles that have transferred through to the current day remarkably, albeit with adjustment along the way.

In the first half of the twentieth century, cultural geography gained greater prominence in the Anglo-American discipline (see Horton & Kraftl, 2013), and social geography was muter, seeming to have lost its sense of purpose and radical potential. Social geographies has since had four notable (overlapping) periods of resurgence and growth, seeing a large increase in scholarship and attention.

The first period of resurgence was during the 'quantitative revolution' of the 1960s and 1970s, when social geographies was reinvented as a spatial science, utilising new techniques to map and analyse social problems. Holloway and Hubbard (2001) call the result a 'dehumanized' geography that mapped and predicted human behaviour at an aggregate level; yet it was open to criticism not only for saying little about causality and ignoring the role of people as agents of change but also for studying social categories that were often reflective of a certain, now outdated, view of the world (Little, 2014).

The second period of resurgence involved the growth of structural explanations such as Marxism, but also humanistic geography, in the 1970s, much of which focused on social issues and developed as a critique of positivist approaches (Relph, 1981b). This was the first sign of a social geography that balanced structure and agency via rich empirical and conceptual study (e.g., Ley, 1983).

The third period involved a longer process of the inclusion of the feminist and postcolonial critiques of knowledge production that we mentioned earlier, beginning in the 1980s, which in time have radically reshaped the interests, theories and methods used by social geographers (e.g., Bondi & Domosh, 1982; Rose, 1993; Tivers, 1978).

Fourthly, dissatisfaction grew with the promised changes that qualitative methods would bring and with the concurrent overly theoretical and apolitical analysis (admittedly, some of this was confined to cultural geography, while social geographies languished) – a feeling that social geographies had strayed too far from its core concern with inequality and oppression (Peach, 2002). From the late 1990s, an impetus to action-oriented research that more directly sought to address social issues developed critical mass and led to a revitalised social geographies (Fuller & Kitchin, 2004; Pain, 2003; see Chapter 3).

with pursuing the new at the expense of pursuing the important (see Bissell, 2019; Pain & Bailey, 2004, on the relationship of social and cultural geographies). Like much of the social sciences, our subdiscipline has also been critiqued by the alt-right for its focus on (among other things) identity politics. But we argue that, as critical sites of social and political exclusion and vitally significant in shaping people's lives, these social divisions remain of fundamental importance, and research examining them is required in order to work for change. In the 'Divisions' part of this handbook, then, we retain separate considerations of gender, age, race, sexualities, class, religion and disability (Chapters 13–19), as well as focusing on their intersections (Chapter 20). Changes in society always impact changes in the fortunes and the nature of fields of academy study, and social geographies continues its resurgence as issues such as migration, racism, feminism, housing, welfare inequalities, climate change and hate crime receive more public and political attention.

What does all this mean for you as a student? As you encounter different ideas and examples in this book, the material may prompt you to respond, feel and act in certain ways. Consider how these responses relate to your own geographical, social and economic positioning and life experiences (England, 1994). As Kobayashi (2010) has noted, being reflexive in this way (see Chapter 3) should have the purpose of stimulating better knowledge rather than reinforcing our own privileged standpoints.

KEY THEMES IN SOCIAL GEOGRAPHY

As it should be clear from our discussion so far, social geographies are dynamic rather than static, changing all the time, shifting in relation both to other academic fields and to events in the world around us. However, there are a number of key themes that characterise the types and subjects of inquiry that social geographers often pursue. We summarise these here, explaining the terms that are used and developed throughout the rest of the book.

Power and Exclusion

Issues of power are at the centre of social geographies – who holds power, how it shapes experiences of space and place, how this affects less-powerful people in society and how social power is contested. As we explained in the first section of this chapter, it is the relation of power to place and space that is of most interest to social geographers. As Trudeau and McMorran (2011: 437) ask, 'How is space fashioned to privilege some groups and marginalise others? How does space contribute to the social exclusion of certain groups?' Power is commonly seen as closely connected to systems of colonialism, class, gender, race, age, sexuality, religion and disability (see Chapter 8 and Chapters 13–19; see also Text Box 1.9). However, neither power nor the meaning and experience of these categories is fixed. Rather, a Foucauldian notion of power views it as continually shifting and resisted in ways that are small and private (such as the tactics of survival of someone targeted by homophobic abuse in the workplace), as well as large and public (Pride marches around the world to celebrate and campaign for LGBTQ rights). Power is always messy and complex, and it has different meanings in different settings (Sharp et al., 1999).

TEXT BOX 1.9 | Ruth Gilmore

Ruth Gilmore is a professor at the City University of New York in the United States. She is a founder of 'carceral geographies', the study of prisons in their wider spatial context. Her work has focused on the intersection of the systems of power, including capital and race, which underpin the provision of prisons in the United States, and the discrimination that leads to high rates of incarceration of Black people (Gilmore, 2007). She is known for her activism on these issues and for founding grassroots social justice organisations, as well as for her influential academic writing.

For instance, one body of work in social geographies has explored how powerful groups construct boundaries that mark out excluded groups as 'othered', in opposition to what is considered 'normal' and at the centre. These boundaries may be created through speech or actions; they may be invisible to many people yet still highly effective in marginalising others. How power practices are challenged and overcome is also a key focus for much work in social geographies (see Chapter 6 on social change). For example, Cloke, May, and Johnsen (2010) have studied how homeless people are forced out of city centres through social and spatial strategies but also exercise tactics of resistance, and Valentine's (2004) work has charted the agency of children and young people in resisting adults' ideas about their use of space.

Justice and Inequality

Often interconnected with debates about power, a mainstay of social geographies over the decades has been the motivation provided by questions of justice and the desire to challenge, overcome and eradicate inequality, oppression and disadvantage. This represents an important ethical underpinning for why social geographers do the work that they do. The focus upon justice is about highlighting the distribution of benefits and burdens among society and across space. As Walker (2012) emphasises, justice is about more than just describing this distribution and demands deeper consideration of how society might be organised differently.

As a collective, we take inspiration from Martin Luther King Jr., who visited Newcastle in 1967 and whose identification of poverty, racism and war has provided three key axes for justice-oriented work. A considerable amount of geographical research has also focused on issues of justice in relation to cities (e.g., Fincher & Iveson, 2012; Mitchell, 2003 [see Text Box 1.10]), gender inequalities (e.g., Wright, 2010), climate justice (e.g., Chatterton, Featherstone & Routledge, 2013) and ecological and interspecies justice (see the section on non-

---

TEXT BOX 1.10 | Don Mitchell

Don Mitchell is a professor of geography at Uppsala University in Sweden. He has published widely on debates about public space, geographies of labour, landscapes and culture. His work pays attention to historical and political-economic processes and how these shape public spaces for particular societies and communities. His 2003 book *The Right to the City: Social Justice and the Fight for Public Space* examines the relationship between struggles over public space and movements for social justice in the United States.

---

humans below), while others have focused on ethical and philosophical debates about justice (Barnett, 2018). However, sometimes the sense is that issues of justice and inequality are more implicit within research rather than explicitly referenced; we contend that justice, as subject and goal of research, might be addressed more directly.

Attention to inequalities tends to focus on examining injustices and inequities between groups and places based on specific factors and resources (such as health, crime or access to work). Significantly, much of this work is about fostering change outside of the academy. Research in social geographies about justice and inequality is diverse and multiscalar, paying much attention to wider structural and political contexts (such as institutional edicts or government policies) as well as to everyday lived experiences. Specific chapters in this book address these issues directly (see Chapter 7 on justice and Chapter 33 on environmental justice), and others offer concepts through which justice can be studied (see Chapter 5 on scale, Chapter 9 on nation/nationalism and Chapter 10 on urban/rural). Social divisions and the exclusions and marginalisations associated with these are inherently bound up with issues of justice and inequality (see Part C, 'Divisions'). Indeed, all of the chapters in this book connect in some way to issues of justice and inequality.

TEXT BOX 1.11 | David Ley

David Ley is professor emeritus at the University of British Columbia in Canada. He has published widely in social geography, particularly on debates about immigration, housing and cities. Some of his recent work has explored issues of religion and immigration. In 2011, he published *Millionaire Migrants: Trans-Pacific Life Lines*, which examined the experiences of wealthy migrants who left Hong Kong and Taiwan to migrate to Canada, Australia and the United States in the 1980s and 1990s.

Communities and Cities

We noted earlier that social geographies interconnects and overlaps with other types of 'geography' rather than existing in a vacuum. Much of our work is interested in specific neighbourhoods and communities, their relationships with other places, the stereotypes and stigma associated with specific localities and how these play out for local residents. Much of this work has been urban in its focus. Indeed, much of the original work that provided the foundations for social geographies was about living in cities (Ley, 1983; Smith, 1987), and so there are overlaps here between urban and social geographies (see Knox & Pinch, 2009). Of course, social geographers also work on communities in rural and semirural areas (see Chapter 10 on urban/rural), as well as on wider issues of nature and environment (see Chapter 32 on sustainability and Chapter 33 on environmental justice).

Earlier work in social geographies had a strong focus on debates about residential segregation, specifically housing and ethnic residential segregation in cities, often using quantitative approaches to understanding social-spatial relations (Peach, Robinson & Smith, 1981). Building upon this earlier work, social geographical research diversified to explore issues such as the contested cultural construction of cities and communities and people's senses of belonging and identification with specific neighbourhoods. Examples include those associated with the LGBT community (such as Nash & Gorman-Murray's [2014] exploration of the 'gay village'). A key strand of work here has focused on public spaces and how 'the street' (Fyfe, 2006) is a key location for protest and for encountering difference, such as Pride parades (Johnston, 2007), or against government policies, such as austerity in the United Kingdom. At the same time, the street is a location that is governed, subject to security controls, and both formally and informally policed.

Many of the chapters in this book focus especially on communities in town and cities, and the relationships between and within them, including Chapter 21 on housing, Chapter 22 on wealth and poverty, Chapter 23 on health and Chapter 25 on policing the city.

Identity and Difference

Much work in social geography pays attention to identities and difference. Identity describes forms of identification that people use to affiliate with (or disaffiliate from) specific social groups, such as those included in the Divisions part of this book. By identities, we mean associations with specific social groupings such as gender, disability, class, religion, age and race. Identities are therefore about similarity and difference and are relational. For example, you may share aspects of your identity with other young working-class women if you identify your age, class and gender in this way. Often, people take up specific identities by disassociating from other identity categories. Panelli (2004: 145) points to five processes that make up identification:

- Identities may be actively conveyed or communicated.
- Identities can be read, recognised and reinterpreted by others.
- Identities may be negotiated – for example, selectively adopted, modified, reconstructed, challenged, contested or resisted.
- Identities may be represented and performed through a variety of texts, practices and personal cues (e.g., hair, dress, body language).
- Identities can take up, employ, affect or even reconstruct spaces.

Our work on identities focuses on the complexities of specific categories; for example, feminist social geographers have undertaken this exploration in relation to the category of gender (e.g., Bondi, 1991; McDowell, 1999), particularly the various ways it plays out in diverse everyday contexts (see Chapter 16 on gender). Informed in particular by Black feminist scholarship, research on the social geographies of identity and difference often draws upon the concept of intersectionality (see Chapter 20), whereby multiple social divisions and their interconnections are analysed in relation to the issues of power, relationality and justice that are discussed above (see Text Box 1.12).

TEXT BOX 1.12 | Gill Valentine

Gill Valentine is a professor of geography at the University of Sheffield in the United Kingdom. Much of her work is situated in debates about identity and difference, particularly in relation to studies of childhood and family and of sexuality and intimacy. Her work develops concepts around encounter, diversity and intersectionality. Her early work on geographies of lesbian identities played a crucial role in shaping studies of sexuality, space and gender (Valentine, 1993).

Global and Intimate

While social geographies are sometimes viewed as overly focused on the everyday rather than on national or global processes, a key feature of much contemporary research is its insistence on the multiple scaling of socio-spatial phenomena, or working across scales. We reflected earlier in this chapter on knowledge hierarchies within geography, and there are still presumptions in some quarters that studying 'big', global and public processes is more important and relevant than studying small, local or private phenomena. These kinds of scaled knowledge hierarchies are easy to unpick, given that many geographers would today agree that multiscalar explanations are often most robust (political geographers' recent adoption of the concept of the everyday is just one example). Presumptions about the different value of analysis at different scales have been critiqued as not only hierarchical but also masculinist, reflecting Western precepts shaped by ideas and practices of empire (Marston, Jones & Woodward, 2005). Of course, it is now generally agreed that these scales are themselves social and political constructs (see Chapter 5 on scale). Still, those areas of geography with a reputation for holding on to masculine and colonial ways of knowing more firmly continue to reproduce them.

As we show in this book, things, events and processes at different scales are so intertwined as to make a nonsense of the idea of these scales as separate (Valentine, 2001). For example, Longhurst's (2000, 2005) research on different aspects of the body (such as those associated with pregnancy and body size) shows clearly the socio-spatial consequences for those whose bodies are deemed out of place. Liz Bondi's (2005) work has illuminated the important role of the psyche to social and spatial life. As we can also see from Gerry Pratt's scholarship (Text Box 1.13), it is feminist work in particular that has most successfully connected global and intimate scales of analysis in ways that do not privilege one or the other but highlight their interdependence. Chapter 11 on everyday and Chapter 12 on emotion detail further recent perspectives and examples.

TEXT BOX 1.13 | Geraldine Pratt

Geraldine Pratt is a professor at the University of British Columbia in Canada. Her work has focused on transnational migration and the resulting separation of families. In *Families Apart* (Pratt, 2012), she identifies layers of violence that follow female migrants who travel from the Philippines to Canada to work as caregivers. Identifying various forms of interpersonal and state violence as connected, Pratt argues for the co-constitution of global and intimate processes.

Relationality and Interaction

As we outlined earlier in this chapter, much work in social geographies focuses on how people interact and interrelate to each other and to the social world in different spaces and at different times. The nature of these interactions, encounters and engagements has been of growing interest. For example, if we think about how people communicate with each other on the bus, in the office, at school or in neighbourhoods, many of the previous key themes identified above come into play. Clearly, interaction is imbued with power and can work to reinforce inequalities, which those people affected in turn resist (see Text Box 1.14). One example of research that centres on these issues is Askins' (2015) work with a befriending scheme for asylum seekers and refugees in the North East of England. Critically exploring the relationships between befrienders and befriendees,

she points to the social politics of the relationships and interactions between each of these people. She refers to the 'quiet politics'
involved in such relationships; in other words, how these everyday
modes of support can be seen as a form of activism.

Another way to think about these interactions is to position them
as relational (Hopkins & Pain, 2007). Relationality describes the
complex two-way relations between individuals, between specific
social groups or institutions, and between and within specific spatial
contexts such as everyday places, neighbourhoods or cities. Elwood,
Lawson, and Sheppard (2016: 745) identify three ways relational
thinking may be used in geography. First, they note that spaces
themselves are 'constituted through relations that extend beyond a
singular place'. Second, they observe the 'multiple intertwined causal
structures, actants, subjects, knowledge and exercises of power' that
can lead us to appreciate different social-spatial contexts. Third, they
point to a 'politics of possibility', whereby relational thinking can
challenge commonsense understandings and enhance new forms of
learning and engagement so that specific social issues are reimag-
ined or reframed. These themes emerge in many of the chapters in
this book, but most notably in Chapter 13 on race, Chapter 26 on
migration and diaspora, Chapter 27 on encounter and Chapter 34
on food (see also the following section on nonhumans).

Nonhumans and the More-Than-Social

Whatmore (2002) issued a challenge to geographers to reconsider
the relationships between the social and natural worlds, leading
to the eventual development of what has been called 'more-than-
human' geographies. For social geographers, this means that 'the
social' as a field of study has broadened to include our relations with
nonhumans – other animals, the natural environment and forms
of artificial intelligence (Lorimer, 2013). This work dismantles the
idea of clear divides between humans, animals and nature, contending that we are ultimately intimately connected and codepen-
dent via social processes such as eating, pet ownership and other
forms of interaction (Srinivasan, 2019; see Text Box 1.15). Indeed,
more broadly, social life is completely dependent for its existence on
earth's ecosystems and natural resources (see Chapter 33 on environmental justice). Élisée Reclus, whom we introduced earlier as one of

| TEXT BOX 1.15 | Alice Hovorka |

Alice Hovorka is a professor at Queens University in Canada. Her work on animal geographies explores how animals shape human society and spatial relations. She argues that the study of animals lends insights into the workings of power in human societies, using as a case study the position and status of women and chickens, and their interrelation, in Botswana (Hovorka, 2015).

the very first social geographers, in the late nineteenth century made exactly this point about the need for reconciliation for both human and nonhuman flourishing.

Human relations with animals intersect other forms of power and exclusion, such as gender, race and class (Gillespie & Collard, 2015). These literatures tend to promote a strong ethic that emphasises care within and for the nonhuman world, and even the idea that its constituents might (unwittingly) exercise agency to participate in our research (Bastian et al., 2017). Issues of justice (see our earlier section) are seen as central to urgent questions around environmental and interspecies violence. Chapter 33 on environmental justice and Chapter 34 on food both develop this theme, which is of rapidly growing interest to social geographers.

OUTLINE OF THE BOOK

We have structured the book into four parts. Dividing up a large subdiscipline into these parts is not an easy task; there are 'issues', for example, that some might feel are 'foundations' (and vice versa), while some might reasonably argue that social divisions are foundational to social geographies.

The first part, 'Introductions', continues with chapters on the key theories (Chapter 2) and methodologies and approaches (Chapter 3) used and developed in contemporary research in social geographies.

The second part, 'Foundations', offers a set of chapters that discuss some of the key principles, concepts and ideas that unite social geographies as a subfield. We intend that these chapters provide the fundamentals or groundwork needed to begin to understand social geographical approaches: space, time, scale, justice, social change, Indigeneity, nation and nationalism, urban/rural, everyday and emotion.

The third part of the book, 'Divisions', focuses upon social divisions. These chapters map out some of the important social categories that are used within societies to differentiate people from each other. We focus upon seven of the key social divisions, taking each in turn – race, religion, class, gender, sexualities, disability and age. We end this section with a chapter on intersectionality in order to reflect on the complex ways that these social divisions transform and re-create themselves as they intersect with each other.

The fourth and final part, 'Issues', focuses on the key social issues studied in contemporary social geographies. Here we examine a selection of topics, analysing them in light of the 'foundations' and 'divisions' covered earlier in the book. Some of them have a long history in social geographies and remain a mainstay of the sub-field, such as migration and diaspora, housing, education, policing, health and well-being, and wealth and poverty. Others represent more recent developments, such as performance, encounter and digital spaces. Towards the end of the 'Issues' section, we include three chapters that focus on environment, sustainability and food, each of which highlights the importance of the interrelationships between the social and natural worlds.

HOW TO USE THIS BOOK

We have not written this book with the intention that you read it from cover to cover. Instead, we imagine that some chapters or parts will appeal more to you than others, depending on your own interests and the focus of your studies. We include a summary of the main points at the end of each chapter, as well as occasional 'real-world' text boxes, where you can read about practical examples of research and theory in action. We also include recommended further reading with each chapter and include articles, chapters, books or reports that we think will be most useful to you in learning more about each aspect of social geographies. These can be read alongside the short summaries of key researchers in social geographies that we have provided in this introductory chapter. We frequently cross-reference chapters in order to connect and relate individual topics to the wider body of scholarship in social geographies, as well as to the past and future developments signalled in this first 'Introductions' part. Each chapter offers a general overview of current work in social geographies, offering a range of examples, in most cases including our own research.

Although the chapters are all focused on specific concepts, social divisions or issues, all of the subjects discussed inevitably overlap and interconnect in people's everyday lives. So each chapter should not necessarily be regarded as a unitary narrative; our hope is that you may learn more about specific social divisions, such as gender and race, by not only reading the chapters with these titles but also engaging with other chapters in which these concepts are often at play.

SUMMARY

- Social geographies is the study of the interrelationships between society and space. It focuses on the implications of these relationships for social identities, social reproduction, social inequalities and social justice.

- Social geographers are interested in social relations – the ways we are social beings and the context in which this is formed and plays out. Social relations are uneven across space and forged through struggles within specific places, producing unequal outcomes.

- Social geographies is expansive, eclectic and not exclusive; yet its study has some important common features. These include a commitment to certain principles and themes, to epistemological approaches and methodological innovation and often to maintaining the relevance of our research so that it can inform or involve action.

- Feminist and postcolonial critiques of mainstream Western academic research have been especially influential in shaping social geographies over the past four decades. And so another key feature of social geographies is its attempts to challenge knowledge/power hierarchies, asking why, how and from what standpoint we create knowledge.

- The idea of the social as 'doing together' has shaped social geographers' ethical commitment to the world and the social problems that we study, and the ways that social geographers conduct research. This is demonstrated in the way that we have authored this book collaboratively.

- Some important cross-cutting themes in social geographies include power and exclusion; justice and inequality; communities and cities; identity and difference; global and intimate; relationality and interaction; and nonhuman and the more-than-social.

FURTHER READING

Del Casino, V. (2009) *Social Geography: A Critical Introduction.* Chichester, UK: Wiley-Blackwell.

Smith, S. J., Pain, R., Marston, S., & Jones, J. P. (2010) *Sage Handbook of Social Geographies.* London: Sage.

See periodic reviews of social geography in the journal *Progress in Human Geography.*

CHAPTER — 2

Theories in Social Geographies

Robert Shaw

THEORY AS A TOOLBOX

'A theory is exactly like a box of tools'.
—Deleuze, in Deleuze and Foucault, 1980: 208

I don't know about you, but my ability with everyday tools just about extends to mild competence with a screwdriver. I'm certainly not a home improvement fan: the knife rack that I put up in my kitchen a couple of years ago wobbles disconcertingly whenever I remove something from it. You might feel somewhat similarly about theory. Perhaps you have some confidence with one or two concepts, but whenever you try and use them to write an essay it feels a little, well, wobbly. The philosopher Gilles Deleuze was right: theory is like a toolbox. And if theory is the toolbox, then concepts (such as place, space, gender or home) are the tools. It's not always clear at first how to use the concepts from the theory toolbox, but, like tools, they help solve or explain a particular problem. Becoming comfortable using a tool takes time and practice, and so you shouldn't feel bad if you don't understand a theory the first time you see it. But just as I can pick up and use a screwdriver without really being able to skilfully use a drill, it's also possible to start using concepts without fully understanding other connected ideas. The more practice that we get with theoretical tools, the more concepts we become familiar with and the better our understanding becomes.

Students sometimes complain that theory is too 'abstract' and, in a sense, theories are always abstracted from, in the sense of 'taken out from', the world. But good theory is also always grounded in research, and – as we hope this book shows – theory and research should inform each other. Theory helps us to understand research: to compare different case studies, to generalise from specific cases, to interpret data and to give our research or writing extra insight and impact. In turn, research can help confirm, challenge and generate theory: some of the most interesting theories have their origins in 'real-world' problems.

Social geographies does not have a single unifying theory, and you'll find a range of theories and theorists discussed in this book, as in the wider discipline. Most social geographers accept that their research can be understood using more than one concept or theory and do not usually rely on one theoretical framework or set of concepts all the time. Used as explanatory tools, theories and concepts in geography are not usually 'proven' or 'rejected'. Rather, the tool is refined or adapted so that it can work better next time. To that end, social geographies operates with a (usually convivial) theoretical pluralism: in other words, different theories will sit alongside each other, informing each other. This pluralism, however, means that researchers face a choice in which theories they use. Introducing choice inevitably introduces a politics of theory, because it opens up the question of why certain theories may be chosen over others. We will return to this issue of the politics of theory later in this chapter.

Chapter 1 introduced a number of schools of thought that have been developed and used over time in social geographies: many of our students describe these as the 'isms' of geography! Table 2.1 outlines how these translate into theories. It's important to stress that these schools of thought are diverse: different branches of feminism, for example, will use different concepts and ideas. Rather than offering strict definitions, then, Table 2.1 instead describes what theory is broadly attempting to achieve. This chapter then goes on to discuss a key concept that connects the application of all of these theories to social geographies in some way – namely, the idea of 'social construction' and how that can be applied to both society and space. The chapter will end with a short section on how to read and access theory.

IS EVERYTHING JUST A SOCIAL CONSTRUCT?

Have a look at Figure 2.1. It's an image of a rather idyllic landscape, ruined only by my presence in the foreground! We might intuitively describe this as a 'natural' landscape: we can see trees, grass and

TABLE 2.1 | Theories in Social Geographies

Theory	Description	Example
Marxism	Named after the economist Karl Marx, Marxism argues that social differences can be explained by control over the economy. In social geographies, it has been useful in showing the connections between economic power and social inclusion or exclusion. Marxists have been accused of giving too much power to the economic over social or cultural parts of life, but many Marxists have shown how their analysis can incorporate noneconomic inequalities (see Chapter 15 on class).	Jou, Clark & Chen (2016)
Feminism and Queer Theory	Feminism explores how gendered inequalities are reproduced and how these inequalities create differentiated experiences of the social world, focusing in particular on how different societies tend to favour men over women (see Chapter 16 on gender). The concept of 'intersectionality' has emerged from criticisms that feminism has too often ignored forms of difference within gender groups, such as racial differences (see Chapter 20 on intersectionality). Queer theories are closely connected to feminist thought and are a loose collection of theories that attempt to explore how behaviours or social groups are demonised and become taboo, particularly in relation to sexuality (see Chapter 17 on sexualities).	Sultana (2009)
Postcolonialism	Postcolonialism analyses how contemporary social relations have emerged out of the experience and legacies of colonialism through the eighteenth to twentieth centuries. Postcolonialism has been used to explore the continuing impact that colonialism has on social relations, even after political colonisation has ended. It can be applied to both the colonised society and the centres of imperial power (see Chapter 8 on Indigeneity and Chapter 13 on race).	Pratt & Johnston (2014)
Postmodernism and Poststructuralism	Both of these approaches deny that there is any one satisfactory explanatory framework for social relations. Instead, they claim that society has always simply been a product of actions and how we interpret them. Postmodernism argues that this is a new feature of the contemporary world, in which society has become increasingly fluid, with identity less connected to 'real' or traditional sources. Though closely related to postmodernism, poststructuralism differs in arguing that there has *never* been a set of rules controlling society and that relations of power are always produced.	Maestri & Hughes (2017)
Nonrepresentational Theories	A set of theories that argue that social geographies has been too focused on analysing how the social world is described or represented, rather than focusing on how it is made through our experiences and actions. These theories are related to 'practice theories' in sociology. Criticised for being overly abstract and ignoring the importance of social differences, nonrepresentational theories have increasingly drawn from feminist and queer theory to help to correct this (see Chapter 29 on performance).	Raynor (2017)
Actor–Network Theory	Actor–network theory offers a radical form of social constructivism, arguing that it is not just people but also objects, ideas, materials and nature that construct society. This theory attempts not to interpret and analyse social relations but to describe how they are connected up and organised.	Shaw (2015)

FIGURE 2.1

Hadrian's Wall, Northumberland. (Credit: Rob Shaw)

hills. Despite appearances, however, this landscape has been subject to major engineering for thousands of years. The wall to the right of where I'm standing is built on the foundations of what was Hadrian's Wall, a Roman border wall constructed in AD 122. The land around the wall was extensively shaped by the Roman military, who enhanced the naturally occurring crags and ridges of an existing geological fault by clearing surrounding land and creating an extensive moat, called the *Vallum*, just to the south of the wall. Trees were cleared from around the wall to ensure good visibility, producing the moorland that has since been maintained by the agricultural practices of sheep farming that continue to this day.

When we start to explore a landscape like this, we quickly find ways the features that we imagined to be natural are in fact *socially constructed*. What we call the 'natural' landscape does not really exist as 'natural', in the sense of being separated from society (see also Chapter 32 on sustainability). These ideas, when applied to social geography, have been described as the *social construction of space*. While this might be obvious when standing among the buildings of a city centre, geographers have shown how it is also the case in rural locations such as that in Figure 2.1, and even in so-called wildernesses. Both rural and urban landscapes are subject to social and natural processes of construction, destruction and change. This understanding of the world is called 'constructivism' and is central to most theories in geography, anthropology, sociology and much of social science, because it describes the causal relationship used by each theory to understand social relations or processes and space. In other words, constructivism means that theories attempt to look at how society and space are coproduced, taking the position that society is constructed spatially and space is constructed socially. As Soja puts it, 'the structure of organized space is not a separate

TEXT BOX 2.1	**Real-World Research: Using Feminist, Postcolonial and Nonrepresentational Theory**

Theories drive the methodologies we use to carry out research (see Chapter 3), and this is one reason why the methods used in social geographies are so diverse. Feminist and postcolonial theories, for example, have encouraged the use of multiple in-depth methods, often with participatory elements in which participants contribute to the design and undertaking of the research. Farhana Sultana explored how the effects of drinking-water contamination in a rural community in Bangladesh had different impacts on men and women (Sultana, 2009). Her participants were generally poor, and all lived in a very remote area. As such, Sultana wanted to avoid repeating the mistakes of many past researchers, who have come from outside such communities and imposed their research onto participants, extracting knowledge without offering anything in return. Sultana used participant observation, focus groups and semistructured interviews to ensure that she properly listened to her participants. She has also written about the various ways her identity, in relation to

the participants, shaped how her data were collected (Sultana, 2007). Intensive, qualitative methods are not the only way to do feminist or postcolonial research, but they are commonly used as a means of undertaking research that is inclusive of participants.

Alternatively, nonrepresentational theories – which explore how society is produced through everyday actions that we barely notice – have encouraged geographers to use embodied methods in their research. Arun Saldanha studies drinking and partying cultures, and in research on the clubbing scene in Goa, India, he conducted in-depth ethnographic studies, including many nights in clubs and bars! This embodied experience of the site of research allowed for a detailed account of how conflict between tourists and local residents plays out in these clubs (Saldanha, 2004).

Both of these methodological approaches are theoretically informed, producing data that are shaped by the theoretical approach to the topic being studied, and which in turn contribute to further theoretical development.

structure with its own autonomous laws of construction and transformation, nor is it simply an expression of . . . social (i.e., aspatial) relations' (1980: 210). Theories in social geographies don't start with social relations and then map them onto space, nor do they start with spatial relations and try to use these to explain society. Rather, geographers use theories to explore how space and society are mutually constituted. The focus on which elements of society and space are constructed will depend upon the different priorities of a theory. For example, feminist geographers may focus on how gender is produced through the different experiences that men and women have in a particular space, or they might look at how certain spaces are 'gendered' – that is, how they become associated with either men or women. By contrast, someone using actor–network theory to study the same site would look to document the range and networks of various 'actors' who have been involved in the construction of that space, with no inherent focus on how the experience is gendered.

We can illustrate the role of social construction in shaping place by returning to the site in Figure 2.1, Hadrian's Wall. During the era of Roman Britain, this was a busy border community inhabited by many thousands of Roman soldiers. At this time, a 'Roman' was not someone from the city of Rome but anyone who had gained Roman citizenship. While you could inherit Roman citizenship in the way that national identity is inherited today, it could also be obtained through work or purchased. As such, it was open to anybody, regardless of ethnicity, and there is evidence that Arabic and Black African Romans lived and worked along Hadrian's Wall. However, contemporary sources did not often describe people's skin colour because this was not thought particularly important. Romans did see cultural differences and stereotypes, but these were not associated with skin colour. In other words, in the society of Hadrian's Wall, what we would today called 'race' did not exist. The concept of race was created only in the seventeenth and eighteenth centuries as scientists started to classify plants and animals and wondered if the same classifications could be applied to humans. Using postcolonial theories, the geographer Divya Tolia-Kelly has explored how the concept of race was applied much later by archaeologists and historians interpreting sites such as Hadrian's Wall. By portraying the Romans as White and overlooking evidence of a more racially diverse society, they actually contributed to the production of the idea of race itself. Specifically, the Roman Empire was used as evidence for the socially constructed belief that White Europeans would naturally conquer people in other areas, and, in turn, this was used to explain geographical differences in terms of power, including the dominant European empires of the nineteenth century (Tolia-Kelly, 2011). So the existence of European empires, together with the particular social geographies that these created, was partially a result of how specific spaces – such as Hadrian's Wall – and forms of social differentiation – such as race – were constructed together.

READING AND USING THEORY IN SOCIAL GEOGRAPHIES

I want to finish with some reflections on reading and using theories in social geographies. Sometimes geographers will have a very clear statement of theory in their work: they will label their analysis 'feminist', 'Marxist' or 'nonrepresentational'. Sultana's interesting article on the role of gender in shaping access to water in Bangladesh, for example, refers to feminism four times in her introduction, clearly positioning her work within that theory (Sultana, 2009). By contrast, other articles will focus on a key concept rather than a theoretical area. For example, Tan's 2012 article, which interviewed clubbers in Singapore about their use of nightclubs to party and to meet people for sex, predominantly discusses the concept of 'affect' (Tan, 2012), a term referring to our immediate emotional responses to a space, person or object. While Tan does not particularly mention a theoretical position, affect is a key concept within nonrepresentational theories, although she also uses concepts from feminist and queer theory. This is a good example of the pluralism of theory in social geographies – Tan uses a key tool from the non-representational theory box while operating within a broadly feminist framework. We need to be careful, then, about labelling work as belonging to particular theoretical areas: try to focus on the core concepts or ideas being discussed and be ready to recognise that much work mixes theoretical approaches.

Earlier in the chapter, I claimed that the choice of theory is political. As research can often be interpreted by using more than one theory, we need to consider why the researcher has chosen the theory that they have. They might be following research traditions, whether in a subdiscipline or perhaps following particularly influential papers or researchers. Often, particular geography departments will develop strengths in certain theoretical areas, so it may be useful to pay attention to the university at which someone is working. It is important to note that this creates social geographies of theory. Simply put, theory has tended to be produced by the powerful and has tended to overlook the experiences of marginalised groups. The majority of the theories introduced in this chapter were conceived of in the Global North and have been created by men. Feminist writers such as Gillian Rose have highlighted that work written by men may mistakenly be understood as more theoretically serious and sophisticated than that written by women (Rose, 1993) because people expect male work to be more theoretical. Similarly, postcolonial writers such as Roy have argued that Western geographers need to make more use of theories from outside the Global North, particularly when studying locations in the Global South (Roy, 2016). These social geographies of theory don't make theories inherently 'biased' but do mean that we should consider the 'positionality' – that is, the identity and the location – of both the individual using a theory and also that theory itself: Where did it come from, what does it prioritise and who has used it? Theory does not sit independently of social and geographical structures.

Geographers will often refer to the philosophers and theorists who originated key concepts in their field. Sometimes, reading these writers may be difficult and intimidating; their work may not have been written for a nonspecialist audience, and you may not be familiar with the concepts, the debates and the examples that the authors discuss. Some philosophers have attempted to make their ideas more accessible – this can often be found in feminist, postcolonial or queer theory, where writers are concerned about the politics of knowledge production and its use. However, some of the concepts that geographers use emerged from the work of philosophers who were writing well before the twentieth century, even back to Ancient Greece: it is perhaps not surprising that their work is not immediately accessible! Nevertheless, it can be valuable to make space to look at this material: you do not need to understand the whole thing, and believe me when I say that the geographers who reference philosophers will not understand everything in their work. There are various resources that make theory or philosophy more accessible. Textbooks such as *Geographical Thought* (Nayak

& Jeffrey, 2011) and *Approaches to Human Geography* (Aitken & Valentine, 2015) offer introductions targeted at geographers, while the Very Short Introduction book series gives broader introductions to a range of theories. Web resources change more frequently; yet they can be very helpful in introducing theories. The online *Stanford Encyclopaedia of Philosophy* offers introductions to philosophers and key concepts, while the Global Social Theory website aims to introduce theories from outside the Global North or from marginalised groups, focusing on feminist and postcolonial thinkers. All of these resources should be read with the same critical eye that you'd apply to more traditional academic work.

SUMMARY

- Social geographies uses a range of theories. These theories can be considered as 'toolboxes' containing conceptual 'tools' that help us explain research findings and that can be refined and constructed based on our research.
- This chapter has outlined some of the key theories used in the subdiscipline, and, in particular, it has explored the concept of social construction and how this connects these theories.
- Finally, some suggestions were offered for students on how to read and use theoretical work.

FURTHER READING

Aitken, S., & Valentine, G. (eds) (2015) *Approaches to Human Geography*, 2nd ed. London: Sage.

Blunt, A., & Wills, J. (2000) *Dissident Geographies: An Introduction to Radical Ideas and Practice*. Harlow, UK: Prentice-Hall.

Special issue, *Environment and Planning D*, 36(3).

Researching Social Geographies

Rachel Pain and Peter Hopkins

UNDERSTANDING SOCIAL AND SPATIAL WORLDS

How do we investigate the many topics covered in this book? This chapter provides a brief overview of how we do research about social geographies. Chapter 2 introduced theories in social geography, or the 'thinking', and this chapter turns to the 'doing'. But theory and methodology should not be seen as separate activities as they are closely connected. The Brazilian educator, researcher and philosopher Paulo Freire (1972) used the Greek term *praxis*; this means that thinking and doing are activities of equivalent value that are interreliant in the research and also take place at the same time. And, as many social geographers acknowledge, feelings are also inherently bound up with the process of producing new knowledge (e.g., Askins, 2009; see Chapter 12).

Social geographers have amassed a rich and diverse toolkit of methods to choose from, as we go on to outline next. However, it would be misleading to suggest that we undertake research very differently from other areas of human geography. Human geography itself is eclectic when it comes to methodology; it is known for drawing on a range of techniques from across the social sciences, sciences, arts and humanities, often taking great delight in adapting and combining them, as well as deploying a range of more specifically geographical techniques. Nonetheless, social geographies has become one of the most methodologically diverse and innovative fields of geography. We suggest that four key features give social geographical research its overall character (you may notice that these all arise directly from our discussions in Chapter 1 about what social geographies is and how it may be characterised):

- First, and fundamentally, what characterises much social geographical research is our wish to engage with people, who are the common subject of the broad span of interests covered in this book. Many of the methods that we use are therefore people-oriented and people-friendly, helping us to elicit stories, descriptions and explanations about various facets of people's everyday social worlds.

- Second, social geographic research is focused on particular features of place and space, the immediate or more distant environments in which people are located. Our methods therefore need to be up to the job of eliciting the relevant aspects of localities and environments to enable us to draw out their connections.

- Third, many social geographers are also concerned with conducting research that is relevant and, in many cases, that makes a positive difference to the social issues and communities that we study. There are particular approaches and methods that tend to lend themselves to these goals.

- Fourth, practices around ethics and positionality, developed in response to critiques of traditional modes of geographical knowledge production, tend to be more prominent in social geographers' methodological practice than in many parts of the discipline.

Rather than write a how-to guide for doing fieldwork (as there are other textbooks that do this well, some of which are referenced at the end of this chapter), we offer a broad picture of the issues involved in researching social geography. First, we outline the range of data and methods commonly used by social geographers. Second, we reflect on broader approaches to research: issues of epistemology and ontology, as well as politics, ethics and emotions. Third, we reflect on two examples from our own research on domestic abuse and ethnic minority youth, discussing the data available to us, the particular issues raised in researching these topics and the methodologies that we have designed for fieldwork. Fourth, we consider the whole process of research, including issues of analysis and meaning-making, and, finally, we summarise the debates around the purposes of research that have been especially vigorous in social geographies.

DATA AND METHODS IN SOCIAL GEOGRAPHIES RESEARCH

A rich and varied range of methods has been developed and used, modified and mixed with others, evaluated and studied in their own right, resulting in social geographies being an exciting field in which to do research. Today, it is full of creative and experimental methods, as well as more conventional ways of finding out about the world. As you will no doubt be told numerous times as you begin to conduct your own research, the key deciding factor when it comes to designing your research is that the methodology must be appropriate to your research questions and be able to answer them. When thinking about data collection, we then ask what data are already available that might be appropriate and what data we can create. A first key distinction between methods is whether you want to use them to collect quantitative or qualitative data. This will depend on whether you are seeking to create an extensive dataset that represents a section of the population and from which you can generalise (in which case you will probably choose quantitative methods) or you want to create an intensive dataset to explore in depth the mechanisms and meanings from a smaller number of cases (which suggests qualitative methods). However, 'mixed methods' are often used together in the same study, and there are methods that produce both types of data.

Table 3.1 lists some common types of methods in social geographies. Bear in mind as you look at these that they may overlap, be adapted or used alongside others in real-life research (see Text Boxes 3.1 and 3.2 later in this chapter). And data can never give us a neutral lens on the world we study; they are contested and contentious, both constructing the world and being constructed by it. Chapter 30, on data, explores these tensions in detail.

FIGURE 3.1

Using art to explore place and identity in Newcastle upon Tyne. (Credit: Rachel Pain)

TABLE 3.1 | Methods for Social Geographies

Type	What Does It Do?	Example	See ...
Secondary methods	Uses existing data to ask new questions	Government statistics, policy documents	Dunn (2004); Catney (2016)
Statistical methods	Analyses large datasets, may include spatial data	Correlation, regression, geographical information systems (GIS)	Dorling (2017); see also Chapter 30 on data
Survey methods	Collects brief generalisable data from people. Usually quantitative, but may also produce qualitative data	Questionnaires, online surveys, postal surveys	Pain (2006)
Talking methods – individual	Collects detailed qualitative data from people one-to-one	In-depth interviews, narrative interviews, biographical interviews	Sandberg & Tollefsen (2010)
Group methods	Collects qualitative data from people in groups	Focus groups	Hopkins (2007a); Hyams (2004)
Mobile methods	Collects data on the move, such as when walking or travelling on public transport	Walking interviews	Warren (2017)
Observational methods	Observes situations and people, with different degrees of involvement from the researcher	Ethnography, autoethnography, participant observation	Longhurst (2011); Olson (2006)
Sensory and visceral methods	Uses the researcher's or participants' senses, feelings or bodies to analyse the world	Psychogeographies, embodied methods, nonrepresentational methods	Macpherson (2008); Duffy, Waitt & Harada (2016)
Online methods	Uses material available 'online' via the internet	Analysis of social media, chatrooms, netnography	Kingsley (2013); Cockayne & Richardson (2017)
Visual methods	Analyses visual forms	Analysis of existing images, artworks, film	Rose (2004)
Textual methods	Analyses texts	Analysis of existing books, news stories, diaries, archival materials	Meth (2003); Mills (2016)
Arts-based methods	Uses creative arts as a research method with participants	Creating drawings, photographs, drama, video	Young and Barrett (2001); Pratt & Johnston (2014); see Chapter 29
Participatory methods	Uses techniques that engage and include participants in data collection and analysis; may be part of a participatory approach	Participatory diagramming, participatory mapping, photovoice, participatory video	Kesby (2000); Kindon (2003); Raynor (2019)

APPROACHING SOCIAL GEOGRAPHIES RESEARCH

It is not surprising that so many textbooks and methods classes at university focus on methods, as these are the hands-on techniques that we use in the field: they may present risks to us and our participants, and, moreover, without data we have no research. However, just as important, if not more so, are our *approaches* to research – the wider philosophies of knowledge that underpin these methods. Here, we want to introduce you to some important terms:

Ontology: a theory or set of beliefs about the way the world is

Epistemology: a theory or set of beliefs about knowledge

Methodology: a research process involving a series of stages of methods and analysis

Method: a technique for collecting data

Generally, a researcher's *ontological* outlook influences their *epistemological* approach, which then shapes the design of their *methodology* and their choice of specific *methods*. And, of course, as researchers we rarely make these choices in isolation because we are situated in certain disciplinary, institutional, geographical and social contexts. In some disciplines and specific fields, there are very few competing ontologies or epistemologies and a narrow range of methods – as we mentioned above, human geography is unusually diverse. Back in the mid-twentieth century, a positivist ontology dominated social geographies, characterised by the belief that the external world has a reality that can be known objectively by researchers (Hoggart, Davies & Lees, 2002). Epistemology was based on the idea that this world is observable without bias, and thus findings should be taken as factual. Most methodologies used were quantitative and extensive, with the most popular methods being mapping, statistics and surveys. Today, these methods remain very useful for answering certain research questions, but positivist assumptions have been much critiqued (see, for more detail, Chapter 30 on data).

A recent example of an approach that is now popular in social geographies is participatory action research (PAR). It is illustrative of how much has changed in the last couple of decades. PAR involves studying a problematic situation or issue in collaboration with those affected by it; people who, conventionally, are 'researched' reposition themselves as researchers (Kindon, Pain & Kesby, 2007). PAR is an epistemology founded on a belief in the potential of shared expertise and the goal of collective nonhierarchical knowledge production. It is underpinned by ontologies, often (though not always) drawn from postcolonial and feminist worldviews. It therefore involves a particular methodological design, where research is planned, designed, undertaken and analysed with participants with the goal of taking action on the issue being studied in order to change it (see Cahill, 2007a). And PAR often involves the use of certain participatory methods that help to

FIGURE 3.2

Participatory diagramming is a common method used to identify key issues in participatory action research. (Credit: Hazel Edwards)

enable these principles (see Table 3.1), although more conventional methods such as surveys and interviews may also be included.

Another example is provided by nonrepresentational approaches to social geographical research, the ontological underpinning of which is that the world is continually brought into being through actions and practices (see Chapter 2). Epistemologically, the world can only be known by attempting to access these practices, and so the methods chosen often seek to uncover bodily habits and performances (Latham, 2003).

In Indigenous research ontologies, by contrast, the worldview of Indigenous people shapes the way that research is approached and conducted. Epistemologies focus on the ownership of knowledge and the control of research agendas and outputs by Indigenous people (Howitt & Stevens, 2010; see Chapter 8 on Indigeneity).

Three other really important and interrelated aspects of doing research also come into play in the design and conduct of research, and social geographers have been especially likely to take account of these in their research practice:

- The politics of research – as is clear from the examples above, knowledge is a hotly contested domain that, for centuries, has reflected the dominant societal power relations. In Chapter 1, we described the dominance of Western (especially Anglo-American) nations in social geographic scholarship. Indigenous approaches have perhaps the greatest claim to shifting the politics of research. The memory and ongoing legacies of settler colonialism (see Chapter 8) and the great harm done to Indigenous people in the name of research feed into decisions about who owns, controls and gets to use the data that are produced in Indigenous approaches to research (Smith, 2007). All of this, in turn, has implications for methodological design.

- Research ethics – ethical protocols are conventionally designed to protect the participants in our research from unintentional harm. Feminist methodologies have had most to say about safeguarding the welfare and rights of participants: humanising research processes rather than conducting 'quick and dirty' data extraction with no benefits to the researched communities (Moss et al., 2002). However, most researchers must also work within ethics procedures at universities, which may run counter to feminist approaches, for example, as they increasingly prioritise protecting the institution from liability if things go wrong.

- Emotions in research – emotions are a powerful force in shaping research encounters, both for the researcher and for the people whom he or she is researching (see Chapter 12 on emotion). Again, feminist and (more recently) nonrepresentational approaches have recognised that emotions come into play in all research. In PAR, emotions may generate research topics and motivations and mobilise for social change (Cahill, 2007b).

THE RESEARCH PROCESS: DOING SOCIAL GEOGRAPHY RESEARCH

Having thought carefully about epistemology, ontology, methodology, data and methods, there are a number of other important considerations when doing social geography research. Ideally, you should have a clear understanding of the relevant debates related to the specific issues in your study, as well as an appreciation of relevant concepts and social divisions. This will enable you to fine-tune your specific research problem and the questions that you will be seeking to address in your research.

Specific ethical considerations then need to be considered. Research ethics is about promoting good and minimising harm. The Economic and Social Research Council in the United Kingdom has six principles for research ethics:

- Research should aim to maximise benefit for individuals and society and minimise risk and harm.

- The rights and dignity of individuals and groups should be respected.

- Wherever possible, participation should be voluntary and appropriately informed.

- Research should be conducted with integrity and transparency.

- Lines of responsibility and accountability should be clearly defined.

- Independence of research should be maintained, and where conflicts of interest cannot be avoided, they should be made explicit.

All universities have specific ethical approval processes and guidance that it is important to comply with.

Part of the process of doing research (and part of your ethical review) is to think about how you will access your participants or the specific data that you require to undertake your study. In some cases, data may be publicly available. When accessing participants, you may need to go through a gatekeeper (for example, a school head teacher or community group leader). The chances are that people will want to know what your research is about, why you are doing it and what benefits may result from it.

Having negotiated access, you will then need to be able to explain your research to potential participants so that they can decide whether they want to participate. Informed consent is an important principle here; this is about participants consenting to participation in your research from a position of being as informed as possible about it. This means that they need to understand as much as possible about your research, questions, motivations and how you intend to use your findings. It is generally best to seek informed consent by using a consent form, and an information leaflet about your research can help to ensure full information.

The process of data collection can then begin. This often takes time, and you need to be organised in how you record data and keep track of the process that you are following. For example, this might involve labelling interview recordings, keeping track of consent forms, ordering your fieldwork notes and keeping in touch with participants. There will then come a point when the main data collection phase will end and you will leave 'the field'. You can then prepare and order your data and move into a more formal phase of data analysis (although, ideally, you should have been analysing and thinking critically about your data as you collect it). If you are following a participatory approach, then these various stages might be undertaken with participants rather than on your own.

What does this last stage of analysis and meaning-making really involve? Rachel tells her students that the process of doing research is like having a baby. Before your first go, there is a period of time leading up to it during which you are encouraged to get as much training as possible, with plenty of books and websites to help prepare for the event itself. But, once the data have been collected (or the baby has been delivered) and all the fuss has died down, you are left with an equally important job to do, and there is often relatively little information to guide you.

Data analysis is often thought of as tedious, but this is a key stage of research when the findings take shape and interpretations are made. In contrast to positivist ontologies, most social geographers nowadays view knowledge as multiple and situated (see Chapter 1) – in other words, there is no single lens on the world we study that provides a single 'truth' that is untarnished by the scientific process.

TEXT BOX 3.1	**Real-World Research: Rachel's Research on Domestic Abuse**

My research with survivors of domestic abuse has aimed to understand the geographies of abuse in new ways (Pain, 2014a), to examine survivors' political agency (Pain, 2014b) and to explore the socio-spatial experience of trauma (Pain, 2020).

There are a number of existing datasets on domestic abuse – from statistics collected by the police, the criminal justice system, and the National Health Service, for example – but all are thought to seriously underestimate its actual incidence. These datasets do not give any texture to the experiences of families behind the statistics and are of limited use to services seeking to improve how they recognise and deal with abuse.

Working from a feminist ontology and a participatory epistemology, I conduct my research with charities and groups of survivors, planning, conducting, analysing and interpreting the research together (Kindon, Pain & Kesby, 2007). The methods we use are interviews, discussion groups and participatory diagramming. In a recent project on trauma, we also used arts-based methods, including drawing, photography and songwriting, to help represent experiences that can be difficult to talk about. The research has resulted in reports and artwork as well as academic publications, and over the years it has been used to influence legislation and practice.

My own family's experiences of domestic abuse give me some understanding of this complex field. This is helpful in research encounters, although my research is not autobiographical in the same way as Tamas' (2011) groundbreaking study. I draw on psychotherapeutic approaches to research (Bondi, 2013) in order to try to mitigate ethical issues and protect the emotional well-being of everyone involved.

TEXT BOX 3.2	**Real-World Research: Peter's Research with Ethnic Minority Young People**

My research about ethnic minority young people has aimed to explore key spaces and times in their lives, such as their family relationships (Hopkins, 2006a), their senses of national and religious affiliation (Hopkins, 2007a) and their negotiations of multicultural encounters (Hopkins, 2014).

There are relatively few existing datasets about ethnic minority young people. Scottish Census data gives a snapshot in time and includes data about religious group membership too. There are also national surveys such as the Scottish Social Attitudes Survey and Growing Up in Scotland. Although these provide useful contextual data, they lack the in-depth insights that can be gained from conducting original qualitative research with ethnic minority youth.

My research practice is informed by feminist and antiracist ontologies, as I believe that Whiteness and masculinity provide a series of privileges for White people and for men that are not often available to women or those of minority ethnicities. I tend to use a social constructionist epistemology, as I seek to understand the lifeworlds of my participants by exploring how they understand their place in the world and their interactions with others. I do this through the use of focus groups and interviews, and sometimes also diaries or participatory diagramming techniques.

I tend to be regarded as an outsider by my participants, given my White ethnicity. However, I attended a large, multicultural high school in Glasgow and worked for a number of years in a residentially segregated neighbourhood in the South Side of Glasgow, both of which I feel give me some insights into these issues. Moreover, we all occupy a number of different positionalities (see the section on situated knowledges in Chapter 1) and so possess a range of similarities and differences to those we research (Hopkins, 2009). So, although my White ethnicity makes me different from many of my participants, my class background, Scottishness and gender mean I sometimes have more in common than people first realise.

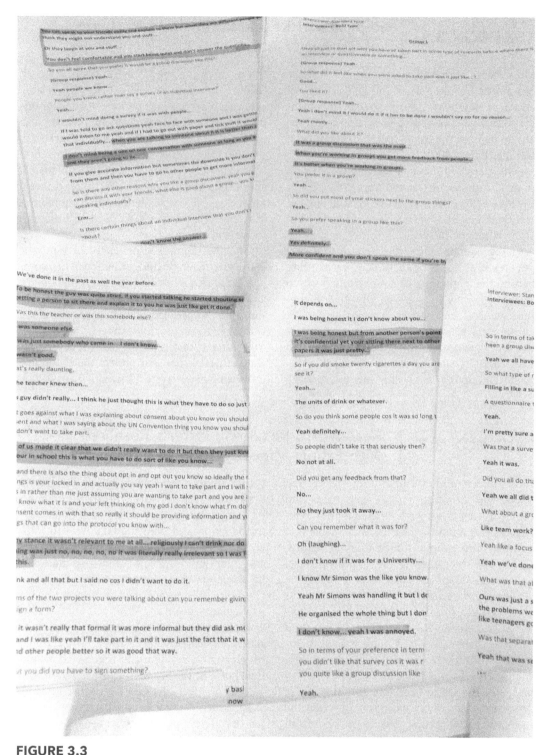

FIGURE 3.3
Coding focus group transcripts from research with young people. (Source: Peter Hopkins)

This is one reason why robust and rigorous systems of analysis are so important, whether you are undertaking statistical analysis or coding interview transcripts. And, as we also discussed in Chapter 1, reflecting on *who* you are and *where* you are is vital to ensuring that these analytical procedures are transparent and accountable and it is clear how your contribution to knowledge acquires its final shape. This is why social geographers place so much weight on carefully considering their positionality in relation to their participants, being reflexive about power relations in the field and analysing data (England, 1994; Nagar & Geiger, 2007).

WHAT'S THE POINT? THE PURPOSES OF RESEARCHING SOCIAL GEOGRAPHIES

Social geographies research has tended to be more oriented than other parts of geography to making some kind of difference. This trend has grown in popularity in recent years, especially in the United Kingdom, where it is now known as 'research impact' since the government introduced measures to count it and distribute partial funding on that basis (Pain, Kesby & Askins, 2011). However, social geographers have a much longer history of engaging with communities, policy makers and other institutions and organisations outside universities, and of seeking positive changes to the many social problems that much of our research focuses on (see Bunge, 1971; Pain, 2003). While we do not believe that this is obligatory or appropriate for all of our research, many of the authors of the chapters in this book and in the contemporary social geographies literature cited here have this commitment at heart.

The endeavour to make a difference with research can take various forms:

Engagement describes interactions and collaborations between academic researchers and other organisations, whether public sector, private sector or 'third' (voluntary) sector, as well as with the general public. For example, geographers are increasingly using arts-based methods or collaborating with artists to produce exhibitions based on their research, as alternative ways to educate, inform or create debate (e.g., Dwyer, 2015).

Policy research is a term used for research that seeks to engage with and influence policy making. This may take many forms, such as critiques of specific policies, recommendations for revision to policies or suggestions for new policy formation. An example is Crawley's (2007) research into the impact of age disputes on the welfare of separated asylum-seeking children. This research identified wide variations in practice and the use of highly problematic means of assessing age. The recommendations led to the introduction of specific guidelines and training for social workers and lawyers, and subsequently a significant reduction in the number of age disputes in the United Kingdom.

Participatory research, mentioned earlier in this chapter, involves the communities or groups that are directly affected by an issue sharing control of the research process to ensure positive outcomes. For example, Askins (2018) assesses the insights and outcomes achieved by PAR on people and place published over twenty-five years in feminist geographies.

Scholar activism is a term used when researchers and their research are actively aligned with a political cause and help to campaign for change. For example, a special issue of the journal *ACME* focuses on challenging food injustice by working beyond the dichotomy of being a scholar or an activist (Reynolds, Block & Bradley, 2018); see also Text Box 33.1 in Chapter 33 on academic activism in environmental justice.

As we suggested in Chapter 1, then, many social geographers are not simply interested in studying the social but in doing so in ways that *are* inherently social. Nonetheless, these approaches to making a difference do not always lead to improvements and sometimes have potential to do further harm (Smith, 2007). There is still a considerable way to go before our subdiscipline is routinely producing social geographic knowledges that address uneven power relations and before it fully recognises that these inequalities also inflect universities and the ways that research is arranged, as well as spaces and social forms in the wider world.

SUMMARY

- Social geographies is one of the most methodologically diverse and innovative fields of human geography.
- Social geographers use a rich range of qualitative and quantitative methods of data collection to study the relations between people and places. These choices are based on underlying ontological and epistemological approaches, which again draw on various traditions. Their deployment should be sensitive to particular research sites, contexts and sets of social relations.
- The politics, ethics and emotions of research are key issues that are often explicitly accounted for in social geographical research.
- Social geographers have also had much to say about the purpose of scholarship and knowledge production, and many of us try to do research that has a positive influence on society.
- In the chapters in this book, you will find many examples of 'real-world research' that show how social geographers have used methods in particular research settings. As you read, you may want to critically reflect on why they chose these methods and what their pros and cons are, remembering that there is no perfect way to design research and that our practice is also situated in and changed by the messy realities of life.

FURTHER READING

Flowerdew, R., & Martin, D. (2005) *Methods in Human Geography: A Guide for Students Doing a Research Project.* Harlow, UK: Longman.

Hay, I. (2016) *Qualitative Research Methods in Human Geography.* Oxford: Oxford University Press.

Hoggart, K., Davies, A., & Lees, L. (2002) *Researching Human Geography.* London: Arnold.

Kindon, S., Pain, R., & Kesby, M. (2007) *Connecting People, Participation and Place: Participatory Action Research Approaches and Methods.* London: Routledge.

Limb, M., & Dwyer, C. (2001) *Qualitative Methodologies for Geographers: Issues and Debates.* London: Hodder Arnold.

FOUNDATIONS

A   B   C   D

PART   PART   PART   PART

Space and Time

Robert Shaw

A television advert for Guinness from 1999 begins with a group of surfers waiting on a beach. A voiceover kicks in: 'He waits, that's what he does. And I'll tell you what. Tick followed tock followed tick followed tock followed tick'. After a while waiting, the perfect wave comes; yet only one of them is able to successfully surf it – and he and his friends celebrate victory. The advert finishes with the slogan, 'Good things come to those who wait'. Running to over one hundred seconds, the advert was unusually long for a television commercial, reinforcing the idea of the value of waiting. The aim was to evoke the longer time that it takes to pour a pint of Guinness compared to most other beers, suggesting that the wait for the drink adds value to the product.

Thinking about this advert as a social geographer, what's interesting is the way that it portrays an engagement with the natural world as representative of something slow. For many people whose hobbies involve nature, slowness or waiting is part of the appeal – the wait for the right wave to surf, for the right fish to bite, for the right birds to appear and so on. Slowness and waiting are connected in popular imagination to nature and the countryside. Indeed, we tend to associate certain places with slowness or fastness, too; contrast the images in Figure 4.1: one might be labelled a sleepy hamlet and the other a hectic urban shopping street. Taking the concepts of

FIGURE 4.1

Places with different speeds. (Credit: Rob Shaw)

space and place, we often find that place and the local are imagined to be slow, whereas space and the global are imagined to be fast.

These associations between speeds and geographical concepts are one way geography intersects with questions of time. We can also think of time in relation to individual experience: How do we perceive and live through time? We've all had moments in exam halls or lying in bed at night when time seems to go much more slowly than usual! Geographers have looked at individual experiences of time over days, weeks and years, and at how this experience is shaped in relation to place and social position. A third approach to time is the consideration of repetition and rhythms: from natural rhythms of days and seasons through to the socially constructed working day (see Chapter 28 on social reproduction). In this chapter, I want to take each of these understandings of time and explore how geographers have integrated this temporal element into the study of space and place.

FAST CITIES, SLOW TOWNS: SPACE, PLACE AND SPEED

Early social geographers imagined time and space to be closely connected. The influential geographer Paul Vidal de la Blache (1926) argued that places and the people who lived in them were inherently related. According to Vidal de la Blache, humans are 'at once both active and passive' (19) in their relationship to place, both changing places actively and experiencing external changes passively. Such changes shape place and people together; for Vidal de la Blache, this was always at a slow and gradual pace, connecting the present day with the history before it. This understanding of place as slow persists, and geographers have studied how activists have tried to use the idea of 'slowness' as a way of facilitating the distinctiveness of the local in the face of globalisation. The Cittàslow ('slow city') and 'slow food' movements are examples of this, created in Italy in the 1990s as ways of arguing for more sustainable, place-based consumption (Pink, 2009). The use of the word 'slow' was inspired by campaigns against fast food and, specifically, the spread of transnational chains such as McDonald's. The slow food movement argued that fast food was environmentally damaging, economically negative for its locations and unhealthy; by contrast, while the use of locally grown products and home cooking might be slower, it has a number of social, economic and environmental advantages (see also Chapter 32 on sustainability and Chapter 34 on food). In applying these ideas to urban life, the slow city movement seeks 'a set of criteria for local urban governance aimed at improving local quality of life, maintaining local uniqueness and supporting sustainable urban economies' (Pink, 2009: 453; see also Chapter 21 on housing). Further 'slow' movements have emerged, such as 'slow fashion' and 'slow beauty', as well as through application of ideas of mindfulness (Lea, Cadman & Philo 2015). Thus, activists have connected slowness with identity, sustainability and 'place'.

By contrast, speed has been associated with loss of place and loss of identity. The philosopher Walter Benjamin feared that the transformations to the landscape of Paris in the early twentieth century were destroying that city's historical characteristics. The medieval streets of the city had been demolished and replaced with wide boulevards (the best-known example being the Champs-Élysées), and these boulevards were now being filled with bikes and cars, displacing pedestrian movement. Since then, other writers have argued that other places have lost their identity as they have 'sped up'. The idea of the nonplace is used to describe sites, such as supermarkets and service stations, in which the dominant interactions are solitary and automated (Auge, 1995). However, most geographers reject the idea that speed destroys the identity of places. Returning to Paris, the boulevards that Benjamin feared would destroy the city have now become a symbolic and integral part of Parisian life. Their wide pavements have allowed cafés to prosper, generating a new form of slowness as people sit, stop and people-watch. So, while places do connect us to traditional and slower forms of living, they should not be understood as static or unchanging; rapid transformations can also form part of the evolving identity of a place.

PERSONAL TIMES: TIME GEOGRAPHY AND EVERYDAY LIFE

'In the persistent present stands a living body subject, endowed with memories, feelings, knowledge, imagination and goals'.

—Hägerstrand, 1982: 324

Torsten Hägerstrand's claim might seem quite obvious: the individuals whom we study in human geography are living people, with all the subjective qualities that that brings. However, much of the human geography that was being produced in Europe and North America at that time made the mistake of forgetting the living human at the heart of its research. Data were 'abstracted' from people, and lives that were lived with memories, feelings and emotions were reduced to points on a map. For Hägerstrand, this meant that important details about the social world were being overlooked. He argued that if we do not consider people's everyday experiences of the world, we cannot understand social relations and organisation, and therefore the inequalities and power structures that pervade it (Hägerstrand, 1970: 8). As Hägerstrand points out, this lived experience takes place in a 'persistent present'. By this, he means that we always experience the world *now*: we are never in the past and never in the future. Hägerstrand thought that by paying more attention to this 'present' he could better understand everyday life. This led to him bringing in questions of time alongside space, developing an approach that came to be known as time geography. Time geography attempted to 'capture the "thereness" of people and objects within their "normal" environmental and social settings' (Gregson, 1986: 189). In other words, time geographers described the social world by looking at the lived physical and social contexts in which people could be found, and they did this by bringing time into study alongside space. A major tool of time geography was the alteration of the representational tools that geography had traditionally used. Specifically, time geographers created time-space diagrams that would show the movement of individuals in time as well as space. In principle, these time-space diagrams could be used to show individual time-space paths and how such paths may come together or diverge across both time and space. An example of these time-space diagrams can be seen in Figure 4.2, which depicts a simple time-space path of an individual's working day involving three journeys: from home to

FIGURE 4.2

A time-space diagram in the style of Hägerstrand. (Credit: Rob Shaw)

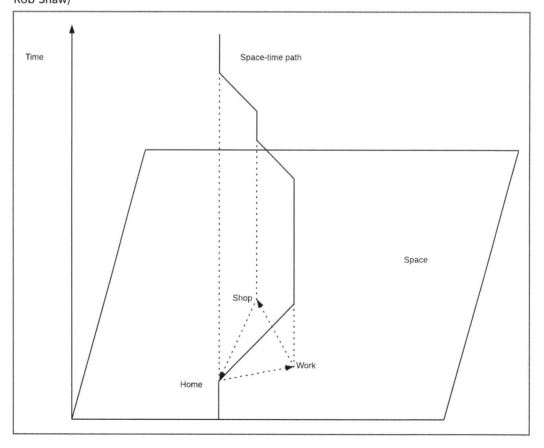

work; from work to a shop; and from the shop to home. This path can be followed along the solid line as the individual 'travels' across the square on the x-axis, representing space, and along the line on the y-axis, representing time.

Although the addition of the time axis conveyed data that a 'flat' map does not, time-space diagrams were still quite abstract. Writers from humanist and feminist perspectives argued that time geography still did not take sufficient account of the individuality of the people that they claimed to discuss. Anne Buttimer is reported as having told Hägerstrand that time geography appeared as a '*danse macabre* – a chilly recording by a detached observer, a hollow rattle of bones, but no communication of the vibrating sound of full orchestra' (Buttimer, in Hägerstrand, 2006: xii), ignoring the liveliness of the social world that she was interested in exploring (Buttimer, 1976). Several years later, Rose also criticised the project, arguing that by reducing lived experience to a single position on a diagram fails to account for gendered difference in experiences (Rose, 1993). This critique has now been largely accepted, and today such time-space diagrams are only rarely used in social geography, although writers such as Gregory and later Latham have attempted to breathe life into time geography accounts by adding photographic and interview data (Gregory, 1994: 252; Latham, 2003). The legacy of time geography remains, however, through greater attention and focus to the study of everyday life.

Time geography had its limitations, but, alongside new forms of feminist geography, it has helped to open up social geographies for

TEXT BOX 4.1 | Real-World Research: Time-Space

What time of day do you shower or bathe? When are you most likely to cook your evening meal? Do you have a time of day when you sit down to watch television? Geographers and sociologists have explored why it is that the time of these events coincides for many people. Our lives at home are shaped by social norms, coordination with others and key events – in the language of time geography called 'pacemakers' – that shape when we do common activities. Key pacemakers might be school opening hours, the scheduling of key television programmes, public transport operating hours and so on (Shove, 2009). While this might seem quite obvious, its importance is often overlooked. The fact that we all follow similar domestic routines creates peaks in the demand for energy; providing for this effect is less efficient than if energy demand was the same across the day; therefore, any 'flattening' of such peaks through behaviour change could reduce carbon emissions.

Powells and colleagues (2014) used geographical theories of time and rhythm to explore which domestic activities are more flexible. They found that practices such as eating an evening meal, which requires coordination with more people and more 'external' forces, are less flexible than activities such as cleaning, which is often done by just one person. They argue that effective interventions to encourage changes in behaviour so that people at home spread their energy use more widely across the day should therefore be targeted at these solitary practices rather than at more communal activities (see also Chapter 32 on sustainability).

more detailed study of everyday life. Dyck (2005) offers two reasons why this has enhanced social geographies. First, it has allowed closer attention to be paid to spaces in which marginalised groups often find themselves, outside more obviously powerful time-spaces. Second, 'taking a route through the routine, taken-for-granted activity of everyday life in homes, neighbourhoods and communities can tell us much about [everyday life's] role in supporting social, cultural and economic shifts – as well as helping us see how the "local" is structured by wider processes and relations of power' (Dyck, 2005: 234). In other words, it is in these routine and taken-for-granted spaces of everyday life that important social changes can happen (see Chapter 6 on social change).

PRODUCING PLACES: RHYTHMS

Imagine spending a day sitting at a busy urban crossroads, as in Figure 4.3. You arrive at 5 a.m.: the place is quiet. It's cold, and dawn is just beginning to break. Streetlights start blinking out, but not many people use the streets: just a few delivery drivers bringing baked goods to the stores and night-shift workers driving home at the end of their day. Slowly, from 6.30 a.m. or so, the streets begin to get busier; as the day gets lighter, commuters start to appear, and eventually there is a busy stream of people in suits, on phones, listening to headphones, going to work. After 9 a.m., it gets a bit quieter than in the rush hour, and now you see the activity of the day: maybe you're joined by someone selling street food or by street entertainment. In the evening, you see the same process in reverse, as workers return home. At some point in the early evening, the cafés and bars on the edge of the crossroads start to fill up, with an audience that is younger, more casually dressed than in the day. The temperature starts to drop and darkness falls again. It's quieter now, but still there are people around. Someone selling plastic flowers walks around the tables of the cafés, and you hear musicians playing for the drinkers and diners. Midnight approaches, and the number of people starts to dwindle.

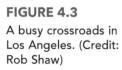

FIGURE 4.3

A busy crossroads in Los Angeles. (Credit: Rob Shaw)

These rhythms seem so natural, but the study of rhythms – which is the third key element in the study of time and space – reveals the ways they are constructed. Social geographers have examined how rhythms, such as those described above, produce places and the lives of the people who inhabit them. The philosopher Henri Lefebvre was particularly interested in rhythm, and he identified two key elements: repetition and difference. 'Repetition' might be obvious as part of rhythm: without repeated actions, there can be no sense of rhythm. However, there is no 'identical absolute repetition' (Lefebvre, 2004: 6); when actions are repeated, they are never exactly the same. So one working week is never exactly the same as the next, and a morning commute at a train station is always a little different from the previous one. This is where, for Lefebvre, difference comes in: a rhythm must contain difference or it is just one action repeated, rather than a proper rhythm. This difference is important, as it creates the possibility for the rhythm to change. Lefebvre conceives of the dominance of rhythms as the dominance of society: 'for there to be *change*, a social group, a class or caste must intervene by imprinting rhythm on an era' (Lefebvre, 2004: 14, original emphasis). Lefebvre analyses the ways capitalist control over the rhythms of rest, sleep and leisure dominates people's lives and entrenches the power held by capital.

Lefebvre's is just one approach to rhythm, but it has been influential in geography in highlighting the possible relationship between rhythms and power. Both feminist and nonrepresentational work have engaged with questions of bodily rhythms, looking at how these shape different people's engagements with particular places and spaces (Duffy et al., 2011). Others have developed the work of time geography to speak more of rhythms: Edensor (2011), for example, has explored the rhythmic qualities of commuting, which connects together multiple locations rather than just one place through a series of repeated practices. Other approaches to studying rhythm have focused on a set of practices rather than on one place, as in Kärrholm's (2009) work on shopping, showing that this practice draws together multiple people and locations. What links these studies of rhythms together is the ways they unpack and explore the apparently natural, recurring sequences of events that produce both everyday life and place.

SUMMARY

- For Vidal de la Blache (1926), the slow evolution of place and the people who live in a place was an almost 'natural' process.
- Whether through the study of fast/slow geographies, of the lived experience of time or of social rhythms, social geographers have shown that this connection between time and space is anything but natural.

- Instead, time is constructed, and in ways that are particularly powerful in producing both people's everyday lives and the places in which they live them.
- By focusing on questions of time, geographers can excavate the constructed origins of the social structures that shape our lives.

FURTHER READING

Edensor, T. (ed.) (2016) *Geographies of Rhythm*. London: Routledge.

Latham, A. (2003) Research, performance, and doing human geography: Some reflections on the diary-photograph, diary-interview method. *Environment and Planning A: Economy and Space*, 35(11): 1993–2017.

Mountz, A., Bonds, A., Mansfield, B., Loyd, J., Hyndman, J., Walton-Roberts, M., Basu, R., Whitson, R., Hawkins, R., Hamilton, T., & Curran, W. (2015) For slow scholarship: A feminist politics of resistance through collective action in the neoliberal university. *ACME: An International E-Journal for Critical Geographies*, 14(4): 1235–59.

CHAPTER — 5

Scale

Quan Gao

Scale is one of the foundational concepts that geographers use to understand social and spatial relations, along with other geographical key terms such as space, place and time (see Chapter 4 on space and time). The concept of scale shapes our geographical imaginaries, enabling us to understand the worlds around us both spatially and differentially. However, scales and their significance to geography and broader disciplines are contested. The conventional classification of scales, such as local, regional and global, are not taken-for-granted categories in which material and social processes take place.

In this chapter I therefore offer a brief introduction to scale. First, I look at the multiple meanings of scale and its status and epistemology; there is no consensus on whether scale actually exists – that is to say, there is no agreement to date regarding whether scale has material and concrete manifestations or is simply a conception imposed by us. Second, I review existing theories and debates about scale. Instead of arguing from one specific standpoint, I emphasise how we can employ scalar imaginaries in real-world research in social geographies.

THE MULTIPLE MEANINGS OF SCALE

Cartographic Scale

In its simplest sense, scale is conceived of as predominantly a cartographic concept; this is the oldest definition of scale, which dates back to the science of cartography in the eighteenth century. In this tradition, scale refers to the ratio between the distance on a map and that same distance on the surface of the earth. According to Sayre (2009), cartographic scale in this sense can be understood as *size*, a quantitative unit of measurement to map out some attribute of an object or phenomenon (e.g., length, volume or mass). Space and time cannot be quantitatively observed unless they are divided into specific units that can be used for measurement. Therefore, cartographic scale implies that the ways we make sense of worlds – that is, what we perceive and understand about the worlds around us – is conditioned on the concepts that we adopt. Cartographic scale actually provides us with a conceptual tool with which to organise what we sense in a spatial and temporal manner and, therefore, to understand particular phenomena. To put it simply, cartographic scale is about how we spatially and quantitatively perceive the world. However, the observational results might vary in accordance with the scale employed. For example, if we explore ethnic minorities' or immigrants' residential concentrations in specific neighbourhoods or cities, we can cartographically represent their patterns of residential concentration and consider this from various scales, such as specific streets, wards, neighbourhoods, postcode districts, cities or metropolitan areas.

Hierarchical Scale

Hierarchical scale is a more qualitative measure, referring to the *levels* at which social practices and physical processes take place. Hierarchical scale raises very interesting questions: Might social and physical processes operate at and be sorted into several levels and categories, such as the local, regional and global scales? To answer these questions, we need first to differentiate hierarchical scale as a way of knowing and as the actual relations among social and physical phenomena.

On the one hand, like cartographical scale, hierarchical scale is also a kind of epistemology – the way that we perceive worlds, albeit adopting a more qualitative and vertical scope. In order to capture the complex phenomena, geographers tend *deliberately* to classify and differentiate phenomena into various scales so that they can be observed and measured more clearly. For example, the hierarchical scales employed by human geographers vary from the body to the globe (see Figure 5.1). Peter Taylor (1982) offered an early social theory of scale by drawing on Immanuel Wallerstein's world-system theory (see Figure 5.1). Taylor argues that world-system theory is deficient in explaining the geopolitics of worlds, for it primarily focuses on the horizontal understanding of space

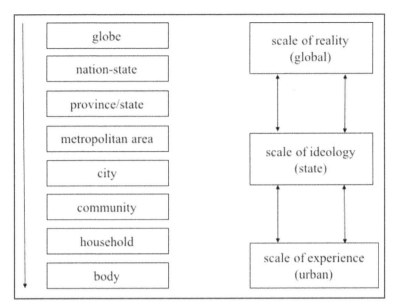

FIGURE 5.1
Hierarchical scale and social theory of scale. (Credit: Quan Gao)

and power rather than on how these operate at different levels. He therefore proposes a political and economic model of scale that can be classified into three vertical levels: 'the scale of reality (global), the scale of ideology (state) and the scale of experience (urban)' (Taylor, 1982: 24). Taylor argues that capitalist accumulation is a global-scale phenomenon, while the scale of experience is the social environment that we live in. The state as an ideological apparatus makes efforts to separate experience from reality to reinforce capitalist accumulation. For example, in an age of globalisation, farmers who plant cocoa in South America might perceive their lived experiences at a village level; yet they are actually involved in the commodity chain at the global scale.

Hierarchical scale is particularly important for social geography. Valentine (2001) suggests that hierarchical scales, from the body to the global, are platforms for analysing specific kinds of socio-spatial activities. For example, home or household is an appropriate site for analysing microsocial dynamics, such as family relationships and gender inequality (see Chapter 16 on gender), while community is often the site at which neighbourhood activism, ethnic congregation and cultural conflicts take place. But it is important to remember that social relations often cut across several scales (more on the social construction of scale below).

Observational Scale and Operational Scale

Scale can also be classified as observational scale or operational scale. Observational scale refers to what *extent* and *resolution* particular phenomena can be observed and measured at (Sayre, 2009). Extent means the overall area and time period that a study intends to cover. For example, small-scale research typically means research conducted in a small area, such as a neighbourhood or city block. Resolution is the basic unit of measurement that the research intends to employ, which determines the precision that the research can capture. For example, an investigation on urban poverty might capture more precise and detailed information if the smallest unit of an investigation were a household rather than a city block or census tract.

Operational scale refers to the spatial and temporal scales at which geographical processes take place, meaning that scale is an actual entity, independent of the way that we observe it. The operational scale might also apply to social and economic processes. For example, the phenomenon of spatial mismatch – the mismatch between where low-income households reside and where suitable job opportunities are available when manufacturing firms move to the suburbs – operates at the metropolitan scale.

SCALE AS RELATION AND NETWORK

In sharp contrast to the ideas of operational and hierarchical scale, some scholars argue that different scales are neither linear nor function independently but are, instead, relational. Understood in this way, it is an oversimplification to view scale as a hierarchical entity or spatially contiguous structure; rather, scale spans the social and biophysical space and functions as a network, stretching across hierarchical space. The most famous metaphor of relational scale comes from Howitt's (1998) examination of musical scales: the overall quality of a symphony is not a mechanical combination of all notes; rather, it is determined by not only the individual quality of each note but also how one note is positioned in relation to others. Thus, a change in any note will affect the symphony at the whole scale. Howitt's central aim is to argue that scale should be understood relationally, as a relational element within a complex system and network, rather than as the sum of its separate elements.

THEORIES AND DEBATES OF SCALE IN SOCIAL GEOGRAPHY

As suggested above, scale is a multifaceted and contested concept. Social geographers are rarely united on what is meant by scale and how or in what ways it should be operationalised. Over the past two decades or so, 'scale debates' have continued as the concept has increasingly proved to have contradictory and problematic meanings. The 'scale debates' in geography have been primarily concerned with three lines of inquiries: (1) whether scales actually exist, (2) how scales come into being and (3) why and to what extent scalar thought is valued in geography. These debates are crucial to justifying why 'geography matters'.

Social geographers who follow a structuralist approach may acknowledge scale's existence and thus view it as an existential element that constitutes space and society. From a structuralist point of view, social and material phenomena are structured by predictable regularities that are superior to any individual or object. Social phenomena cannot be explained unless they are understood in relation to other phenomena and within a systematic structure. For example, structuralists tend to break down society into social, economic, political and cultural dimensions, within which each domain generates meanings only by interacting with another. Some key thinkers on theories of scale (e.g., Peter Taylor and Neil Smith) are influenced by this approach, acknowledging that production activities and their organisation under capitalism are structured by a scaled system. Taylor's theory of scale is primarily concerned with the various scales, like urban, nation-state and global levels, at which capitalism is organised.

Another important contributor, Neil Smith (1984), advances Taylor's arguments by elaborating on how various scales come into existence. For Smith (1984: 135), scale is the outcome of the uneven development of capitalism: 'Capital inherits a geographical world that is already differentiated into complex spatial patterns. As the landscape falls under the sway of capital … these patterns are grouped into an increasingly systematic hierarchy of spatial scales'. For Smith, capitalism is constantly caught up in the geographical tension between two opposing needs: capital seeks to be fixed in particular locations in which accumulation can take place (e.g., capitalism must take advantage of local labour forces), and simultaneously capital needs to level its economic space across wider locations to achieve optimal allocation of various resources and thus maximise the rate of profit. In this sense, it is the very structure of capitalism itself that results in the existence of various scales.

Inspired by Smith's thoughts, human geography has been increasingly concerned with how and why scales are produced by economic, social and political processes. Many human geographers therefore interpret scale more as a result of social construction than as an externally given category. Overwhelmingly, this set of thoughts reflects a social constructionist approach. Although many human geographers accept the constructionist framework, it does not mean that they achieve consensus on the status of scale's existence, because constructionism itself consists of diverse standpoints (see Text Box 5.1 regarding the social construction of scale).

As we see in Text Box 5.1, political-economic and poststructural approaches are divergent about the nature of scale (scale as a set of material relations and structures versus scales as social representations and discourses). Some geographers therefore started to reflect on the very question of whether scale is a valuable analytical frame. The most extensive critique came from Marston, Jones and Woodward's (2005) article 'Human Geography without Scale'. They argue that scale is not an analytically specific concept because it does not have a causally grounded foundation. The primary difference between vertical geographies of scales and a horizontal geographies network reflects only researchers' several epistemologies and spatial imaginaries (see Table 5.1).

TEXT BOX 5.1 | What Is the Social Construction of Scale?

Social Constructionism

Social constructionism claims that the things we experience in the world are merely constructed by society and it is our ideas or conceptions that form the basis for assumptions about fact and reality. For example, race and ethnicity are not biologically predetermined categories but rather constructed by society (see Chapter 13 on race). However, there is both a weak and a strong social constructionism: the weak one acknowledges the existence of factual knowledge, while the strong one views reality as a purely social construct.

The Social Construction of Scale

Viewing scale as a social construct might be inspired by Henri Lefebvre's (1992/1974) theorisations about the production of space, which argue that space is not a physical container but a production of social relations. Likewise, scale is not necessarily a preexisting hierarchical structure that orders the world. Instead, it is an outcome of the social, economic and political processes per se. According to Marston (2000), early research on the social construction of scale addresses at least three sets of theorisations. First, the differentiation of scale produces and is produced through 'the geographical structure of social interaction' (Smith, 1992: 73): scale is an outcome of the structure. Second, the production of scale has material consequence in the real world. Scale is not purely a tangible conception of reality but has real impact on the ways that social and material worlds are organised. Third, the framing of scale is not necessarily fixed and enduring but always open to transformation in accordance with social and material processes.

Different Approaches to the Social Construction of Scale

Political and economic approach: This approach engages in examining how scales are constructed as material entities in political and economic processes. It does not deny the existence of scale but does reject scale as a pregiven container in which human activity takes place. 'Something is a social construct' does not mean that it does not exist, because social constructs might have material consequences or manifestations in the real world (weak constructionism). The key figures of this approach are Neil Smith (1984, 1992) and Erik Swyngedouw (1997, 2007). For example, Swyngedouw (1997) argues that scales such as 'the local', 'regional' or 'global' are shaped by the political and economic forces of globalisation. Global capital has simultaneously made both the global scale and metropolitan regions more important for capital accumulation, while the national scale is less significant. Moreover, scales are also shaped by particular actors, organisations and movements. Local and regional actors might construct 'spaces of engagement' (Cox, 1998) that link them to superior levels of institutions and thus enable them to gain more power and resources.

Poststructural approach: This approach considers scale as fundamentally a conceptual representation of specific socio-spatial relations and orderings (Moore, 2008; MacKinnon, 2011), which rejects not only a pregiven sense of scale but also the existence of scales altogether. Scholars of this approach are concerned more with how social practices and discourses shape scales than with the wider political and economic structures. For example, Deckha (2003) argues that scale might be a discursive tool deployed by different actors to achieve particular forms of power and recognition. He examines the contested scalar narratives between community and government in urban regeneration, with local actors resisting governments' agenda of reinserting 'the local' into wider global capital.

TABLE 5.1	Spatial Association of the Horizontal and Vertical (Marston, Jones & Woodward, 2005: 420)
Horizontal Geographies	**Vertical Geographies**
Network	Scaffold
Extensive	Layered
Horizon	Summit
Distance	Elevation
Milieu	Dominion
Dispersed	Stacked

Are political-economic and poststructural approaches to scales really so incompatible? MacKinnon's (2011: 23) recent work seeks to reconcile and combine scale 'as a set of material relations with an interest in the epistemological construction of scale through particular social representations and discourses', drawing on a critical realistic philosophy. Critical realism acknowledges the objects and relations constructed by social actors, discourses and representations, while arguing that social construction may, in turn, produce regularities or material differentiations independent of an individual's conception (see Andrew Sayer's 2010 accessible introduction to critical realism). Scale is not restricted to an 'epistemological construct', as social construction itself may fix scales as the material expression of power relations and structures – the consequences of social construction actually exist. MacKinnon (2011: 21) therefore proposes a more compatible theorisation of scale: 'It is often not scale *per se* that is the prime object of connection, but rather specific processes and institutionalized practices that are themselves differentially scaled'.

Finally, to what extent has scalar thought added value to social geographies? Regardless of whether scales exist, we cannot deny that they are geographical imaginaries that shape how we view the social world. Moreover, our geographical imaginaries are themselves often organised according to scale. As we can see in Text Box 5.2, scalar imaginaries not only influence the way we view the world but also have real, material impact on the real world. This is evident in the development of cities (see Chapter 10 on urban/rural), which is influenced by urban planners and policy makers, whose ideas are unescapably organised in scalar terms. In other words, we could assume that scalar thought is inherent in our social imaginaries, which constitutes an intrinsic element of our perception of space.

TEXT BOX 5.2 | Real-World Research: Scale and Social Relations in Spain and China

Case 1: Scalar Narratives in Bilbao, Spain (González, 2006)

Gonzalez's research on Bilbao's urban regeneration project provides a vivid description of how different conceptions of scales are narrated by social actors and how the scalar narratives in turn shape the material processes of urban development.

Bilbao is an old industrial city in Spain which was undergoing an extensive urban regeneration during the 1990s to early 2000s. During this process, policy actors, including the city council, different levels of governments and planning agencies, used scalar narratives to justify an entrepreneurial urban policy and reinforce Bilbao's competitiveness in the global economy. The local policy makers produced three forms of the scalar narrative about Bilbao. First, the scalar political project sought to discursively construct 'the global Basque city region'. The government therefore made efforts to promote Bilbao from a local city to a global scale by redesigning the urban landscape. Second, the values of locality were highlighted as key resources to compete in the global economy (the 'glocalizing Bilbao' narrative). The city therefore made efforts to produce a set of distinctive 'local' values. Third, the scalar narratives of the 'space of flows' and 'network' were adopted by policy makers to construct different layers of material infrastructure, including information technologies systems and the nodes and hubs that supported this system.

This case study shows not only that scales were socially constructed by different actors who sought to gain specific power and resources but also that, once particular scalar narratives are established, they shape the material configuration of the city.

Case 2: Multiscaled Secularisation in China (Gao, Duo & Zhu, 2018; Gao, Qian & Yuan, 2018)

Secularisation is a social process whereby religious beliefs and practices decline and become increasingly individualised in society. In China, however, secularisation is a state-endorsed policy and a top–down ideological process engineered by political elites. Gao and colleagues' research suggests that the process of secularisation is differentially scaled and its effects vary differently at national and local scales.

Taking the case of a 'gospel village' (in which most villagers accepted the missionary work from the West), they find that secularisation in ideological campaigns at the scale of the nation-state is not homogenous but negotiated by members of the local community. At the scale of the local community, while most villagers accepted secular ideologies and were uninterested in Christian belief, the inflow of rural migrant workers engaged in Christian belief reinvigorated the Church, which was declining. It is the very secular condition of being (the massive industrialisation and exploitation among workers) that enabled migrants to seek meaning form Christianity and therefore revitalise religion at the local scale. Therefore, a scalar perspective might help us better understand the contingency and tension existing between broader social processes and their impacts on local practices of human beings. In this case, nation-scaled secularisation has a contradictory effect on the local community.

SUMMARY

- Scale does not have absolute manifestations, although it provides a way to observe and measure particular phenomena in terms of size, level and relation.
- Scale is produced by social processes and relationships, so it is subject to change and revision. Therefore, there are no necessarily fixed scales that structure the world.
- Scale is socially constructed yet also has material consequences. Social geographers often focus on how social processes are differentially scaled in unequal ways.
- While suspending scale's status regarding its existence, we cannot deny that our social imaginaries are organised in scalar terms.

FURTHER READING

Gao, Q., Qian, J., & Yuan, Z. (2018) Multi-scaled secularization or postsecular present? Christianity and migrant workers in Shenzhen, China. *Cultural Geographies*, 25(4): 553–70.

MacKinnon, D. (2011) Reconstructing scale: Towards a new scalar politics. *Progress in Human Geography*, 35(1): 21–36.

Marston, S. A. (2000) The social construction of scale. *Progress in Human Geography*, 24(2): 219–42.

Moore, A. (2008) Rethinking scale as a geographical category: From analysis to practice. *Progress in Human Geography*, 32(2): 203–25.

Social Change

Alastair Bonnett

This chapter looks at the social geographies of social change and transformation. It addresses social change and transformation in terms of three geographical themes (globalisation, the environment and racialised cities) before turning to the social geographies of one particular consequence of rapid social change – namely, nostalgia.

All four of these topics evidence the importance of geographical perspectives on social shifts and transitions. We shall see that social geographies does not just take the sociology of 'social change' and politely scatter a few spatial footnotes beneath it. It expands and reconstitutes the concept of social change, remaking it for a form of scholarship where places and environments matter. Many social geographers insist on the international and transnational nature of social change and transformation; they stretch these ideas across the world at the same time as they try to grasp their local character. In this way, the social is situated and placed and our knowledge of it transformed. Let me take one of the examples I touch on in this chapter briefly to show what I mean. A sense of loss in the face of social change is called nostalgia. This word, derived from Greek, literally means homesickness. Nostalgia is not always about home; yet it is always, in small or large part, about places and environments – the landscapes, streets, fields – now gone but fondly thought of (see also Chapter 12 on emotion). Geography is not just a 'frame' or a 'context' here – it is integral; not an addendum, but part and parcel of the idea.

GLOBALISATION AND THE SCALES OF SOCIAL CHANGE

Our understanding of the tiniest scale to the grandest is socially constituted (see Chapter 5 on scale). The meaning and apprehension of the intimate geographies of our bodies and of interstellar distances have changed over time, sometimes quite suddenly. Cosgrove (2001) argued that the first photograph of the whole Earth, taken by Apollo 17 some 29,000 kilometres away on 7 December 1972, was a simultaneous social, scientific and cultural transformation. Our planet, in an instant, was seen as nothing more than a small 'blue marble', alone in an inky nothingness. The 'blue marble' image provided a fillip to the nascent environmental movement, for it offered a stark reproof to those bent on using up Earth's finite resources. There is no Planet B.

Most social geographers have been concerned with more familiar scales – notably, the local, regional, national and inter- and transnational. These scales have been connected by social geographers through a wide range of engagements with contemporary social changes, including migration patterns (King, 2012a) and the rise of activism around social discrimination and marginalisation (Wright, 2008; Routledge & Cumbers, 2009). One of the most pressing changes that has provoked research over the past forty years has been globalisation, a topic that is usually allied to the rolling out of neoliberal models of governance, economy and behaviour. Social geographers have been interested in globalisation as a planetary process and also in how it has been adopted, adapted and resisted at smaller scales. An increasing focus for social geographers has been the capacity of those subject to global capitalism to reshape or even reject its expectations and restrictions. For example, Routledge and Cumbers' (2009) study, *Global Justice Networks: Geographies of Transnational Solidarity*, addresses the emergence of a 'global justice movement' as a 'translocal and transnational' phenomenon (see also Perrons, 2004). Drawing on examples from across Asia and Latin America, especially those that concern Indigenous struggles over land resources, Routledge and Cumbers (2009) evidence the interconnectedness of disparate campaigns, noting that 'increasing global convergence between movements [has] signalled a scale shift in what had hitherto been largely disconnected struggles' (11). However, Routledge and Cumbers are also keen to draw out the continuing and sometimes growing salience of the local. The term 'glocal' has been devised to capture this paradoxical combination. Many studies of the glocal address 'the local' in terms of geographical proximity and 'the global' in virtual terms, as accessed and engaged through the internet. For example, Schnell's (2016) study on glocal 'lifestyle' in Tel Aviv observes two distinct spatial scales: 'corporeal daily life' and 'virtual space'. The result, he says, is an 'estrangement from home spaces' that 'enables easy residential mobility' (58).

CONNECTING SOCIAL AND ENVIRONMENTAL CHANGE

The social changes occasioned by environmental change have not always been to the fore in social geography. The subdiscipline has, sometimes, exhibited an anthropocentric disposition; construing 'the social' as a purely human arena disconnected from 'the natural world', which, in any case, is claimed to be a human construct (Demeritt, 2002; see also Chapter 33 on environmental justice). However, the importance of connecting environmental and social change is gaining attention as various crises concerning the environment have ever more profound social impacts. Climate change–induced migration has become a key area of concern, especially when compounded by regional conflicts (Selby et al., 2017; Farbotko, Stratford & Lazrus, 2016). Some of the most far-reaching and interesting work that links environmental and social change addresses the question of how 'change' is conceptualised. Thus, for example, Shove (2010) has written extensively on how best to conceptualise the social changes required to mitigate climate change. She points to the titles of UK environmental policy statements to indicate the individualistic paradigm of social change within which they work:

> In the UK, the Framework for Pro-environmental Behaviours produced by the Department for Environment, Food and Rural Affairs (DEFRA) (2008) represents one of a slew of recent reports dealing with issues of lifestyle, behaviour, and climate change. Others include 'Creatures of Habit: The art of behavioural change' . . . 'I Will If You Will' . . . 'Changing Behaviour Through Policy Making' . . . 'Motivating Sustainable Consumption' . . . 'Driving Public Behaviours for Sustainable Lifestyles'. (Shove, 2010: 1274)

Most of us are familiar with the way that our responses, or nonresponses, to environmental crises are soaked in the language of individual behaviour change and of guilt. No matter how much we recycle, or buy organic, or refuse to fly, and so on, it is never enough. Shove's point is not that people should not be changing their behaviour, but rather that a singular focus on individual behavioural change is unlikely to be sufficient or productive (see Chapter 32 on sustainability). She says that such a focus 'marginalises and in many ways excludes serious engagement with other possible analyses' (1274). Shove proposes other models, such as those that address the way 'institutions, infrastructures, and daily life interact' and an understanding that 'certain forms of demand are unavoidably inscribed, for example, in the design and operation of electricity and water infrastructures and in the architecture of the home itself' (1274) (see Chapter 21 on housing). Rather than positing the social response to environmental crises as something grounded in individual choices, Shove is asking that we frame it more broadly. The 'relevant societal innovation', she says, 'is that in which contemporary rules of the game are eroded; in which the status quo is called into question; and in which more sustainable regimes of technologies, routines, forms of knowhow, conventions, markets, and expectations take hold across all domains of daily life' (Shove, 2010: 1278). In part, Shove's argument is mirrored in work by social and environmental geographers on community 'resilience' and adaptation in the face of environmental degradation and climate change. Cote and Nightingale (2012) argue both for the importance of seeing the connection between social and environmental change and for a shift towards understanding 'political and ethical questions as crucial drivers of social-ecological outcomes rather than "inconvenient" politics' (484). Brown (2014) extends and challenges this insight when she responds to Adger's (2000) examination of the 'co-evolving' nature of social and ecological resilience, drawing attention to the way that environmental crises are likely to be radically destabilising and difficult to plan for. 'Global environmental change', Brown notes, 'will enforce radical, unplanned and detrimental transformation, especially through impacts of climate change' (2014: 112). In our hubristic age, it is common to imagine that 'change and transformation' are things that we can control and master. Brown reminds us that, when it comes to the relationship between humans and the environment, it would be wise to recognise the limits of our knowledge and power.

RACIALISED URBAN CHANGE

The city may be thought of as a national stage for social change and transformation. It is certainly the epicentre for many events that capture the headlines, such as protests, violence and social experimentation. For social geographers, however, it is more than just a stage: change and transformation have an intimate relationship, not just with 'the city' as a generic context but also with particular cities and particular neighbourhoods and streets. The social changes that I am interested in here concern the racialisation of city space. Although this is a topic that can be examined in many parts of the world, Anglophone social geographers have tended to approach it by looking at the cities in their own countries of origin. Although such a focus limits the geographical scope of such work, it reflects the politicised nature of the topic and the desire to engage in questions of social justice that are near at hand.

From the 1970s onwards in the United Kingdom, and earlier in the United States, what Cohen (1993: 7) called the 'spatialisation of race' led to the inner city becoming territorialised in terms of specific minority ethnic groups, as well as in terms of general levels of 'diversity' (see also Chapter 13 on race). Watt (1998: 688) argued that this process 'reflects the racialised, and in certain cases, racist pathologisation of urban areas'. Stanton (2000: 129), writing about the United States, suggests that 'conceptually the city is left to the poor and racially marginalized' and that, for 'the media, the barometer of the national consciousness, the American city is now "the black city"'. The racialisation of the inner city's image is associated by Stanton with the devaluing of the city: its demotion to a hopeless and irrational landscape. To illustrate this process, he offered the following anecdote: 'Canal Street, the teeming main downtown New Orleans, was described as "dead" by white residents when I arrived in the city. The energetic "Third World" and African-American commercial presence there was not registered as a realm of the living' (Stanton, 2000: 129). The partial revitalisation of many US urban cores and the suburbanisation of non-White Americans suggests that Stanton's assessment is somewhat simplistic. However, neither revitalisation nor suburbanisation necessarily signals a weakening of the spatial confinement of non-Whiteness. Indeed, Logan's (1988: 352) research suggested that 'the status of black suburbs in relation to the rest of suburbia is very much like the status of black ghettos in relation to the rest of the inner city'.

More recent work has focused on the conflict and connections between gentrification and racialisation. Writing about English cities, Rhodes and Brown (2019) depict 'shifting understandings of the "inner city"', from 'a pathological, racialised space subject to particular modes of institutional regulation' to a more recent phenomenon, which they depict as 'the relative fragmentation of the "inner city" . . . through urban regeneration and changes in the spatialisation of "race" and ethnicity'. Rhodes and Brown point to the development of a complex pattern in which enclaves of racialised gentrification and racialised poverty sit cheek by jowl. This kind of proximity also attracted the attention of Shaw in her research on the power of Whiteness in the context of gentrification in Sydney. Shaw (2001, 2007) notes how White urban identity only becomes visible in relation to a ghettoised Black presence, in this case the presence of 'The Block', an Aboriginal-identified zone of inner Sydney. 'My observations of the spaces near The Block', Shaw writes, 'lead me to think about how whiteness strengthens and consolidates against the presence of The Block' (2001: 8). Shaw highlights the way property is valued in terms of detachment from the presence of The Block and concludes that 'negotiations' over property values 'occur at the expense of entitlement of the residents of The Block to live in a place designated as Aboriginal' (2007: xx). Work by social geographers on the impact of gentrification on Black and Latino residents in cities across the United States has also unpicked the confluence of rising property values and racialised communities (Glick, 2008; Brenner & Theodore, 2002; Wyly & Hammel, 2004; Maharawal, 2018).

At the same time and, sometimes, in the same place as the impacts of gentrification are debated, social geographers have written about the racialisation of policing and the rise of antiracist activism in the city. Referring to Ferguson, the city in Missouri where disturbances were sparked by the police shooting of Black suspects, Derickson (2017) considers that, 'politically and culturally, the Age of Ferguson holds the potential to force a reckoning' with 'the inadequacies' of the 'post–Civil Rights racial détente' (231). The Black Lives Matter movement is the best-known example of this new form of mobilisation. The diffusion of this movement across the borders of the United States, with Black Lives Matter protests appearing in London and other cities, tells us that American antiracist activism is being adopted and adapted in numerous urban contexts.

RESISTING CHANGE: SOCIAL GEOGRAPHIES OF NOSTALGIA

One response to urban diversity and change has been 'White flight' and other forms of self-imposed segregation, such as gated communities. These are movements in space yet, in the sense that they are seeking to re-create a purportedly lost sense of community, also in time. However, the geography of nostalgia has diverse political pathways: it can represent an attempt to turn one's back on diversity, 'foreigners' and incomers, but it can also reflect a rejection of neoliberal globalisation; it can be right wing and it can be left wing, and sometimes it is both or neither. The diversity and importance of nostalgic responses to social change has been coming to the fore in the work of a number of social geographers, in part in response to the realisation that many types of activism and politics contain not just a critique of the present but also a sense of a valued past (Blunt, 2003; Wheeler, 2017). This work is likewise responding to that fact that nostalgia is not just a passive sigh of regret: it also provokes action. People move to 'unspoilt' places and buy 'authentic' things: nostalgia is an active component in socioeconomic change. Stewart (1988: 227) argues that, today, 'Nostalgia, like the economy it runs with, is everywhere'.

I shall take one particular example to explore nostalgia – namely, the loss and yearning that often accompanies migration. It sounds paradoxical, but one of the things that connect those hostile to migration and the immigrants themselves is a sense of loss. The migrant leaves behind a great deal: sometimes almost everything, and very often a house, a community, a language, a landscape. The greater the cultural gulf between home and destination, and the less economic power the migrant has upon arrival, the greater the likelihood that migration results in the experience of vulnerability and loss. Nostalgia has been studied among migrants in various ways, and I shall briefly introduce two: material objects of remembrance and long-distance nationalism.

The valued objects that migrants carry with them from 'home' are often handed on to younger generations. Turan's (2011) study of family heirlooms among Armenian and Greek migrants who fled Turkey reveals a distinct female heritage and lineage of objects and remembrance. She cites a New York–born Armenian American, a forty-two-year-old called Carine, talking about some photographs of a piece of lacework that her grandmother had made and that she is to inherit: 'Look at this handiwork. . . . She did not come from anything; she struggled a lot, but she was still able to have so much richness inside her, not material things but as a person who is rock solid and wise' (Turan 2011: 173). Rather than seeing the lacework as a symbol only of loss, Carine draws strength from it, looking backward for inspiration and connection. A similar dynamic can be heard in the narrative of Catherine, a seventy-two-year-old second-generation Greek American whose parents came from present-day Turkey. The object she speaks about is a large grater that hangs on her wall and that was her grandmother's: 'It is almost sacred, that is, it will never be thrown away. . . . There is drama in the family history; the burning of the city, my father leaving the city when he was 16 – it reminds me of all. It is a tangible I can touch and hold. Sometimes when I pass by, I touch it' (Turan, 2011: 182). The materiality that is being described here turns nostalgia into a physical presence; the felt reality of distant places and times is established through the fingers.

Turning to long-distance nationalism, we find a more symbolic and less tactile sense of the valued past (see also Chapter 9 on nation and nationalism). Fuglerud's (1999) study of Sri Lankan Tamil nationalists in exile in Norway points to the development of increasingly self-conscious and explicit attempts to reclaim a proud past, based around an 'ideal of authenticity'. This identity is constantly being provoked into existence by a hungry search for news from 'home'. Bock-Luna's (2007) study, *The Past in Exile*, a portrait of Serbian long-distance nationalism in the United States, shows that the attachment to the homeland and the development of a specifically Serbian identity gathered pace in the context of perceived affronts to Serbian national pride during the Balkan wars of the 1990s. Bock-Luna refers to her fieldnotes to describe her study group's reaction to the 1999 NATO bombing of Serbia:

> The priest's wife tells me about a protest . . . partly organized by the Serbian Orthodox church in San Francisco, where she appeared in traditional folklore fashion. Showing me a photo of herself, face held up and looking content, holding in front of her *corso* a banner with the sentence 'I am proud to be Serbian'. 'I always feel as if I am there', she states, 'I share their pain. My heart has never left Serbia'. (196)

These brief examples are not meant to be representative (there are numerous other ways objects of remembrance and long-distance nationalism express themselves), but, hopefully, they serve to indicate not only the prevalence but also the importance of nostalgia in the story of migration. And migration is just one of the areas of social life where loss and yearning have a part to play. In rapidly changing societies, where in a single lifetime one can witness considerable change and where human mobility is growing, the geography of nostalgia is becoming an important research agenda.

TEXT BOX 6.1 | Real-World Theory: Nostalgia, Geography and Modernity

Fritzsche (2002: 62) tells us that 'nostalgia stalks modernity as an unwelcome double'. It is a point echoed in Latour's (1993: 76) formulation: 'The modern time of progress and the anti-modern time of "tradition" are twins who failed to recognise one another'. The idea behind both remarks is that yearning for the past is a product of a modern age. It is only when 'tradition' is gone, or in danger of going, that it comes into visibility as something of value. In this way, the modern age can be said to have created 'tradition', 'heritage', 'authenticity', 'the unspoilt' and related ideas. Although, as Blunt (2003: 735) notes, 'nostal- gia is more usually understood in temporal terms rather than in spatial terms', mobility, landscape, environment and the hunger for the place called home provide the most characteristic and powerful themes of the nostalgic imagination. In *The Geography of Nostalgia* (Bonnett, 2015), I draw on accounts of environmentalism, migrants' sense of loss and the commodification of authenticity in the global economy to argue that geography is integral to the nostalgic condition. It seems that nostalgia cannot be understood as a footnote to modern geography, nor as a minority concern, for it shapes all our lives.

SUMMARY

- This chapter has shown that social change and transformation are profoundly geographical. It may be possible to approach social change and transformation purely from a sociological perspective, to abstract them from issues of place, environment and migration, but it is far more convincing and interesting to see them as embedded in the world, as formed in and by geography.

- Social geographers' engagement with social change and transformation will continue to evolve, adapt and be challenged. Social geographers tend to be concerned with research on pressing and topical matters: as Chapter 1 contends, it is perhaps one of the least 'ivory tower' pursuits in the discipline. The examples of social change and transformation discussed here are just a window into the field, but they all share a sense of immediacy and currency.

- The examples also hint at some of the ways that social geographies could and should develop in the future. The word 'social' in 'social geographies' has sometimes been interpreted as indicating that the subdiscipline is exclusively concerned with relationships between human beings. As 'the environment' continues to become a site of wide-ranging crisis, it is wise to keep opening out 'the social' to include our relationship with 'nature' and the 'nonhuman' (see Chapter 33 on environmental justice and Chapter 34 on food). In this regard, we should welcome new work that emphasises the 'multispecies' nature of the social environment (Gillespie & Collard, 2017).

- Another area where social geographies could usefully develop is in its internationalism. The Anglo-American focus of much Anglophone work in social geographies, reflected in this chapter most clearly in my discussion of the racialised city, is a self-imposed limitation and out of keeping with the intellectual promise of geography to be 'the world discipline'. This suggests the importance of new research that emphasises how ideas of change and transformation can themselves be changed and transformed when looking at 'cities elsewhere' (Robinson, 2016; Parnell & Robinson, 2012).

FURTHER READING

Perrons, D. (2004) *Globalization and Social Change: People and Places in a Divided World*. London: Routledge.

Shove, E. (2010) Beyond the ABC: Climate change policy and theories of social change. *Environment and Planning A: Economy and Space*, 42(6): 1273–85.

Wheeler, R. (2017) Local history as productive nostalgia? Change, continuity and sense of place in rural England. *Social & Cultural Geography*, 18(4): 466–86.

CHAPTER —— 7

Justice

Craig Jones and Michael J. Richardson

For Marxist geographer David Harvey, justice is 'essentially to be thought of as a principle (or set of principles) for resolving conflicting claims' (Harvey, 1973: 97). For us, justice is about treating individuals and groups in a morally right and nonarbitrary way. A defensible justice is one that treats a person or group of people consistently over time and ensures consistency in the treatment *between* people. For example, if you, the reader, have the same qualities or have behaved in the same way as we authors, we should receive the same benefits or the same punishment, depending on the circumstances (Miller, 2003). But justice is not easy to define – it is a slippery concept. Here are two statements about justice:

> Justice, far from being some abstract notion, is never something that is remote from our daily consciousness. (Davies, 2011: 380)

> Injustice anywhere is a threat to justice everywhere. (King, 1963)

Justice means different things to different individuals, groups and societies, and its meaning is historically and geographically contingent; it changes across space and time (see Chapter 4 on space and time). Justice haunts the distinctions between right and wrong, moral and immoral, fair and unfair, legal and illegal, but it also exceeds and escapes them. Justice is more than righteousness, lawfulness and fairness; it is at once something that is felt, thought and perceived, but it is also remarkably concrete, embodied and lived – especially by those who fight for it (see Chapter 11 on the everyday).

Geographical approaches to justice are less interested in describing the world as it is and are more invested in (re)making the world as it *should* be. Indeed, Alex Jeffrey (2016) suggests that we can understand the geography of justice in three ways. First are the spatial aspects of claims to justice, which examine fundamental questions of inequality and the uneven distribution of resources, opportunity and harm across the world at various scales (see Chapter 5 on scale). Second are the mechanisms employed to address injustice and inequality and to resolve conflict – in essence, this is about redistributing resources and harms in a fair and equal way (or a fairer and more equal way). And finally, we can think about the geography of justice in terms of our own scholarly methods and modes of inquiry, asking ourselves, 'what would a just geography discipline look like, and what can we do to realise it?'

Issues of justice are central to geographical enquiry and have animated the discipline since the late 1960s and 1970s. The urban geographer and explorer William Bunge (1969) and David Harvey (1973) were early pioneers of what became known as social justice approaches in geography (see Table 7.1). These and other works invigorated the discipline, and, over the last fifty years, geographers have approached questions of justice from a rich, diverse and intersectional set of perspectives (see Chapter 20 on intersectionality). In one way or another, this work is motivated by a sense of injustice – whether that be economic, social, sexual, gendered, racial, religious, generational, legal or political injustice (see Part C on divisions).

Geographers have studied a variety of types of justice, including social justice (Smith, 2000), inequality and justice (Dorling, 2018), urban justice, fear and the right to the city (Pain, 2001; Reynolds & Cohen, 2016), women, gender and justice (Wright, 2010), nature and environmental justice (see Chapter 33 on environmental justice; Swyngedouw & Heynen, 2003), and intersectionality and justice (Hopkins, 2019), among many other studies. Honouring the normative tradition of geographical approaches to questions of justice, this chapter explores two sites and spaces of in/justice. The first is the prodemocracy movement Occupy Hong Kong, and the second is the ongoing fight for justice in contemporary Occupied Palestine. These examples speak to the sites that motivate us as researchers, but they also provide an interesting exploration of justice in relation to contemporary spaces of occupation. This chapter could usefully be read alongside Chapter 33 on environmental justice.

TABLE 7.1 | Definitions of Justice

Key Term	Concepts in Action
Justice: Justice is a broad term with varying definitions. It is regarded as more foundational than morality though less precise than legality.	Established as a working group in 2010 and awarded full research group status in 2012, the Geographies of Justice Research Group (of the RGS-IBG) is a collection of scholars who prioritise studying, teaching and researching 'justice': https://research.ncl.ac.uk/geographiesofjustice/. Key thinker: Jeffrey (2016)
Injustice: A sense of injustice fuels the work of much social geography: geographers seek to tackle elitism, exclusion, prejudice, greed and despair.	The Joseph Rowntree Foundation is an independent organisation for social change. It champions eradicating injustice and funding projects, with a specific focus on the issues of poverty in the UK: www.jrf.org.uk. Key thinkers: Dorling et al. (2007)
Transitional justice: A range of legal and nonlegal processes associated with a society's attempts to come to terms with past abuses, such as mass killings, forced disappearances, rape, and torture. Often associated with accountability, reconciliation and prevention.	The International Center for Transitional Justice (ICTJ) works for justice in over forty states that have endured massive human rights abuses under repression and in conflict. It works with victims, civil society groups and national and international organisations to ensure redress for victims and help prevent atrocities from happening again: www.ictj.org. Key thinker: Nagy (2008)
Justice in law: Justice and law are not one and the same thing, but they are certainly related. Justice is a moral ideal that the law seeks to uphold in the protection of rights and punishment of wrongs. Legal geography often engages with questions of justice, while recognising that the law is one tool among many that can be employed to prevent or achieve justice.	Established in 1978, Human Rights Watch is a nonprofit nongovernmental organisation that focuses on fact-finding, reporting and advocacy for human rights issues: www.hrw.org. Adalah, which means 'justice' in Arabic, is a legal centre for Arab minority rights in Israel. It advocates for the 1.5 million Palestinians who live in Israel (around 20 perent of the population): www.adalah.org. Key thinkers: Blomley, Delaney & Ford (2001)
Social justice: With roots in Marxist philosophy, geographers often look to overturn place-based inequality. Social justice is the application of these ideas to identified areas of need.	The Centre for Social Justice and Community Action, based at Durham University, brings together researchers, community members and voluntary-sector organisations to promote social justice. Often, this work prioritises participatory action research as a methodology: https://www.dur.ac.uk/socialjustice. Key thinkers: Harvey (1973); Smith (2000)
Spatial justice: Spatial justice is shaped by inequalities in how resources are distributed (known as distributional justice). Spatial justice is equally concerned with how we decide who gets what (known as procedural justice).	The Hong Kong Public Space Initiative is a charitable nonprofit organisation founded in 2011. Through research, education and engagement, it raises awareness of the rights to, and resourcing of, public space: www.hkpsi.org. Key thinker: Massey with the Human Geography Research Group (2009)
Environmental justice	See Chapter 33 on environmental justice.

JUSTICE AND OCCUPY HONG KONG?

In this section we discuss the prodemocracy movement Occupy Hong Kong. The global Occupy movement originated in Wall Street, New York, in 2011 in resistance to socioeconomic injustice. It draws on a longer history of anticapitalist and antiglobalisation movements and emerged in a specific political climate that followed the Arab Spring and the Spanish *indignados* (antiausterity) protests (Abellán, Sequera & Janoschka, 2012). First, though, we will explain Hong Kong's democratic history.

Since the handover of British colonial rule to China in 1997 (established through the 1984 Sino-British Joint Declaration), democracy in Hong Kong has been repeatedly questioned. The people of Hong Kong campaigned for universal suffrage, challenging a process that sees the chief executive (the leader of the country) elected from just 1,200 members of an electoral committee in a city of over seven million people. Occupy Hong Kong, which came to be known as the Umbrella Revolution in 2014, is deeply rooted in Hong Kong's protracted democratisation process.

TEXT BOX 7.1	Real-World Research: Social Justice and Hong Kong

The ability to claim space is always power laden, and, in this example, various groups in Hong Kong have attempted to reclaim space to highlight their claims against injustice. This raises the question: For whom is justice being sought?

For example, the lack of citizenship rights among migrant domestic workers has been extensively documented (Constable, 2009). They receive on average less than half the statutory minimum wage and are not eligible for permanent residency (see Chapter 9 on nation and nationalism). Paradoxically, these domestic workers *are* able to unionise and publicly protest (unlike in other areas with high proportions of foreign domestic workers: Singapore, Taiwan, Malaysia and the United Arab Emirates). Equally, they have a long tradition of publically occupying space less politically, in sharing their days off together every Sunday. These mass congregations of workers have become a rendered part of everyday life in Asia's global city.

Physically occupying space has long been a tactic of social justice movements. It channels what Scott (1985: xvi) calls the 'weapons of the weak': 'the ordinary weapons of relatively powerless groups: foot dragging, dissimulation, desertion, false compliance, pilfering, feigned ignorance, slander, arson, sabotage, and so on'.

More recently, Michael's research has helped to reveal how the Umbrella Revolution in 2014 was shaped by its middle-class Hong Kong Chinese demographic. This factor helped ensure that the movement gained traction, with the collective mobilisation of professional and politically oriented Hong Kong Chinese altering the power structures to make these occupations the 'weapons of the well-educated' (Richardson, 2018: 489). Justice was being called for by locally born Hong Kong citizens, many of whom were students from the city's universities, which made the movement harder to ignore and more difficult to silence. When protests over the Chinse Extradition Bill emerged in 2019 and into 2020, the movement was reinvigorated by further support from much of the city's expatriate elite – as well as the UK government – which caused tensions with the Chinese ambassador in London.

For follow-up reading, see Richardson (2018).

FIGURE 7.1

Hong Kong's
occupation in physical
and material protest.
(Credit: RL Visuals)

A student strike in late September 2014 saw the birth of Occupy
Central with Love and Peace (OCLP). This was to take the form of
an occupation of a main road in Hong Kong's central commercial
district if the government refused to implement universal suffrage.
What followed OCLP's conception was a series of public debates, a
well-received – yet unofficial – referendum, scenes of civil disobedience and what became the largest mass protest movement Hong
Kong has ever witnessed (see Figure 7.1).

SPATIAL JUSTICE AND HONG KONG

The occupation took hold of several areas of the city in 2014, with
campaigners employing nonviolence and civil disobedience. It offi-
cially lasted for seventy-nine days (from 28 September to 15 December 2014), although remnants of the movement remain and its legacy
is still being written. The movement focused on the right to universal suffrage, a fair and transparent electoral system and, ultimately,
an open democratic process. Embodied symbols of pacifism (yellow
umbrellas, protective face masks and protective eye goggles) were
employed against police aggression (pepper spray and tear gas); thus
the Umbrella Revolution of Occupy Hong Kong was born. Lying
beneath the broader political calls for democratic change was an
emphasis on injustice. The movement also became representative of
calls to redress socioeconomic inequality, particularly intergenerational concerns over the lack of affordable housing and wider opportunities for social mobility (see Chapter 21 on housing and home).
This justice movement was using a struggle for increasing suffrage

also to call for the greater distribution of wealth and resources (see Chapter 28 on social reproduction).

Whether via Twitter revolutionists or traditional street protestors, #Occupy has a significant global presence and continues its transnational journey across multiple political climates (see Chapter 31 on the digital). The term and the hashtag have become synonymous with social movements worldwide and carry with them a call to action. The movement raises questions of citizenship and human rights and functions at and across different scales (see Chapter 5 on scale). For example, Occupy can serve the needs of localised issues, such as protests against student tuition fees (see the work of Hopkins, Todd & Newcastle Occupation, 2012). At both the global and the local levels, then, it is the embodied practice of occupation that challenges the status quo in calling for justice. While movements often fail to achieve the full suite of their goals (implementing universal suffrage or scrapping university tuition fees), the ignition of citizenship struggles represents a clear desire for a more just society. A sense of justice in Hong Kong is dependent on democracy, representation and rights to the city, while geographies of occupation more generally can represent geographies of possibility.

JUSTICE IN OCCUPIED PALESTINE?

In this section we examine questions of justice in Occupied Palestine through the analytical lenses of social and legal justice. We ask: What might justice look like in Occupied Palestine? And what might a 'just' solution to the Palestine–Israel conflict entail?

First, a brief context: The state of Israel was established in 1948 following World War II and the Holocaust. In 2018, Israel celebrated seventy years of 'independence', and, to mark the occasion, the United States moved its embassy from Tel Aviv to Jerusalem. Palestinians were not celebrating: they see Jerusalem as their capital and refer to 1948 as *al-Nakba* (the catastrophe), because seventy years ago many Palestinians were forced to flee their homes, never to return (Pappé, 2007). In 1967, following a war with neighbouring Arab states, Israel seized control of the Gaza Strip and the Sinai Peninsula from Egypt, the West Bank and East Jerusalem from Jordan, and the Golan Heights from Syria. The Sinai was returned in 1982 – and the Golan effectively annexed – but Gaza, the West Bank and East Jerusalem remain occupied. In the 1980s and 1990s there were many peace talks, which ultimately failed in 2000 and led to the second Palestinian *intifada* (uprising). Since then, Israel claims that a state of war has existed between Israel and the Occupied Palestinian Territories, and so it continues to launch successive bombing campaigns and a punishing regime of sanctions against Gaza (Jones, 2015). Palestinians have fought back with suicide bombings, rocket attacks and various forms of peaceful and nonpeaceful protest. The occupation of the West Bank and Gaza continues, and there appears to be no viable solution to a conflict that is now over seventy years old. Justice has been elusive, while cries of injustice have been many.

FIGURE 7.2

'Disappearing Palestine', a map series representing the loss of Palestinian land to Israel from 1946 to 2012. (Source: Palestine Awareness Coalition, https://palestineawarenesscoalition .wordpress.com)

SOCIAL JUSTICE AND PALESTINE

Where do you stand on the question of Palestine? The late Palestinian American postcolonial theorist Edward Said once called this a 'shamelessly provocative question' but one that reveals an important truth: 'there can be no neutrality or objectivity about Palestine' (Said, 1986: 29–30). This is not to say that all positions are equally valid; it is to suggest, rather, that Palestine is an ideologically and politically charged space. For example, if we want to debate the conflict, do we refer to it as the 'Israel–Palestine conflict' or the 'Palestine–Israel conflict'? Even the syntactical order is political. Justice is also inescapably political; indeed, this is one of the key lessons that has emerged from the literature on social justice in geography since the 1970s.

The geographical literature on social justice begins with the premise that we live in a world of unevenly distributed resources, opportunities and harms. The task for social justice, therefore, is to think critically about 'who gets what, *where*, and how' (Smith, 1974: 289) and to propose how human societies at and across different scales might arrive at a 'just distribution' (Harvey, 1973: 116–17, quoted in Smith, 2000: 1149) (see Chapter 5 on scale). There are complex questions here about what resources, needs or rights could and should be redistributed, but a broad section of geographers agree that social justice should serve to empower, assist or otherwise benefit those who are worst off (and this can be defined in a number of ways). That is, social justice may not be able to achieve equality in the full sense of the term; yet it must nevertheless be a vehicle for what Smith (2000: 1156) calls 'equalisation'.

A just solution to the Palestine–Israel conflict must account for the power relations that have historically played such a defining role in determining 'who gets what, where, and how'. The history of the conflict reveals what Edward Said once called a 'completely asymmetrical record . . . of destruction' (Said, 1992: xxxvi). Justice, in relation to Palestine–Israel, cannot therefore be about 'meeting in the middle' or somehow arriving at a 50–50 split of land, resources and people. A just solution must surely deal with the grievances of both sides, but not necessarily equally (see 'transitional justice' in Table 7.1). Following the lessons of social justice, it is those who have been most disadvantaged who must gain the most from any attempt to restore or create justice. As Edward Said (1986) suggests, it may be impossible to be impartial about the question of Palestine; yet this fact must not blind us from being able to identify injustice and attempting to remedy it: 'we must be able to see that the justice and truth of the oppressor – for there is one here – and that of the oppressed are not interchangeable, morally equal, epistemologically congruent' (33).

LEGAL JUSTICE AND PALESTINE

Law and justice are related, but they are not one and the same. In their ideal form, law and legal systems are designed with justice in mind, and they may help to deliver something perceived by some as 'justice'. But laws can be unjust, and they can and do create and perpetuate injustice. There are many historical and contemporary examples of exclusionary, unjust and indefensible laws, and Palestine reveals some especially acute issues in relation to law and justice.

When a territory is occupied, a special set of laws called the Laws of Belligerent Occupation apply. These laws came into effect in the West Bank and Gaza in 1967 and still apply today (Ben-Naftali, Gross & Michaeli, 2009). One of their key components is the Israeli military court system, designed to govern Palestinians living in the West Bank and Gaza. These courts are different from civilian courts in several ways: they employ military rules, where military commanders' orders become law; they are presided over by military – not civilian – judges; and often the system allows for indefinite detention without trial. This violates the basic principles of *habeus corpus* (the right to a speedy and fair trial). According to sociologist Lisa Hajjar (2005), since 1967 'hundreds of thousands of Palestinians have been arrested by the Israeli military [and] of those who are charged, approximately 90 to 95 percent are convicted. Of the convictions, approximately 97 percent are the result of plea bargains' (3). These rates are alarming, but the injustices perpetuated by the law are not limited to the military court system alone.

The actions of the Israeli military are subject to judicial review and oversight from the highest judicial authority in Israel, the Israel Supreme Court (ISC). This means that Palestinians who are subject to military rule in the West Bank and Gaza are allowed to bring cases to the ISC, for example, if the military has destroyed their home, killed or injured a family member or built a separation barrier on their land. In Israel, this development is hailed as a sign of judicial independence and inclusive democracy; yet, far from guaranteeing the rights of Palestinians, the ISC has rejected over 99 per cent of Palestinian petitions. This has prompted scholars to argue that the main function of the court has been to legalise and legitimise Israel's military activities in the Occupied Palestinian Territories (Ben-Naftali, Gross & Michaeli, 2009: 44). Indeed, Nimer Sultany (2007: 84–85) claims that

> a sophisticated system of oppression has developed in the Occupied Palestinian Territories. Confiscation of land and colonization . . . two different systems of law applying to two populations within the same territory (the Palestinians on the one hand and the privileged Israeli settlers on the other hand) . . . a widespread and long-standing policy of house demolition; extrajudicial executions . . . inhumane conditions of incarceration and torture; expulsion and deportation; curfews and closures; and killings with impunity are the highlights of this system.

You can – and should – read more about systems of legal oppression, both in and beyond the Palestine–Israel context (see "Further Reading" on the next page), but what we hope to have highlighted here is the simple fact that law and justice do not always go hand in hand, and sometimes work against each other. There is a need, therefore, both to simultaneously engage with law and legal systems in the pursuit of justice and to be aware of the limitations of law as well as the fact that justice cannot be achieved by legal means alone.

SUMMARY

- The Occupy Hong Kong movement suggests that space can be occupied for emancipatory purposes and can serve as a medium and catalyst for struggles against injustice.
- As the Occupy movement gained momentum over the last several years, local issues of injustice were put in conversation with global inequalities and systemic injustice. This provides activists, publics and social geographers around the world with a shared language with which to fight injustice – 'we are the 99 per cent'.

- To the contrary, occupation can serve as a tool that causes, perpetuates and proliferates injustice. We saw in this chapter how the law can be used to bolster, enable and legitimise the occupation of Palestine and Palestinian lives.
- This means that we must not equate law with justice or justice with law, and we should always think critically about the question 'justice for whom, and under what conditions?'
- The continuums of oppression and liberation, and exclusion and inclusion, are inherent to much social and spatial research. Explorations of justice, then, as explored in this chapter, are foundational to our understandings of social geographies.

FURTHER READING

Jones, C. (2015) Frames of law: Targeting advice and operational law in the Israeli military. *Environment and Planning D: Society and Space*, 33(4): 676–96.

Pickerill, J., & Krinsky, J. (2012) Why does Occupy matter? *Social Movement Studies*, 11(3–4): 279–87.

Richardson, M. J. (2018) Occupy Hong Kong? *Gweilo* citizenship and social justice. *Annals of the American Association of Geographers*, 108(2): 486–98.

Sadurski, W. (1984) Social justice and legal justice. *Law and Philosophy*, 3(3): 329–54.

Smith, D. M. (2000) Social justice revisited. *Environment and Planning A: Economy and Space*, 32(7): 1149–62.

Indigeneity

Stefan Rzedzian

In its broadest sense, the term 'Indigeneity' refers to the inherent quality of 'being indigenous' (Radcliffe, 2017a). However, what exactly does it *mean* to be Indigenous (that is, what characteristics pertain explicitly to being Indigenous), who defines this, and are these characteristics the same across geographical places and time? As I shall explain throughout this chapter, Indigeneity is a complex and contested concept, embedded in historical trajectories and problematic power relations between peoples and cultures. Furthermore, we shall explore the ways that Indigeneity has been approached and the issues that are faced in studying or doing research around it.

Indigeneity can be used to refer to notions of identity, culture, ways of knowing and ways of being (Zimmerer, 2015). This chapter touches upon all these aspects, but, for social geographers, issues of identity and ways of knowing have been the most important. The term 'Indigeneity' can be used to empower, but it can simultaneously be used to oppress and to marginalise (Postero, 2013). In a historical sense, the term 'Indigeneity' is inherently political and bound by contested power relations of colonialism and empire, particularly in the context of how colonised groups of people have been, and are, represented by those who have sought to occupy their land, appropriate their resources and 'civilise' their ways of knowing and being. This happened across the world, affecting peoples such as the Maori in New Zealand, the First Nations in Canada, the Incas in the Andes and many more. Consequently, when we think about Indigeneity we must also think about the historical processes (such as empire building, colonisation and subjugation) that underpin the emergence of classifications such as 'Indigenous' and 'non-Indigenous' in reference to groups of people. However, Indigeneity has also come to represent a form of identity around which groups of people from all over the world have united in order to fight for greater political representation, resources and respect (Lawrence & Adams, 2005).

Furthermore, it is important to remember that Indigeneity is always relational (De la Cadena & Starn, 2007; see also Chapter 1). This means that the notion of being 'Indigenous' stems from being compared to something or someone that is *not* Indigenous, such as a settler identity, or to modernity (Dove, 2006). Therefore, it is useful to think of Indigeneity as a term that is not static, or fixed, in its meaning, but rather one that is used by different people in different ways across a multitude of times, moments and places and through numerous frameworks of knowledge (or ways of knowing). This fluidity and diversity has real-world implications for the ways Indigeneity functions as a form of identity. For example, in Bolivia more people than ever before are currently identifying themselves as Indigenous, whereas previously many simply identified as farmers (in rural areas) or city dwellers (in urban areas) (Canessa, 2007). This is due to recent changes in the Bolivian political landscape, which have led to the popularisation of Indigeneity as a cultural and political identity (Burman, 2014).

It is only recently that social geography has sought to account for, acknowledge and incorporate the idea of 'Indigeneity' into its frameworks of critique and inquiry, as across human geography more broadly Indigenous issues had often been ignored (Frantz & Howitt, 2012). This reflects the social marginalisation faced by Indigenous peoples in settler societies. Greater attention is now being paid to the ways Indigenous peoples exist as part of wider problematic social relations. For example, human geography scholarship on Indigenous peoples and Indigeneity has often come to analyse and critique issues around modernity (Radcliffe, 2018), coloniality (Barker & Pickerill, 2019) and the environment (Kitossa, 2000). However, the concept of Indigeneity, and the way it is treated by human geographers, has only recently been acknowledged as fundamentally problematic in and of itself (Barker & Pickerill, 2019). This change in the conversation around Indigeneity has been assisted by the rise of Indigenous scholars in academia, particularly in human geography (de Leeuw & Hunt, 2018). Such debates and discussions are now highlighting the risk of treating Indigeneity as a static concept and of romanticising and essentialising both it as a term and the people to whom it pertains (Radcliffe, 2017a).

Throughout this chapter we shall cover some introductory issues relating to the study of Indigeneity. First, I consider some key terms that are useful to understand when approaching Indigeneity as a topic and as a concept. Following that, I elaborate upon the connections between Indigeneity and colonialism, paying particular attention to issues of exploitation and appropriation that characterised the relationship between settler and Indigenous groups. Then I discuss Indigeneity and power, highlighting how Indigeneity has been mobilised as a form of identity in order for communities to gain better access to political resources, representation and rights. Finally, I consider some of the practical and ethical issues arising in research on Indigeneity, including that which is conducted with and by Indigenous individuals.

In order to better understand 'Indigeneity' as a concept, it is useful to consider first some of the key terms used in geographical literatures, sometimes in problematic ways (see Text Box 8.1).

TEXT BOX 8.1 | Key Terms in Debates on Indigeneity

Essentialisation: Essentialisation refers to the process by which Indigenous peoples are reduced to certain specific characteristics that they are deemed to possess purely by virtue of 'being indigenous'. Indigenous groups from all across the world are highly diverse, both in comparison to one another and within those groups themselves. For example, Indigenous groups in Ecuador are very different from Indigenous groups in Norway or in the United States or in Canada. In Ecuador alone there are over twelve Indigenous languages spoken (Haboud, 2009).

Traditional: Indigeneity can often be associated with 'traditional' societies and ways of life (Valdivia, 2005). This could include assumptions that Indigenous peoples live subsistence lifestyles, do not make use of advanced technology, maintain highly spiritual cultures or have other social practices that are not perceived as 'modern'. However, being Indigenous does not inherently mean that a person or a group of people is not 'modern'. For example, many Indigenous peoples live in highly urbanised areas, use mobile phones and computers, own businesses, work in offices and so on.

Romanticisation: This refers to the process by which Indigeneity and Indigenous peoples are thought of in idealised forms by non-Indigenous groups (primarily White or settler colonial societies). This occurs through generalisations that *essentialise* Indigeneity to be inherently *traditional* and therefore representative of the antithesis to the woes of modernity and late-stage capitalism.

Knowledge(s): The existence of multiple knowledges is one of the central tenets that guides the understanding of Indigeneity within human geography. Indigenous *knowledges* (sometimes referred to simply as IK) have been referred to in the contexts of climate change, sustainability, land and rights, among other things (Watson & Huntington, 2008). The pluralisation of knowledge is significant in the sense that it rejects the assumption that knowledge itself is universal, homogenous and monolithic – that is to say, that all knowledge (or ways of knowing) is the same across peoples, cultures and places.

Coloniser/Colonised: The concept of Indigeneity is intricately intertwined with colonial histories of settlement, oppression and exploitation. Consequently, much scholarship in social geography draws upon the coloniser/colonised binary to refer to the relationship between Indigenous peoples and the settler colonial societies that attempt to exert power over them. Given that the coloniser/colonised binary is often central to social geographical perspectives on Indigeneity, it is no surprise that postcolonial theory (see Chapter 2) is a common lens through which the topic is explored.

INDIGENEITY AND COLONIALISM

When European powers colonised much of Africa and the Americas, for example, the seizing of land and the enslavement of peoples were systematic and violent. This resulted in the impoverishment, disempowerment and marginalisation of Indigenous populations. Its effects can still be seen today through issues such as land laws that date back to the colonial period, taking from Indigenous peoples and placing in the hands of settlers land and territory that, over the years, have seldom returned to Indigenous ownership. For this reason, the subject of land reform remains a deeply important political issue for many Indigenous groups (Johnson, 2011).

In addition to the appropriation of their land and resources, Indigenous populations were, and remain, subjects of intense racism. Often referred to as 'savage', 'uncivilised' and 'barbarous' by White settler societies, Indigenous populations were deemed less advanced, less intelligent and, put simply, less *human* than their settler counterparts in colonial society. This racism sought to justify the domination, subjugation and exploitation of Indigenous populations and continued the narrative of the 'civilising mission' that underpinned the supposed ethical and moral reasonings behind colonisation and the expansion of empires. For example, during the nineteenth and twentieth centuries, the US, Canadian and Australian governments were responsible for the forced separation of hundreds of thousands of Indigenous children from their families, predicated on the idea that they were helping them (Jacobs, 2005). These forcible removals resulted in immeasurable physical and mental trauma and the fragmentation of families, cultures and generations (Palmiste, 2008).

Racism towards Indigenous populations stems from colonial attitudes towards Whiteness and difference (see Chapter 13 on race). Fundamentally, Indigenous populations were regarded as non-White and therefore inferior. This practice resulted in radical inequalities between Indigenous and settler groups, maintained and reproduced by oppressive colonial states through narratives of citizenship, nationality and otherness (Johnson, 2011). These issues of race and Indigeneity persist to the present day, particularly through the racialisation of Indigenous populations by settler states. This notion of racialisation refers to the process by which certain peoples are subject to categorisation by more powerful groups in society according to perceived racial characteristics.

Consequently, an integral part of Indigeneity as a form of identity (particularly in a politically mobilised sense – an issue that we shall explore in the next section) is the anticolonial ethos underpinning the wider struggles that unite many of the diverse Indigenous populations that may be brought under its umbrella. This anticolonial stance has proven to be one of the key driving forces in the rise of the international Indigenous movement and has shaped its position on issues such as land rights, cultural rights, language rights and the protection and promotion of Indigenous knowledges (Johnson et al., 2007). Building on this, in the next section, we shall explore how the concept of Indigeneity is mobilised by Indigenous movements in order to afford them greater political representation and resources.

INDIGENEITY AND POWER

In recent years, many Indigenous groups have actively mobilised around the concept of Indigeneity in order to increase their political power, visibility and reach. This is made possible through the unifying potential offered by Indigeneity as a form of identity. For example, over recent decades, Indigenous social movements have advanced themselves both nationally and internationally, allowing them to achieve greater recognition of Indigenous rights on national and international platforms (Davis, 2008). This process of unification, however, has in some cases relied on the construction of an 'Indigeneity' to which not all those who might be described as 'Indigenous' subscribe (Burman, 2014). Therefore, the use of 'Indigeneity', both as a term and as a form of identity, must often be recognised as deeply political and also subjective.

At the national level, one clear example lies in the case of Bolivia, where President Evo Morales, an Indigenous former coca grower, has shaped his presidency and initial rise to power around the perception of his own Indigeneity. In 2005, Evo Morales campaigned on an agenda which sought to 'decolonise' and 'refound' Bolivia, espousing the role of Indigenous empowerment as central to his political ethos (Postero, 2010). However, President Morales promoted a specific type of Indigeneity in his political discourse, one based on the assumption that all Indigenous groups could be presented as a homogenous category, unified by shared traditions and beliefs (Canessa, 2014). This was disputed by some Indigenous groups in the country, particularly in the context of interregional tensions between the highlands and lowlands populations (Lopez Pila, 2014). Many Indigenous groups in Bolivia felt that the Indigeneity espoused by the Morales administration prized certain types of Indigenous cultures over others. For example, groups from the country's lowlands felt that the Indigeneity of highlands groups (particularly coca growers) was celebrated more than their own (Canessa, 2014). This reflects how the concept of Indigeneity can be seen as contested, dynamic and inherently political, in the sense that it can be used by different people in different ways in order to make political claims.

At the global level, a good example of how Indigeneity has been politically mobilised can be found in the case of the international Indigenous movement, a collective group that has gained significant recognition in recent decades. Promoting issues such as anti-colonialism, anti-imperialism, cultural rights and water rights, the movement has positioned itself as the force behind the advocacy of Indigenous issues on the global stage (Feldman, 2002). Take, for

FIGURE 8.1

Indigenous peoples from the Azuay province of Ecuador, protesting in the city of Cuenca. (Source: pixabay.com / Royalty Free images–Creative Commons)

example, the impact that it had on the political representation of Indigenous peoples at the United Nations. Under pressure from the increasing power of internationally networked Indigenous groups, the United Nations established the Working Group on Indigenous Populations in 1982. Since then, the space has become a place where representatives from Indigenous populations from all over the world have met to discuss issues pertaining to them collectively and to advocate for them on the global stage (Muehlebach, 2001).

In 2007, the United Nations then established the Declaration on the Rights of Indigenous Peoples; once again, this brought issues of Indigeneity to the forefront of international politics. Crucially, though, the United Nations refuses to provide any official defini-tion of what it means to 'be Indigenous'. This was at the request of representatives within the international Indigenous movement, who instead favoured a system of self-identification (Escárcega, 2010). This system is predicated on criteria such as 'historical continuity with precolonial/settler societies; strong links to natural resources of homelands; and distinct social, economic, or politi-cal minorities with distinct language, culture and beliefs' (Davis, 2008). Therefore, the United Nations' perception of Indigeneity remains relatively ambiguous due to the incredibly wide range of peoples and groups who could align with these criteria. However, it is vital to note that it was Indigenous groups themselves that were at the forefront in presenting these terms. Consequently, the international Indigenous movement has played a key role in establishing the definitional boundaries at the global level for what it means to be 'Indigenous', and the parameters upon which they decided were deliberately chosen so as to be globally minded and inclusive across places and cultures.

RESEARCH AND INDIGENOUS PEOPLES: ETHICS AND RESPONSIBILITIES IN THE PRODUCTION OF KNOWLEDGE

Doing research that is focused on the topic of Indigeneity, or Indigenous peoples more broadly, has important methodological implications. Perhaps most visible in social geographical scholarship is the notion of 'producing knowledge'. In recent years, much research focused on Indigeneity has provided poignant critiques of how our role as writers and researchers bestows upon us a responsibility for the material we produce and how we produce it (for deeper discussions, see Chapters 1 and 3). In researching Indigeneity, this means acknowledging the historical legacy of colonialism that has shaped the world within which we live and how the production of knowledge has served as a tool through which power has been (and still is) exercised.

Geography, as a discipline, has a distinct relationship with colonialism and, through the production of knowledge regarding 'unexplored' and 'uncontacted' lands and peoples, has functioned as a method of domination and subordination (Robbins, 2012). This arose through European explorers writing about their experiences of other cultures, making judgements according to their own frames of reference and their own knowledges. Furthermore, given that colonialism and the expansion of empire were predicated on an idea of European superiority, the materials produced by these explorers often promoted these same narratives, positioning non-European peoples as needing to be 'civilised' by the colonial powers. This mentality was predicated on the belief in a universal (inherently eurocentric) knowledge and a universal way of being, where European systems of thought and social and political organisation were the benchmark against which all else is measured.

In light of these issues, it is important for researchers to reject the reproduction of such power relations in their scholarship. This might involve acknowledging one's positionality in relation to Indigeneity; using participatory methods and collaborating with Indigenous groups; recognising Indigenous research and the plurality of knowledges, and rejecting a hierarchy of knowledges based upon eurocentrism; or ensuring the dissemination of research findings in a way that benefits research participants (see Text Box 8.2).

TEXT BOX 8.2	Real-world Research: Co-becoming and relationality in Northern Australia

In their work on co-becoming and relationality in Northern Australia, Country et al. (2016) take an important step in breaking down hierarchical power relations in the production of knowledge. Their collaboration in authoring a journal article is between university researchers and community (in both human and more-than-human forms). When detailing the authors' biographies, the (human) contributors state:

> Bawaka Country is an active partner and leader of our research collaboration. Located in northeast Arnhem Land, Australia, Bawaka Country incorporates people, animals, plants, water and land. For Laklak and her family, it is what connects them to each other and to multiple spiritual and symbolic realms. It encompasses and (re)creates Laws, custom, movement, songs, knowledges, relationships, histories, presents, futures and spirit beings. Country can be talked to, it can be known, it can itself communicate, feel and take action.

This approach subverts conventional Eurocentric perceptions of knowledge by drawing on the interrelatedness of humans and the more-than-human world in the process of knowledge production. It is underpinned by the respect and acknowledgement of the ways of knowing held by the Indigenous peoples living in northeast Arnhem Land, and it uses these in research and scholarship in a way that disrupts conventional understandings and divisions between 'the researcher' and 'the researched'.

SUMMARY

- Indigeneity may be thought of as identity, culture, ways of knowing, being and more. Recognition of this is having an increasing influence on social geographical research.
- Indigeneity is a deeply political concept characterised by social divisions and political claims. It may also be deployed by communities to self-empower through social activism.
- Place is significant, as Indigeneity is so often dependent on local social and political processes and forms of identity and connected to land claims.
- All researchers must be acutely aware of the power dynamics that underpin Indigeneity and its study as a concept. We need to acknowledge both the contemporary and historical power relations that influence the production of knowledge and our own role within this process.

FURTHER READING

Clement, V. (2019) Beyond the sham of the emancipatory Enlightenment: Rethinking the relationship of Indigenous epistemologies, knowledges, and geography through decolonizing paths. *Progress in Human Geography*, 43: 276–94.

Country, B., Wright, S., Suchet-Pearson, S., Lloyd, K., Burarrwanga, L., Ganambarr, R., Ganambarr-Stubbs, M., Ganambarr, B., Maymuru, D., & Sweeney, J. (2016) Co-becoming Bawaka: Towards a relational understanding of place/space. *Progress in Human Geography*, 40: 455–75.

Radcliffe, S. A. (2017) Decolonising geographical knowledges. *Transactions of the Institute of British Geographers*, 42: 329–33.

Watson, A., & Huntington, O. H. (2008) They're here – I can feel them: The epistemic spaces of Indigenous and Western knowledges. *Social & Cultural Geography*, 9: 257–81.

Nation and Nationalism

Matthew C. Benwell

A social geography strongly informed by attention to (geo) political issues associated with nations and nationalism is of vital importance at a moment when the world appears increasingly fractured along national lines. This work can draw attention to the objects, practices and performances through which citizens are reminded of their national identities (as distinct from the identities of those from other nations) as well as to the multiple ways that citizens engage with and experience the nation in their everyday lives. These are not inevitable or uniform and are influenced by the intersections of national identity with other markers of social identity, as well as (geo) political events. The chapter draws on case studies in South America (Argentina and Chile), a region that has attracted limited attention from geographers interested in nationalism.

A BORDERLESS WORLD?

'Each of us here today is the emissary of a distinct culture, a rich history, and a people bound together by ties of memory, tradition, and the values that make our homelands like nowhere else on Earth. . . . America is

governed by Americans. We reject the ideology of globalism,
and we embrace the doctrine of patriotism'.

—President Donald Trump, address to the
UN General Assembly, 25 September 2018

'I've always been a patriotic American citizen. I've always
believed in the American way of life; the values that are
embodied in the Constitution and I believe ultimately that it
will be these values, values like diversity, religious freedom,
equality, justice, humane treatment of prisoners which holds
the United States together. I'm a wrongly accused terrorist
spy and I'm a patriotic American'.

—James Yee, US Muslim Army Chaplain, wrongly detained
as a US enemy combatant, 2008 (from Weber, 2011)

It has become almost routine for political leaders like the president of the United States or the British prime minister to reject globalism and a sense of global citizenship in favour of patriotic identification with the nation. This patriotism is frequently lauded as a positive and beneficial means of expressing one's allegiance to the nation and its associated traditions and values. Meanwhile, in popular understandings, the concept of nationalism has tended to be associated with expressions of extreme nationalist sentiment. However, the academic study of nationalism, 'the modern social and political formations that draw together feelings of belonging, solidarity and identification between national citizens and the territory imagined as their collective national homeland' (Sparke, 2009: 488), continues to attract significant attention from geographers. This chapter emphasises its continued relevance in the contemporary world. A critical social geographical approach to nationalism can highlight how it simultaneously includes and excludes selected people as part of the national collective (including the Indigenous peoples of nations that pre-dated settler states like Australia, Canada or the United States; see Chapter 8 on Indigeneity); it can help us comprehend why some bodies are seen to belong in the nation while others do not; and it can enable more sensitive understandings of the diverse ways people identify with, and feel about, nations and nationalism.

With the benefit of hindsight, the heady predictions of a 'borderless world' that were prevalent at the turn of the twenty-first century appear increasingly distant in the contemporary era, when questions related to national sovereignty and identity tend to dominate (geo)political debate and discourse (Antonsich & Skey, 2017). The opening quotes of this section are useful for a number of reasons and are used to frame the following discussion of nations and nationalism. First, they show how the nation can be reproduced in the political arena, influenced by the political speeches or tweets of elite figures like President Trump. However, social geographers, in particular, have also shed light on the everyday practices, performances and objects through which national citizens are reminded of their nationhood. The second quote, from James Yee, who was wrongly detained by the US government during the so-called War on Terror, starts to tease out the differing social conditions that give rise to people's identification with and experiences of the nation. National identity is not abstract, uniform and constant for all citizens living in or along the borders of the nation-state. Social and embodied markers of identity like gender, sexuality, ethnicity, religion and age (see Part C on divisions), can directly shape people's experiences of the nation.

Second, these quotes draw attention to the geography of debates about the nation and nationalism. Nationalism in the United States has often gone unnoticed by geographers because of problematic assumptions regarding how and where nationalist sentiment is highly visible and can be investigated. This saw research on nationalism typically drawn to so-called hot regions where nationalist conflict had broken out (e.g., the Balkans) and not to 'established' nations like the United States or the United Kingdom (Billig, 1995). Although this is changing, there remain parts of the world that have received relatively sparse academic interest from scholars of nationalism, and the final section of this chapter draws on my own research in South America (although see the excellent study by Radcliffe & Westwood, 1996).

(RE)PRODUCING THE NATION

Our national identities are often seen as natural elements of who we are – most of us are born in a particular state that endows us with a nationality. Some scholars have theorised the production of the nation by emphasising these natural 'ethnic ties and sentiments' and 'popular ethnic traditions', which are shared and expressed through language, religion, customs and traditions (Smith, 1998: 12). These ideas, linked to ethnic nationalism, are often set up in opposition to civic nationalism, which sees nationhood as being formed around shared citizenship within a state and determined by its political institutions rather than selective cultural characteristics. In keeping with these more liberal interpretations, scholars of nationalism have become increasingly attuned to the fact that nations are not inevitable and are regularly being (re)produced. National citizens need to be constantly reminded of their nationhood in order to reaffirm their loyalty and allegiance to the nation, and this is done through a multitude of daily routines and practices. An influential text penned by Michael Billig (1995) on what he called *Banal Nationalism* drew attention to the mundane, everyday ways that the nation is 'flagged' to its citizens (as well as to those who are not national citizens). It is now commonplace for research by geographers and other social scientists to attend to the production, dissemination and negotiation of the national through discourse, objects and practices, including unremarked-upon features of everyday life such as the flags fluttering from public buildings.

As Billig noted, 'The unwaved flag, which is so forgettable, is at least as important as the memorable moments of flag waving' (1995: 10). Since then, a plethora of work has emerged exploring the reproduction of the nation through things like postage stamps, licence plates, music and various other aspects of everyday popular culture (e.g., Edensor, 2002; Leib, 2011; Raento & Brunn, 2005). This work has also examined the national objects (e.g., textbooks and teaching resources), practices and performances (e.g., assemblies, ceremonies and commemorations) that present particular stories about the nation to children and young people in both educational settings and organisations such as Cub Scouts (Benwell, 2014a; Mills & Waite, 2017; Scourfield et al., 2006).

SOCIAL GEOGRAPHIES OF NATIONALISM

These studies have subsequently been critiqued for overlooking the agency of human subjects and the various ways that they can engage with the nation and nationalism (Antonsich, 2016). Heated debates in the United States on appropriate embodied practices and postures before sporting fixtures during the playing of the national anthem and unfurling of the flag illustrate the contentions that can surround the disruption of 'expected' national performances (Lyons, 2019). Social markers of identity and their intersection with (practices and performances of) national identity are brought to the fore in this example, as these protests have focused on the racial inequities inherent to policing in the United States. The United Kingdom's European Union referendum unveiled schisms among British citizens along generational lines – just over 70 per cent of eighteen- to twenty-four-year-olds voted to 'remain', whereas 60 per cent of those aged sixty-five and over voted to 'leave' the EU – which led to impassioned debates and soul-searching about British national identity and the United Kingdom's (geo)political future. Other work has explored the experiences of minority groups (see Chapters 13 on race and 14 on religion), such as British Muslims and Sikhs, showing how their lives and experiences of nationhood can be affected by geopolitical events and the foreign policies of the state in which they live (Hopkins et al., 2017; Hopkins, 2007b). Additionally, some people may have dual national citizenship or live near borders that lead to them having strong economic, social and cultural connections with more than one nation (Radcliffe & Westwood, 1996). Nationhood is not uniformly experienced by all national citizens, then, and investigations of the social geographies of nationalism enable us to identify and explore some of these variations.

EVERYDAY NATIONALISM

Banal signifiers of the nation can also instil a range of emotions and feelings (e.g., pride, embarrassment, annoyance and so on), depending on things like social identity and the context in which

FIGURE 9.1
Outline of the Falklands-Malvinas on a school uniform in Santa Fe, Argentina. (Copyright: Matthew C. Benwell)

they are encountered (see Chapter 12 on emotion). Recent work from geographers has tried to explore the emotional charge of nationalism and its ability to move people in diverse ways in everyday life. Rather than looking at an object like a flag or a performance like a war commemoration and assuming how national citizens might or might not respond to them, these studies look to investigate 'how nationhood "feels", expanding the focus from what we think about national symbols to what emotional responses accompany them' (Sumartojo, 2017: 207). This body of work has looked not just at objects, practices and performances where the nation is explicitly represented or commemorated. Instead, authors like Militz (2017) show how the performance of things like national dances in Azerbaijan can perpetuate feelings of collective belonging to the nation, as well as alienation of those who are not familiar with their rhythms and steps. Emotional interrogations of nationalism offer social geographers the opportunity to interrogate how the nation can be reproduced, resisted and rejected in unexpected and lively ways, which may actually take us (in the sense of both citizens and academics) by surprise.

FIGURE 9.2

Young people in Rosario, Argentina, take part in a commemoration ceremony to mark the Falklands-Malvinas War of 1982. (Copyright: Matthew C. Benwell)

CONCLUSION

This chapter has illustrated the continued relevance of social geographical research that examines the nation, national identity and nationalism. Far from diminishing in importance, national borders and distinctions appear to be depressingly common reference points in political and popular discourses in the twenty-first century. The challenges posed by alt-right and far-right nationalist organisations and the increasing visibility of their exclusionary rhetoric are topics that are ripe for geographical research on everyday nationalism. The work presented in this chapter shows how a sensitivity to the social and political geographies of the nation can shed light on the diverse ways people experience and express their nationhood. A sense of national belonging is not inevitable or uniform, given the various ways that people encounter the nation in their everyday lives. Geographical research undertaken alongside citizens across a range of spaces is showing how they can reproduce, resist, rework and even reject nationalism and its associated narratives, practices and performances.

TEXT BOX 9.1 | Real-World Research: Everyday Nationalism in Chile and Argentina

Citizens' Active Engagements with Everyday Nationalism in Patagonia, Chile

While we may become accustomed to the presence of national objects like flags in our everyday lives, the ways that citizens respond to and appropriate them are far from inevitable and stable. They can make, improvise, deface and burn national signifiers to make (geo)political points directed at different audiences, particularly during moments of sociopolitical tension. These kinds of appropriations can shed light on how people feel about and relate to their national identities, but they can also be highly contentious, given that many states have laws dictating how the national flag should be displayed. In 2012 in the Aysén Region of Patagonia, Chile, communities deployed flags to draw attention to their socioeconomic grievances, which broadly revolved around the perceived neglect of the region by the centralised Chilean state. In order to apply political pressure, citizens from the Aysén Region made and flew the flag of their near neighbour, Argentina, in part because of the solidarity and material support that they felt that they received from the other side of the border. In contrast, the flag of Chile was flown upside down or next to black flags, evoking the despair associated with citizens' perceptions of the regional decline, exacerbated by the national government. Examining the legacies of events like the 2012 protests and citizens' creative engagements with national flags enables an interrogation of their everyday identifications with nations (plural). It also sheds light on the political agency of citizens and their ability to disrupt certain national codes and etiquettes in order to draw attention to particular political reclamations (Benwell, Núñez & Amigo, 2019).

Engaging Territorial Nationalism in Argentina

Narratives about the nation are often bound up with historical and contemporary geo-political events. In many states, young people are reminded about national histories of warfare, independence struggles and the territorial extent of the nation in the classroom and through participation in ceremonies that require them to sing national songs and salute the national flag (see Figure 9.2). For instance, children in Argentina learn about the territorial extent of their nation through objects such as maps that visually represent the national territory. These include territories such as the Falkland Islands, or Islas Malvinas (as they are known in Argentina), considered integral parts of the nation that are, according to the Argentine state, illegally occupied by the United Kingdom. The national maps also include Argentina's Antarctic sector, notwithstanding the lack of international recognition of this or any other state's territorial claims in Antarctica (Benwell, 2017). The reception of this kind of territorial nationalism is not inevitable or uniform, however, and research has begun to recognise the various ways that young people interpret (and teachers present) national and geopolitical subjects in the classroom. Investigating everyday (territorial) nationalism in different geographical contexts, and alongside young people, facilitates our understandings of how they respond to and feel about the nation (Benwell, 2014a). While research in social and political geography has typically focused on the school as a significant site where young people engage in nationalism, domestic spaces and intergenerational relations with family members can also be influential in their learning and engagement of national histories and nationhood.

The undertaking of qualitative research requires constant self-reflection on how the researcher's identity (or positionality) may influence interactions with respondents and, ultimately, the conclusions that are drawn (see Chapter 3 on researching social geographies). Methodological accounts examining researcher positionality regularly interrogate identity markers such as gender, ethnicity, age, sexuality and their intersections. However, much less attention is drawn to national identity, despite the important role that it can play in shaping relations between the researcher and the researched. Nowhere is this more apparent than in studies of everyday nationalism, where questions relating to national identity and nationalism are central. This can be even more pronounced when the subject of research focuses on sensitive geopolitical claims that have been nationalised. My research on the Falklands/Malvinas sovereignty dispute in Argentina and the Falkland Islands required me to think self-reflexively about my identity as a British researcher. While we all have national identities, we can 'perform' these in several ways, depending on the context in which we find ourselves through our use of language, our reference to national customs and terminology and our expression of geopolitical views. These can all reinforce or disrupt expectations associated with our national identities when we carry out research. For these reasons, nationality and its performance by the researcher and researched should not be overlooked in discussions of positionality (Benwell, 2014b). The writing of fieldnotes that reflect on research interactions is a useful way to chart your observations and negotiations of national identity in ways that remain attentive to the intersectional nature of (researcher) identities.

SUMMARY

- Social geographers are well placed to critically engage the nation, national identity and nationalism in an era marked by increasing levels of exclusionary political rhetoric expressed along nationalist lines.

- People experience the nation in different ways, and the sense of belonging to a nation is not inevitable or uniform, given the many ways that people encounter the nation in their everyday lives.

- National citizens can reproduce, resist, rework and reject nationalism and its associated narratives, practices and performances in creative and provocative ways that unsettle notions of nationhood as somehow natural or inevitable.

FURTHER READING

Closs Stephens, A. (2013) *The Persistence of Nationalism: From Imagined Communities to Urban Assemblages.* London: Routledge.

Edensor, T. (2002) *National Identity, Popular Culture and Everyday Life.* Oxford: Berg.

Radcliffe, S., & Westwood, S. (1996) *Remaking the Nation: Place, Identity and Politics in Latin America.* London: Routledge.

Skey, M., & Antonsich, M. (eds.) (2017) *Everyday Nationhood: Theorising Culture, Identity and Belonging after* Banal Nationalism. London: Palgrave Macmillan.

Urban/Rural

Wen Lin and Ruth McAreavey

Today we live in an urban world. The year 2007 was the first in which more people lived in urban areas than in rural areas, and it is expected that by 2050, 66 per cent of the world's population will be living in cities (UNFPA, 2017). According to the Organisation for Economic Co-operation and Development (OECD), just over a quarter of the OECD population lives in a predominantly rural region, and, of them, 80 per cent live close to a city. Recent urban growth, evident since the twentieth century, is characterised by the rapid urbanisation of less-developed countries. For example, sub-Saharan Africa is expected to have a greater percentage of the world's urban population than Europe by 2030 (Soja & Kanai, 2007). There are many factors contributing to this growth, one of which is the significant level of rural-to-urban migration arising from better employment opportunities in the city (see Chapter 26 on migration and diaspora).

Traditionally, a rather two-sided approach was used to label urban and rural areas. Whereas urbanity represents technological progress, openness, diversity and sophistication vis-à-vis culture and living conditions more generally, rurality is often associated with parochial and insular communities. In short, rural has frequently been viewed as an oppressive space, in contrast to the progressive nature of the urban environment.

And yet the way rural and urban areas are designated has important implications for the people living in those places, as it often determines policy approaches and, ultimately, access to resources. In this chapter, we provide a short introduction to these competing categorisations and grapple with key concepts associated with the urban and rural in relation to social geographies. It is impossible to cover such a diverse field comprehensively in the space of this chapter. Rather, we hope to use this as an entry point to invite you to think more about these issues critically and where you might be able to find more resources to further your enquiry.

DEFINING THE URBAN AND THE RURAL?

A dualism existed between the city and the rural in early writings in both urban and rural studies, with the rural often being understood as a counterpoint to the urban – parochial, backwater, socially conservative and ethnically homogenous, in contrast to a cosmopolitan, progressive, liberal and ethnically diverse urban society. Increasingly, it has been recognised that it is no longer useful to separate the two. Scholars point out that the artificial division between rural and urban society creates separate entities and fails to take account of the flows between the two (see, for instance, Copp, 1972; Hoggart, 1990). As this chapter will reveal, both urban and rural areas in themselves are incredibly diverse. Making sweeping generalisations across wide geographic areas is neither accurate nor helpful. In the field of urban studies, a growing body of work has engaged with 'relaxed urban theories' to grapple with the 'more interrelated and more differentiated' urban areas in the emerging urbanised world (Harding & Blokland, 2014: 222–23). This body of work, rather than producing 'overarching, synthetic accounts of urban "spikiness"', has sought to 'present more or less empirically evidenced accounts of its causes and/or consequences for or within particular types of urban settlement, in certain respects, over various time periods' (Harding & Blokland, 2014: 223). An important issue regarding the current rapid urbanisation process worldwide is informal settlements (see Text Box 10.1), 'raising questions of displacement and replacement of populations and of tactics and trajectories of agency, accommodation, recombination, and reappropriation' (Bach, 2017: 162). In a similar vein, over twenty-five years ago Halfacree observed the growing realisation in the literature that the quest for any single, all-embracing definition of the rural is neither desirable nor feasible (1993: 34). It is much more fruitful to determine whether there are significant structures that are solely associated with a particular (rural) locality and to understand if and how they are distinct to their urban counterpart.

Defining a city is notoriously difficult. Among many definitions, the level of population density has often been used to define urban areas (Bluestone, Stevenson & Williams, 2008). However, there is no universal threshold of the size of population for defining a city.

Other theorists focus on conceptualising and characterising urban life. For example, Karp, Stone and Yoels (1991) provide a useful review of classical conceptions of urban life, including Louis Wirth's work (1938) on urbanism as a way of life, which is considered the classical view of urban sociology. Conceptualising urbanism as a mode of life, Wirth (1938) seeks to provide a generic definition of the city through identifying three key attributes of urbanisation: the increased size, density and heterogeneity of urban populations. These three attributes serve as independent variables from which characteristics of the urban mode of life can be deducted (Karp, Stone & Yoels, 1991; Knox & McCarthy, 2014; Parker, 2015). Such a deductive approach has been critiqued (Knox & McCarthy, 2014; Pacione, 2009). It is also important to point out that Wirth's work is based on a particular phase of urbanisation (Knox & McCarthy, 2014) and has been confined to Western contexts and influenced by the time of his writing (Karp, Stone & Yoels, 1991). As such, one may argue that 'the urban mosaic sustains many different "ways of life"' (Knox & McCarthy, 2014: 366). In a similar vein, Karp, Stone and Yoels (1991: 108) note that the city 'is large, dense, and composed of groups with heterogeneous lifestyles'.

In an attempt to determine the meaning of rurality and to distinguish between types of rural areas, in the past the UK Department of Environment used a classification scheme based on the index of rurality for England and Wales (Cloke, 1977, 1978; Halfacree, 1993). Of late, policy makers are more attuned to how rural–urban binaries may hide important practical and ideological connections between regions, obscuring relationships within and between hinterlands. In recognising the limitations of population density, researchers in Europe have coined the term 'population potential' to categorise areas according to the number of persons residing within a certain distance (Gløersen et al., 2006; Copus & Hopkins, 2017). This allows for population density but, importantly, access to adjacent populations as well. Many countries are now adopting definitions that help to understand urban–rural linkages, including Scandinavian countries, England, Scotland and Germany. For instance, in England the 2011 Census recognised ten different categories, including major conurbations, towns and fringe, and hamlets and isolated dwellings. However, there is tension between recognising urban–rural links and upholding administrative boundaries for political accountability (see Chapter 30 on data). One of the ways of addressing this tension is to gather information at a local level, as it creates building blocks for policy makers and provides a more nuanced understanding of localities. This approach is adopted by the OECD: if, at the local level, the population density is less than 150 people per square kilometre, the area is broadly rural (OECD, 2011). These data are combined to create predominantly urban, intermediate and predominantly rural regions and are adjusted if those regions contain urban centres. Three types of rural areas exist, according to the OECD (2016) typology: rural inside a functional urban area, rural close to cities and remote rural, as shown in Figure 10.1.

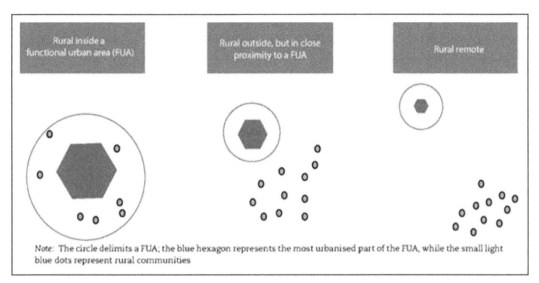

Note: The circle delimits a FUA; the blue hexagon represents the most urbanised part of the FUA, while the small light blue dots represent rural communities

FIGURE 10.1

OECD's typology of three types of rural areas. (Source: http://www.oecd.org/regional/oecd-regional-outlook-2016-9789264260245-en.htm)

THE INDUSTRIAL REVOLUTION: RURAL AS THE ANTITHESIS OF URBAN

Despite the shift in conceiving the rural and urban, traditional impressions persist. Understanding those viewpoints is important, as it can help us to appreciate potential conflicting interests. For a long time, rural was viewed as everything that urban is not. Debates about rural society from the nineteenth century were rooted in a fast-changing world. This was largely driven by the Industrial Revolution, which created jobs in urban centres and provided opportunities for agricultural workers to improve the quality of their lives through better and more secure wages and superior housing. This shift in society provoked wider discussions about archetypal or ideal-type societies. Emergent debates often placed rural in direct opposition to urban. If the urban was gritty, smelly and dirty, the rural was picturesque, fragrant and clean. These idyllic constructions of the rural are evident more widely, in literature and the arts, noted here in an English context. Just consider the works of Elizabeth Gaskell as an example. Gaskell was writing during the industrialisation of Manchester; not only does she depict tensions between mill owners and workers, but she also conveys a rural way of life that was being eroded by industrialisation. Meanwhile, nineteenth-century rural natural artists depict a sentimental but very real rural life, including people, activities and landscapes. This nostalgic rural idyll is very aligned with a rustic and simple way of life, rooted in a pastoralism where people are in touch with nature. It continues to be held by some groups and individuals in society.

Writing in Germany during the Industrial Revolution, towards the end of the nineteenth century, Ferdinand Tönnies studied social relations between individuals to understand the threats arising from modernity as society shifted from a rural base to become more urban and industrial. The terms *Gemeinschaft* and *Gesellschaft* encapsulate the transition from an informal community base to a more formal

TABLE 10.1	*Gemeinschaft* and *Gesellschaft* Relations	
Gemeinschaft Context and Relations	**Gesellschaft Context and Relations**
Traditional social relations: 'organic and natural', close knit	Social relations created: loose, impersonal and perfunctory
Closed, homogenous communities	Diverse, heterogenous communities
Individuals consider the 'greater good'	Individuals motivated by self-interest
Governed within the locale	Governed by remote state
Superstition and irrationality	Reason and scientific enquiry (the Enlightenment)
Family life, folklore, religion	
Customs, values dictate behaviour	Convention, legislation, public opinion
Predominantly agricultural	Protection of individuals' personal property and freedom key function of state
Human will equates to *Wesenwille* – that is, natural and innate	Predominantly industrial
	Human will equates to *Kurwille* – that is, rational and arbitrary

society, reflecting the shift from a rural base and reliance on agriculture to dependence on commerce in an urban setting. Broadly, *Gemeinschaft* highlights community relations from a preindustrial, agrarian society, while *Gesellschaft* is presented, on the whole, as a critique to modernity, depicting looser and impersonal perfunctory relations. Tönnies (2002) was concerned with how modern societies could retain stronger *Gemeinschaft*-like relations in the new world order. A summary of both is presented in Table 10.1.

Gesellschaft relations were considered problematic due to the shift away from family life, close relations within a locality and more formalised social relationships, overall. Tönnies maintained that society will progress from a period where *Gemeinschaft* relations predominate to one epitomised by *Gesellschaft*-like relations, before evolving into a new society. He went on to clearly state that both elements are simultaneously present in society. Nonetheless, *Gemeinschaft* relations are often associated with rural society and *Gesellschaft* relations with urban society. In reality, both relations can be found in the modern world, the extent to which they are confined to urban and rural contexts is not a given. Knowledge of context – locality, economy, culture – is important for helping to establish the prevailing social relations.

LOCAL CONTEXT

Getting to grips with the local context is important for uncovering local nuances, such as poverty and social inequality, which exists in both urban and rural areas. However, there is often an emotional response (see Chapter 12 on emotion) to social conditions in rural communities, where powerful lobby groups effectively advance a particular understanding of the rural – that is, one of poverty and exclusion (see Chapter 22 on wealth and poverty). In some jurisdictions, this can lead to rural proofing, a tool used by government to ensure that their policies do not adversely affect rural society (and raising a set of complex challenges; see Shortall & Alston, 2016). The evidence suggests that poverty exists in both urban and rural areas and that it is an 'ecological fallacy' to think that all people in the most deprived areas are deprived (Pateman, 2011). 'Ecological fallacy' refers to the mistake of assuming that results found at a higher level hold at a more detailed level. In fact, the majority of deprived people do not live in deprived areas, and there is often more variation within areas than between them. Social conditions are, therefore, not uniform across rural or urban areas, as we show below.

Understanding Urban Society

As noted above, urban society is often associated with individuality rather than community, emphasised by thinkers such as Émile Durkheim and Louis Wirth (Pacione, 2009). However, there have been alternative views, including recognition of the existence of close social bonds in urban neighbourhoods, as well as attempts to expand the notion of community to address different forms of social interaction and communication (e.g., Karp, Stone & Yoels, 1991). The Chicago School is well known for its ecological investigations of urban spaces, arguing that the city is organised in the form of natural areas, habitats in which different groups dominate, such as ethnic enclaves and income groupings (Knox & McCarthy, 2012). While the ecological approach has been criticised for its 'Darwinian metaphors' (Jonas, McCann & Thomas, 2015), studies by Chicago School sociologists paid attention to 'the rich texture of urban life' (Pacione, 2009: 369). Subsequent efforts have been made to modify the ecological approach, one of which is the social area analysis (Shevsky & Williams, 1949). Social areas can be delineated using three constructs: 'socioeconomic status (based on such indicators as rent, education, and occupation), familism (based on such indicators as fertility ratios and women not in the labour force), and ethnicity (based on such indicators as race and nativity)' (Karp, Stone & Yoels, 1991: 59). The social area analysis approach has been influential in studying residential differentiation in the North American city (Pacione, 2009).

Researchers have pointed out the inadequacy of these above approaches in taking into account the roles of symbolism and sentiment in shaping urban community (Knox & McCarthy, 2012). The qualitative aspects of urban community can be studied through the notion of sense of place (Pacione, 2009), which includes two related meanings: 'the intrinsic character of a place' and 'the attachment that people have to a place' (Pacione, 2009: 374). For example, the first meaning can be reflected in how the Tyne Bridge in Newcastle upon Tyne, North East England, has been used as an iconic image for the city to form a distinctive character of the place. Yarker's (2017) study underscores the second meaning, in which she explores how comfort serves as a key dimension of people's attachments to place using a case study of a neighbourhood in Newcastle upon Tyne.

Negotiating Diverse Rural Interests

There are many different interest groups or stakeholders with a legitimate claim to the countryside: people live, work and play in the countryside. Environmental groups, farmers, landowners, workers, commuters, leisure seekers, retirees, migrants and entrepreneurs are among the many who seek to influence what happens in rural areas, bringing with them differing agendas relating to conversation, preservation, production and consumption. Some of these individuals are long-standing residents of the rural space in which they live, while others are more recent arrivals. 'Whiteness' has for a long time been a symbol of rurality for many Western economies (see, for example, Philo, 1992; Panelli et al., 2009). This has led to the observation that much of the literature has underplayed or simply ignored the importance of rural ethnic heterogeneity (De Lima, 2012). Some recent literature has challenged that idea, with the arrival of international migrants into rural space (see, for instance, Krivokapic-Skoko, Reid & Collins, 2018).

Negotiating between differing interests can be very tricky indeed. For instance, a retiree newcomer who is pursuing an idyllic retirement in the countryside, complete with the romanticised notion of what the rural life entails, may heavily resist change within that community, such as building homes for local people. Locals can challenge the legitimate entitlement of international migrants to access local services and the labour market (McAreavey & Krivokapic-Skoko, 2019). This raises questions about the extent to which rural areas are defensive sites or inclusive areas and shows how tension can arise in rural spaces due to clashes between reactionary and progressive values.

GLOBAL FLOWS, MOBILITIES AND MIGRATION

The way global flows have impacted rural areas demonstrates how it is not possible to reduce rural and urban areas to binaries (see Chapter 26 on migration and diaspora). Woods' (2007) 'global countryside' sought to rectify the notion of the rural and stagnant backwater, cut off from global forces. He argued that, in the same way as urban areas, rural spaces and places are active sites in the reproduction of globalisation. They are implicated in capital flows and central to the exchange of ideas and the movement of people that characterise the world today (Woods, 2007). International migration is one of the defining features of his global countryside, and in this section we use the example of international migration to demonstrate uneven social relations across rural and urban spaces, showing how it is not possible to generalise about social relations in either place.

Migrants' lives involve the everyday negotiation of cultural difference and transnational mobility, and it is not surprising that there are geographically variable responses to migration. Urban areas have traditionally been gateways for migrants, as evidenced by the large migrant communities in major metropolitan areas, such as Italian and Irish migrants in Boston. These places have established networks that support migrants' settlement, but not without challenges for those communities, as residential segregation remains a key challenge for urban policy makers (Parisi, Lichter & Taquino, 2011). Uneven reactions are evident in newly emerging rural migration destinations: Some rural communities display negative attitudes to newcomers, creating legal barriers to employment, among other measures of resistance (Popke, 2011; Pruitt, 2009). Other areas demonstrate warmth, embracing newcomers, often despite little history of international migration and minimal knowledge in how to support new arrivals (Jensen, 2006; McAreavey, 2012).

Positive responses to international migration in rural areas have been associated with cosmopolitanism (see, for instance, Woods, 2018; Krivokapic-Skoko, Reid & Collins, 2018). A concept that has largely been associated with urban society, cosmopolitanism conjures up notions of sophistication, openness and tolerance to new ideas, people and experiences, contrasting sharply with stereotypes of rural society. Woods (2018) shows how cosmopolitanism can be deployed at individual and community levels. Individuals act in a way that allows them to resolve their cosmopolitan openness in a context of a parochial institutional infrastructure. Meanwhile, rural communities may display cosmopolitanism as they seek to develop positive intergroup relations. A wider interpretation of cosmopolitanism as an ethical endeavour suggests that it is manifest distinctively in rural places compared to urban areas (Johansen, 2008; Woods, 2018).

CONCLUSION

In conclusion, researchers have pointed out that a binary view on the urban and rural is not helpful. In an increasingly urbanised world, it is important to view the urban and the rural as highly connected and mutually influenced by each other. Both have distinctive features, and social relations can be manifest in distinct ways. However, social geographers need to understand the specificity of the locale if they are to fully appreciate and unravel complex social relations. In Text Box 10.1, we present a real-world case study of urban regeneration to illustrate the complexities of these two interlocking realms.

TEXT BOX 10.1 | Real-World Research: Shenzhen – A Metropolis with Hundreds of Urban Villages

Shenzhen, a city in the Pearl River Delta region in China, embarked on implementing the so-called reform and opening policy initiated in the late 1970s to reform the planning economy of the Maoist era into a market-oriented economy, which also set forth profound urban transformation in China. Designated as one of the first four special economic zones (SEZs), Shenzhen has grown from a fishing town of thirty thousand in the late 1970s to a major metropolis in China with a population of more than twelve million in 2017, with one of the highest GDP among Chinese cities according to Shenzhen Statistics Bureau's data. Shenzhen also has one of the highest Gini coefficients among Chinese cities, showing a high level of inequality (Chen, Liu & Lu, 2017). Shenzhen's rapid growth and urbanisation underpin many themes illustrated in this chapter, one of which is informal settlements, elaborated further in this text box through its urban villages.

The so-called urban villages landscapes in China, a form of informal settlements, emerged where the expansion of urban area engulfed areas that were owned by rural collectives. Original rural land users transformed these dwellings into six- or seven-story buildings that provide low-cost accommodation (Figure 10.2). In addition to providing affordable housing for migrant workers, they are also sites in which migrant workers enact agency in establishing vibrant social networks (e.g., Liu, Li & Liu, 2015). Shenzhen has more than two hundred urban villages, and they house half of Shenzhen's population. However, urban villages are under constant threat of redevelopment given the rising price of land in the city. These villages may also appear as eyesores to urban elites. One recent manifestation of these threats is Shenzhen's attempt to upgrade its urban villages starting in 2017. This initiative has been met with resistance as reported on mainstream media and social media. Most recently, the Shenzhen city government released an announcement in November 2018 that suspended a large number of the urban renewal projects involving urban villages. Resistance reported earlier might have contributed to such a position shift by the government.

Roy (2005) argues that although existing studies might have contrasting frames of informality as either one of crisis or one of heroism, they tend to frame informality as separate from formality. Roy suggests that informality should be considered as a mode of urbanisation rather than a separate sector, which can be well reflected in the case of Shenzhen. However, it remains to be seen how these various informal settlements might evolve in different geographical contexts and how the marginalised groups might be able to contest against state and corporate-led initiatives that often result in displacement of the have-nots and to develop a more inclusive and sustainable urban world.

FIGURE 10.2

Looking up from one of the urban villages in Shenzhen. (Credit: Wen Lin)

SUMMARY

- The Industrial Revolution created a context for debates on the archetypal society. It led to the emergence of the concept of the rural idyll in many parts of Western Europe. Accordingly, the rural is typically constructed as something in opposition to the urban.

- It is important not to make sweeping generalisations, and it is not helpful to treat the urban and the rural as two dichotomic realms. Urban and rural areas both encompass incredibly diverse social relations and interactions.

- The urban and rural are linked not only through internal migration and individual mobility but also by global forces and flows.

- Paying attention to local contexts is important to understand poverty and social inequalities in both urban and rural society.

FURTHER READING

Fyfe, N., & Kenny, J. (2005) *The Urban Geography Reader*. New York: Routledge.

LeGates, R., & Stout, S. (2011) *The City Reader*, 5th ed. New York: Routledge.

McAreavey, R. (2017) *New Immigration Destinations: Migrating to Rural and Peripheral Areas*. London: Routledge.

Pahl, R. (1966) The rural–urban continuum. *Sociologia Ruralis*, 6(3–4): 299–329.

The Everyday

Alison Stenning, with Leah Chan,
Lottie Rhodes and Katy Smith

For many of us, thinking about the everyday starts with thinking about our own everyday lives. On the day I started to write this chapter, working at home, I juggled my attempts at writing with, among other things, dropping my daughter off at school, going for a short run, waiting for a handyman to come to sort out a few jobs, negotiating utility bills and eating and drinking. All these took place in an area of not more than a square mile, but they drew in diverse relationships and spaces – with my daughter's teachers and classmates, and their parents; with the streets around my house as I ran; with the cooperative, its staff and customers as I bought eggs on the way home from my run; with the handyman and his assemblage of tools and materials and his tales of his own everyday life; with the big corporations that provide me with gas, electricity, broadband, television and a phone; and with the call centre operators in County Durham and India.

Of course, it is not enough just to describe and map out the geographies of my everyday life. For the everyday to be a useful concept for geographers, we need to be able to connect to key geographical debates and questions. So we might want to ask, as Doreen Massey (1991b) does, how global is my everyday life and what power geometries shape my everyday relationships (see Chapter 1)? Or, following Erving Goffman (1959), how do

I negotiate, materially and emotionally, the different roles I perform in different spaces, as a mother, an academic, a customer, a runner, for example? Or, building on the work of generations of feminist geographers, how does gender shape and become written into my everyday geographies?

The everyday is often a starting point for geographical enquiry, a way into thinking about another issue – globalisation, power, identity or gender, for example (Clayton, 2013; Holloway & Hubbard, 2001). But it also reflects a set of related ontologies that hold in common certain ideas about space, place and humans. With three students who studied everyday emotional geographies, I worked to develop this chapter, reflecting on what the everyday means to us, whose ideas we find helpful in understanding the everyday, what geographers in particular can gain from and offer to ideas of the everyday and how we can think about the politics of studying the everyday.

WHAT IS THE EVERYDAY?

As I suggested above, most of us first identify the everyday as personal, intimate, ordinary and taken for granted. At the beginning of our conversations, the everyday emerged as a scale and space that felt quite stable and secure, based on routines and rituals that we engaged with, often without much thought, on a daily basis. Perhaps reflecting our own gender identities, we saw the everyday as a feminine space at small scales, focused on social reproduction, in complex articulation with the apparently more masculine spaces of politics and infrastructure (Mitchell, Marston & Katz, 2004). Because the everyday was imagined as so personal and intimate, it was seen as extraordinarily diverse, reflecting perhaps phenomenological and humanistic approaches to geography (Jackson, 1981; Ash & Simpson, 2016). Everyone's everyday would be different, reflecting their life histories and experiences, their personal geographies and their intersecting identities. And each everyday is intertwined with and overlaps with others, and with diverse sites, spaces and relationships, in quite ordinary, unremarkable, yet complex and multiple ways. This presents an intellectual challenge – how can we usefully think about the everyday when it's made up of so many relational components?

As we talked, I asked how change fits into the everyday if we first conceive of it as stable and routine. We explored how different scales and rhythms of change work in different ways with thinking about the everyday. We identified how growing up and older might expand the spaces of our everyday lives but also transform our emotional attachments to and experiences of those spaces as they become more familiar or we integrate new spaces. We also talked about breaks, ruptures and endings, such as holidays, ill health or the end of a degree, and how these might reshape the everyday and the spaces and relationships within. At perhaps the smallest scales of time, we also explored how shifts from day to night, or within days, as we move, for example, from home to university to the city, are interwoven with intricate time geographies that illuminate much about the everyday.

THE IDEA OF THE EVERYDAY

The idea of the everyday appeared in social thought in the years of the 1920s. Its integration into academic geography came considerably later; yet much of the work in geography has its roots in this earlier work and in the early human geographies of Elisée Reclus and Paul Vidal de la Blache (Smith et al., 2010). The idea of the everyday is profoundly connected to the work of György Lukács and Henri Lefebvre, two Marxist theorists writing in the 1920s and 1930s in the context of economic and political crisis. For them, 'everyday life' was an attempt to capture the limits of daily routines for working people, tied as they often were to long hours in factories. At the same time, in very different ways, sociologists working in Chicago were also developing perspectives on everyday life. The so-called Chicago School is well known among many geography students for its creation of the concentric zone model (Park, Burgess & McKenzie, 1925), but this model was part of a much larger body of work that sought to develop insiders' perspectives on urban social worlds through ethnographic methods that were both radical and innovative at the time.

Two other American sociologists, Harold Garfinkel (1967; Laurier, 2009) and Erving Goffman (1959), shifted the focus to even smaller scales of everyday life – to the body and to language – and drew attention to the many unconscious and taken-for-granted moments, acts and rules that shape our experiences of everyday life. These taken-for-granted routines and habits formed the focus of Pierre Bourdieu's contribution to the study of everyday life developed through the 1970s and 1980s (Bourdieu & Nice, 1977; Painter, 2000). For Bourdieu, our ability to negotiate everyday life depends on our habitus, the practical and embodied skills, knowledges and ways of being that we develop from childhood onwards, reflecting, among other things, our family history, class, ethnicity and geography. Writing at a similar time, Michel de Certeau (1984) explored how everyday practices like 'living and cooking' come to be seen as tactics through which individuals, households and communities contest and subvert the agendas of powerful actors. Alongside these developing perspectives on everyday practices, routines and norms, we can also identify a developing academic tradition that focuses on everyday things. In part, this emerged with the new discipline of cultural studies in the United Kingdom from the 1960s (Bell, 2009), which focused on urban subcultures, popular culture and media. This focus on everyday cultures was enriched by the increasing attention paid to the cars, homes, food, clothes and music, among other things, that we engage with and value in our everyday lives.

The increasing influence of feminism reinforced a material perspective on everyday life but also emphasised strong corporeal and emotional angles. Not only did feminist writers seek to document and explain the differential everyday experiences of men and women, but they also developed strong critiques that shifted our thinking about everyday life (see Chapter 16). First, feminists argued that the personal is political: what happens in intimate, domestic, everyday spaces and moments both reflects and shapes 'bigger' political questions (Bowlby & McDowell, 1987). Second, they argued that everyday life is embodied: who we are and what our bodies are shape, and are shaped by, our everyday lives. Third, feminists argued for the virtues of routine and repetition; some feminists argued strongly that 'everyday life' need not be seen as negative, and this opened up a space to think about the value of stability and security in everyday life.

All of these perspectives have something to say about place, space and scale. Many emphasise the very local spaces of everyday life – the home, the street, work, for example – and highlight the interrelationships between private and public spaces. Others map the crossing of scales and spaces at the heart of everyday life, as people, places, things, institutions and ideas from more proximate and more distant worlds collide in the everyday.

GEOGRAPHIES OF EVERYDAY LIFE

This begs the question: What, in particular, do geographers have to contribute to the study of everyday life? In our conversation, we argued that geographers' desire and skills to hold the different parts of everyday life together and to map the intricate components of the 'tangled webs we weave' (Jarvis, 1999) were critically important. This connects to questions of scales and spaces, as we seek to integrate geographies of everyday life from Robyn Longhurst's 'geography closest in' (1994) – the body – to the planetary scales of Doreen Massey's 'global sense of place' (1991b) and to pay attention to the conflicts and contradictions in living life between these scales. Massey's work was very much an attempt to hold together these different scales, and she latterly developed the idea of throwntogetherness: 'the way that very diverse elements that cross categories such as the natural or social come together to foster a particular "here and now"' (Anderson, 2009: 232; Massey, 2005).

The mapping of the ways the intricate geographies of everyday life come together is often first connected to Torsten Hägerstrand's time geography (1982). Hägerstrand sought to record the paths of everyday life within the wider contexts of socioeconomic structures, power and the built environment. Key sites were connected by individual movements, and these were represented by space-time maps. Individual paths included connections to other people and things and mapped the ways that individuals navigated their everyday environments. The centrality of this question to human geography is reflected in the work developed from Hägerstrand's, placing particular emphasis on power and on gender to account for the uneven paths of everyday life.

Much social geographical research at this time was influenced by wider humanist and phenomenological approaches (Jackson, 1981), which sought to focus on lived experiences and lifeworlds to map the 'plurality of worlds' (Relph, 1970: 194) and to explore the meanings and values that shape our experiences of everyday life. This work was a key step in Nigel Thrift's move from time geographies towards the development of nonrepresentational theory, through which he focused on the 'mundane everyday practices that shape the conduct of human beings towards others and themselves in particular sites' (Thrift, 1997: 142; see also Chapter 2). In this work, 'the focus falls on how life takes shape and gains expression in shared experiences, everyday routines, fleeting encounters, embodied movements, precognitive triggers, practical skills, affective intensities, enduring urges, unexceptional interactions and sensuous dispositions' (Lorimer, 2005: 84). More recently, work in this vein has focused on mapping and interpreting affective atmospheres, defined as 'a distinctive kind of mood or shared corporeal phenomenon' (Gandy, 2017: 353). In some ways, this echoes work by psychogeographers (Richardson, 2016), who developed playful, exploratory strategies for investigating the city and sought to feel and record the less tangible aspects of places, the ambiance, feelings, essences, memories, light, sound and rhythm, and these have all been part of a wider move to focus on the noncognitive, emotional and embodied aspects of everyday life (see also Chapter 12 on emotion).

INTERSECTIONS

Perhaps one of the strongest themes that run through these varying and developing takes on the everyday is the necessity and the possibility to map and explore the ways our everyday lives are produced through the coming together of multiple spheres and spaces. All of the approaches explored above insist that attention is paid to the past and the present, the intimate and the more distant, the socioeconomic, the cultural and the political, the myriad and multiple objects of everyday life; and geographers' contributions reinforce this perspective by stressing the interwoven paths of everyday life.

This idea of intertwining practices, dynamics, things and bodies was central to our conversations about the everyday too. And with this, we explored the diversities and intersections that are highlighted by looking at the geographies of everyday life. The articulation between our biographies and the shape of our everyday geographies was a key theme to which we returned repeatedly. As feminist geographers have long argued, men's and women's experiences of public space vary considerably, reflecting gender norms, discrimination, the nature of the built environment and much more (McDowell, 1983). More recently, geographers have also explored how class, sexual identity, religion and age have shaped our negotiations of public space (Pain, 2001), and these ideas have attracted considerable popular attention through campaigns to document everyday sexism (Bates, 2015); the idea of a so-called hostile environment is one that profoundly connects race to the spaces of everyday life, such as schools, workplaces and hospitals.

TEXT BOX 11.1 | Real-World Research: Researching Austerity and Everyday Life

Ideas of everyday life have been invoked by the architects of British austerity. In 2011, Nick Clegg, then deputy prime minister, talked about 'alarm-clock Britain' to depict the grinding, repetitive experience of hardworking life, while George Osborne, then Chancellor of the Exchequer, attacked a so-called 'benefits lifestyle', characterised by the idea that 'some claimants were able to lie in with their curtains closed while "hard-working families" headed off to work' (BBC News, 2011).

In this context, many social geographers have turned their attention to researching the everyday experiences of cuts, economic crises and welfare reforms. This research has taken various forms. For example, Sarah Hall (2018) has used a 'zine' (https://e.issuu.com/anonymous-embed.html?u=everydayauster ity&d=everyday_austerity_full_zine) to rep-resent what austerity looks and feels like for families in the northwest of England, focusing on the complexities of small moments. Esther Hitchen (2019) developed a detailed, yearlong ethnography in a northeast library service, exploring the emotional and affective presence of austerity in the many spaces of work, volunteering and transformation. And Sander van Lanen (2020) used in-depth interviews and the concept of 'lifeworlds' to research the everyday geographies of young people in two disadvantaged urban neighbourhoods in Ireland. Together, this research and more like it employs the concepts, framings and methodologies developed over more than a hundred years to explore the interplay between the intimate spaces of everyday life and the multiple scales of economy and politics, documenting the inequalities and intersections that shape and are shaped by these geographies.

All of this work clearly and emphatically links studies of the everyday to class (see Chapter 15), bringing us full circle to the Marxist theorisations of the early twentieth century. What all these perspectives have in common, perhaps, is the reclaiming of the banal, taken-for-granted, unseen spaces of everyday life as the spaces in which so many of us spend our days. As Doreen Massey put it, 'Much of life for many people, even in the heart of the First World, still consists of waiting in a bus-shelter with your shopping for a bus that never comes' (1994/2013: 163). Moreover, waiting in bus shelters is an act that rests on our gender, class, age and ethnic identities, such that it reveals everyday questions of power and intersectionality that cannot be ignored (Moran, 2005; Wilson, 2011).

Many of the ideas explored here highlight the profoundly political nature of work on the everyday. At times, paying attention to the minutiae of everyday life has been critiqued for being too ephemeral and too trivial to matter, in contrast to the more influential spaces of national politics and global economics. But this, by definition, is the stuff of everyday life, and in it we can find questions and answers that challenge, engage and remake those bigger processes. What sense can we make of public transport cuts, or new rounds of foreign investment, or exiting the European Union, if we don't also ask what these shifts mean for people negotiating the changing spaces of their everyday lives? The everyday is a profoundly political space – it answers back, and this is why it sits at the heart of such radical work as feminism, cultural studies and subaltern studies. Work with such political intent inevitably carries with it enormous responsibility, all the more so since it demands that we engage so intensely with the messy, vulnerable, intimate spaces of people's everyday lives, whether that is their shopping habits, their care routines, their activism or their mantelpiece.

SUMMARY

- This chapter has introduced key ideas and perspectives that help us to understand the everyday as an important focus for social geographers and as a scale that is inherently connected to wider spatial processes.
- Feminist, humanist and phenomenological approaches have had particular influence on social geographers' conceptions of everyday geographies.
- Geographies of everyday lives are produced through the coming together of multiple spheres and spaces.
- Many of the ideas explored here highlight the profoundly political nature of the everyday and of research that examines it.

FURTHER READING

Clayton, J. (2013) Geography and everyday life. In B. Warf (ed.), *Oxford Bibliographies in Geography*. New York: Oxford University Press.

Holloway, L., & Hubbard, P. (2001) People *and Place: The Extraordinary Geographies of Everyday Life*. Harlow, UK: Prentice-Hall.

Moran, J. (2005) *Reading the Everyday*. London: Routledge.

Moran, J. (2008) *Queuing for Beginners: The Story of Daily Life from Breakfast to Bedtime*. London: Profile Books.

Emotion

Matej Blazek, with Katy Smith, Lottie Rhodes and Leah Chan

Like Chapter 11 on the everyday, this chapter is based on discussions with students who have studied everyday emotional geographies with Alison Stenning and me, exploring *how* we can make sense of emotions and also *why* this is important for us as social geographers.

Imagine the moment when you enter your house after a long day. What do you feel? Perhaps it is a cold, rainy day, and you cannot wait to sit down in the warm living room and have a cup of tea. Perhaps you are looking forward to sharing the news of the day with your friends. Perhaps you are focused on leaving the stress of university behind, sitting down on the sofa and watching television. Or perhaps your first impression is the stressful view of dirty dishes, the sound of a noisy neighbour and a reminder that you need to spend the rest of the evening working on your essay.

Now imagine that you walk down a busy street, such as Grey Street in Newcastle upon Tyne (see Figure 12.1). And consider how various things are *deliberately* placed and designed to make people feel in a certain way. Consider businesses as they seek to grab your attention with colourful visuals and groovy music and get you to step inside. Consider the benches, encouraging you to sit for a while but not to get comfortable enough to take a nap. Consider signs placed to help those unfamiliar with the

FIGURE 12.1

Grey Street, Newcastle upon Tyne. (Credit: Matej Blazek)

city to navigate their way around. And consider people: the police officers whose presence should make you feel both alert and secure; the busker letting you take pleasure in his music and perhaps consider giving him some money; and all the anonymous people who do not want to incite any particular feelings in you – they just wish to pass by unnoticed as they are getting on with their daily errands.

These examples tell us something about why emotions should matter to geographers. First, *we feel differently in different places*. Those differences in feelings might have to do with the physical environment (your house is warm, the street is cold), social relationships (the housemates awaiting you at home), everyday objects and activities (the comfort routine of sofa and television) or with deeply grounded inscriptions of identity – how who we are is linked to our belonging to places (the importance of this being *your* home and *your* city).

These examples also show us that the links between emotions and places are not random. *Places are made to elicit certain feelings* and *emotions have certain politics*. The downtown street is designed to make you spend time (and money) there and not feel overly concerned about the others around you. This process does not have a single architect; the emotional dynamics are produced by a range of actors, from city planners and local entrepreneurs to visitors like you. Indeed, we all contribute. In a public place like Grey Street, we might do so just by following unwritten rules of polite but oblivious interactions with strangers, but at home our imprints are much larger. We work (hard) every day to feel comfortable, safe and happy in our homes.

But *how we feel also depends on who we are*. For some, home is not associated with comfort and peace but with violence, trauma and loss (Brickell, 2012). For some, busy streets are not places to be but places to get away from – whether due to fear of racially motivated attacks (Hopkins, 2016) or punitive policies against rough sleepers (Mitchell, 1997). Home or busy streets are not welcoming – or neutral – spaces for everyone, and emotional geographies are concerned with the question of links between who we are, where we are, how we feel and what we do.

If you are reading this book, you probably agree that geography matters (Massey & Allen, 1984; see Chapter 1). And so do emotions. They 'produce real effects, with significant and often severe consequences' (Askins, 2019: 107). Emotions also have their geography. They emerge through affective capacities of places, while at the same time impacting social and spatial processes. This chapter explores how emotions and geography come to matter together. We discuss key ideas from three theoretical approaches: feminism, phenomenology and theories of affect. This focus does not capture everything there is to say about emotions, and we do not even get to talk about key perspectives on emotions such as psychoanalysis (Bondi, 2005) or participatory research (Askins, 2016) – these were mentioned in Chapter 3. Rather than seeing our discussions as detailed overviews, this chapter offers a set of key ideas that help us to highlight why emotions matter for social geography.

Like other social scientists, social geographers are 'more concerned with what emotions do than what they are' (Walby, Spencer & Hunt, 2012: 5), exploring them in the contexts of experience embedded in places, social organisations and everyday activities (see Chapter 11 on the everyday). Geographers have been rather cautious in endorsing a single definition of emotions, but, for the purpose of this chapter, we will understand emotions as *experiences of embodied presence in the world*. This gives us a few ideas from which we can work further. One is that emotions are always felt through the body; yet they are not the same as bodily sensations – feeling hot is not an emotion, but feeling frustrated because of that is. The second is that emotions need to be explored in relation to their contexts, not on their own. And the final one is that thinking about emotions as experiences draws attention to links between thoughts and emotions, rather than viewing the two as separate elements. Our thoughts elicit emotional responses ('happy thought' or 'scary thought'), while emotions prompt thoughtful reflections ('why do I feel scared when I talk to my neighbour?').

FEMINIST EMOTIONAL GEOGRAPHIES: CHALLENGING THE DUALISM OF REASON AND EMOTION

In the early 2000s, geography witnessed an effort to evolve from 'an emotionally barren terrain, a world devoid of passion [and] spaces ordered solely by rational principles' (Bondi, Davidson & Smith, 2005, 1; see Chapter 1). The impact and role of feminism in this so-called emotional turn go well beyond the space this chapter offers (see Bondi, 2005), but there is one specific point that will open our further discussion.

A key contribution of feminist geographers in the 1990s was a critique of dualist or binary thinking (e.g., Rose, 1993; see Chapter 16 on gender). Dualism defines one subject as a superior model and another one as its inferior opposite. By deconstructing binaries such as man/woman, culture/nature, public/private or mind/body, feminists showed that these dichotomies are politically charged because the marginalised subject (woman, nature, private, body) is defined in relation to, and as a negation of, the dominant model (man, culture, public, mind). A clear-cut division puts one side of the binary – associated with men, cultural rationality and public politics – in a position of significance and power, and it diminishes the importance of the other one – associated with women, nature, embodiment and the private sphere.

One of those problematic dichotomies is that of reason and emotion. Western thought has traditionally identified human subjectivity with the presence of reason, while emotions became seen as a sign of imperfection and the imprint of natural forces that humans should seek to control. This division is fundamentally gendered:

> Whereas mind has been associated with positive terms such as rationality, consciousness, reason and masculinity, the body has been associated with negative terms such as emotionality, nature, irrationality and femininity. Whereas Man is assumed to be able to separate himself from his emotions, experiences and so on, Woman has been presumed to be 'a victim of the vagaries of her emotions, a creature who can't think straight as a consequence'. (Valentine, 2001: 17, citing Kirby, 1992: 12–13)

By critiquing not just the dichotomies of man/woman and reason/emotion but also their political impact when working together, feminist geography laid the grounds for further developments of emotional geographies in at least three ways:

1. It articulated the importance of emotions in processes shaping society. Furthermore, it showed that disregarding the importance of emotions is not just an epistemological omission but also a political act reinforcing the hierarchical gendered order (Bondi, 2005).

2. It highlighted the importance of emotions in our understandings of the world and accentuated embodied and emotional forms of knowing (Thien, 2005). The concept of 'objective thought' cannot fully encapsulate our experience of the world, and knowledge production needs to incorporate embodied and emotional knowledge.

3. By drawing attention to intersubjectivity and knowing as 'among others', feminist geography established the grounds for collective engagement, interdependence and ethics of care as strategies to explore the world (Askins, 2019).

PHENOMENOLOGY: THE WORLD, THE FEELING AND THE BODY

Joyce Davidson's (2003) research on the experiences of women with agoraphobia links feminist perspectives on emotional geographies with those of *phenomenology*, a philosophical tradition concerned with the process rather than the object of experience. Davidson explored links between agoraphobic experience and one's control over, and security in, spaces such as home, street or shopping mall. She argued that the lack of attention by geography to these spaces stemmed from their historically feminised character. She also argued that the emotional and embodied nature of agoraphobic conditions requires methodologies that would be attentive to the felt experience of bodies placed in social space.

Davidson thus brings together emotions, body and 'lived' space as joint foundations of experience. For phenomenology, our experience is neither just a physiological perception nor a construct of the intellectual mind. Rather, the body, the mind and the environment are in ongoing engagement, and our experience is simultaneously embodied, emotional(ised) and rational(ised): 'the body and world, subject and object, are conjoined as flesh' (Wylie, 2006: 525). An example is given in Text Box 12.1.

TEXT BOX 12.1 | Real-World Theory: Therapeutic Landscapes

An example of phenomenological work in geography is in the concept of therapeutic landscapes (see Chapter 23 on health). Therapeutic landscapes emerge at the intersection of the material, social and spiritual worlds, at which body and mind are actively intertwined with their immediate surroundings. As David Conradson (2003) points out, a key aspect of physical and mental well-being is the 'relational dimensions of the self-landscape encounter' (346). For instance, Jennifer Lea's (2008) work on outdoor yoga retreats illustrates the importance of nature in what is otherwise an individual bodily and spiritual practice:

- The uneven floor of the yoga platform amplifies the sensation through touch and the bodily experience of yoga positions.
- Seated meditation at the sunrise connects the perceived energy of natural forces and the mobilising role of yoga exercise on one's body.
- The presence of wind-bent trees and other Earth surface forms creates a visual parallel with the changing posture and shape of the body.

Earlier phenomenological work in geography has been criticised for paying little attention to questions of difference and power, assuming the universality of embodied experience (Ash & Simpson, 2016). However, linking together the critical conceptions of bodies as always socially inscribed with the phenomenological attentiveness to situated embodied experience creates a more critical framework for close investigation of emotional life as always situated in an embodied moment.

AFFECTIVE GEOGRAPHIES: THE PREINDIVIDUAL CONSTITUTION OF FEELING

Lea's (2008) example of yoga retreats suggests that emotions emerge through the body's engagement with the environment but also that, while everyone feels differently in these situations, certain forces are affecting the feelings of many. And this brings us to the idea of affect.

The geographical understanding of affect refers to the seventeenth-century philosopher Baruch Spinoza, who saw affect as the force by which 'the body's power of acting is increased or diminished' (Spinoza, 1677/2001: III, 56). This definition implies that our experience happens through the body, as changing the state of the body produces an emotional experience. But it also implies that, unlike emotions, which are located within an individual, affect is preindividual, as it emerges outside oneself (although it comes to act through individuals' embodied interactions with the world).

Imagine sitting on a sofa in your home, watching a comedy show on television. What are the elements that *affect* how you feel? Perhaps they are:

- the solitude, or the presence of others
- the lack of immediate pressure, associated with your time to unwind
- what happened earlier that day
- the physical comfort of the sofa, room temperature, light and acoustics
- the programme itself
- the fact that you are (not) hungry or thirsty

All these elements constitute an affect. They are *preindividual* because they exist outside yourself before your emotions emerge through their impact on your body. But they are also *transindividual* because they impact other people too, even if in different ways. Indeed, if someone else was on the same sofa, in the same time and watching the same show, they would be affected by the same aspects but differently. Imagine how one would feel if they were a stranger to the house, they did not like the show, they had had a difficult day or they did not understand the language of the show.

Affect can also be an adjective. We can consider your living room to be an *affective space* or *an affective condition*. Affective conditions can be very different in kind. Consider how the affective power of the nighttime city emerges through the assemblages of embodied practices of partygoers, taxi drivers, street cleaners and police officers (Shaw, 2014). The nighttime city impacts on the emotional experience in a way that is different from its daylight equivalent. And then consider how the idea of childhood has an affective power, as portrayals of children often serve as vehicles of sympathies, mobilised in humanitarian campaigns (Manzo, 2008). In the example of the nighttime city, it is the space, bodies, objects and practices that constitute an affect. In the example of childhood, it is only a visualised idea, a representation of children in need that moves us, makes us feel and act.

Feminist geographies showed that emotions matter politically. Theories of affect further emphasise that, because of the pre- and transindividual nature of processes that produce emotions, emotions may become subjects of governance. They are regulated, modified and manipulated, not necessarily through direct control over an individual's feelings but through the production and management of wider affective conditions to which people are exposed (Jupp, Pykett & Smith, 2017). Affect, geographers have argued, therefore becomes a useful tool for governance.

For example, Janet Newman (2017) suggests that the governance of austerity is predicated on the politics of rage. She argues that in order to secure voters' support and to compensate for austerity's negative effects on their socioeconomic situation, the UK government has generated an affective condition that produces anger against welfare, bureaucracy and irresponsible citizenship. Through the 'scapegoating of migrants, the demonization of welfare recipients, and the intensification of the language of security/insecurity' (Newman, 2017: 32), such an approach seeks to create a state where the emotional response to the impacts of austerity does not target the government but is channelled as rage against others.

SUMMARY

This chapter has introduced the growing importance of emotions to social geographers' understandings of how society and space interrelate. By exploring feminist, phenomenological and affective approaches to emotions, this chapter offered the following key ideas:

- Privileging uncritical rationality over emotions reproduces dualistic societal hierarchies. Problematising the superiority of reason and 'thinking emotionally has a vital role in progressive approaches to destabilizing normative, exclusionary structures and discourses' (Askins, 2019: 109).

- Emotional forms of knowing require attentiveness to the conjoined presence of the body, mind and environment. Emotions emerge through the body, but they are relational to the world.

- While emotions emerge from individual bodies, they are produced through wider affective conditions. Because emotions are fundamental to social relations and yet are also produced by those relations, they are inevitably a subject of politics and governance.

FURTHER READING

Askins, K. (2019) Emotions. In *Antipode* Editorial Collective (eds.), *Keywords in Radical Geography*, pp. 107–12. Oxford: John Wiley & Sons.

Davidson, J., Bondi, L., & Smith, M. (eds.) (2005) *Emotional Geographies.* Aldershot, UK: Ashgate.

DIVISIONS

A
PART

B
PART

C
PART

D
PART

Race

Raksha Pande

As human beings, we make sense of the world by ordering it. One of the earliest attempts to classify humanity was based on a set of observable criteria of skin tone, leading to the development of 'race' as one of the lasting myths of humanity. In this chapter, I examine what 'race' is and how it is a social construct and not a biological category. I also discuss how racism is conceptualised, before moving on to explore some key examples of social geography research on 'race' and racism.

RACE AS A SOCIAL CONSTRUCTION

At the outset, it is important to state that scientists are unanimous in their assertion that 'race' does not exist as a biological category among human beings. In fact, in 1950 the United Nations Educational, Scientific and Cultural Organization (UNESCO) issued a statement that all humans belong to the same species and that race is not a biological reality but a myth. However, you might argue that you can see racial difference, as people have 'black' and 'white' skin tones and all the shades in between, so how can we say that 'race' does not exist? What scientists mean when they say that 'race' as a category does not exist is that the variations in skin tone on which racial classification is based are not linked to any substantive genetic differences. Simply put, if we want to use 'race' as a mutually exclusive category, then we would need to show that there is a great deal of genetic difference between people with different skin tones. However, this is not the case; there is so little genetic diversity among humans that genetic differences are not fixed along racial lines. Moreover, scientists (Tishkoff & Kidd, 2004) have proven that there is more genetic variation within populations than between them, which means that you may share more genes with a person whose skin colour is different from yours than with a person who has a similar skin colour. Consequently, classifying people along racial lines does not serve any meaningful purpose; there is simply far too much overlap and very little difference in genes between people with different skin tones.

It is worth mentioning here that the question is not whether differences in skin colour are genetic, because they are. We know that, because these traits are passed from parent to child. The important question is what else the genes for skin colour relate to. Scientists have confirmed that they do not relate to people's intelligence, their ability to do certain jobs or their overall behaviour. The association between the genes that determine skin colour and human traits such as intelligence has no basis in biology. With advancements in genetic mapping and genome research, 'racial science', the branch of science that established racial classification and its links with human intelligence and potential, has been proven to be wrong. However, we still live with its legacy inasmuch as racial classification continues to exist as a social category.

'Race', then, is best understood as a social construction (see Chapters 15 on class and 16 on gender). This implies that racial categories such as 'Black' and 'White' do not capture biological truths about human ability (other than skin colour) but are products of social contexts. People's understanding of racial differences is shaped by the culture and era that they live in. Who is counted as 'Black' or 'White' has not been fixed through human history and national cultures. For example, Irish immigrants to the nineteenth-century United States were not always considered 'White'. The historian Noel Ignatiev in his 1995 book *How the Irish Became White* shows how in the first few years of their arrival in the United States the Irish were treated as racially different from the wider population of Anglo-Saxon heritage. This was because these immigrants were Catholics in a primarily Protestant country. This religious difference, coupled with the fact that the influx of migrant labour was seen as a threat to the jobs of existing unskilled American labourers, contributed to this social classification of Irish as non-Whites. He goes on to show how the Irish *became White* and found acceptance among an initially hostile population through contributing to the oppression of African Americans by keeping them out of the labour market and by opposing abolitionism. For us today, it may be difficult to imagine a time when fair-skinned people of Irish descent were not considered

White. However, as Ignatiev's study proves, definitions of 'race' have changed over time and are rooted in a complex interplay of other social categories, such as class and religion.

Moreover, what the Irish example also shows is that, while 'race' categories do not exist in any real objective sense, 'race' can still be *made to exist* to form the basis for exclusionary practices. The process through which it is brought into existence through cultural or political processes is termed *racialisation*. Racialisation is a key concept through which race and ethnic relations are understood. It refers to the processes where it is invoked as an explanation for a social phenomenon and is associated with ideological practices such as racism. Racialisation is the process though which race is socially constructed and comes to be regarded as a meaningful category (Murji & Solomos, 2005). It primarily involves the attribution of racial categorisation to a previously racially unclassified relationship, such as in the Irish example above and, more recently, in calls for conceptualising Islamophobia as anti-Muslim racism. Even though Muslim is a not a 'race' category, the irrational fear of Islam (Islamophobia) comes to act in ways that are very similar to racism by marginalising Muslim populations. The notion of racialisation helps us to understand how racial meaning pervades social life and to appreciate how 'race' continues to exist in a globalising world.

To summarise, 'race' is a social construction because the definition of what counts as 'Black' and 'White' identity is prone to change, in keeping with changes in the socioeconomic and cultural landscape of society. However, to say that something is a social construction does not mean that it not real or is insubstantial in its impact. Race may be socially constructed yet still be embodied – meaning that individual bodies are racialised in their experience of racism and discrimination. In fact, race is the ultimate sticky category. Even though its scientific basis was debunked a long time ago, its social import persists in the form of racist ideology. Writing in 1981, the public intellectual Stuart Hall (1983: 269) alerted us to the significance of race as a social category: 'Instead of thinking that confronting the questions of "race" are some sort of moral intellectual academic duty which White people with good feelings do for Blacks, one has to remember that the issue of "race" provides one of the most important ways of understanding how this society actually works and how it has arrived where it is'.

The social construction of 'race' is underpinned by an ideology that favours White and lighter-skinned people. Racial categories serve the function of justifying social inequalities; it is always easier for some politicians to explain why Black people are disproportionately represented in the poorer sections of society by attributing it to their 'race' than by acknowledging the structural disadvantage that they face in accessing resources and opportunities to advance their education. The experience of racism is a daily reality for many people, and in the next section I explore how racism is conceptualised in social geographies.

FIGURE 13.1
Anti-racism activism at the Monument, Newcastle upon Tyne, 12 January 2019. (Credit: Raksha Pande)

RACE MATTERS: UNDERSTANDING RACISM

Racism can be defined as an ideological position where racial and ethnic categories, such as Whiteness, are employed as the basis of a social hierarchy. The categories are a result of social construction or biological determinism. It is important to stress the point that racism is an ideological stance (meaning that it is based on a set of beliefs and ideas) about the superiority of one racial (White) and ethnic identity over others. White identity can be understood as a location of sustained social privilege that exceeds what is accorded to non-White people. The notion of Whiteness and its supremacy is also a social construct. The social construction of the supremacy of White identity owes its origin to the legacy of colonialism, slavery and the now-discredited 'racial science' theories. Whiteness, as a racial category, works through being invisible and universal at the same time: as Dyer (1988: 45) puts it, 'In the realm of categories, black is always marked as a colour (as the term "coloured" egregiously acknowledges), and is always particularizing; whereas white is not anything really, not an identity, not a particularizing quality, because it is everything – white is no colour because it is all colours'. The power that comes with being regarded as representing the norm (hence normal) and universal (so not different) is what gives White supremacism and racism their pernicious edge. Racism exists in many forms, depending on the basis of classification. In social geography, there are two primary ways racism is identified, the first based on social classification – individual and systemic – and the other on historical classification – new and old.

Individual and Systemic Racism

Individual racism refers to an individual's racist beliefs and behaviours and is a result of conscious or unconscious personal prejudice against a specific racial or ethnic group. This form of racism is usually stated as a personal opinion, where an individual may defend their right to free speech and express their prejudice, then discriminate against a person of another race or ethnicity. For example, shouting racial libels is a typical form of individual racism. Individual racism rarely functions on its own, but is part of and reinforced by systemic racism. Systemic racism refers to the policies and practices entrenched in societal institutions that result in discrimination against certain racial groups and the promotion of others. The term 'systemic' helps to distinguish this form of racism from individual racism by focusing on the wider institutional (political, educational and economic) and structural basis of discrimination. When systemic racism is related to the discriminatory actions of an organisation(s), it is referred to as institutional racism; when it refers to sociocultural norms and representations that reinforce racial inequality at a systemwide societal level, it is called structural racism. The fact that more Black people are stopped and searched by the police in the United Kingdom is an example of institutional racism within the police force. Structural racism is more difficult to locate in a specific example because it involves the reinforcing effects of sociocultural and historical factors that privilege the White identity over others. Structural racism is evident in the society-wide inequality in power, opportunities and policy impacts and outcomes for non-White people.

The relationship between individual and systemic racism highlights the fact that racism is not merely the problem of holding offensive or discriminatory opinions about someone, but it is a question of power – the power (bestowed through institutions or wider social structures) to act upon those opinions and include or exclude people based on their race or ethnicity. For example, a teacher may hold a prejudiced opinion about a student because of their ethnic and racial identity (an example of individual racism), but if that teacher is allowed by the school education system (institutional racism) or, in other words, *given the power* to exclude that student from certain lessons, then it becomes an example of systemic racism. Over time, if all students belonging to that racial group have poor educational outcomes, they are then seen as experiencing structural racism, as their discrimination is sanctioned by the sociopolitical system.

From Old to New Racisms

Within the social sciences, scholars also distinguish between old and new forms of racism. Their argument is that blatant forms of biological racism, which include stereotyping, overt discrimination and notions of racial inferiority, are on the decline in Western societies. This is a result of changing social norms that render it no longer acceptable to express racist views in public, and these norms are further reinforced by legislation that restricts such behaviours and practices within workplaces. Instead, scholars (Barker, 1981) argue that newer and more subtle forms of racism are on the rise. This 'new racism' is rooted in prejudice based on cultural difference rather than racial difference. Consequently, the older forms of racism based on the biological superiority of the 'White race' have fallen out of favour; a new racism, driven by a belief in the superiority of Western culture over others, has taken its place. These new forms of racism can be symbolic or aversive. Symbolic racism (first theorised in the context of the United States) is also known as modern racism, defined as a belief that promotes negative feelings against Black and minority ethnic people and is characterised by resistance to changes in race relations (resulting, for example, from equality legislation and affirmative action). The resistance is justified by the argument that racial discrimination is no longer a problem and that ethnic minorities are unjustly benefiting from these legislations. In the United States, this belief is also coupled with notions of Black inferiority and seeing Black people as departing from the so-called traditional American values of hard work and self-reliance. Symbolic racism can be seen at work when media reports single out Black or minority ethnic people as benefit cheats. Many people cheat the benefits system, but Black and minority ethnic cheating is most often reported, as Black people are seen as abusing the system more than

| TEXT BOX 13.1 | Real-World Research: Researching Race and Ethnicity—What's in a Name? |

You may have noticed that, increasingly, people shy away from using the term 'race' and that, in public and academic discourse, the term 'ethnicity' is used instead of, or alongside, it to distinguish between White and non-White populations. It is important to remember that, although these terms are sometimes used interchangeably, they are not one and the same.

Race is a socially constructed category based on skin colour differentiation and its unscientific correlation with human behavioural and psychological capabilities. Ethnicity is a term used to describe a category of people who identify with each other based on similarities of culture, language, religion and a belief in a shared real or perceived common origin. Another key difference between race and ethnicity is in terms of who is doing the classifying. Race is usually an externally attributed category, based on the observable trait of skin colour. Ethnicity, however, may also be self-attributed where individuals ascribe to a group identity based on shared beliefs in common origin and culture. So, for example, all Black people do not share the same ethnicity, depending on ancestry and cultural roots; Black racial identity can include many different ethnic groups. Due to the misuse of the term and the changing understanding of race in our societies, some groups that were previously identified as a 'race' are now seen as an ethnic group. For example, in Nazi Germany the Jews were classified as a race, but now scholars agree that they are a distinct ethnic group, sharing a common ethnicity.

Although 'race' and ethnicity can be defined as distinct categories, there is also considerable overlap between the two and it is not always easy to clearly distinguish between them or to promote the best use of these terms, even among scholars. There is a dense relationship between the two categories. Some scholars favour the use of the term 'ethnicity' over 'race' to signal the demise of 'race' as a useful scientific category. Others indicate the nonscientific and problematic nature of race by always writing it within inverted commas. Still others argue that the social construction of race and the process of racialisation intimately tie race and ethnicity together. What is important to keep in mind is that changing the term from 'race' to 'ethnicity' to capture the experience of racism does not in any way change its harmful impact. Moreover, some scholars have argued that our well-intentioned desire to discredit the use of the term 'race' by renaming racial issue as ethnic problems depoliticises the problem of racism, whereby racial problems are seen not as expressions of inequality and power imbalance in society but as benign forms of difference.

In your own research and writing, you will also need to be clear about the terminology that you use. While there are no prescriptive guidelines on whether you use the term 'race' or 'ethnicity', within social geography it is conventional to use the terminology of 'race and ethnicity' to signal the complex relationship between biological and cultural markers of difference implicated within the two.

For further reading, see Gunaratnam (2003).

others due to symbolic racist attitudes. Aversive racism is another form of this new racism. First conceptualised in social psychology (Gaertner & Dovidio, 1986), it can be defined as exhibiting racist tendencies while denying that those thoughts, behaviours and motives are racist. Aversive racists express egalitarian views; yet, deep down, unconsciously, they will exhibit racially discriminating behaviour in certain circumstances. Aversive racism is most evident in organisational hiring practices – a hiring committee will consistently discriminate against a particular ethnic group but will rationalise its discrimination with reasons other than 'race' – for example, businesses not hiring people from a particular ethnic group while justifying that decision as a business need. Aversive racism is also sometimes called unconscious bias. The difference between symbolic racism and aversive racism is that in the former the person is aware and takes ownership of their socially acceptable form of racist prejudice, while in the latter their racism is a result of unconscious bias.

This examination of the various forms of racism highlights the pernicious and deeply engrained nature of racism in our societies. The task of social geographers has been to theorise 'race' and racism, to reveal racial inequalities thorough an analysis of the lived experience of 'race' and racism in various places and across time and to conceptualise how an antiracist geography can be advanced in research and teaching.

'RACE' IS SOMETHING THAT WE DO RATHER THAN WHO WE ARE: GEOGRAPHIES OF 'RACE' AND RACISM

The precursor to current social geographical scholarship on race and racism can be identified as Peter Jackson's pioneering edited collection of essays, *Race and Racism*. This book established the agenda for future research on critical geographies of race and racism. It signalled a transition in social geography scholarship from quantitative and descriptive studies of immigration and residential segregation towards a more critical attempt to deal with the political dimensions of race and ethnicity. In short, Jackson's challenge to social geographers was to ask them not to just count and describe where people of various 'races' and ethnicities live but also to ask why they were residentially segregated. In this way he helped to establish a radical edge to social geography and attuned it to capture more effectively the political and social realities of living with racism. Since then, his call for social geography scholarship has developed into a dynamic field of study that engages with questions of how geographical imaginaries come to be racialised and, more significantly, how we can advance an antiracist geographical scholarship. To further explore the field of social geography research on race and racism, we can examine it under two main themes: theorisations of race and ethnicity and understanding the lived experience of 'race'. I will cite key representative research work that has contributed to these themes, but it is by no means an exhaustive list.

Theorisations of 'Race' and Ethnicity

The social construction of 'race' continues to be explored by social geographers in the form of critical inquiries into Whiteness (Bonnett, 2016), postrace thinking (Nayak, 2006a) and the new materiality of 'race' (Saldanha, 2006). One of the major attempts to understand critically how 'race' is brought into being has been through the research of Alastair Bonnett (2016), who explores how Whiteness operates as a central symbol of the power of Western culture and modernity at large, while at the same time is portrayed as a vulnerable racial identity under threat from migration and globalisation. Nayak's theorisation examines how the category of race can be emptied of any intrinsic analytic value while also trying to understand how racism operates and racialisation takes place. He theorises 'race' within the postrace paradigm by arguing that it is something that we do rather than who we are (Nayak, 2006a: 424). Similarly, Saldanha's work also contributes to what can be understood as the antifoundational perspective on 'race' by conceptualising it as a material process. His focus is on understating how different human bodies (economically and physically different) become grouped together in certain places, and which groups benefit from this 'race'-based grouping over time (Saldanha, 2006). These three approaches, among others, have contributed significantly to social geographical engagements with the difficult question of how to continue researching 'race' without contributing to its revitalisation as a concrete category.

Understating the Lived Experience of 'Race' and Racism

Social geographers have also examined how 'race' continues to exist as a social category through processes of racialisation and the ideology of racism on an everyday scale. For example, Ash Amin (2002) has emphasised the importance of understanding how racial and ethnic differences are negotiated in everyday life by focusing on the daily encounters and routine practices through which 'race' and racism operate in a given society. Geographers have also analysed the experiences of racism in both the rural (Neal & Agyeman, 2006) and the urban landscape (Cross & Keith, 2013). They have also explored how 'race' is implicated in the production of the ideas of national heritage and belonging (Tolia-Kelly, 2011). As Muslim identity has become racialised in the aftermath of 9/11, geographers have explored debates around the veil (Dwyer, 1999), the impact of Islamophobia (Najib & Hopkins, 2019) and wider debates around multicultural encounters (Wilson, 2014). They have also raised questions of how we do geographies of 'race' by turning a critical eye to the politics of 'race' and ethnicity in geographical fieldwork (Abbott, 2006) and in the spaces of the university itself (Mahtani, 2006) by developing the agenda for an antiracist geography (Peake & Kobayashi, 2002).

This brief discussion of research on 'race' and racism shows that questions of how 'race' is manifested in our lives and continues to structure unequal power relations have been central to human geographical scholarship.

SUMMARY

- Race is not a biological category. It is a social construction. The social construction of 'race' is underpinned by an ideology (racism) that favours White and lighter-skinned people.
- Racism functions at individual and institutional levels and racial categories serve the function of justifying social inequalities.
- Social geographers have contributed to our understanding of 'race' and racism by examining how 'race' is made real in everyday life and by researching the lived experience of 'race' and racism.

FURTHER READING

Dwyer, C., & Bressey, C. (2008) *New Geographies of Race and Racism*. London: Routledge.

Mahtani, M. (2006) Challenging the ivory tower: Proposing anti-racist geographies within the academy. *Gender, Place & Culture*, 13(1): 21–25.

Meer, N., Nayak, A., & Pande, R. (2015) Special issue: The matter of race. *Sociological Research Online*, 20(3): 1–5.

Peake, L., & Kobayashi, A. (2002) Policies and practices for an antiracist geography at the millennium. *Professional Geographer*, 54(1): 50–61.

Religion

Kawtar Najib and Robin Finlay

While race, ethnicity, gender and sexuality have been regular foci of social geography, religion has traditionally received less attention. However, since the early 1990s the topic of religion has started to receive greater attention, and it is now considered a 'burgeoning sub-field' (Stump, 2008; Wilford, 2010) of social geography. This interest in religion is illustrated by numerous geopolitical issues and events (such as 9/11, the Paris attacks, antiabortion violence, the burka ban in France, anti-immigrant protests against the 'Islamisation' of Europe, the Trump Muslim bans, etc.) in which religion has been cast as a central issue. Moreover, a reemergence of religions in the public sphere is noted, with religious institutions and faith groups having a greater presence in everyday spaces and providing certain social and community provisions that are no longer provided by the state (Beaumont & Baker, 2011).

Broadly speaking, the study of religion in social geography focuses on the ways matters of religion, faith, belief and spirituality interconnect with societies and shape everyday landscapes and spaces (Kong, 1990, 2001, 2010). An important aspect of social geographies of religion is how it has taken influence from and developed core themes about race, racism and ethnicity (see Chapter 13 on race). Given the rise in religious hate crimes such as Islamophobia and anti-Semitism,

TEXT BOX 14.1 | Religion, Spirituality, Faith, Belief, Secularism and Postsecuralism

Religion is the belief in and worship of a superhuman controlling power, especially a personal God or gods. It is also considered a particular set of faiths and worship practices. Therefore, in simple terms, religion tends to involve communities that share a belief in a God, and it tends to involve shared practices and faiths in the worship of such a God.

Spirituality is essentially about the human spirit and the state of being spiritual. Just like religion, spirituality also questions the relationship between the known and the unknown, the real and the unreal, but it is not confined to traditional religious rituals and sacred spaces (Bartolini et al., 2017).

Faith refers to a belief in the doctrines of a religion or spirituality.

Belief refers, in religious terms, to the acceptance that a God and the spiritual aspects of a religion exist.

Secularism refers to the disappearance, or reduction, of religious beliefs and practices in society. In political terms, it denotes the separation of the state and government institutions from religious institutions and religious beliefs (Wilford, 2010).

Postsecularism is where religion is considered to be playing a renewed role in the public sphere. It describes a shift from a less religious secular period to a period where religion has a renewed voice and role in society (Beaumont & Baker, 2011).

discrimination based around religious identities has significantly increased, and, for some scholars, religion has replaced race and ethnicity as the most significant interest in minority populations (Peach, 2006b; Gale, 2013). Therefore, in recent decades we have seen a significant growth in geographical research that focuses on discrimination, segregation and identity formation in relation to religious identities. Given the politicisation of the Islamic religion, much of this research has tended to focus on Muslim identities. However, as religion impacts on many aspects of contemporary society and everyday spaces, a wide range of issues and themes has come to be explored in social geographies of religion, such as alternative spiritualties, gendering of religion, the religious-built environment, migration and religious belonging. Although we cannot cover all topics under study in social geographies of religion, we start by providing definitions of key ideas before discussing the core themes of research.

RELIGIOUS SPATIAL DISTRIBUTION AND SEGREGATION

At the global scale, large regional areas are often associated with dominant religions, such as in Europe Christianity, in the Middle East Islam and in parts of East Asia Buddhism. However, throughout history religions have been on the move and have migrated (see Chapter 26 on migration and diaspora), creating multifaith spaces in many nations around the world. At the national and urban scales, large cities often include spaces where religious groups have been primarily studied (such as New York and London), and, within these cities, there are often ethnically and religiously segregated neighbourhoods that raise questions about the spatial concentration of specific groups. Indeed, certain neighbourhoods can be associated with believers of a particular religion, such as the association of Borough Park in Brooklyn in New York City and Pletzl in Paris with the Jewish religion. As such, there are several works focusing on mapping Jewish populations and their patterns of segregation (Valins, 2003; Watson, 2005). These Jewish neighbourhoods are sometimes represented as ghettos, based on ethnic and religious gatherings. Therefore, religion can be an important factor that determines boundaries and segregation in urban places.

Different religious groups are sometimes considered to live parallel and separate lives, leading to social tensions between such groups. These kinds of narratives and discourses have mainly been assigned to Muslim populations – notably, with the Cantle Report (2001) in the United Kingdom on the 2001 riots in Bradford, Oldham and Burnley, which refers to Muslims and Whites as two distinct groups, leading separate lives. However, to be able to make such conclusions, it also has been important to draw on large datasets, such as the 2001 and 2011 England and Wales Censuses, which include new data on religion. Peach (2006a, 2006b) used this new material and mapped the spatial distribution of various religious groups, superimposing other relevant criteria (see Figure 14.1).

The study of ethnic and religious residential segregation has a long history in social geography, but the monitoring and the mapping of segregation levels came later in the early 2000s and primarily focused on Muslim residential settlement. The cartographic analyses stemming from these maps allow us to better understand the spatial logics of specific religious patterns and neighbourhoods, and Peach (2006b) was able to state that Muslims in London, as a whole, are much less segregated than Sikhs, Jews or Hindus. Similarly, Phillips (2006) also analysed the residential choices of Muslims in Bradford in the United Kingdom and challenged discourses of Muslim self-segregation. Building upon these works, Gale (2007) provided a geographical analysis of the spatiality of Islam by mapping out its two key trends (the sacred geography and topography in Islam and the politics of Muslim space).

RELIGIOUS DISCRIMINATION

The dominant religious groups in Western countries may be more powerful in terms of political leadership, but they remain less studied in geography. There is nevertheless some research on the geographies of Christianity and Christian identities, but they are less explored since the tendency is rather to focus on the margins than on the dominant centre. Indeed, the minority status of religious

FIGURE 14.1

Distribution of Muslims in England and Wales in 2001. (Source: Peach, 2006a)

groups can create a context of marginalisation and exclusion, leading to experiences of discrimination and violence. Some tensions and conflicts can take an international dimension, and a territorial and political dispute can therefore emerge. This is the case of sectarian disputes between Catholics and Protestants in Northern Ireland or between Shiites and Sunnis in Iraq, for example.

Religious discrimination in the United Kingdom is mainly explored as a new form of racism, especially against Muslims or those who are mistaken as such. Islamophobia appears as a racialisation process of people, essentialising a group of highly diverse individuals under one single religious attribute (Runnymede Trust, 1997; Allen, 2010; Sayyid & Vakil, 2010). Studies on Islamophobia have been theorised primarily in sociology and the political sciences, but, with the rise in anti-Muslim attacks and sentiment, the concept of Islamophobia is becoming a growing area of research in geography. A special issue on 'Geographies of Islamophobia' recently focused on the spatial dimension of Islamophobia while discussing its definition. In brief, Islamophobia is the hatred of, or prejudice against, the Islamic religion or Muslims in general (for a broader discussion, see Najib & Teeple Hopkins, 2020).

The reasons for the dominant focus on Muslim populations in the United Kingdom and Western Europe are multiple. First, there has been a significant rise in Islamophobic hate crimes, which is often linked to global political events such as terrorism. Just in the United Kingdom, there has been a 30 per cent increase in religious hate crimes between 2016 and 2017, and abusive behaviour represents the most common incident, according to the last two reports of Tell MAMA (2017, 2018) (see Table 14.1). Second, there has been significant growth in Muslim populations in Europe, with Muslim minorities often representing the largest minority religious group (Peach, 2006a). Third, many Muslims come from marginalised backgrounds, are often socioeconomically disadvantaged and suffer high levels of male unemployment and low female participation in the labour market (Peach, 2006b). Therefore, these factors have made Muslims highly susceptible to religious discrimination, and, as a result, Islamophobia is emerging as an important topic of research within social geographies of religion.

TABLE 14.1	Rise in Anti-Muslim (Offline) Incidents Recorded by Tell MAMA from 2016 to 2017 (Najib and Hopkins, 2020)	
	2016	**2017**
Abusive behaviour	349	441
Physical attack	120	149
Vandalism	43	81
Discrimination	46	72
Threatening behaviour	49	57
Anti-Muslim literature	32	28
Hate speech	3	11
Total	642	839

TEXT BOX 14.2 | Real-World Research: Geographies of Islamophobia in London and Paris

An important contribution of research in geography is the mapping of Islamophobia, which can provide innovative spatial readings and demonstrate the types of spaces where anti-Muslim acts occur. The SAMA (Spaces of Anti-Muslim Acts) project conducted at Newcastle University presents a comparative case study of spatialised Islamophobia in London and Paris, two European capitals where high rates of Islamophobic acts have been recorded, especially since the recent terrorist attacks (*Charlie Hebdo* attack, the London Bridge attack, etc.). The project uses both quantitative and qualitative methods (such as the exploration of the statistical databases from associations fighting against Islamophobia and from the Metropolitan Police, and sixty individual interviews with victims of Islamophobia).

The maps from the project show that in Paris anti-Muslim acts take place more in the centre, and they decrease progressively as we move towards the suburbs. In London, the phenomenon seems to be more spatially spread than in Paris, and the map highlights the importance of some horizontal and vertical lines corresponding to the places where anti-Muslim acts occur. Indeed, in the United Kingdom anti-Muslim acts often occur in everyday spaces (public areas and transport hubs), while in France the majority occur in public institutions, which can draw a more central geography. Finally, Islamophobia shows a clear impact on everyday spaces and people's everyday lives, especially for veiled Muslim women, who are forced to reinvent new mobility in order to avert potential situations of discrimination (Najib & Hopkins, 2019).

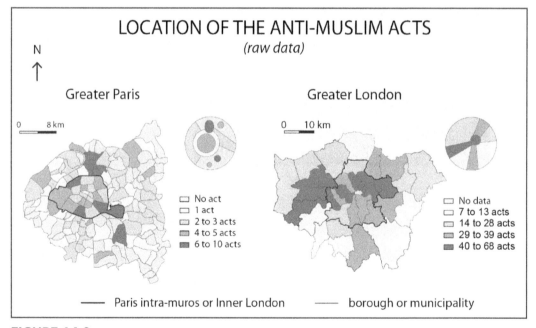

FIGURE 14.2

Location of anti-Muslim acts. (Source: CCIF and Metropolitan Police, 2015)

IDENTITY, BELONGING AND CITIZENSHIP

An important area of research in social geography is religious identities and how they are performed and represented in various locations and contexts. Such research has been attentive to the intersections of religious identities and the role of religion in the formation of communities and senses of belonging and citizenship (Kong, 2001). Research on the geographies of religion mostly focuses on identities of ethnic and religious minority communities, most notably Muslim identities, which present a great variety of cultural diversity. Therefore, the relationships among 'religion', 'identity', 'belonging', 'citizenship', 'multiculturalism' and 'integration' are often explored in research about Muslim populations (Nagel & Staeheli, 2008; Dunn, 2005). In addition, Peach (2006a) and Modood and colleagues (1997) have shown that, for Muslims, religion is considered more important to how they live their lives than for other religious groups in Britain. Religious belief and observance among British Muslims represent a big part of their identity, and they can play an important role in the formation of Muslim diaspora communities (see Chapter 26 on migration and diaspora). Thus, the significance of studies on Muslim identities is understandable in geography, notably with the contributions of Hopkins (2017), who examines Muslim identities in the context of Scotland, and Hopkins and Gale (2009), who focus on how identities of British Muslims intersect with race and place. That said, there is also important research on other religious identities, such as those looking at young Christians (Sharma & Guest, 2013) or Sikh men (Hopkins, 2014).

Drawing on debates in feminist geographies (see Chapter 16 on gender), there is a significant body of scholarship that examines the intersections of religious identities with gender (Morin & Guelke, 2007; Gökarıksel, 2012). In particular, Falah and Nagel (2005) have conducted important work on the contested geographies of Muslim women with reference to debates about mobility, discourse and representation. The integration of Muslim women is associated with their religious practice, particularly their dress, which can be seen as a measure of national belonging (Bowen, 2007; Listerborn, 2015). There has also been a focus on Muslim men, with research examining the intersections of Islam and masculinities (Hopkins, 2006a; Dwyer, Shah & Sanghera, 2008). Finally, a person's religious identity can impact how they negotiate citizenship and participate in society, so another important issue is the relationship between citizenship, everyday participations and religion. Much of the existing research has focused on immigration and diaspora communities and how religious minorities negotiate everyday participations and citizenship (e.g., Finlay & Hopkins, 2020; Nagel & Staeheli, 2006, 2008).

URBAN ENVIRONMENT, RELIGIOUS LANDSCAPES AND RELIGIOUS BUILDINGS

Social geographers have also explored the role of religion in shaping the built and physical environment, notably in urban contexts. Much of this work has explored the contested ways religious bodies negotiate cities, such as Gökarıksel (2012) and Listerborn (2015), who discuss issues of veiling in Istanbul (in Turkey) and Malmö (in Sweden), respectively. In addition, landscapes are impacted by religious architecture (places of worship, cultural buildings, pilgrimage roads, etc.). Indeed, geographers of religion have drawn significant attention to issues associated with the religious landscape in various urban contexts. There are important works on Muslim faith organisations and buildings, such as the work of Naylor and Ryan (2002) on London's first mosque or the influential work of Dunn (2005) on the problematic and racist ways mosque development is resisted by the national government and local communities in Australia. Here this focus allows the development of discussions about urban design and planning, but it is also connected to other debates on multiculturalism and citizenship.

That said, there are also works focusing on other religious buildings. Ehrkamp and Nagel (2012) have explored how Hindu places of worship act as an important location for citizenship in the US South. Ley (2008) has shown how immigrant churches help minority religious groups to settle into their new lives, and Sharma (2012) has explained how the space of the church offers a sense of family and community to women churchgoers.

EMERGING ISSUES

Within the field, there are several areas of emerging interest. First, religion sacralises places through rituals, performances, practices and representations. Sacred places are often sites of pilgrimage (i.e., ritual places to visit) that people seek to travel to and visit. Important sites of pilgrimage include Mecca (in Saudi Arabia) concerning Islam, Lourdes (in France) concerning Christianity, the Wailing Wall (in Jerusalem) concerning Judaism and the river Ganges (in India) concerning Hinduism. Given its geographical nature, research in geography has focused on scared places and pilgrimage (Scriven, 2014).

Second, religion marks landscapes with burial places. Indeed, religion has a strong link with the evocation of death and grief, and geographers have started to explore these topics. For example, Kong (1999) has developed the notion of 'deathscapes', focusing on cemeteries, memorials and mausoleums, while Maddrell and Sidaway (2010) provide a significant set of insights into the space of death and bereavement. Maddrell (2009) has shown how grief practices and expressions of belief are marked out in the landscape of the Witness Cairn in Scotland.

Third, an emerging set of debates in geographies of religion focus on forms of postsecuralism, particularly in urban environments. Much of this research either maps out the meaning of the term 'postsecuralism' (Beckford, 2012) or explores emerging postsecular spaces in cities (Beaumont & Baker, 2011). The latter offers an examination of the growing role of faith- and religious-based organisations in welfare and charity provisions in the city. For example, Cloke, May and Johnsen (2010) illustrate the role of faith-based organisations in providing provisions, such as soup kitchens, for homeless people living in urban areas in the United Kingdom.

Fourth, another growing body of scholarship looks at the rise of alternative spiritualties, which is an umbrella term for a range of spiritual practices and beliefs that are not necessarily part of mainstream and traditional religions. For example, Holloway (2003) looks at how new age spiritual seekers create spiritualised spaces through everyday objects and practices such as meditation, bodily movements, candles and incense.

SUMMARY

- Religion has become a significant area of analysis in social geography.
- Social geographers have examined issues as diverse as religious segregation, religious discrimination, religious identity formations and religious landscapes. Muslim identities have been a dominant focus in research.
- Geographies of religion interact and overlap with various other concerns studied in geography, especially those associated with race and ethnicity.
- The centrality of religion in numerous sociopolitical issues and events around the world means that it is of increasing relevance and should continue to grow as an area of research.
- With the rise in religious hate crimes and religious discrimination, social geography has a particularly important role to play in understanding the socio-spatial manifestations of such discriminations.

FURTHER READING

Gale, R. (2007) The place of Islam in the geography of religion: Trends and Intersections. *Geography Compass*, 1(5): 1015–36.

Hopkins, P., & Gale, R. (eds.) (2009) *Muslims in Britain: Race, Place and Identities.* Edinburgh: Edinburgh University Press.

Kong, L. (2010) Global shifts, theoretical shifts: Changing geographies of religion. *Progress in Human Geography*, 34(6): 755–76.

Najib, K., & Teeple Hopkins, C. (2020) Introduction. Special issue: Geographies of Islamophobia. *Social & Cultural Geography*, 21(4): 449–57.

Stump, R. (2008) *The Geography of Religion: Faith, place and space.* Lanham, MD: Rowman & Littlefield.

Tell MAMA. (2017) *A Constructed Threat: Identity, Prejudice and the Impact of Anti-Muslim Hatred.* Tell MAMA Annual Report 2016. London: Tell MAMA.

Tell MAMA. (2018) *Beyond the Incident: Outcomes for Victims of Anti-Muslim Prejudice.* Tell MAMA Annual Report 2017. London: Tell MAMA.

Class

Anoop Nayak

Broadly speaking, class is a division in society primarily based on one's economic and social status. It can refer to a person's occupation and cultural dispositions, but it can also be thought of as a set of social relations. What should also be remembered is that patterns of class are geographically variable and may operate differently across the globe. Given this, interpretations of class remain diverse and deeply contested. For some, class remains a key locus of how social inequality and power are expressed. Harvey (1989) has rigorously used key Marxist conceptualisations of class relations to challenge postmodern perspectives. In contrast, in his later work on the reflexive project of self as a condition of late modernity, the sociologist Giddens has been accused of rendering class as an antiquated and increasingly obsolete category (see Atkinson, 2007, for discussion). In between these poles, numerous other positions emerge in geography – for example, Massey (1991b) has adopted a critical Marxist-feminist approach to consider class alongside gender and ethnicity, while McDowell's (2003) research on unemployed young men combines economic approaches to class with gender theory and work on masculinities.

It is worth noting, too, that race was the beating heart of capitalism and the class system, and several merchant businessmen owed much of their wealth to imperial trading and the profits deriving from the slave trade (see Chapter 13 on race). While the class system is power laden and exploitative, it is formed through global interconnections between nation-states. This is evident in recent geographical accounts of the 'ex-patriate bubble', where class, cosmopolitanism and White privilege intersect (Cranston & Lloyd, 2018). It is also found in global cities such as London, where May and colleagues (2007) found a new 'migrant division of labour' shaped by the nation-state is polarising communities around lines of ethnicity and class.

In light of the 'cultural turn', geographers have been interested in the *cultural* inflections of Marxist theory. For example, one of the primary ways middle-class people assert their status is through 'taste', or what the sociologist Bourdieu (1984) depicts as practices of distinction. This encompasses the types of food we eat, the programmes we watch, how we decorate our homes, the books we read, the music we listen to, clothes we wear and our sporting and leisure interests. Like contemporary urban hipsters, who may enjoy freshly ground coffee, craft ales and underground music, taste and consumption become a central means through which class values are made known. As Bourdieu succinctly notes, 'Taste classifies, and it classifies the classifier' (1984: 6). While the distinction between what is 'good' taste and what is 'vulgar' is often arbitrary, it works to consolidate what Bourdieu regards as a class habitus. He describes the habitus as a system of tacit dispositions that shape our viewpoints, perception, tastes and actions. In doing so, subjects distinguish themselves by the distinctions that they make, marking out who they are and who they are not. Over time, these practices become habitual, subconscious reactions that can be embodied in the way we walk, talk or dress, as we will go on to see.

The chapter begins by briefly documenting some of the ways that ideas of class have changed from the nineteenth century to the present. I then investigate how the geography of social class can be traced in homes and neighbourhoods, education and embodied forms of consumption. To develop deeper critical thinking around class, I also turn to the tricky issue of studying class to encourage you to consider the ethical, analytical and methodological issues of researching class in a sensitive and meaningful way (see Text Box 15.1). While there are numerous ways class is understood and researched, it remains a critical concept in geography as it is a prism through which much social and spatial inequality is refracted.

CHANGING CONFIGURATIONS OF CLASS

In the wake of the Industrial Revolution, there appeared to be a number of discernible class stratifications. This included, for example, the aristocracy or upper-class elites, who inherited wealth and owned large amounts of land; a rising middle class or bourgeoisie, which included business entrepreneurs and various professionals; and a working class or proletariat, who had nothing but their labour to sell. This varied third group was employed as scullery maids, servants, factory workers, nannies, stable hands and so forth.

Alongside these early class demarcations of a working, middle and upper class was also to be found a further stratum of society, the urban poor, often known as the 'casual residuum' or 'underclass'. This included vagrants, beggars, paupers, orphans, street performers, small vendors, washerwomen and 'mud-larks' – scavengers who perused the local riverways, knee deep, for discarded goods that they could reclaim and sell (Mayhew, 1985). This early anatomy of class is insightful in showcasing the hierarchical aspects of the class system, where a number of Victorian bourgeoisie regarded the lower orders as subspecies or a race apart (Steadman Jones, 1992).

As social reform and changes in work-based practices began to develop in the late nineteenth century, a more basic distinction between 'blue-collar' workers (manual labourers and tradespeople) and 'white-collar' workers (managers, professionals and office staff) emerged. However, these typologies themselves proved increasingly ambiguous in the postwar era, as coal mines, shipyards, engineering plants and large-scale factory industries were dismantled in a move towards a postindustrial service-sector economy and later technological innovations. For Savage and colleagues (2013), class not only concerns occupation and economic wealth but also is about cultural knowledge, taste and social networks. Analysing the BBC's 2011 Great British Class Survey, it contends that there are now seven class demarcations within the United Kingdom, with some of the main categories making up a wealthy 'elite', an established middle class, new affluent workers, an ageing traditional working class and a fragile 'precariat'. Though this work has proved controversial, having been subject to much sociological critique (see Bradley, 2014; Dorling, 2013; C. Mills, 2014), it does impart insight into the continuing salience of class in British society. For example, we might consider how at one end of the spectrum in society there is the 'super rich', who are rapidly shaping world cities and displacing preexisting elites in the search for what Webber and Burrows (2013) term 'Alpha territory' (see Chapter 22 on wealth and poverty). At the other end there is a growing number of precariat who are employed on zero-hours contracts and involved in protracted periods of unpaid and low-paid work. Using multiple statistical indices, Dorling (2014a) argues that the 'super rich', whom he categorises as the top 1 per cent of earners in society, are damaging life for the other 99 per cent, as inequality has grown from a gap to a chasm. It is these class inequalities, taking place on a global scale, that create and exacerbate issues related to climate change, housing, education, health and food poverty – all of which are key areas of research in social geography. Text Box 15.1 demonstrates some of the new approaches to class when it comes to researching working-class subjects and developing new methodological and conceptual tools for exploring contemporary class relations.

TEXT BOX 15.1 | Real-World Research: Researching Class

There are many ways of researching class, including the use of numerical data, surveys, interviews and ethnographies. However, class can be a sensitive area to study, so ethical care and methodological rigor are required to research it in a meaningful way. What the examples in this section will show is the importance of designing research methodologies and practices that do not objectify working-class people but provide a means for their experiences to be heard and engaged with.

An innovative methodological approach to class is deployed by Arthurson, Darcy and Rogers (2014), who explore how social housing tenants in western Sydney respond to representations of class. To elicit responses to class, the authors screened sections from a satirical parody, *Housos*, set in the fictional housing estate of Sunnydale. The show focuses upon the everyday lives of Australian 'housos' – social housing tenants – whom the authors depict as a form of 'underclass'. This televisual representation is underpinned by their repetitive associations with crime, drugs and unemployment welfare benefits. The show draws upon class caricatures embodied by stereotypically named characters such as Dazza, Shazza and Franky. Arthurson, Darcy and Rogers use the show to prompt responses from actual social housing residents as well as local community workers.

The aim of the project is to develop opportunities for social housing residents to express their own knowledge of the connections between place and disadvantage. To achieve this, the authors instigated collaborative tenant–academic research teams, with tenants recruiting people in their neighbourhoods to take part as well as shaping many of the research questions for discussant focus groups. Participants were sent a weekly episode of *Housos* with a set of research questions they could respond to by writing or recording an audio or video diary. In this study, researching class involves a participatory approach, working with tenants who shape the focus of the study, help recruit participants and make sure their voices,

and those of other tenants, are clearly heard. Reflecting on the methodology, Arthurson, Darcy and Rogers note how, 'The deliberately highly exaggerated characters and scenarios in Housos provided an excellent vehicle for resident researchers on the team to explore their own reactions to being represented in this way' (2014: 1347). The researchers utilise participatory visual elicitation techniques to develop more enriched, multilayered understandings of social class relations.

Nevertheless, class remains a slippery topic to study and ethically complex terrain to tread when it comes to analysing people's responses. This is made evident in Skeggs' (1997) research, which involved interviewing a number of White working-class women in northern England. When asked directly about what class they were, Skeggs found the majority of her respondents claimed to be middle class. As Skeggs goes on to show, this was in part because most of the women did not regard themselves as poor but 'somewhere in the middle', in large part because they were involved in acts of appearing 'respectable', which itself is driven by class desire. Skeggs deliberately reads the experiences of her participants 'against the grain', as on all visible social indicators they would present as working class. This can create ethical difficulties for the researcher, but Skeggs skilfully handles this by making transparent how and why she interprets their lives through the lens of working-class experience. She explains:

Questions of epistemic responsibility and the ethics of this interpretative process were most obvious in relation to social class. The women did not want their actions interpreted as class responses for this reproduced the position they wanted to disassociate from. However, their rejection of class did not lead me to abandon it. In fact, it did the opposite. It heightened my sensitivity to its ubiquity and made me construct theories to explain the responses. (1997: 30)

Skeggs writes of the ethical responsibility she has to make class visible, shedding light on the hidden insecurities, ambivalence and resentment that form a psychic part of the 'emotional politics of class' (1997: 162) (see Chapter 12 on emotion). Skeggs demonstrates how forms of working-class identity are stigmatised, and due to this many respondents may disassociate from this identity. As she explains, 'Even though they dissimulate from class, their dissimulations are produced through it' (1997: 94). Writing class back into the accounts of these women's lives is then part of a critical project that recognises class is structural, informs the interview process and should be formative of the analysis.

THE SPATIALITY OF CLASS

'The class struggle is inscribed in space'.

—Lefebvre, 1992/1974: 55

Homes and Neighbourhoods

A good example of how class struggle is inscribed in space can be seen in the study of New York gentrification undertaken by Zukin in her book *Loft Living* (1989). Zukin explores how a number of New York workers in the creative arts were drawn to renting studio lofts in the SoHo district. The lofts were relatively cheap, had good floor space and got plenty of light. Many of the apartments had bare polished floors, exposed brickwork and cast-iron facades, a functional design suitable for craft designers, workers and artists. This creative class was willing to endure dirt, noise and the inconvenience of being some distance from services. Zukin, herself a loft inhabitant of Greenwich Village, observed the dramatic transformations that occurred when capital interacts with space. A few upper-middle-class people who desired a bohemian lifestyle, rubbing shoulders with sculptors, dressmakers, craftworkers and other creatives, moved into the district. The practical, minimalist design soon became part of a new urban aesthetic, transformed into what Zukin calls 'bourgeois chic' (1989: 2).

The consequence of this growing population movement was that many of those in the arts and creative sector were forced to relinquish these work spaces as their rent increased. For Zukin, 'The residential conversion of manufacturing lofts confirms and symbolises the death of an urban manufacturing centre' (1989: x). In this example, capital accumulation can create a terrain of conflict between different social actors, including independent artists and designers, middle-class tenants, small manufacturers, real estate developers, local politicians and financers. The value of Zukin's study is seen where similar forms of gentrification and successive rounds of regeneration are now commonplace in most Western industrial cities. In this way, class struggle is contingently, but emphatically, inscribed in space, impacting as it does upon people's mobility.

A vivid example of the way urban landscapes are class-divided terrain can be traced in Edensor and Millington's (2009) study of

Christmas decorations in the UK cities of Manchester and Sheffield. Here, they identify a particular 'geography of illumination'. This is illustrated by 'modest, chic white and blue lighting illuminating middle class housing areas', while 'more colourful extravaganzas pervade working-class residential districts' (2009: 104). The markers of taste are seen in the choice of decoration, how particular aesthetic items are produced and consumed and the ways these material objects disclose the contested landscapes of class in British society (see Figures 15.1 and 15.2).

These creations of an aesthetic of loft living or the penchant for particular Christmas illuminations connect to Bourdieu's idea of how taste can be an expression of class. For example, Edensor and Millington (2009) found that a number of people on internet forums expressed class disgust at what they perceived as gaudy, garish, environmentally polluting and excessive lighting and decoration. These remarks reveal the middle-class values and broader habitus of the complainants. However, when interviewing working-class residents, the authors found that many displayers saw the illuminations as a convivial statement of neighbourliness, warmth and generosity. In exploring the disconnection between the comments on internet forums and the perspectives of the exhibitors, Edensor and Millington ultimately reveal the spatially 'contested landscapes of Christmas' (2009: 103).

FIGURE 15.1
Illuminating class: Soft white lighting decorations in a middle-class neighbourhood in Royal Leamington Spa, UK. (Credit: Anoop Nayak)

FIGURE 15.2

Bright, colourful, flickering Christmas decorations in a working-class suburb of Birmingham, UK. (Credit: Anoop Nayak)

Education

One of the primary ways class privilege is reproduced in the United Kingdom is in the education market (see Chapter 24 on education). Ball (2003) argues that state education was historically constructed around the needs and interests of the middle classes. In interviews with middle-class parents and pupils, he demonstrates how the middle classes consolidate and enhance their social advantages through education. This is done through developing social capital, drawing up markers of social closure and progressing particular class values. For many middle-class families, 'school choice' is a critical decision, one that is enabled by educated parents making informed choices about schooling. As Ball's work in the UK state sector has shown, middle-class parents will look at performance indicators, move house to be in close proximity to high-performing state schools and play an important role in their children's wider development. They are more likely to encourage and enforce rules around homework and personal study, employ tutors, monitor academic progress and sit on the board of school governors. Success can also be achieved when middle-class parents avoid the state sector altogether and pay to send their children to private and boarding schools.

Although school choice is pivotal to class reproduction, Reay, Crozier and James (2011) explore a rather unusual group – White middle-class parents who send their children to non-fee-paying urban schools. For some of the parents, this was a political act to support free schooling, for others it was about putting into the local community rather than withdrawing their children from it and for others still it was a means of adding a type of 'worldly' capital to the experiences of their children, who would mix with ethnic minority and White working-class young people. As Reay, Crozier and James argue, these practices are a way of doing Whiteness and performing as middle class. For example, in the following excerpt an interviewee describes her son's 'advantageous' friendship circle: 'incredibly ethnic range of friends and it's a marvellous advantage, I mean it's not something that most people of my generation would have I think. At his 15th birthday party last year 19 friends came and they were from nine different ethnic origins from all around the world and I found it rather moving actually' (Reay, Crozier & James, 2011: 85). Some middle-class parents then saw value in a cosmopolitan experience, regarding it as a means through which their children could become global citizens and rub along with racialised and classed Others through institutional encounters. While not all children were content with their schooling experience, Reay, Crozier and James (2011) reveal the complex ways school choice is used as a means for consolidating social structures. They reveal how the middle classes are adept at erecting symbolic and geographical boundaries that expose how schooling is a site for class formation and contestation.

The Body and Consumption

So far, we have looked at how class is enacted across time and space, considering changing typologies of class over time along with illustrations of the spatial manifestation of class in homes, schools, neighbourhoods and cities. To develop a fuller account of class, it is important to consider how class is lived on the body and intersects with other identities, such as ethnicity, gender, sexuality or disability. The body has become an important scale in contemporary geographical analysis when it comes to interpretations of gender and masculinities, disability, pregnacy, racialisation and sexed bodies (Rose, 1993; McDowell, 1997; Hansen & Philo, 2007; Longhurst, 2001; Tolia-Kelly, 2011; Cream, 1995).

The intersections between the body, class and age (see Chapter 20 on intersectionality) can be seen in research conducted by Nayak and Kehily (2014) exploring two marginalised youth groups – unemployed young men, who in policy terms are defined as NEETs (not in education, employment or training) and were stigmatised as 'chavs' or 'charvers', and young women who were teenage mothers or pregnant and were rebuked as 'pramface'. These two groups embodied class stigma in particular ways that marked them out as victims for disparagement. The authors developed a class analysis of youth to consider what lies beneath these derogatory labels:

> chavs and pramface girls are relational constructs emerging within the context of social change and the growing cleavage between rich and poor in Western late modernity. The figure of the chav and the teen mother exists in the representational sphere

as 'abject others', a repository of fear and anxieties concerning the corrosion of white respectability and social class mobility. . . . As such they serve to maintain the boundaries of the 'normative', holding in place otherwise fragile configurations of class, ethnicity and gender. (Nayak and Kehily, 2014: 1335)

Chavs were depicted by young people as having 'rough accents', a limping, 'knuckle-dragging' walk, and were thought to be further identifiable through their dress. Many 'chavs' wore branded sports clothes, such as Reebok trainers, Kappa tracksuits or Nike running bottoms, and felt aggrieved when they were the recipients of humour and abuse. Their attempts to appear respectable by wearing expensive branded clothes only served to evince the negative class credentials that they sought to escape. Here we can see how a particular class habitus is embodied through speech, deportment, dress and demeanour. Simultaneously, these markers of class were deeply racialised. Several 'chavs' sported brassy sovereign rings, large hooped earrings and other accoutrements stylistically derived from Gypsy, Romany and traveller communities. Like traveller communities in the United States, the term 'trailer park trash' or 'white trash' signifies class status through nonhomeownership, a theme that was attributed to 'chavs', who were designated as living in social housing and on welfare benefits. Furthermore, the etymology of 'chavvy'/'chavi' in part derives from a Romany word for a small child, a lineage that further displaced them from the borders of White respectability. This, compounded by the fact that a number were perceived to be associated with crime, have large families and are feckless, meant that they were frequently racialised as 'filth', 'scum' and 'dirty whites', the 'not-quite-white' of Britain's dark imaginary.

Similarly, where new motherhood is celebrated in women's magazines as the apex of feminine achievement and romantic coupledom, this was not the case for teenage mothers. They were found to be absent from mother and baby magazines, with early pregnancy deemed a thoroughly working-class affair. Instead, for teenage mothers-to-be, 'the pregnant tummy was a potential source of *shame*, the locus of attention and judgement' (Nayak and Kehily, 2014: 1339–40). Respondents spoke about being morally judged by people whom they didn't know in parenting classes or on public transport, who would openly stare or make comments about their pregnant bodies. In an effort to displace class-based stigma, many young mothers were invested in acquiring expensive commodities for their impending offspring: 'Mumtaz: I'm gonna buy the nicest pram, my pram has to be wicked. I don't wanna be walking down the street with a bad pram. Don't want people to think, you know, I can't provide for my baby. Oh my God, of course I can provide for my baby'. The comments of Mumtaz echoed those of many working-class young mothers, who refused hand-me-downs. By contrast, middle-class mothers sourced a number of baby items from eBay, friends and family or vintage shops, entirely unburdened by the potential of being seen as poor or stigmatised as 'bad mothers'.

SUMMARY

- Class is a dividing line marked by power and inequality. It is linked to monetary power, status, consumer taste and culture. Above all, class is a structural force that is lived out over time and space.
- The social geography of education, housing, work and consumption is inscribed not only through patterns of income but also through class.
- Academics suggest that societies that have the widest inequality are likely to be among the most damaging to live in.

FURTHER READING

Arthurson, K., Darcy, M., & Rogers, D. (2014) Televised territorial stigma: How social housing tenants experience the fictional media representation of estates in Australia. *Environment and Planning A: Economy and Space*, 46: 1334–50.

Dorling, D. (2014) *Inequality and the 1%*. London: Verso.

Edensor, T., & Millington, S. (2009) Illuminations, class identities and the contested landscapes of Christmas. *Sociology*, 43(1): 103–21.

Nayak, A. (2006) Displaced masculinities: Chavs, youth and class in the post-industrial city. *Sociology*, 40(5): 813–31.

Gender

Michael J. Richardson, Raksha Pande and Ged Ridley

There has never been a more important time to study gender. In 2018, Hungarian Prime Minister Viktor Orban banned all gender studies programmes at universities. In the same year, the election of Brazil's President Jair Bolsonaro was labelled a serious threat to women's rights. Meanwhile, Donald Trump's successful 2016 US presidential election campaign – and, indeed, his term in office ever since – was marred by sexism and misogyny. More broadly, this rise in right-wing political leadership has brought gender back onto the public agenda, threatening to reinforce long traditions of gender inequality, sex-based violence and discrimination. In this chapter, we explore the spatial implications of gender-based divisions and of the inequalities they produce. We illustrate why studying social geographies is so important to understanding the gendered world we live in.

Gender and geography have a fractious history (e.g., Maddrell, 2011). In 1830, the United Kingdom's Royal Geographical Society was formed on the basis of discovery and exploration of other countries, but it was not until 1913 that it admitted its first woman member, Isabella Bird. Later work of the Women and Geography Study Group (1997/2014; WGSG) from the 1980s exposed how pervasive sexism was in the discipline, including how women were systematically excluded from geographical research and marginalised within geography departments and related communities (e.g., McDowell & Peake, 1990; Rose, 1993). The study of gender and feminist geographies is now far more common in social geographies than it was in the 1980s and 1990s, and there are more women geographers working in geography and leading social geographies. However, significant gender disparities remain within the discipline (Maddrell et al., 2016).

Doreen Massey's pioneering contributions (see also Chapter 1 and Text Box 1.1), including her book, *Space, Place and Gender* (1994), bolstered the success of social geographies as a subdiscipline. The WGSG has since been renamed the Gender and Feminist Geography Study Group to better reflect a more inclusive approach (see the section on social geographies of masculinities towards the end of this chapter). It is clear that geography has been irrevocably changed by the inclusion of women and the range of feminist perspectives that have since developed. As Chapter 1 made clear, this current book and this chapter owe a great deal to feminist contributions to the discipline.

GENDER INEQUALITY

Gender-based divisions are enforced through a set of established power relations. This can be expressed in the form of blatant discrimination as well as unconscious bias. We refer to this set of relations as patriarchy (a system of male dominance). According to Sylvia Walby (1990), patriarchy is supported by and manifest in six structures – paid employment, household production, culture, sexuality, violence and the state. Its influence over our institutions shapes, for example, how we experience school, the media and the workplace.

It is a common mistake to think that the concept of patriarchy involves the belief that all men are involved in oppressing all women. As a group, men (and women) are differently privileged in their access to power (see below). Gender inequality affects both men and women, as not everyone conforms to roles ascribed by gender and many resist them. Recent campaigns for gender equality (such as http://everydaysexism.com and #MeToo) are based upon notions of human decency, fairness and justice for all. It is important to note, therefore, that feminism is not about 'man hating' but instead about redressing the balance of structural inequalities. It is also important to note that women are still adversely affected by these societal pressures and suffer more under a patriarchal system. This is not to suggest that men do not suffer too; they do, but due to the nature of these systems of oppression as multifaceted, the disadvantage is felt unevenly (e.g., Rose, 1993).

As Figure 16.1 shows, gender still matters and, for social geographers, place matters too. Research on gender in social geographies focuses on geographical variations in gender relations and its outcomes; space, place, environment and social difference influence who is most affected by sexism. The concept of intersectionality describes this interconnectedness with other relations, including those of race,

TEXT BOX 16.1 | Gender Pay Gap

What Is It?

Women earn significantly less than men over their entire careers, as reflected in the gender pay gap. The gender pay gap is defined as the difference in median pay between men and women.

How Much Is It?

According to the Office for National Statistics, across the UK the gender pay gap in 2019 was 18.4 per cent. This means that for every £100 that a man earns a woman in the same sector earns £81.60.

Why Does It Exist?

According to the Fawcett Society, a leading gender equality campaigner in the UK, the gender pay gap is a result of several interconnected factors related to men's and women's roles in society and the labour market:

1. Discrimination: Although it is illegal, some women are still paid less than men for the same work. Discrimination, particularly around pregnancy and maternity leave, remains common, with many women forced to leave their jobs after becoming mothers.

2. Unequal caring responsibilities: Women play a greater role in caring for children. As a result, more women work part time, and these jobs are typically lower paid with fewer progression opportunities.

3. A divided labour market: Women are still more likely to be in low-paid and low-skilled jobs. Women disproportionally make up most of the workers in the low-paid care and leisure sector, while men are overrepresented in the better-paid skilled trades.

class and age (see Chapter 20 on intersectionality). Understanding that gender plays out differently depending on who you are becomes ever clearer when we look at the intersections of gender and race. We note that while women in general experience an 18.4 per cent gap, Black African women experience a 24 per cent gap compared to White British men, while for Pakistani and Bangladeshi women the disparity is even worse, at 26 per cent (Fawcett Society, 2017).

Gender bias is a cause of this gender inequality, and it makes it very difficult to challenge the injustice that sexism and other forms of oppression produce. We can see this in the work of MP Stella Creasey (2018), who has raised concerns about the treatment of women in the UK Parliament. As a woman who has campaigned on issues of gender equality, she has been labelled 'difficult', and raising concerns about inequality becomes labelled as 'women's problems', irrespective of the nature of the concern. Through the patriarchal norms of the political system and political debate, the debate becomes gendered. This is why feminist interventions often point out structural inequality and advocate tackling the system, not the individual.

Gender bias is found in many other sites, whether unconscious or otherwise. Even student evaluations of university-taught modules have been found to be gendered, according to research in France and the United States, which shows a statistical bias against female

FIGURE 16.1
Gender pay gap.
(Source: https://www
.fawcettsociety.org.uk/
close-gender-pay-gap)

instructors. The most damning aspect of these findings is that gender bias can be so strong that less effective teachers may receive better feedback than more effective teachers who are the 'wrong' gender. This raises serious concerns about student expectations about knowledge and expertise and the value that universities place on flawed evaluation methods (see Boring, Ottoboni & Stark, 2016).

DEFINING GENDER (AND SEX)

In order to define the term 'gender', it is important to note that it is not a natural category but a socially constructed one. The term 'gender' is derived from an ancient Proto-Indian-European word root, *gen*, which means to produce or to beget, as in generate, genesis, oxygen. It is also related to the Latin genus and Old French gendre, meaning a kind or class of things that share similar characteristics. As understandings of how biological and social processes influence identity formation have evolved, so has the usage of the term 'gender': from its early roots – meaning to produce or generate (e.g., engender) – to its modern and most common usage – refering to the cultural distinction between women and men (e.g., masculinity and femininity).

In social geographies, 'gender' is defined as a social variable that refers to the understanding and representations of what it means to identify as a man or a woman (what has come to be known as masculinities and femininities). It is a social variable because gender works to place stereotypical assumptions onto those who are male or female, and this then structures their lives and shapes the expectations placed upon them. Men and women are still channelled into certain jobs deemed either masculine or feminine, for example, which is why there are far more female carers and male bankers in most societies. Such divisions are based on social assumptions and meanings rather than on biological differences. Gender is also a key feature of our identity; we are encouraged to associate our primary sense of self with how we see ourselves as masculine or feminine, often to the exclusion of other gender identities, such as trans or nonbinary identities (see later section).

The concept of gender as different to sex is often contested. In common parlance, the terms 'gender' and 'sex' are sometimes used interchangeably. However, in Western societies, it is generally thought that 'sex' describes biological characteristics and 'gender' the social characteristics associated with masculinity and femininity. Thus, sex is assumed to be a 'natural' category, while gender is socially constructed (a similar theme is discussed in Chapter 13 on race). This means, over time, people acquire a gender identity that may be masculine or feminine (WGSG, 1997/2014). The French feminist Simone de Beauvoir put it succinctly: 'One is not born, but rather becomes, a woman'. So, being a woman, or a man, is a state of becoming, a condition actively under construction. A person's sense of self as masculine or feminine also depends on cultural interpretations of what it means to be masculine and feminine in a particular society and geographical location, and these may differ widely and shift over time in response to historical and political changes. Imperialism and colonisation have been key amongst these changes (see Text Box 16.2).

Recent research, not only in feminist and queer theory but also in medical science, likewise challenges the straightforward definition of sex that we suggest above. It is becoming increasingly clear that sex is socially as well as biologically constructed. Sex is commonly determined on the basis of whether a baby has a penis or a vagina at birth, but biological traits such as chromosomes, genitals, reproductive organs, hormones and secondary sex characteristics are much more diverse and do not always align with our designation of male or female. Recent controversies over intersex athletes demonstrate this point.

These contestations of sex/gender distinctions are the bedrock of feminist politics because they imply that we are not defined by our sex, which in most cases is difficult to change; furthermore, gender roles are often used in problematic and discriminatory ways to shape people's lives and access to specific spaces. Since these gender roles

TEXT BOX 16.2 | **Real-World Theory: The Coloniality of Gender**

Mainstream gender theory owes its origin to the cultural and social experiences of people from the Global North. Feminist geographers (Raju, 2002; Johnston, 2018a) have called for a rethinking of the priorities and agendas of such theorising by asking who is excluded from mainstream gender theory and in what ways can we recover those lost voices. Their contention is not to mechanically insert gender analysis and research in issues related to the Global South but to fundamentally challenge the Northern bias of gender theory and to rethink how knowledge about gender is produced.

A leading theorist who has taken on this task is the late Argentinian feminist philosopher María Lugones, who developed the concept 'coloniality of gender' that proposes that gender is a colonial construct. She argued that coloniality (understood as the current logic, culture and structure of the world derived from colonialism) permeates all aspects of social existence and leads to gendered identities intersecting with race, class, sexuality, ethnicity and location. For Lugones, the coloniality of gender manifests itself not only in the violent suppression of women and Indigenous peoples along racial lines (as a continuing legacy of colonialism; see Chapter 8 on Indigeneity) but also in the persistence of the hegemony of heterosexual patriarchal systems (derived from and solidified under modern capitalism) around the world. She

argued that 'unlike colonization, the coloniality of gender is still with us; it is what lies at the intersection of gender/class/race as central constructs of the capitalist world system of power' (Lugones, 2010: 746).

When viewed as a colonial construct, gender as a concept opens up to many challenges. For example, Lugones' work alerts us to the diversity of gender identities and knowledges about the body and self that existed in precolonial times and their total suppression because of the colonial/modern project, thereby challenging the eurocentric binary understanding of gender identities as male and female. It enables us to understand gender inequality as a complex interaction of economic, racialising and gendering systems (see Chapter 20 on intersectionality). It urges scholars to reconsider and then rework ideas related to gender and feminism in relation to the different sites of knowledge production. As Lugones (2010: 747) said, 'It must include "learning" peoples'. The coloniality of gender thesis also implies that all forms of gender analysis need to be attentive to neocolonial global power relations, which shape the lives of women and men *in both* the Global South and the Global North. Lastly, it sets into motion a call for decolonising feminism that decentres the dominance of eurocentric ideas of gender by recognising the continuing legacy of colonial oppression and its impact on the development of those ideas.

have been socially constructed, they can also be deconstructed and challenged, thereby opening the possibility of changing the power imbalance between men and women (Massey, 1994/2013). We advocate moving beyond treating gender as a binary and support the need to see gender identities as multiple and complex, open to change and transformation, and variable across space and time.

GENDER-DIVERSE GEOGRAPHIES

The subfield known as gender-diverse geographies is a recent development in feminist social geographies that develops the ideas we have just discussed. This area of research builds, first, upon the historic roots of gender in geography: for example, Gill Valentine's (1989) work on women's fear in public space and Linda McDowell's (2003) research on gendered workplaces both demonstrated the spatialised and gendered ways that especially women's bodies are affected by geography. Second, gender-diverse geographies encompasses research on LGBTQ geographies, such as Bell and colleagues' (1994) engagement with Butler's (1990) poststructural idea of gender as performance (see also Chapter 17 on sexualities). The dialogue between research on sexualities, gender and feminist geographies highlights that not only gender but also perceptions of gender change the ways that bodies interact within space.

Recent engagement with gender in social geographies has focused on the ways that gender is performed differently in various spaces. Rather than focusing simply on men or women, masculinity and femininity are inhabited and experienced by a variety of bodies (Bain & Nash, 2007; Noble, 2002). Other social geographers' research has looked at the unique experiences of trans bodies in different spaces (Doan, 2010). The emergence of nonbinary as an underresearched group of people is also becoming a focus, as in Johnston's (2018a) book, which examines the key role that space plays for people whose gender does not fit into a neat gender binary. Through this strand of work, existing categorisations of gender and sex are further challenged. For instance, many definitions of gender do not take into account intersex bodies or fully engage with trans bodies. If a trans woman has undergone medical transition (taking cross-sex hormones or having surgery), then her gender is that of a woman, but it could be argued that her biology is also now closer to that of a cis-gender woman than a cis-gender man (i.e., those who identify with the gender given at birth). In this way, sex and gender become further blurred. The suggestion that gender should be viewed as a spectrum might also be applied to ideas about sex, as research is now suggesting.

Both Doan (2010) and Johnston (2018a) question any simplistic understanding of gender as simply including male or female. Doan (2010) takes an autoethnographic approach, using the case study of her own transition and the differing ways and spaces in which her body was seen as 'female enough' or not. Johnston (2018a) makes conceptual suggestions for the direction of what she calls 'gender-queer' geographic research. Both propose that gender as it is lived and experienced is a spectrum encompassing a complex and diverse set of ideas about masculinity and femininity. They both argue that the ways gender is seen and interpreted are highly spatialised.

However, Browne, Nash and Hines (2010) offer a cautionary note, suggesting that gender research that engages with trans people often uses them more as a tool to make a broader point about gender, particularly how their existence affects cis bodies. An example of this is the attention in geography to drag. Meanwhile, popular media tropes reflect this same tendency – for example, the unsubstantiated idea that trans women using toilets are somehow a threat to cis women's

FIGURE 16.2
A gender-neutral toilet.
(Credit: Ged Ridley)

safety. In future, social geographers might pursue further engagement with trans issues as a research interest in its own right – seeing trans people as more than simply a strategy to make gender (especially ideas about performative gender) more comprehensible.

SOCIAL GEOGRAPHIES OF MASCULINITIES

'Normative gender roles and performances are acquired through socialisation within the context of institutions such as the family, school, media and workplace'.
—Gorman-Murray & Hopkins, 2014: 6

These words from social geographers Andrew Gorman-Murray and Peter Hopkins' introduction to their book *Masculinities and Place* are significant for two reasons. First, they point out where understandings of gender come from, and, second, they are writing about men and masculinities. Too often, gender is labelled a wom-

| **TEXT BOX 16.3** | **Real-World Research: Gender Identity and the Debates around 'Gender-Neutral' Toilets** |

Ged's PhD thesis extends examination of issues of gender and geography through his study of trans identities and public toilets. The research involved interviews with twenty-five trans and gender-nonconforming people about the provisions and experience of gender-neutral toilets. These toilets are designed with the intention to help make life – and access to public space – easier for not only transgender people but also a wide range of gender-diverse identities and bodies. A feminist geographic perspective argues that toilet spaces not only act as microcosms of societal fears about the unknown and encounters with other bodies but also say something more about public participation. Early feminist work (Pain, 1991) highlighted the ways that public space may be hostile to women's bodies, and so too with toilets. Without adequate provision of public toilets for all bodies, whole groups of people are disenfranchised and restricted from fully participating in public life and spaces.

While Ged's study focuses specifically on trans and gender-nonconforming bodies, gender-neutral toilets also have implications for other people. Bathrooms that are not split by the binary of male and female can enable a more equal division of labour – fathers with young children often struggle to find or use appropriate bathrooms, as many men's bathrooms do not provide baby-changing facilities (this prompted a viral social media campaign, #SquatForChange). Equally, people with carers of a different gender to themselves can struggle to find bathrooms that are simultaneously accessible to both bodies. Creating more spaces that are more accessible for all bodies is a project that social geographers concerned with inclusion and social justice should be especially invested in (see Cavanagh, 2010).

en's concern, and, as we mentioned earlier in this chapter, this can lead to debates being shut down and campaigns for gender equality being dismissed. Work on masculinities in social geographies has grown rapidly in recent years (see Berg & Longhurst, 2003; Hopkins & Noble, 2009; Hopkins & Gorman-Murray, 2019; Van Hoven & Horschelmann, 2005, for overviews of the field). Gorman-Murray and Hopkins (2014) observe that work about masculinities in social geographies has included a focus on issues as diverse as intersectionality and relationality (see Chapter 20 on intersectionality), home (see Chapter 21 on housing), domestic labour, place and care, the family, health and well-being, and work (see Chapter 28 on social reproduction). Some specific examples of work about the social geographies of masculinities include research about working-class masculinities (e.g., McDowell, 2003), migrant masculinities (e.g., Datta et al., 2009) and the masculinities associated with the surfboard industry (Warren, 2016).

The work of gender theorist Raewyn Connell helps us to understand the extent and power of patriarchy. Connell (1995) developed 'hegemonic masculinity theory' and later developed with sociologist James Messerschmidt the idea of 'hegemonic masculinities': 'Hegemonic masculinity was not assumed to be normal in the statistical sense; only a minority of men might enact it. But it was certainly normative. It embodied the currently most honoured way of being a man, it required all other men to position themselves in relation to it, and it ideologically legitimised the global subordination of women to men' (Connell & Messerschmidt, 2005: 832). This hierarchy of power and control not only separates masculinity from femininity but also establishes patterns of dominance within men as a group. There have been critiques of hegemonic masculinities, primarily concerned that the theory is too reductionist and ignores nuances arising from those who are able to deviate from this framing (see Anderson & McCormack's [2018] work on inclusive masculinity theory). The relevance of the theory remains, however; in practice, patriarchal power and control still exist in all major nations and institutions around the world. The theorisation works within socially constructed gender norms, and its dominance is inscribed through an embodiment of race (Whiteness), class (middle-class aspiration), sexuality (heterosexual, ideally confirmed through marriage and children), age (working population is not too old and not too young) and physicality (height, strength, muscularity). We can better understand these overlapping and interlocking layers of oppression through the conceptualisation of intersectionality (see Chapter 20). Key to the later development of Connell and Messerschmidt's work – and, indeed, subsequent critiques – is the plural recognition of different forms of masculinities. These more variegated approaches do not, however, equate to a rejection of the hegemonic framework. Importantly, as social geographers have helped to point out, localised hegemonic masculinities have emerged, and there is now much empirical work mapping these particular sites of masculinities (for example, in the journal *Gender, Place & Culture*).

Research has also focused on the so-called crisis in masculinity, the idea that boys and men are now being left behind in Western societies: for example, being outperformed at school and university, including in traditionally male subject areas such as medicine and law. Sometimes biological 'facts' are attributed to the innate nature of masculine 'failings', reflecting much earlier, gendered ideologies. However, social geographers, including Anoop Nayak (2003) and Linda McDowell (2003), have helped to expose the unhelpfulness of this framing, as it places blame for men's 'failures' on women's 'successes'. As the example of the gender pay gap in Text Box 16.1 shows, this binary approach to gender difference is damaging and dangerous. This chapter has endeavoured to understand its limits and to highlight contemporary conceptualisations and lines of research.

SUMMARY

- Gender is a major source of inequality that structures our daily experiences of space. Ideas about gender are used to exert control over men as well as women, and feminist interventions are important in campaigning for gender equality for all.
- Gendered divisions exist across numerous sites, including social and built environments and institutions.

- Gender is nonbinary; it is multiple, and it varies across time and space. Gender intersects with other forms of social difference to create oppression in different places.
- Today, research on women's experiences in social geographies is joined by the growing fields of geographies of masculinities and gender-diverse geographies.

FURTHER READING

Datta, A., Hopkins, P., Johnston, L., Olson, E., & Silva, J. M. (2019) *The Routledge International Handbook of Gender and Feminist Geographies.* London: Routledge.

Massey, D. (1994/2013) *Space, Place and Gender.* London: Wiley-Blackwell.

Oberhauser, A. M., Fluri, J. L., Whiston, R., & Mollett, S. (2018) *Feminist Spaces: Gender and Geography in a Global Context.* London: Routledge.

See also the journal *Gender, Place & Culture: A Journal of Feminist Geography.*

Sexualities

Graeme Mearns and Carl Bonner-Thompson

During the 1980s, the phrase 'sexuality and space' was popularised to refer to a field concerned with the mapping of residential neighbourhoods in which sexual minorities lived (Adler & Brenner, 1992). Castells (1983) identified spatial clusters of residences and businesses of lesbians and gay men in San Francisco's Castro District while detailing prejudice, legal repression and political violence. Visibility is important. As Bell (1991: 323) notes, it 'demands recognition of norms that construct public space as heterosexual, heterosexist and heteronormative'. Geographies of sexualities emerged in the early 1990s as a research field, in part enabled by the cultural turn (see Chapter 1 on creating more social geographies). The establishment of this field was to move beyond 'simplistic' maps of sexual minorities and develop a fuller understanding of how different sexual identities are performed, negotiated and contested in and across space.

Warner (1993) coined the term 'heteronormativity' to highlight the inescapable – and often invisible – norms of heterosexuality ingrained in the institutions of most societies. Heteronormativity is the process of reproducing heterosexuality as 'normal'. This assumes heterosexuality and a strict adherence to a male/female binary, devaluing lives outside such a system, including lesbian, gay, bisexual, trans and queer (LGBTQ)

TEXT BOX 17.1 | Stonewall

Stonewall is shorthand for the rebellion of men, women and trans people (including Black trans sex workers erased from the event's history) who fought a police raid on New York's Stonewall Inn on 28 June 1969. Stonewall resulted in a visible gay male culture of men seeking equals: 'clones', 'machos', 'leather' men and others in specialised bars, darkrooms, cinemas, saunas and gyms. Having long felt threatened by family, friends, neighbours and institutions, these individuals created a patchwork of sexual and romantic relations that was crucial in lessening the pressures of the outside world. Stonewall is now a national charity that works to end discrimination against LGBTQ people.

people (Binnie, 2007). Text Box 17.1 discusses the Stonewall Inn incident that challenged the stigmatisation of sexual minorities.

Mapping Desire was published in 1995 by David Bell and Gill Valentine. It was the first book on geographies of sexualities, containing many contributions from other feminist geographers who use queer theory to challenge normative ideas of gender and sexuality. The category of 'queer' became a 'disruptive' concept used to subvert heteronormative assumptions in lesbian and gay rights discourses at this time (Oswin, 2008). In a twentieth-anniversary review, Peake (2016) argues that *Mapping Desire* highlighted the privileging of heterosexual bodies. *Mapping Desire* also clarified the relevance of Butler's (1990) 'performativity' for considering the fluidity of sexuality, while challenging 'masculinity' and 'femininity' as rigid ideas that neatly map onto sexed bodies (see Chapter 16 on gender).

In short, for over three decades geographers have worked to understand how sexualities reproduce unequal power relations that manifest socially and spatially. While there have been positive political and social changes for sexual minorities in recent years, discrimination remains, and equality is not geographically even. New norms have also formed, and LGBTQ people still experience implicit and explicit marginalisation, violence and abuse. So, the field is not 'just' focused on LGBTQ lives but also on heteronormativity (the cultural domination of heterosexuality as normal and accepted).

In this chapter, we introduce the core concepts and interrelated debates in the social geographies of sexuality. We start by explaining heteronormativity before engaging with the key political tensions that have framed the field so far.

HETERONORMATIVE SPACES, BODIES AND DISCIPLINES

Heteronormativity is the normalisation of heterosexuality and associated practices. It assumes that bodies are either male or female, with opposite-gender desire becoming 'normal' and same-gender sex, intimacy and love 'abnormal', 'unnatural' or 'deviant' (Weeks, 1995). In other words, heterosexuality *becomes* the norm, as it is assumed to be natural. Entangled within binary expectations of gender is the reinforcement of heterosexuality as *the* default sexuality. Particular femininities and masculinities are celebrated by heteronormative discourses, fixing ways of doing gender to sexed bodies (Cream, 1995). For example, men are assumed to walk, talk and dress differently from women. Heteronormativity organises daily lives and is reproduced through bodies, homes, institutions, nation-states and globalisation – for example, through parenting practices, children's books and sex education (see Chapter 19 on age). Not only does heteronormativity shape normative identities, but sexual practices do so as well. Sex is constructed as something occurring only between two people in a private, monogamous relationship. Threesomes, group sex, outdoor sex, sex in clubs and nonmonogamous relationships are among the practices understood as immoral, deviant, disgusting and shameful. Heterosexuals who engage in these practices can also be said to disrupt heteronormativity (Hubbard, 2008).

Spaces are likewise 'sexed', meaning that they become imagined as heterosexual or homosexual, as with the designation of 'gay bars' as opposed to 'straight bars'. These spatial manifestations can be understood as fluid and act as sites where genders and sexualities are performed, negotiated and contested (Bell et al., 1994). 'Gay' spaces in the nighttime economy are often seen as a 'claiming space' – for example, Poke in Newcastle upon Tyne (see Figure 17.1). In other words, the sexualisation of space is not 'natural' but a product of socialisation. Geographers work to understand how these processes render some bodies invisible in/from space while rendering others (hyper)visible (see Text Box 17.2). This has occurred mainly in the context of commercial 'gay villages' and Pride spaces (Valentine & Skelton, 2003) and also in homes, gyms, toilets, saunas and spaces of the countryside (see, for instance, Nash & Bain, 2007; Waitt & Gorman-Murray, 2008).

Notwithstanding greater amounts of research on sexuality, geography as a discipline – and set of practices – has been critiqued for being heteronormative. Early work often did not challenge constructions of sexuality, allowing heterosexuality to pass as the norm. Both the geographies of sexualities and the subfield of queer geographies work to 'queer' the discipline (Brown & Browne, 2016). This means that they disrupt how knowledge is produced, including foregrounding the lived experiences of LGBTQ people to underline how heteronormativity shapes daily lives (see 'queer geographies'). However, there remains a scarcity of research on the material and fleshy aspects of sex itself and the places through which sex occurs to further contest heteronormativity.

FIGURE 17.1

Poke, Newcastle's longest-running queer club night. (Credit: Adrian Martin)

INDIE · ELECTRO · HIP-HOP · PUNK · POP FOR QUEER FOLK

10PM – 3AM

 @POKENEWCASTLE
@KOMMUNITYNCL   £5 adv £7 door £4 NUS

TEXT BOX 17.2	Real-World Research: Geographies of Sexualities in North East England

In the North East there has been a shift from manufacturing (which shaped the dominant 'working class' identity) to the service, culture and tourism economic sectors. This shaped how gendered and sexual lives are embodied (Casey, 2010). Certain city centre zones have been noted as uncomfortable for younger queer people due the heterosexual masculinities celebrated there (Coleman-Fountain, 2014). The 'gay scene' in the city, the 'Pink Triangle', also produced exclusions, as it is a commodified celebration of young white gay male culture. This has led to exclusions of a variety of identities (for example, older lesbian women and gay men and trans people), or the 'queer unwanted' (Casey, 2010). Pride celebrations have also been commercialised and remain contested due to formal policing and normative ideas of lesbian and gay identity embedded by business. Both the Pink Triangle and Pride have been used as 'spectacle' to attract tourism. The entanglement of sexualities and city rebranding can further idealisation of young, white, able-bodied and affluent men. Bonner-Thompson (2017) provides recent commentary, exploring how masculinities unfold on Grindr (a gay dating app) in Newcastle. There remains much research to be done to diversify the geographies of sexualities in the region, as with other provincial towns and cities of the United Kingdom.

POLITICAL TENSIONS

Understanding sexuality and attempting to create equality and disrupt heteronormativity are not straightforward tasks. A central tension is between LGBT- and queer-identity politics. LGBT politics tends to approach sexuality as being about the labels of gay, lesbian, bisexual and transgender and how these identity markers can be used to make change. By contrast, queer politics seeks to unpick the labels and categories, due to their essentialising nature. Queer theorists seek to deconstruct categories and resist their formation. This section will explore some of these tensions.

Duggan (2002) coined the term 'homonormativity' to understand the normalisation of particular (usually young, White, affluent, able-bodied gay man) nonheterosexual, queer and LGBTQ identities. This process involves the assimilation of heteronormative ideals (monogamy, same-generation pairings, marriage) into LGBTQ cultures, normalising *particular* queer identities. Some theorists are sceptical of the concept, arguing that homonormativity labels LGBTQ people in a generalised way that diverts the necessary attention away from biphobia, homophobia and transphobia (Brown, 2008). However, the concept is still viewed as useful in aiding reflection of how different queer people can become unwittingly complicit in heteronormative, patriarchal and racist institutions (Oswin, 2008).

Marriage claims have caused significant tension between advocates of LGBT and queer politics (Podmore, 2013). Crudely, this can be summarised as a concern that nonheterosexual couples who conform to heteronormative standards of sex, romance and love gain recognition as 'normal' in a way that produces a 'good gay citizen' (see Text Box 17.3), versus a radical 'bad queer' who steps or falls outside conformist ideas of sex/uality (Bell & Binnie, 2000).

Assimilation is the term used to describe a nonheterosexual person or group that conforms to normative ideas of sex/uality (Bell & Binnie, 2000). Debates surrounding gay marriage are tied to this, suggesting that equal marriage does not disrupt heteronormativity but extends it. Transgression, then, is about the resistance of heteronormativity and attempting to live beyond its restraints (nonmonogamous relationships are one example). Sexual citizenship is important here. People who may be understood as 'assimilating' arguably become 'better'

TEXT BOX 17.3 | Sexual Citizenship

The 'sexual citizen' is now a common category among those who have claimed rights based on sexuality (Weeks, 1998). The concept can refer to the rights people have – or not – to enact sexualities in and across multiple spaces, as well as legislative rights. Hubbard (2013) examines, for example, the rights of two gay-identified men removed from a Soho pub in London for kissing each other in public, highlighting how shifting legislative spaces in the British context (equal age of consent, marriage rights, adoption and so on) often do no correlate with positive treatment in public spaces.

sexual citizens – or good gays – and enjoy increased recognition of their sexual identities as 'legitimate'. Those who resist may not benefit from the same rights and be constructed as 'bad gays', therefore deviant, immoral and shameful (Bell & Binnie, 2000).

Nonnormative sexual practices and identities have dominated scholarship on sexual citizenship, particularly those of lesbian and gay communities (Browne & Ferreira, 2015) but also bisexual (Maliepaard, 2015), trans (Stryker & Whittle, 2006) and intersex peoples (Grabham, 2007). There remains a tendency to sexualise nonnormative groups while desexualising 'normative' ones. Therefore, marriage and nuclear family formation are constructed as legitimate forms of adult relationship. Dreher (2017) suggests that this is why campaigns for institutional change in marriage and other areas have presided over, say, confronting government about the impacts of funding cuts on LGBTQ services. Debate continues about the precise nature of gains and losses in seeking comparable rights to heterosexuals, which is the main reason heterosexualities are crucial research foci too (Beasley, Holmes & Brook, 2015).

Feminist, postcolonial (see Chapter 2 on theories in social geographies) and queer scholars have critiqued many of the concepts, theories and activisms underpinning sexual citizenship, showing the limits of the Western basis of sex-gender categories in non-Western places (Sabsay, 2012). Much of this work queries 'global' lesbian and gay political agendas due to their frequent grounding in the United States and Europe, wherein 'a universal' has been inset into 'sexual minorities'. One argument is that this has led to lesbian and gay scripts (fashions, tastes, imagery) being interpreted as 'adopted' rather than 'adapted' outside the Western world, reproducing Altman's (1997) homogeneous 'global gay' culture that overrides alternative and hybrid identities and ways of politicising (Binnie, 2004). How sexual rights struggles uphold particular performances of the nation-state warrant making these universalising processes clearer, as 'progressive' states are sometimes distinguished from 'intolerant' others by means of a racialised account of sexual democracy that masks neo-orientalist and -colonial practices (Kulpa & Silva, 2016). As the next part of this chapter clarifies, there remains an uneven geography to 'homonormativity' and the kinds of discrimination that LGBTQ people are still confronted with.

GEOGRAPHICAL UNEVENNESS AND LIMITED DEPICTIONS OF SEXUALITY

As lesbian and gay spatial visibility grew during the 1980s in Amsterdam, Berlin, Paris and New York, geographers questioned how markers of 'gay culture' were being used to strengthen the economic vitality of cities. This pushed sexuality into urban, economic and political geographies while underlining how the 'cosmopolitan city' is implicated in – and by – stereotypes of lesbians and gay men as uniformly affluent, with 'dual incomes and no kids' ('DINKs'). Demand for Albert Kennedy Trust (UK) services and those of other charities proves that poverty and homelessness are still unduly high among LGBTQ people, in spite of the image of wealth and 'excess' purported by media and business (Hollibaugh & Weiss, 2015).

Even preausterity, Binnie and Skeggs (2004) wrote about how Manchester's gay village had been woven into city marketing and regeneration strategies to project to a global audience an image of the city to compete for new residents, tourists and businesses. While this indicated positive attitude change, it also curtailed diversity. Even in one of the twenty-five countries now with full or partial equal marriage laws, 'being out, proud and visible' in sexualised spaces remains impossible for many people. Such geographical unevenness is shifting rapidly; yet questions remain in respect of the possibilities of a more inclusive 'sexual citizenship' than is currently on offer to queers, who by and large still find their identities and bodies articulated in respect of consumer spending power.

TROUBLING TIMES: FUTURES OF GEOGRAPHIES OF SEXUALITIES

Longhurst and Johnston (2014) suggest that, although work in geography concerning sexualised and gendered bodies has become more mainstream, sexist, racist and homophobic structures still need to be challenged. Johnston (2018a) contends that attention to emotions could further trouble masculinist knowledge production. Through a 'precarity' lens, she contends that emphasis on the moments that make people uncomfortable, anxious or vulnerable could illuminate how discursive sexual and gender categories exclude particular bodies. We suggest three other topics that could be similarly provocative.

Johnston (2015) details the main approaches used in geography to 'trouble' gender, arguing trans subjectivities are only beginning to be given fuller attention (see Chapter 16 on gender). Doan's (2010) *Gender, Place & Culture* article has drawn attention to the limits of deploying queer theory to highlight the instability of gender and sexuality, contending that the category of 'trans' has been used only as a disruptive tool rather than to explore everyday lived experiences (Browne, Nash & Hines, 2010). Trans people do not live lives only as unstable bodies, so it is important to attend to the ways that trans people materially experience space and place. Doan (2010) contends that most places are constructed from the gender binary, fuelling vulnerability for the trans body, which is understood as not 'fitting in'. As trans geographies gathers momentum, scholars may wish to reflect more on how gender-variant people experience specific places to detail how these sites can work to affirm or resist the gendered norms and expectations that are enmeshed with heteronormativity (Nash, 2010).

The prevailing 'squeamishness' on being able to research and write about sex has been criticised. Longhurst (2004) is among those who have advocated for more focus on the 'sexy', 'dirty' and 'messy' materialities of sex within geography to develop an understanding of the manifold ways bodies and places are perceived and experienced. Both Binnie (2004) and Longhurst (2004) suggest that geography risks reproducing heteronormativity by not addressing 'pervy sex' lives in favour of sexual identities. Consequently, some have foregrounded sex to challenge the silencing and to confront heteronormativity through research praxes, but such work remains marginal. For instance, Brown (2008) explores the smell, touch and sound of gay men's cruising practices. Beyond touch and haptic geographies (mediated bodily contact), Misgav and Johnston (2014) stress the relevance, both in and to the field, of considering bodily fluids. People have sex in multiple places, not just in bedrooms. There are spatialities to sex, and feminist, queer and other geographers are well equipped to develop an understanding of how places figure in people's sex lives, as well as to determine how this resists or remakes heteronormative discourses.

DECOLONISING THE FIELD

As well as being heteronormative, the discipline of geography is a White and colonialist project (Lennox & Waites, 2013) (see Chapter 13 on race). The geographies of sexualities and queer geographies are part of this. The majority of sexualities research is conducted from the perspective of and about the Global North. Feminist, antiracist and postcolonial theorists are among those who have challenged the sameness of experience implied by scholarship that is anchored in and by the Global North and have included work on queer diaspora, queers of colour and queer religiosity (Valentine et al., 2016). The geographies of sexualities can result in a colonising way of *doing* geography, supporting the dominant epistemological and philosophical standpoints (Maria & Jorge, 2014).

The categories of LGBTQ are produced through the Global North, meaning that they do not always map onto understandings of sexualities in the Global South (Brown & Browne, 2016). For example, Rodó-de-Zárate (2016) argues that using the word 'queer' in her research with lesbian women in Catalonia is met with confusion, as it sounds like the word *cuir*, which translates to 'leather' in English. For Rodó-de-Zárate (2016), 'queer' does not represent a disruptive tool but a colonialist and elitist one that seeks to undermine her feminist work. Therefore, geographies of sexualities research *can* become a colonising way of working, reproducing the epistemologies of the Global North (Maria & Jorge, 2014). Geographers must be sensitive to Other experiences, knowledges, desires and bodies by reflecting on positionality and the design of academic practices – for example, by means of engagement with research *by* scholars in postcolonial contexts and attention to those articulating 'glocal' expressions of sexuality.

CONCLUSION

Social geographies of sexualities are perhaps more relevant than ever now, in light of the political climate. The fallout from the 2008 financial crash and subsequent austerity measures imposed across many of the economies of the West has still not really been fully understood in the context of queer lives, nor has the lurch to the political right that has occurred in numerous states (a precursor to Brexit in the UK context) (Nash et al., 2019). Reported hate crimes against LGBTQ people have surged in England and Wales, and there has been significant media coverage of the backlash to #NoOutsiders, a schools project that aimed to help diversify curricula to increase awareness of LGBTQ lives and relationships in schools. These are just a selection of current topics that could be studied in geographies of sexualities.

At the same time, the penetration of digital technologies, mobile dating and sexual networking ('hook up') applications (see Chapter 31 on digital) into the everyday lives of vast numbers of people holds the potential to remap all social spaces in ways that 'prove' the public sphere to be less heteronormative than purported (Ferriera & Salvador, 2015). The field developed from an engagement with feminist and queer theory that started to challenge heteronormativity in society and knowledge in the discipline. Since then, work in geographies of sexualities has expanded to interrogate multiple spaces, places and bodies. There remain tensions between LGBTQ and queer identity politics and over the most effective ways to bring about equality. This 'messiness' may be part of the strengths of the field, as it keeps debates lively. There are now further challenges and questions to explore. Gender variance and decolonisation are central to challenging the ways gender and sexuality in the West are understood, providing exciting new avenues of research that can inform parallel fields of social geography.

SUMMARY

- The geographies of sexualities are multifaceted and operate at numerous sites and scales, from the body outwards.
- Lesbian and gay geographies of the city were a key focus, but geographies of sexualities now focus on challenging heteronormativity.
- Trans geographies have become important, while current scholarship is beginning to engage more fully with nonnormative sexual practices, sexualities within postcolonial contexts and articulations of genders and sexualities within digital spaces.

FURTHER READING

Bell, D., & Valentine, G. (1995) *Mapping Desire: Geographies of Sexualities*. London: Routledge.

Binnie, J., & Valentine, G. (1999) Geographies of sexuality – A review of progress. *Progress in Human Geography*, 23(2): 175–87.

Brown, G., & Browne, K. (2016) *The Routledge Research Companion to Geographies of Sex and Sexualities*. London: Routledge.

Johnston, L. (2015) Gender and sexuality I: Genderqueer geographies? *Progress in Human Geography*, 50(5): 668–78.

Disability

Janice McLaughlin

If you are a wheelchair user or have a visual or hearing impairment, your ability to participate in society will be strongly influenced by whether you can easily, reliably, efficiently and safely access key aspects of social space. This includes transport systems, public buildings and general social space, such as streets or parks (Gaete-Reyes, 2015). Disabled people's underrepresentation in education and employment and their overrepresentation in poverty and as victims of crime have much to do with the difficulties that they face in navigating social space (Smith, 2016). Some of the issues that disabled people confront have been reduced due to greater investment in accessibility, legislative protections and changes in planning/ building regulation. However, it remains important for social geography to study the impact of disability on people's experiences for several reasons. First, improvements in accessibility are not uniform across the Global North and Global South. In contexts where extreme poverty is prevalent and public-sector investment minimal, the most basic infrastructures of public space are limited and commitments to accessibility negligible (see Chapter 22 on wealth and poverty). In addition, at moments of crisis such as climate extremes, warfare or civil unrest, disability is produced and, in addition, disabled people are most at risk of further harm. That disabled people bear the brunt of environmental crises such as extreme climate events is, of course, not just found in the Global South, as the events of Hurricane Katrina in New Orleans in August 2005 show (National Council on Disability, 2006). Second, the most common displayed symbol of accessibility provision is the wheelchair, as seen in Figure 18.1. This points to a general presumption that disability equals wheelchair user, meaning that accessibility equals a designated car-park space close to a building with a ramp and powered door. While these things are important, the range of impairments and the issues created by the lack of fit between different impairments and different social spaces are far greater and more complex. Physical disabilities are more varied than the examples that I gave above; indeed, the resources to help one group can make things more difficult for another. For example, wheelchair users can find it difficult to get across the bumps on pavements that are there to help someone with a visual impairment safely identify the difference between the road and the pavement. Going further, understanding the relationship between the environment and disability is about more than physical disability; the social environment can create many problems for people with learning disabilities. For example, signs directing people

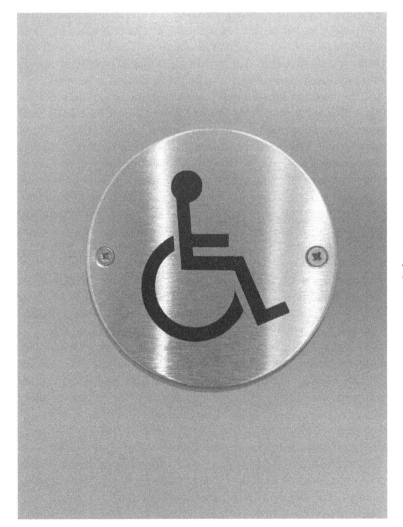

FIGURE 18.1
Accessibility symbol.
(Credit: Janice McLaughlin)

may not be understood by everyone; in addition, people with learning disabilities can find access to public space challenging because other people do not take the time to communicate with them in ways that they understand or may react to them with stigma and even violence. Bringing in the problems that people with learning disabilities face highlights a central concept of social geography – *what happens in any space is a product of the interrelationship between its materiality and the interactions of those within it.*

This chapter explores the varied ways an environment can be disabling; it does so by showing how *geographies of disability* has emerged as an important subdiscipline in social geography. This development has been hugely influenced by disabilities studies. The chapter begins by briefly showing how disability studies conceptualises disability before mapping out how geographies of disability has adapted that understanding to study the importance of social space in its production.

DISABILITY STUDIES

The key concept from disability studies that has shaped geographies of disability is that of the 'social model' (Barnes, 2012). The social model has its origins in British disability politics in the 1970s and 1980s, but its influence is international. Disability activists, mostly with physical impairments, drew from Marxism to redefine disability. They rejected medical explanations that associate the problems that a disabled person faces with the limitations of their body. This understanding had led to disabled people being treated as tragic figures, to be either cured by medicine or locked away from society in oppressive institutions. In 1976, an organisation called UPIAS (Union of Physically Impaired Against Segregation), led by key actors such as Ken Davis, Liz Finkelstein, Vic Finkelstein and Paul Hunt, proposed the 'Fundamental Principles of Disability'. Their document made a distinction between impairment and disability: impairment is aspects of the body that are limited in their functionality; disability is the creation of social disadvantage due to the inability of the environment to adapt to those limitations: 'it is society which disables physically impaired people. Disability is something imposed on top of our impairments, by the way we are unnecessarily isolated and excluded from full participation in society' (UPIAS, 1976: 4). A simplistic way to understand this is that someone who uses a wheelchair is not disadvantaged by the fact that they need a wheelchair to be mobile; they are disadvantaged by the presence of stairs and doors that do not open easily. This definition also explains why British disability studies uses the terminology of 'disabled people' rather than 'people with disabilities'. While the latter is preferred in disability politics in other countries (for example, the United States), the British movement argues that the language of 'with' still positions disability as in the person rather than in the social environment. Text Box 18.1 gives a summary of key points within the social model.

TEXT BOX 18.1 | Key Aspects of the Social Model of Disability

- Disability is not a property of the individual. Instead, it is a social construct produced by multiple barriers in society.

- Society is designed around the assumption that people are nondisabled; this means that the problems are material, structural, economic and institutional, as well as being about personal attitudes or prejudice.

- The priority should therefore be 'fixing' those social barriers rather than the individual with impairments.

- Disabled people have a right to an independent life, which the state should support.

- Disabled people should have much greater say in things that affect them (for example, in what kind of support will enable them to live independently). This includes playing a key role in organisations said to represent and advocate for them. This concept is often represented by the phrase 'Nothing about us without us'.

Given that the social model has been around for some time, it has been critiqued, including within disability studies. Disability researchers have sought ways to open up the structural focus to create more space to recognise the relational and cultural aspects involved in the production of disability (Garland-Thomson, 2011). Researchers are also keen to bring in greater recognition of the ways the other aspects of who someone is – their gender, race and ethnicity, age, sexuality – influence the ways they are disabled by society (Thomas, 1999). Greater recognition is now given in disability studies to learning disability as both an impairment (although its status as an impairment is also contested [Goodley, 2001]) and a socially produced disability. Geographies of disability has made significant use of the social model in addition to becoming important in its further development and revision.

SOCIAL GEOGRAPHIES OF DISABILITY

Given the focus on the environment as the producer of disability, it is no surprise that social geography, particularly from the 1990s onwards, picked up the arguments of the social model (useful summaries of the development of the subdiscipline can be found in Hansen & Philo, 2007; Imrie & Edwards, 2007). One of the key early interventions was by Brendan Gleeson, who incorporated a geographical emphasis into the social model by arguing,

> Far from being a natural human experience, disability is what may become of impairment as each society produces itself socio-spatially: there is no necessary correspondence between impairment and disability. There are only historical-geographical correspondences which obtain when some societies, in the course

of producing and reproducing themselves, oppressively transform impaired first nature as disablement. (1996: 391)

Since then, a variety of themes has developed: the significance of the built environment as an important barrier to people participating in a range of social activities; the massive limitations of public transport across the globe (Lubitow, Rainer & Bassett, 2017; Pyer & Tucker, 2017); the work that disabled people must do to 'work around' the inadequacies and 'ableisms' of their environment (Blewett & Hanlon, 2016); and the financial penalties that disabled people experience, both because such issues are a barrier to education and employment and because of the additional costs that they face in negotiating their way through social life. In doing so, what geographies of disability highlights is that '*many* bodies, not just a few bodies, share some problems with disabling design, spatial organisation, etc.' (Freund, 2001: 693). Freund (2001: 695) also quotes Relph's observation that 'Modern landscapes seem to be designed for forty-year-old healthy males driving cars' (1981b: 196).

Let's look at one example in a bit more detail.

TEXT BOX 18.2 | Exercise: Student Task about Disability

If you are able, take a trip around your university/college campus and think about the following questions. How often is the disabled access (particularly in older buildings) round the back or separate from other access points? How many lecture rooms have induction loops (for people with hearing impairments) and how many of them are working? Are the signs directing you around campus easy to follow if you have a visual impairment or have restricted growth? Thinking about these questions (and others), who is the expected user of a higher education space?

TOILETS

A major problem that disabled people face is being able to find accessible toilets. People with a range of impairments can find that mainstream toilet facilities, including some toilets that are labelled accessible, are inadequate for their needs. While disabled toilets are often assumed to be designed for wheelchair users, this does not mean they do not face difficulties. The most common design of accessible toilet is one that assumes either the ability to lift oneself from a wheelchair onto the toilet or the availability of someone strong enough to lift the person onto the toilet (imagine doing this for an adult rather than a young child). Someone with a colostomy bag does not need just a toilet and sink but also shelf space so that they can empty and change their bag hygienically. A parent/carer with an incontinent child needs to have space in order to safely and hygienically change them. The lack of toilets that have such space leads to children being changed on dirty toilet floors or them wearing double nappies to avoid the need to change them (Timms, 2017). A contemporary toilet issue found across the Global North is the declining availability of freely available public toilets; if people's impairments mean that they need to go to the toilet more frequently, then this withdrawal of provision limits their access to public space. Declining access to appropriate public toilet facilities is also a problem in public transport systems in the United Kingdom. On social media and news outlets, disabled people have shared stories of having to relieve themselves where they sat because the disabled toilet on their train was out of service (BBC News, 2017). There is increasing evidence that disabled women are 'choosing' to have surgery to have a catheter fitted, due to being unable to guarantee that when they are out or travelling they will be able to access a toilet, a situation sometimes referred to as 'social incontinence' (Ryan, 2018). This is a clear example of the problem not being the impairment but the failure in social space to provide the facilities that can enable someone to participate in an equal way. A final problem is that, due to the common presumption that accessible toilets are for wheelchair users, non-wheelchair-using people who use an accessible toilet can be challenged when using such provision. For example, people with restricted growth can be questioned when using disabled toilet facilities, even though the lower position of the sink (to make it accessible to someone in a wheelchair) can be helpful (and although the higher toilet can create its own challenges). This final example points to the importance of encounters with others in the production of disability in social space.

SOCIAL ENCOUNTERS

A common theme across the book you are reading is that space is not made just of buildings and physical environments; crucially, it is a space of people, and therefore of encounter (see Chapter 27 on encounter) (J. Allen, 2004). In these encounters, disabled people can find their social presence confirmed as outsider and Other, or they can participate in moments of recognition and resistance. The importance given to encounters in social spaces has become more pertinent to geographies of disability as it has expanded on the criticisms of the social model for being too structural and universal in approach. Edward Hall and Robert Wilton (2017) argue that geographies of disability has become more focused on the relational production of disability as it has explored the intersectional, intersubjective and embodied dimensions of disability.

Relationality is used to capture that, while broader social structures such as economic inequality and lack of expansive public transport systems are important, the specificity of how those issues are lived will be varied. It depends on how their influence is mediated by intersectional interactions between people and the materiality of social space. For example, Vera Chouinard (1999: 150) discusses how women whose disabled embodiment is read as outside bodily norms are positioned as 'out of place' in spaces that assume a male, able body. Louise Holt (2004, 2007, 2010) has done crucial work looking at the experiences of disabled children in mainstream school environments in the United Kingdom and argues that such environments produce the 'socio-spatial constitution' (Holt, Bowlby & Lea, 2017: 1362) of differences. She argues that although, formally, education policy favours the inclusion of disabled pupils into mainstream provision, the spaces of education and the interactions that occur within them create dynamics of 'micro-exclusion'. This happens through the demarcating of space – for example, disabled pupils sitting separately in the classroom – and social interaction – for example, bullying and name-calling by other pupils on the playground.

One important benefit of incorporating a relational perspective is that it can also help to identity moments in mainstream space where norms are challenged and reinvented to be more inclusive. In an ethnographic study of deaf people's use of public transport systems in India, Annelies Kusters (2017) argues that they make use of distinct spaces for disabled people to create a mobile community, where the journey to work involves not just movement but also the creation of the opportunity for friendship, solidarity and belonging. A focus on social encounters is particularly important in research looking at learning disability (Cresswell, 1996; Hall, 2005; Wiesel & Bigby, 2016). Power and Bartlett (2018), focusing on the United Kingdom, argue that contemporary welfare narratives of disabled people as welfare scroungers lead to people with learning disabilities being targeted by hate crime, as people question their right to 'take up' space. Drawing from research undertaken in Canada, Wilton, Schormans and Marquis (2018) show how opportunities to participate in shopping in public space can create moments of inclusion or exclusion for people with an intellectual disability depending on the way that people engage with them. For example, staff who recognise someone with a learning disability as a regular customer or give them extra time to complete their task create a space of inclusion and belonging. Sara Ryan (2005) has highlighted how food outlets like McDonald's in the United Kingdom can be more welcoming to children with the label of autistic spectrum disorder because the chaotic nature of such spaces means that the different way that they engage with the world is not positioned by others as problematic.

REASONABLE ADJUSTMENTS AND UNIVERSAL DESIGN

In the United Kingdom and elsewhere, equalities legislation (the relevant legislation in the United Kingdom is now the Equality Act [2010]) emphasises the requirement for organisations to ensure that their environments are accessible to disabled people. However, the key phrase that is used in the United Kingdom is 'reasonable adjustments'. This gives the impression that architects and planners can approach it as an additional task rather than a central requirement of good design. One approach to design, held up as an inclusive alternative to reasonable adjustments, is 'universal design'. Universal design, which has been around since the 1980s, argues that if you create spaces that imagine from the beginning a broad range of uses and users, it will be more inclusive because, rather than looking at the questions of inclusion as an afterthought, it sits at the heart of design. The concept has been built into design practices, particularly in Scandinavia and other European countries such as the Netherlands. Seven key principles (Story, 1998) are associated with it, including equitable use, flexibility in use, simple and intuitive design and size and space for approach and use. While social geographers see universal design as having an inclusive aspiration, they still query how socially inclusive it can be. In particular, writers such as Rob Imrie (2012a) argue that it does not do enough to really engage with the social model's emphasis on the social production of disability. Specifically, Imrie argues that the design approach sees the problem as one of getting the right kind of technical fix. This lays bare the key concept of geographies of disability: that disability is a product of the relationship between social interaction and environment. The same space can be made inclusive or exclusive, depending on what happens

TEXT BOX 18.3 | Real-World Research: Challenge of Shared Space Environments

Rob Imrie is an important researcher of geographies of disability. One area he has looked at is what is known as 'shared space environments' (2012b), a concept of urban design that has been around since the 1960s (the Netherlands being an early location). The concept is now being picked up across the Global North as part of contemporary regeneration and gentrification practices. It involves blurring the distinction between road and pavement to encourage the different users of public space to integrate together and create a more aesthetically pleasing space. Planners believe that colocating vehicles and pedestrians encourages both to work together to negotiate movement, rather than relying on ugly signs and barriers. Imrie undertook research in the United Kingdom on the topic in 2009 and 2010. It involved ethnographic observation and qualitative interviews with national and local government actors involved in design and NGOs who work on disability access issues. He argues that such planning initiatives prioritise both normal bodies and vehicles and, in the process, produce 'auto-disabilities'. Such spaces serve to 'reproduce auto-dominated environments that are creating, potentially, new spaces of disablement in towns and cities, particularly for vulnerable pedestrians, such as the elderly and vision-impaired people' (2012b: 2261). Shared space requires that the individual takes on the responsibility of negotiating their safe movement, generating vulnerability and disability in the removal of the usual signs and demarcations people rely on. Innovations like this point to the continued marginalisation of people whose bodies do not match the norm, to the benefit of a narrower group of users.

FIGURE 18.2

Luggage stored in space allocated to disabled passengers. (Credit: Janice McLaughlin)

within it. While particular configurations of different spaces can solve some practical issues and can encourage particular kinds of interactional dynamics, on their own they will not guarantee a significant change in whether spaces are disabling. One example is the presence of wheelchair spaces and ramps on buses and trains. The availability of the technology and spaces has potential to improve wheelchair users' access to mobility, but what happens is that they become contested spaces in the social interactions with other users (for example, wheelchair spaces on buses are used by adults with children in buggies and wheelchair spaces on trains are filled by luggage, as seen in Figure 18.2). If drivers or train staff do not assert the rights of wheelchair users to those spaces, the social reality is that disabled people are still second-class citizens when it comes to mobility access. If the technological or other material solutions of universal design are to create the values that lie behind it, they need to include explorations of the social dynamics of design and living in inclusive spaces. As is picked up elsewhere in this book, this point importantly involves the participation of disabled people in shaping the priorities of design and research in this area.

SUMMARY

- Social geography is contributing much research to understanding what produces disability in contemporary societies.
- While relatively new, geographies of disability is an important body of work, asking us to evaluate just who is welcome in the social world.
- It examines disability alongside sources of marginalisation such as gender or race and ethnicity and, in doing so, highlights how the 'normal' human actor who navigates through different social spaces unhindered is not representative of the majority seeking to do so.

FURTHER READING

Chouinard, V., Hall, E., & Wilton, R. (eds.) (2010) *Towards Enabling Geographies: 'Disabled' Bodies and Minds in Society and Space.* Farnham, UK: Ashgate.

Gleeson, B. (1999) *Geographies of Disability.* London: Routledge.

Imrie, R. (1996) *Disability and the City.* London: Chapman.

Watson, N., Roulstone, A., & Thomas, C. (eds.) (2012) *Routledge Handbook of Disability Studies.* London: Routledge.

Age

Peter Hopkins and Rachel Pain

What is your age, and how does it influence your experience of the world around you? There has been less explicit attention paid to *age* in social geographies than to some of the other identities in this part of the book. This is perhaps surprising, as 'age' is an aspect of our identity that is almost guaranteed to involve major shifts as we move throughout our lives. Cindi Katz (2004) showed in her book *Growing up Global* that the meaning of childhood varied widely for young people living in New York City and Sudan, and yet related global processes had structured their experiences of these places. In past decades, social geographers might have argued that factors such as income are more pivotal in determining our life chances; yet, as Katz and a wealth of other researchers have demonstrated, age is not a fixed social category but has shifting meanings and influence across cultural and spatial contexts. It is therefore deeply embedded in space and place. This chapter provides an overview of research on age in social geographies. As we go on to discuss, however, there has been a very uneven representation of age groups, with most attention being given to the very young rather than to wider consideration of age itself. We briefly consider the geographical experiences of various age groups and outline an approach that seeks to integrate our comprehension of age across the lifecourse.

TEXT BOX 19.1 | Four Common Approaches to Understanding Age

Chronological age: the number of years a person has lived, or the length of time that has passed since they were born. This is the most basic form of age categorisation, common in the analysis of social surveys, for example. It might lead us to uniform (and, in reality, quite limited) descriptions of where people of different ages live and their use of different spaces.

Embodied age: the condition of the body, and the ways that bodily appearance is read by others as having markers of 'youthfulness', 'elderliness' and so on. This often underpins discrimination, especially against people whose bodies are read as old, as Western cultures celebrate visible signs and the maintenance of youthful bodies.

Social age: the social values, attitudes and beliefs that are held about people in particular age groups. This approach views age as largely socially constructed rather than a real or concrete set of characteristics. It considers that

many age-related barriers to certain spaces – such as those that restrict access to certain educational, employment and leisure spaces – are ageist and thus discriminatory rather than reflecting people's abilities and desires.

Being and becoming aged: the question of whether adulthood is viewed as a fully formed norm around which other age groups are analysed. Many children's geographers have worked from the premise that children should not simply be viewed as in process of *becoming* adults but are already social *beings* who are worthy of study in their own right. Indeed, people within any age group may have distinct lifeworlds, cultures, attachments and relations to particular spaces and places. As Kesby (2007) points out, perhaps it is more realistic to view both adults and children as beings and becoming simultaneously rather than continually seeking to establish differences between them.

First, we should define what we mean by 'age'. Our understandings and assumptions about age are always subjective, produced by the contexts that we work and live in. There are several key approaches that social geographers have applied over the years to the interrogation of age. Text Box 19.1 summarises four such approaches (and a fifth is detailed later in the chapter).

The approaches in Text Box 19.1 provide a way into investigating the key focus of the geographies of age literatures, which is that 'people have different access to and experiences of space and place on the basis of their age' (Pain et al., 2001). Social geographers have explored a wide range of spaces and places, from the marketing of retirement communities to interactions on the school playground, to transitions from school to university and work, to the sites of parenting. Below, we summarise some of the key areas of scholarship about children, youth and older age. Following this, we consider contemporary debates, which argue for a fifth approach to age known as the relational approach.

CHILDREN'S GEOGRAPHIES

The subfield known as children's geographies emerged in the 1990s and early 2000s (Matthews & Limb, 1999; Holloway & Valentine, 2000). Drawing on ideas from the field of childhood studies (e.g., James, Jenks & Prout, 2001), its key principles were that childhood is a social construction and that children have agency, should be listened to and should be actively involved in research and decision-making processes (Punch, 2003). Social geographies, with its interest in social divisions, and feminist geographies, with its focus on gender roles, the family and social inequalities, informed the development of this new field. Children's geographies has identified the ways society is adultist – that is, controlled and shaped by adults so that children are subject to regulation in and exclusion from certain spaces (e.g., Matthews, Limb & Taylor, 1999). Despite challenges to these dominant orthodoxies and frames of reference within children's geographies (e.g., Ansell, 2009; Horton & Kraftl, 2005; Vanderbeck, 2008), the field has remained rather consistent in terms of its conceptual focus over the last twenty years or so.

While it is a large field, its common focus is on the importance of space, place and time to the everyday lives of children, and especially the interrelation of constructions of childhood and understandings of place. Research has tended to emphasise children's agency as 'beings', not just 'becoming-adults' (see Text Box 19.2), and has focused on its expression in specific places, such as children's negotiations of classroom spaces or the journey to and from school (Hemming, 2007; Ross, 2007; see also Chapter 24 on education). Other approaches to studying childhood focus on children being out of place in specific contexts and how this is governed or controlled. For example, Van Blerk (2013) explores the impact of urban governance on street youth in Cape Town, while Beazley (2015) assesses the experiences of children who migrate independently for work in Southeast Asia.

In the last few years, children's geographies has continued to develop and explore the diverse and complex spaces of childhood. Some of the most important work here has explored issues and contexts often overlooked or not associated with childhood. For example, a notable set of developments includes children's connections

TEXT BOX 19.2 | Exercise: Mapping Your Childhood

Draw a 'map' of your childhood. How and where did you travel to school? Who were you with? Where did you 'play' and why? What places did you visit on a daily, weekly or fortnightly basis? Were you with other children there or people in different age groups? As you read the next section on youth geographies, think about how this changed for you as you became older. And when you reach the section of the chapter about old age, how much do you imagine that your map will change in future?

with political issues (e.g., Wood, 2012), such as their relationships in geopolitics (Benwell & Hopkins, 2016), borders (Spyrou & Christou, 2014) and debates about climate change (Stratford & Low, 2015).

YOUTH GEOGRAPHIES

Youth is the stage in the lifecourse between childhood and adulthood (Aitken, 2001; Skelton & Valentine, 1998; Hopkins, 2010). In the United Kingdom, it tends to be defined as those aged sixteen to twenty-five years, but this varies considerably across the globe (Evans, 2008). Young people are a very diverse constituent of the overall population and do not map neatly onto legal definitions and entitlements associated with age. Youth geographies is sometimes seen as part of children's geographies, using similar frameworks and approaches (see above). However, other researchers approach youth as distinct from childhood and draw on the field of youth studies for inspiration, where studies tend to focus on either youth transitions or youth subcultures. Thus, a number of social geographers have studied the multiple and complex transitions made towards adulthood, including transitions in relation to housing, education, employment and personal relationships (Bennett, 2000, Henderson et al., 2007; Holdsworth & Morgan, 2005). In contrast, youth subcultures research focuses on the specific styles, behaviours and interests of groups of young people, such as goths, emos, skaters and skinheads. Although youth transitions feature in social geographical work about age (e.g., Hopkins, 2006b; Van Blerk, 2008), there is relatively little about youth subcultures.

Again, social geographers draw attention to the spaces and times of youth and the specific practices associated with young people. For example, there is important work about young people, clubbing and the nighttime economy (e.g., Chatterton & Hollands, 2003), including critical reflections on gendered drinking cultures in various urban and rural contexts (e.g., Leyshon, 2008). Other research draws attention to young people's engagement in volunteering, including the Woodcraft Folk (S. Mills, 2014), international volunteering (Hopkins et al., 2011) and student volunteering (Holdsworth, 2010). Indeed, 'student geographies' has emerged as an important subfield over the decade (D. P. Smith, 2009), investigating diverse aspects of student experience relating to differing forms of mobility (Waters, 2017), purpose-built student accommodation (Kenna, 2011) and debates about student belonging and identity (Holton & Riley, 2016).

In a recent review, Smith and Mills (2019) observe that young people are more likely to be segregated in specific urban neighbourhoods, experience increased mobilities (regional and international) and have increasingly commodified lifestyles. They also note that there are more spaces available to, or created by, young people; that they are more often positioned as stakeholders in decision-making in contemporary Western societies; and that they are more politicised. These are key issues for the future study of young people in social geographies.

THE SPACES OF OLD AGE

When you think about older people (for the purposes of this discussion, people aged sixty and above), what, who and where do you think of? Are your perceptions shaped by the media, by your own experiences or by people you know? To what extent has your geographical education to date covered issues associated with later life? And how far do these various sources of knowledge either promote stereotypical views of older people (for example, viewing them as frail, vulnerable and needing support) or challenge these views?

A small body of work in social geographies has focused on people in the later years of life. Its modest size belies the urgency of social debates around the issue of ageing populations and the crises of economics, welfare and care facing many Western societies (Harper, 2005). However, positioning older people only as a demographic problem is an ageist trope that reflects the particular political economies of the West, where value comes primarily from participation in the workforce, which is regulated by barriers of chronological age (Harper & Laws, 1995).

While some older people are just as mobile as the young, for others those spaces close by become increasingly important as they age. Buffel, Phillipson and Scharf (2013) show the continuing significance of neighbourhoods to older people's experiences of inclusion and exclusion because of factors such as crime and safety, community change and the governance of local spaces. Other research has focused on the importance of the design of buildings, institutional and public spaces for 'successful' ageing. Such planning goals can enable social as well as environmental inclusion; for example, intergenerational spaces can bring benefits to younger people too (Rowles & Bernard, 2012).

Age-related segregation is also present at different scales. Oliver, Blythe and Roe (2018) compare two examples of age-segregated environments, retirement migration to Spain and older people's centres in London, to consider how older people negotiate sameness and difference in these environments. A related seam of work focuses on the meaning and representation of places that become associated with old age, such as retirement communities (Laws, 1995) and leisure spaces (Pain, Mowl & Talbot, 2000). Here, social geographers have identified the ageist processes and barriers to feelings of comfort and to participation that operate in particular sites. Importantly, one's sense of one's age is rarely fixed but shifts according to where we are and who we are with, as well as the broader social and political context (Laws, 1995).

Since these ideas developed in the 1990s and 2000s, the field of social geographies of old age has remained surprisingly static. Recent commentators have called for more conceptual development of our understanding of ageing spaces and for geographers studying old age to engage with the field of emotional geographies (Pain & Hopkins, 2010; see Chapter 12), theories of embodiment (Schwanen, Hardill & Lucas, 2012) and nonrepresentational theory (Horton & Kraftl, 2005;

Skinner, Cloutier & Andrews, 2015; see Chapters 2 and 11). Social geographers have also asked why it is that the further end of the life-course receives less attention than the worlds of young people (Pain et al., 2001; Skinner, Cloutier & Andrews, 2015), speculating that the explosion of research on children's geographies might mirror the societal value that we place on the young as opposed to the old.

RELATIONAL GEOGRAPHIES OF AGE

These seams of research continue on the social geographical experiences of particular age groups. How do they relate back to the four approaches to examining age that we introduced at the start of the chapter (Text Box 19.1)? You may have noticed that many of the examples we have given in the sections above would align with the second, third and fourth approaches listed there – that is, viewing age as embodied or socially constructed and, certainly in children's and youth geographies, seeing younger people as 'beings' in their own right. However, it is also noticeable that geographical research has been reluctant to dispense altogether with the first approach, the chronological approach to age, as this produces categories that are the basis of much research and analysis. Since the mid-2000s, a fifth approach has emerged as a popular framework for the study of age in social geography, which we have called the relational approach to age.

We have observed that there is a tendency to 'fetishise' the chronological margins of age; in other words, there is plenty of work in social geographies about children and young people, rather less on older people and very little on those in between (Hopkins & Pain, 2007). Yet specific age groups are not separate in real life but mutually constitutive. We propose three concepts that might help social geographers to achieve these more relational geographies of age: lifecourse, intergenerationality and intersectionality.

Lifecourse

This concept recognises that people tend not to experience fixed and stable life stages but, instead, negotiate lifecourses that are varied, dynamic and flexible. Hockey and James (2003: 5) describe this as viewing 'the passage of a lifetime less as the mechanical turning of a wheel and more as the unpredictable flow of river'. For example, Worth (2011) uses a lifecourse approach in 'life-mapping' the transitions to adulthood of visually impaired young people in the United Kingdom. In Evans' (2011) work on sibling-headed households in Tanzania and Uganda, she explores transitions into sibling care, changing family roles and young people's positioning within the community.

Intergenerationality

This means focusing on relations between generations: the idea that interactions between age groups shape our identities, regulation and

TEXT BOX 19.3 | Real-World Research: Young Scottish Christians and Intergenerational Relations

Our research explored intergenerational relations between young Scottish Christians and their parents/guardians or other adults and the impact of these on the religious identities, beliefs and practices of the young people (Hopkins et al., 2011). The research, involving in-depth interviews and focus groups, challenged the predominant previous assumption that religion is simply transmitted (or not) down the generations. We identified four modes of intergenerational relations present in this context:

- Correspondent: Religious beliefs are shared with the adults who have influenced young people (not always parents). Religious identities are likely to be similar but are never identical.

- Compliant: Some young people comply with parental religious traditions while showing an interest in other forms of religion or spirituality. They actively seek their own routes through traditional religions.

- Challenging: Some young people did not comply with their parents' or grandparents' religious traditions but asked questions, negotiated alternative positions and actively challenged the practices, values and beliefs of their elders.

- Conflicting: Struggle and conflict characterised some young people's accounts, where one or more of their parents showed no interest in their religiosity or were openly resistant. Differences in religious observance, decisions to switch affiliation and sectarianism were all sources of intergenerational conflict.

The research showed that young people's religiosity is shaped by multiple factors, only some of which involve intergenerationality (relations between generations). Other importance influences were intragenerational (relations within generations), in that religiosity is shaped by the other people, places and practices that young people encounter in their daily lives.

use of space. Since the mid-2000s, research has used an intergenerational approach (e.g., Vanderbeck & Worth, 2015). A useful example is Anna Tarrant's (2013) work, in which she explores the intergenerational caring practices of grandfathers in their interactions with grandchildren in North West England to understand these men's ageing masculinities. A further example from our own research is given in Text Box 19.3.

Intersectionality

More relational geographies of age require us to develop intersectional accounts. You can read more about intersectionality in Chapter 20, but the main point here in relation to age is to ask who else people are, other than people of a certain age, and how this alters the experience and meaning of their age. Being an affluent older woman, for example, might mean encountering an 'old age' that is quite different in nature and meaning than that of a less-affluent older woman.

Paradoxically, geographers tend to be adults in midlife themselves yet have tended to ignore this centre ground when analysing age (Hopkins & Pain, 2007). Vincent Del Casino is one of few to directly address this gap, arguing that midlife is 'the hegemonic elephant in the room. . . . Adult life, particularly those practices associated with people in the mid-life period, is *the* naturalised norm around which others, such as children and the elderly, are often constructed' (2009: 212). Del Casino makes the point that midlife is a life stage of concentration of the activities of both spheres of production and reproduction, with domestic and public spaces intersecting. Middle-aged adults are often heavily involved in both paid work and caregiving. Of course, the reality is almost always a more complex separation of age-segregated activities. Outside the West, there are different cultural expectations of childhood and old age (see Evans, 2011), and within the West youth–adult transitions are becoming less clear-cut due to changing patterns of housing, work, further study, relationships and so on. As Mike Kesby (2007) reminds us, old age, midlife and youth are performative, messy and always shifting. A relational approach to age opens up fruitful pathways for further research that might unpick these complexities, revealing how changes to age are experienced and lived across the lifecourse and the significance of the contexts and sites in which this occurs.

SUMMARY

- Age identities are always culturally and geographically specific and include longer-standing and more recent ideas of what it means to be a certain age. These identities are lived, reproduced, resisted and remade in specific spaces and places.

- Most research on age in social geographies has focused on both ends of the lifecourse – the very young and the very old. In particular, geographical research on children has proliferated at the expense of other age groups.

- Most recently, social geographers take a critical and relational approach to age itself. This approach focuses on the relations between age groups rather than studying them in isolation, highlights intersectionality and asks us to reflect on changing lifecourses in various geographical contexts rather than in fixed categories of age.

FURTHER READING

Ansell, N. (2009) Childhood and the politics of scale: Descaling children's geographies? *Progress in Human Geography*, 22(2): 190–209.

Harper, S. (2005) *Ageing Societies*. London: Hodder.

Hopkins, P. (2010) *Young People, Place and Identity*. London: Routledge.

Hopkins, P., & Pain, R. (2007) Geographies of age: Thinking relationally. *Area*, 39(3): 287–94.

Horschelmann, K., & Van Blerk, L. (2011) *Children, Youth and the City*. London: Routledge.

Intersectionality

Alessandro Boussalem, Nathar Iqbal and Peter Hopkins

The previous chapters in this part of the book have looked at specific social divisions associated with race, religion, class, gender, sexualities, disability and age (see Chapters 13–19). Understanding the complexity of specific social divisions, the exclusionary processes that make these matter (such as those associated with racism, homophobia and sexism) and the ways that these vary across space together constitute one of the most significant challenges that social geographers address in their work. This chapter introduces the concept of intersectionality to show how these processes of exclusion and domination are not isolated from each other: they intersect and interact in complex ways. Sexism, for example, often does not take place in isolation from, say, racism, homophobia or class discrimination. The concept of intersectionality is useful in allowing social geographers to recognise and analyse such interactions. Rather than viewing sexism, racism, homophobia or classism as separate and independent processes, intersectionality involves understanding that these specific forms of discrimination alter as they interact with each other.

In this sense, intersectionality provides a way of understanding the complexity of social relations in particular places at different times. The development of intersectionality is often attributed to the socio-legal scholar Kimberlé Crenshaw

(1989), who applied it to the discriminatory labour market experiences of Black women in the United States. Legislation about gender was seen to protect White women, while that about race was seen to protect Black men; as such, Black women were excluded from protection. Such one-dimensional approaches to identity and power relations were criticised by Crenshaw, who recognised that all our lives are shaped by interdependent and multiple axes of social difference, such as race and ethnicity, gender, sexuality and class (Collins, 1990; Crenshaw, 1991). The intersection of social divisions has the potential to change how each category is experienced and negotiated. This is important, particularly when it comes to exploring the strategies of political action that can counter discrimination.

In addition to defining intersectionality as a way of understanding complex social relations, it is important to highlight what intersectionality is not. Intersectionality is not only about multiple identities, and it is not a simple way of solving problems connected to equality and diversity. It is not merely connected to oppression and marginalisation, as it is also applied to understandings of domination, such as those associated with masculinity, Whiteness and heterosexuality. Intersectionality is useful as it encourages us to focus on institutional structures and exclusions rather than simply on individuals. It can also help us to improve our research, as it inspires us to listen carefully to others, to examine our own privileges and to ask questions about who is excluded or adversely affected by new initiatives and what can be done to challenge this.

While a reflection on the construction of various identities is certainly an important part of many intersectional analyses by social geographers to date, intersectionality itself is much more than this. To help appreciate the complexity of intersectionality, Collins and Bilge (2016) identified the six key principles that underlie it: social inequality, power, relationality, social context, complexity and social justice (see Table 20.1).

CHARTING THE HISTORY AND ORIGIN OF INTERSECTIONALITY

Intersectionality originates in Black feminist activism and academic scholarship. While the concept of intersectionality has been an important expression of research and activism oriented towards social justice, some critics now suggest that its popularity has led to it being 'Whitened' and depoliticised (Bilge, 2013; Hopkins, 2017). By providing a short overview of the historical contours of intersectionality, we argue for more sensitive scholarship that acknowledges the histories and legacies of Black activism and feminism.

Intersectional thought manifested long before Crenshaw coined the term in the late 1980s; it can be seen in both early Black activism movements and Black academic feminism itself. Evidence of social and political struggles that employ intersectional thinking goes back to the nineteenth century. At a women's rights convention in Ohio in

TABLE 20.1	Key Principles Underlying Intersectionality (Collins & Bilge, 2016)
Social inequality	An intersectional study sees social inequalities as comprising multiple interlocking factors rather than being related to only race or gender or class, for example.
Power	Intersectionality is about how the mutual constitution of inequalities and power relations can be analysed via specific intersections as well as in relation to domains of power (such as structural, interpersonal, disciplinary and cultural).
Relationality	Relationality between and within different domains of power – such as race, class and gender – is important. This focuses attentions on the interconnections between categories, and a 'both/and' frame of reference, rather than binary thinking.
Social context	Intersectionality produces social inequalities in particular political, institutional or intellectual contexts, and attending to these contexts is important.
Complexity	The principles of social inequality, power, relationality and social context are all interconnected, meaning that there is an explicit complexity to intersectional analyses.
Social justice	Ideas of social justice are fundamental to much work about intersectionality, given the attention to social inequality and the promotion of fairness.

1851, Sojourner Truth, an enslaved Black woman, spoke out against the apparent stability of the category 'womanhood' as it was represented in women's struggles and highlighted the routinised forms of oppression that she faced (Collins, 1990). Cooper (1988: 134) noted that women of colour faced interconnecting obstacles associated with race and gender, suggesting that they were 'an unknown or an unacknowledged factor in both'. These examples show that 'the *do*-ing of intersectionality has a far longer history' (Mollett & Faria, 2018: 567) than is generally suggested, and that lived experiences were an elemental foundation of the Black feminist epistemologies that underpinned Crenshaw's contributions (1989, 1991).

Centring the lived experiences of intersecting oppressions and their historical, structural and political contexts has been key to the Black feminist movement (Combahee River Collective, 1982/2019). Black feminism has sought not only to highlight the suppression of Black women in the United States but also to reflect upon their absence from mainstream academic feminism and the related forms of knowledge produced, which seldom acknowledged the particularities of Black women's issues (Davis, 1981; hooks, 1981).

The spread of this idea of intersectionality into diverse academic disciplines – including social geographies – has created challenges. A number of analyses that use an intersectional framework have been criticised for moving away from the origins of intersectionality in Black feminist critique, particularly for relegating the category of race (Hopkins, 2017). It is therefore important to acknowledge the complex origins of intersectional thought, which has a history beyond its 'naming' and its travels within social science research today (Hancock, 2016), and this includes its use in social geographies.

INTERSECTIONALITY AND COMPLEXITY

Complexity is a central aspect of any intersectional analysis; the ways various elements interlock must be taken into account. Critics of intersectionality, including those who see it merely as a way of observing and analysing multiple identities, often fail to recognise this complexity. An analysis that takes complexity seriously would include the key principles outlined in Table 20.1, in addition to other factors that are found to be shaping the specific case studies being examined. Examples from our research with LGBTQ Muslims in Belgium and the United Kingdom demonstrate the various power dynamics, intra- and intergroup social relations and the issues pertaining to social context that emerge when applying an intersectional framework (Text Box 20.1).

TEXT BOX 20.1	Real-World Research: Lived Intersectionality and LGBTQ Muslims in Belgium and the United Kingdom

Alessandro and Nathar have applied an intersectional lens to their analysis of the lived experiences of LGBTQ Muslims in Belgium (see Figure 20.1) and the United Kingdom, respectively. Drawing from data collected through interviews with LGBTQ Muslims, an intersectional lens allows us to observe the complexities that shape the ways individuals experience the different spaces they move through, as well as their relations with different groups they encounter in their daily lives. LGBTQ Muslims living in Europe can often experience specific kinds of oppression, resulting from the interlocking of Islamophobia, racism and homo/bi/transphobia. None of these systems of power alone can explain the specific lived experiences of LGBTQ Muslim people living in Europe.

Across our interviews, we often heard participants recounting episodes in which they felt that their interactions with White non-Muslim members of the LGBTQ community revealed the presence of racist and Islamophobic stereotypes and prejudices. One of the spaces where racist and Islamophobic remarks are common is the dating apps targeted at gay and bisexual men. When talking about his experiences on Grindr and Planet-Romeo, two popular dating apps, in Brussels,

Youness, a twenty-six-year-old gay man from a Moroccan background, says, 'I've already had for example people calling me "dirty Arab". Or "yet another Arab". . . . But, on the other hand, there is, I think, in Belgium . . . In Brussels, they love Arabs. You see? There's this thing of the Belgian guy who loves Moroccans'. Many of the gay and bisexual men that were interviewed in Brussels had similar experiences. The reactions of the people that they were chatting with often seemed to oscillate between open racist remarks and statements that betray a certain (racialised) exoticisation of the bodies of Arab men. This exoticisation shows how racism and stereotypes about gender and sexuality work together in producing the specific oppression that some gay and bisexual Arab men face in their daily lives. Hamid, a twenty-five-year-old gay man from a Tunisian/Indian background, says,

> So . . . I felt discriminated in . . . some bars. . . . Because I'm an Arab, I represent the . . . fantasy of an Arab? You know? So, like, people seem to think that whenever I want to have sex with someone . . . they always think I'm like a violent person, and like sex is always . . . that kind of stuff. So, yeah, that's for me discrimination. And making

me an object of . . . violent sex, because I'm an Arab, is not acceptable for me.

Our participants also reported fears of being rejected in their communities of origin because of being LGBTQ, or more generally for not conforming to the norms that shape social relations in such groups. Barwaqo is a twenty-eight-year-old Somali Djiboutian lesbian woman living in Brussels. When describing the building where she lives, she says, 'Inside the building you have to be quiet about being gay. Because there is a lot people from immigrant background, from . . . you know, religion. They're very religious, so . . . So, in order not to shock them, you have to be very quiet . . . about your sexuality'. She then goes on to explain that people who are White or not from a migratory background do not need to worry in the same way: 'In the case of white people, they tolerate it more. I think that they tolerate it more because white people are . . . Let's say that it's OK for a white person to be gay, inside. . . . Like, if you ask an immigrant person to draw you someone that is gay, it's always going to be white. Never a person of colour'.

Migrant non-White communities are not the only ones that often imagine LGBTQ people to be White. In many of their interactions,

participants felt that they were neither part of migrant Muslim communities nor LGBTQ communities. Their identity as LGBTQ Muslims was met with surprise, shock or disbelief. According to Siddique, a twenty-six-year-old gay man from North London, 'You're asked so many questions . . . people are shocked to find that you can be gay and Muslim, Asian. . . . I find that people are almost suspicious that you can want to be gay and Muslim and not necessarily see these at odds with one another'. Siddique's account demonstrates how dominant perceptions of Muslim, ethnic minority and nonheterosexual identities see these as mutually exclusive. However, for many of the participants in both studies, Islam could often be a source of strength; though they may have initially grappled with heteronormative religious discourses of sexuality, they forged reflexive adoptions and adaptations of Islam that maintained their sense of religiosity.

These examples show how the everyday experiences of LGBTQ Muslims cannot be understood through a single-lens analysis that only focuses on one category at a time. Participants' lives are shaped in complex ways by Islamophobia, racism and homo/bi/transphobia; these interact to produce specific experiences that transcend simple understandings of racism and homophobia.

FIGURE 20.1

Mural art painted by Ralf König, inaugurated in celebration of Brussels Pride 2015, in collaboration with the network of LGBTQ organisations RainbowHouse Brussels. (Credit: Alessandro Boussalem)

INTERSECTIONALITY AND POWER

According to Collins and Bilge (2016), a concept that is central to intersectional theories, analyses and activism is that of power. Power operates *along* different yet interlocking axes – for instance, racism, sexism, Islamophobia, homo/bi/transphobia (see Figure 20.1) – and *across* different yet overlapping domains. By 'domains of power' (Collins & Bilge, 2016: 7), we mean the different roles that power plays in society and the different layers of social life in which we can observe its operation. Here power means the interpersonal relations between individuals and groups (the interpersonal domain); the rules that govern such relations, which are applied differently to different people (the disciplinary domain); the cultural representations and ideas about different groups of people (the cultural domain); and the way that society is organised to the benefit of some and the disadvantage of others (the structural domain) (Collins & Bilge, 2016: 7–13). As social geographers, we have an especial interest in attending to the interplay of systems of power across these various domains in order to observe the emergence of intersectional political projects and collective identities.

For example, Gökarıksel and Smith (2017) focus on the women's demonstrations organised across the United States after Donald Trump's election as president and the symbols that were deployed to protest against the president's sexist, racist and Islamophobic rhetoric. Gökarıksel and Smith (2017) argue that the use of these symbols during the protests – the image of a woman wearing a *hijab* on a stars-and-stripes background and the wearing of 'pink pussy' hats – shows the extent to which work is still needed to establish an intersectional framework for political action and change in American mainstream feminism. They suggest that the juxtaposition of the image of a Muslim woman wearing a *hijab* inscribed with the national flag reinforces a nationalist narrative, hiding the complexities and contradictions that shape the relationship between US foreign and internal policies and Muslim communities. Through the deployment of this image, 'we see erasure of the religious significance of the headscarf and an insistence on enveloping difference *within* the nation rather than the much more difficult task of challenging exclusionary and violent politics of nation-states' (Gökarıksel & Smith, 2017: 634). The pink pussy hat, worn in protest against Trump's use of sexist expressions, works to exclude from this counternarrative the experiences of sexual violence and abuse lived by women of colour and transwomen. The hat suggests a 'pink vagina' to be a marker of womanhood, excluding all those women who do not see their bodies and experiences as represented by such a symbol.

This example allows us to see how different systems of power – in this case sexism, racism, Islamophobia and transphobia – interlock to produce difference among the individuals and groups that feel alienated by Trump's words and actions. These categories of power, in turn, work across various domains. The most intuitively recognisable, in this case, is probably the one that Collins and Bilge (2016) call 'cultural domain'.

It is on the cultural representations of womanhood, and Muslim womanhood, that Gökarıksel and Smith (2017) focus their analysis. This cultural use of images and symbols also speaks of the interpersonal and structural power relations at work in the organisation of such demonstrations. Relations between White cis-gender women and other protesting groups of women are mediated and shaped by the privileges and advantages that the first enjoy. Rather than seeing the issues and debates that emerge from the use of this partial and exclusive symbolic representation as an insurmountable obstacle, Gökarıksel and Smith (2017) suggest that it is a fundamental moment in which to rethink and rebuild counternarratives to a sexist, racist, Islamophobic and nationalist presidential discourse. This can be done only by embracing difference and using it as a tool to disrupt the power systems at work in society – in other words, by finding 'in these uncomfortable conversations and spaces the possibility of dismantling the structures of power, willful ignorance, and feigned innocence that brought us to our current political moment' (Gökarıksel & Smith, 2017: 640).

This example also shows that intersectionality cannot be understood solely as a theoretical concept. Intersectionality is both a way of theorising social relations and a means of devising political actions and strategies towards social change. The two fields, theory and praxis, feed into each other in advancing knowledge on the intersecting ways axes of power shape social worlds.

INTERSECTIONALITY AND SOCIAL CONTEXT

Social context is another fundamental concept in intersectional analyses. In this sense, intersectionality requires us to look at the specific institutional, political and cultural context in which various axes of power interact in producing specific experiences. This focus on the social contexts, places and locations in which people live is, of course, close to the heart of social geographies (see Chapter 1). Indeed, the origins of the concept of intersectionality lie within ethnically segregated neighbourhoods in US cities. An intersectional analysis should always be sensitive to the multiple roles that social context can play, whether the contexts in questions are specific neighbourhoods and communities, political movements or transformations or other local–global issues.

Social geographers have been employing intersectional thinking since the 1990s. For example, Kobayashi and Peake (1994) explored the connections between race and gender; Jackson (1994) discussed gender, sexuality, race and the body; and Ruddick (1996) investigated the intersections between class, race and gender. More recently, Valentine (2007) highlighted the need to employ the concept of intersectionality more frequently in feminist geographies. Peake (2010) provided a useful set of insights into the intersections of race, gender and sexuality, and others have been exploring the intersections of youth with gender, race and religion (e.g., Hopkins, 2007c; Nayak,

2006b). More recent work has also explored the intersections of masculinities, race, ethnicity and Black geographies (e.g., Hopkins & Noble, 2009; Shabazz, 2015).

One example of intersectionality being used in a way that is attentive to social context can be found in Anthias' (2001) work with Greek Cypriot young people who were born in the United Kingdom. Anthias (2001) talks about 'narratives of location' as a way of explaining the stories people tell about the categories that we place ourselves in, such as those of gender, race and class. These stories are about social context, as they are placed in time and space. Narratives of location are also about dislocation, as often people identify in ways that are about what they are not rather than what they are. Anthias proposes the idea of 'translocational positionality', where translocational refers to the multiple places that people may identify with (particularly migrants) and positionality as encompassing an individual's social identifications and their lived practices.

In another example, Mollett (2017) uses the term 'postcolonial intersectionality' to consider the diverse and ongoing forms of power and inequality that have their origins and remain embedded in the experience of White supremacy and European colonialism. Arguing that intersectionality has always been a deeply spatial concept, Mollett and Faria (2018) point out that interlocking systems of racism, patriarchy and heteronormativity constitute a spatial formation. Furthermore, challenging the assumption that intersectionality is only about Black women in the United States, they point out that the concept travels and can be applied in different contexts. They utilise it through consideration of what they refer to as 'the power of colonial past-presents in and through the Global South' (Mollett & Faria, 2018: 571), developing the term 'postcolonial intersectionality', which is

> a concept that moves beyond US based racial and gender hierarchies to acknowledge the way patriarchy and racialized processes (including whiteness) are consistently bound up in national and international development practice. This approach compels us to talk about the power of race and not just the difference of race. (Mollett & Faria, 2013: 117)

They use this framework to explore privilege and oppression in the lives and land tenure issues negotiated by Miskito women, an Indigenous ethnic group in Honduras. Employing postcolonial intersectionality enables the decentring of Whiteness and acknowledgement of the multiple spaces of violence in processes of development and the ways such spaces are imbued with inequalities. This concept also assists in challenging ideas about racial equality among communities in Latin America and the rejection of European racism, and it reminds us of the significance of caste in South Asia. Overall, then, postcolonial intersectionality is a very useful tool for attending to the significance of social context.

SUMMARY

- Intersectionality can be defined as a way of understanding the complexity of social relations in particular places at different times.
- Intersectionality has its origins in Black feminist scholarship and social justice movements, and it is important to acknowledge these origins when using it in other contexts.
- Intersectionality is not simply about multiple identities. There are six key principles that underlie any intersectional project: social inequality, power, relationality, social context, complexity and social justice.
- Intersectionality is a key concept in social geographies and can be applied to a range of socio-spatial issues.

FURTHER READING

Collins, P. H., & Bilge, S. (2016) *Intersectionality*. Cambridge: Polity Press.

Crenshaw, K. (1989) Demarginalizing the intersections of race and sex: A black feminist critique of antidiscrimination doctrine, feminist theory and antiracist politics. *University of Chicago Legal Forum*, 1: 139–67.

Hopkins, P. (2019) Social geography I: Intersectionality. *Progress in Human Geography*. doi: https://doi.org/10.1177/0309132517743677

ISSUES

A

B

C

D

PART

PART

PART

PART

Housing

Julia Heslop and Helen Jarvis

Housing is a key issue for social justice in society. If people were housed on the basis of what is fair or just, we would not be witnessing homeless rough sleeping; overcrowded, unsanitary and unsafe accommodation; or housing costs that are so high, relative to income, that some people must choose between buying food or paying rent. This suggests that we must explain how some people and areas are 'kept behind', with reference to past and present social and spatial structures of inequality.

The term 'housing' combines three interrelated attributes: the basic needs of shelter and capacity for survival, a property-based resource for speculative wealth creation and a source of emotional attachment and connection to place. Social geographers contribute to all three strands by engaging with housing as an essentially *interdisciplinary* field of concern. Exploring 'where' and 'how' people live alongside neighbours and their immediate environment begins with the premise that multiple meanings cannot be reduced to a housing 'industry' producing units of housing or to residents consuming a commodity, or a title or 'right' to legal occupation. The holistic approach adopted in much of the social geography literature can be distinguished from vocational housing studies in which technical emphasis is placed on socio-legal or administrative issues of planning and policy implementation.

As Perkins and Thorns (2011: 74) observe, 'we all live somewhere, and a place to live allows us to connect with people, the wider community and natural environment, and for many of the world's people, the source of their livelihood'. Yet, very often, relationships between housing, employment, welfare, family support and community cohesion are underdeveloped or fragmented in the literature. This is because houses are typically treated by states and markets as commodities to be traded rather than spaces and places for living. Similarly, debates on living environments frequently neglect housing inequality as a vital piece in the puzzle of poor mental health, low social mobility, loneliness and economic exclusion. As we highlight in this chapter (see also Chapter 1, and Chapter 7 on justice), these are key social justice concerns in relation to housing, but they have different spatial manifestations.

In this chapter, we focus on 'all that is solid' in the fixed attributes of dwelling and permanent address (to paraphrase Dorling, 2014b) to emphasise the social justice significance of 'location' (status, stigma, neighbourliness and isolation) and material standards of living (space, access, comfort, health and cost). In so doing, we begin by outlining the connection between housing, geography and social justice to highlight how housing provision has transformed in the United Kingdom over the past century. We then discuss crisis discourses of housing, highlighting the role that housing plays both in the household and in the macroeconomy, and discuss how housing connects to livelihoods and life transitions. Finally, we offer a global perspective on housing through the lens of housing informality. While we focus primarily on the UK housing context, we offer secondary international examples to highlight how housing differently links to issues of social justice, culture and economy around the world. Furthermore, while we offer a historical analysis of housing transformations, particularly in relation to the development and residualisation of social housing policy in the United Kingdom, we bring this up to date by examining present-day housing crises and contemporary alternatives to market- and state-delivered housing.

Before considering the social and structural anatomy of housing inequality in more detail, we need to define some key terms and concepts that are used widely in housing literature and debate (see Text Box 21.1).

HOUSING GEOGRAPHIES OF SOCIAL JUSTICE

The size, type, condition, tenure and sense of permanence of housing represent significant markers of social stratification in all parts of the world. Yet, in advanced capital economies, it is a well-established cliché that 'real estate' (residential property value) relies on three factors: 'location, location, location'. This helps to explain the apparent anomaly that a studio apartment in a high-demand 'hotspot' (such

TEXT BOX 21.1 | Selected Key Terms and Concepts

Eviction: the action (usually legal, but also at times physically violent or emotionally threatening) of forcing someone to move out of a property. Tenants typically have less power than landlords, whereby eviction will result from a tenant falling behind on their rent or a landlord choosing to sell up, perhaps to realise profit from neighbourhood gentrification.

Gentrification: a process of area upgrade whereby the superior purchasing power of one social class overwhelms and displaces another. Hallmark characteristics include the upgrading of vintage property and the proliferation of coffee shops, wine bars and pricey independent boutiques. Historically, economic geographers have tended to offer 'demand-side' accounts of new capital attracted to undervalued land, resulting in upgrading and profit from the so-called rent gap. Social and cultural geographers have tended to emphasise 'supply-side' accounts of shifting lifestyle and habits. The process of gentrification is now so generalised that attention has turned to the experience and outcome of those who are displaced (Lees et al., 2013).

Homelessness: the circumstance in which people do not have access to a permanent dwelling. Homelessness is both visible (rough sleeping) and hidden (sofa surfing: sleeping on a friend/family member's floor). The causes of homelessness include eviction and a lack of affordable or social housing, as well as reasons of substance addiction, family breakdown, welfare state cutbacks for people who are unemployed or service-dependent, deinstitutionalisation of psychiatric patients, and people in states of transition, such as ex–service personnel or prison leavers, those migrating for work and those seeking asylum or refugees fleeing from war.

Tenure: the legal status and financial arrangements by which residents occupy a house or apartment. The etymology of the word is 'to hold' from the Latin *tenere*. The most common way of 'holding' property is ownership (outright or through a long-loan 'mortgage') or renting (tenants pay rent to the owner as landlord). Renting is further differentiated by private (landlord) and public (local government or nonprofit housing association) arrangements and by short-term contracts (whereby rents can increase annually) and secure tenancy. Underpinning these multiple ways of holding and occupying property are powerful social norms of privacy, individualism and materialism that stand in opposition to alternative ideas of communality (sharing) and cooperation.

as London, England, or Sydney, Australia) costs more to buy or rent than a more substantial family house in a less desirable, less populated area. This is another way of describing the concentration and distribution of individuals and families according to a hierarchy or 'ladder' of income, wealth and power.

Wealth is an important function (or dysfunction) of market-led economies where home ownership is promoted over other tenures, whether through fiscal policy (tax benefits) or the language of individualism, 'choice' and social status (see Chapter 22 on wealth and poverty). Housing wealth serves to reinforce increasingly unequal material standards of living between owners and tenants, within and between generations. This has led to the popular impression of the family home functioning like an ATM wealth dispenser, or the 'bank of mum and dad', to be drawn down in times of ill health or retirement, to support adult offspring through education or to pay for end-of-life personal care (Searle & Smith, 2010). This is why it is important to consider housing, jobs and wealth as interconnected spatial systems, while also recognising that housing and employment opportunities rarely intersect seamlessly in one place.

Socially stratified and segregated housing markets are largely determined by historical patterns of land ownership and the political economy of state intervention, whether this is to support people (by subsidising their rent) or places (by building social housing or undertaking area-based regeneration) or both. State interventions are remarkably uneven between national welfare regimes. In the United States, less than 1 per cent of households live in social rented housing, and the few inner city 'projects' built in the 1960s are widely stigmatised as 'housing of last resort' (Pacione, 2009). By contrast, the UK government launched a major programme of building 'homes fit for heroes' after the First and Second World Wars, providing high-quality, general-needs social rented housing in new towns and 'garden suburbs'.

The profile of housing tenure has changed dramatically in the United Kingdom since 1918, whereby social renting initially replaced private renting, through slum clearance, followed by the expansion of owner occupation as the 'tenure of choice'. In 1918, when there was little by way of state welfare provision, 70 per cent of households in England rented from private landlords. By 1981, private renters accounted for barely 10 per cent of households, while owner-occupiers accounted for 60 per cent and social renters 30 per cent of all households. When Prime Minister Margaret Thatcher introduced legislation in 1979 allowing local authority tenants (and, later, housing associations) the 'right to buy' their home at a considerable discount, some tenants benefited from occupying an attractive asset; yet others lived in property that no one would want to buy. Between 1980 and 1990, a million of the best-quality council houses were sold through right-to-buy legislation. This began a process of 'residualisation' that continues today. By the time of the financial crisis in 2008, owner occupation had reached a peak in most advanced economies (accounting for 70 per cent in England). Yet, since this time, there has been a growth of private rental housing on short-term contracts. This growth reflects an affordability crisis, as well as the difficulty for those on low incomes to access mortgage finance (see Text Box 21.2). This pattern differs from that in other European countries. For example, in Germany over 50 per cent of the population rents, and rental figures are tightly controlled and unlimited contracts are standard.

HOUSING AND THE CRISIS DISCOURSE

History tells us that housing has always been in a state of crisis around the world. Structurally, the stock of accommodation will constantly fall short of need, whether in absolute numbers or in

TEXT BOX 21.2 | Housing Inequality, Stigma and Austerity

The human cost of housing poverty was first brought to public and political attention in the 1966 television play *Cathy Come Home*, directed by Ken Loach. A quarter of Britain's population tuned in to be confronted with evidence of deep-rooted squalor and deprivation – conditions that should have improved, in line with the founding ideals of the welfare state.

Full of youthful optimism, Cathy moves to London, where she meets and marries Reg. When Cathy is pregnant with their first child, Reg is injured in an accident at work. Reg loses his job and they can no longer afford the rent, and so begins the family's slippery descent towards homelessness. Cathy and the children end up in a hostel, while Reg is left to fend for himself. In the final, heartrending scenes, Cathy's children are wrenched from her and placed in local authority care. The viewing public was outraged that this could happen in modern Britain (Jarvis, Cloke & Kantor, 2009: 194): the charity Shelter was founded in the same year to help to eradicate the injustices portrayed.

More recently, the stigma associated with social housing was laid bare in the aftermath of the Grenfell Tower fire tragedy. In June 2017, a fire blazed through a twenty-four-storey social housing block in London, causing seventy-two deaths (mainly people from ethnic minority groups). The Grenfell Tower

Inquiry began in September 2017 to investigate the causes and response to the fire. The rapid spread of the fire has been attributed to the plastic cladding on the outside of the building and the failure to install a sprinkler system, as well as ongoing safety issues (such as problems with fire doors and the smoke venting system). Occupying a site in the Royal Borough of Kensington and Chelsea (one of the wealthiest local authorities in the country, where the gap between rich and poor is the highest in England), Grenfell has come to signify the damaging effects of austerity and deregulation of the building industry (MacLeod, 2018). Some commentators suggested that this amounted to 'social murder' (Chakrabortty, 2017).

In the aftermath of the Grenfell Tower tragedy, and as a result of growing media attention with regard to the housing and homelessness crisis, public attitudes have begun to see housing more sympathetically as a basic human right (as they did previously, after *Cathy Come Home*). Far more people are aware of the problems linking housing, inequality, austerity, gentrification and homelessness today. This has led to the founding of a number of housing activist groups such as the Radical Housing Network, which aims to coordinate groups fighting for housing justice and campaigns to reverse a culture of indifference and to make social housing dignified and not second rate.

size, condition and location. The social history and geography of housing is a story of unresolved inequality: increasing numbers of homeless people, the perpetuation of substandard dwellings or insecure occupation and a general retreat of governments from responsibility. However, the crisis discourse surrounding housing cannot be simplified – it varies both spatially and socially and is real, felt and lived (such as homelessness) as well as being socially and politically constructed (through, for example, the media, as well as government policy).

In *The Housing Question* (1872/1997), Engels (cofounder of modern communism alongside Karl Marx) discussed how to respond to the poor housing conditions of workers in Western Europe. But, for Engels, it was not housing per se that was in crisis; instead, he believed that the housing crisis coincided with an overarching crisis of capitalism, which is then physically manifest in the urban environment through cyclic processes of decay, boom and bust (a point later reiterated through Neil Smith's [1987] work on rent gap theory). As a result, housing is just one section of a much more pervasive crisis-prone capitalist system (Hodkinson, 2012). While much of Engels' work still resonates today, housing is arguably much more central to class (and gendered) struggles in contemporary capitalism (Saegert, 2016). Furthermore, housing is not merely shelter; it also acts as a pension, an inheritance, collateral and an investment commodity.

Housing's role as an economic asset can be seen most distinctively through its role in the 2008 economic crisis. The overextension of mortgage finance, mortgage-backed securities and mortgage deregulation, beginning in the 1980s, created a subprime mortgage crisis in the United States in 2007. When house prices started to decline and borrowers could not sell their houses at a higher price (what is termed 'negative equity'), they were forced to default. In some cases, the banks repossessed homes, which was seen most prominently in Spain and the United States. But the financial crisis, which began in the US subprime mortgage market, rippled out around the world into the real economy, causing a decline of economic outputs and rising unemployment, which was dealt with in most Western countries through austerity policies. Some authors state that austerity has been 'used' in order to open up new avenues for regressive forms of housing commodification, privatisation, deregulation and financialisation (Marcuse & Madden, 2016). However, taking a longer view, housing financialisation has a much longer history and is connected to the deregulation of banks, allowing those who could least afford it to own their own homes (Malpass, 2005), creating precarious home ownership and a rise in the private rental sector in the United Kingdom.

HOUSING AND LIFE TRANSITIONS

Conventionally, housing is understood to be fundamentally linked to demography though a relationship between the dwelling stock (number of houses in a defined area) and the number of people or households to be housed. This relationship has changed in recent years, not least because of shrinking household size (more people living alone, fewer children, relationship breakdown). Separate households typically require separate accommodation. This explains why household demand for housing outstrips population growth. People are increasingly likely to live alone at both ends of the age scale. Different stages of life are typically associated with different types of housing, whereby a 'housing career' appears to coincide with personal biography and milestone events, such as leaving the parental home, marriage and family, job relocation, retirement and older age. Young singles may gravitate to city-centre apartments, and middle-class families may graduate to suburban housing with access to green spaces and 'good' schools, while older people living alone may leave a cherished family home because it becomes too difficult to manage (see Forrest & Yip, 2012).

The picture that is often used, of housing as a ladder to climb, encourages us to think about changing circumstances over the lifecourse, of the intersections of personal biography and housing 'career'. Yet it is also the case that this metaphor is too simplistic, as it appears to assume that the only way is up. We saw above that a more accurate way to visualise entry and exit from precarious housing would be a game of snakes and ladders. Housing careers are socially constructed, in the sense that a 'normal' housing career is bound up with expectations of partnering and parenting and accumulating wealth over the lifecourse (see Chapter 19 on age).

INFORMAL HOUSING IN THE GLOBAL SOUTH

While the private house-building sector reigns supreme in the Global North and is an increasingly powerful government lobby,

TEXT BOX 21.3 | Real-World Theory: Degrowth

Degrowth is an academic and political movement that offers a critique of economic growth as a social objective and the conversion of social processes into commodities with a monetary value (D'Alisa, Demaria & Kallis, 2014). It seeks a radical transformation of the capitalist system so that, instead of modifying existing ways of living (building smaller homes or insulating existing stock to reduce energy consumption) or making tweaks to the economic system, societies use fewer natural resources and organise and live differently (see also Chapter 33). The emphasis is on *different*, not just *less*. In so doing, it challenges norms of behaviour and habits of consumption.

For housing, this may offer new opportunities for living differently and less wastefully through processes of cooperation, mutualism and 'purposeful sharing' (Jarvis, 2017). This is illustrated in Text Box 21.4 in the way that grassroots community-led housing (including

collaborative forms of cohousing) are practising degrowth to a varying extent. Collaborative housing arrangements aim to use fewer resources and are grounded in forms of social conviviality. In practice, this may take the form of shared forms of production, such as energy, food and employment; consumption, such as car-pooling and facility sharing; and caring, such as communal caring activities for older people or children. This thinking can be extended into the production of homes that are more conducive to change over time, as families change and grow, through processes of flexibility and adaptability (see Till, 2014). This may also involve participatory processes of design and building that create social networks, opportunities for learning and education and that make use of reused, reclaimed or locally sourced materials (see Nelson & Schneider, 2019).

TEXT BOX 21.4 | Community-Led Housing

As mainstream housing methods fail to cater for those who wish to live more communally, or for those on low incomes who cannot access the social housing sector, there is more interest in alternative approaches to housing such as community-led housing (CLH). CLH broadly refers to housing that is designed and managed by local people to meet the needs of the community, as opposed to housing for private profit. Today this accounts for just 1 per cent of UK homes, compared with 18 per cent in Sweden and 15 per cent in Norway (Commission on Co-operative and Mutual Housing, 2009). Despite this, it is a diverse and growing sector which incorporates many different financial and governance structures, property tenures, processes and outcomes, from community land trusts to self-help housing, cohousing, self-build and cooperatives. Accounts of CLH are diverse, foregrounding issues such as choice and control in housing, individual and community well-being, ecological sustainability, problems of 'failing' housing markets and housing affordability. CLH also allows for more low-impact, low-maintenance housing design and the creation of shared spaces for everyday interaction, which are able to open up all sorts of additional community-building potential – with food-growing spaces, shared meals and cultural diversity.

CLH has opened new possibilities for what a house is and could be, pushing back against the concept of housing as a mere product or asset, as a space to live in, and instead reconceptualising it as something that encompasses wider aspects of dwelling – such as building, managing and caring for homes. By understanding housing as a process, there is potential to challenge the commodification and financialisation of housing, restating it as a basic human right and a key social justice concern.

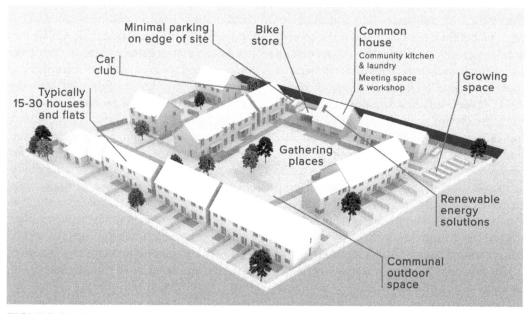

FIGURE 21.1

Example of a cohousing cluster. (Source: Newcastle University)

FIGURE 21.2

Bathore, Albania –
an informal housing
neighbourhood. (Credit:
Julia Heslop)

in the Global South and, increasingly, in Eastern Europe housing is predominantly self-produced through the so-called 'informal' sector. Informal housing refers to housing that has been constructed by people who need a home, often on illegally squatted land and often when the state cannot or will not provide housing or is absent. Today, 30 per cent of the global population lives informally – over one billion people. It is widely recognised that informal building does not function in isolation from formal systems of state intervention. This suggests that informality is better understood as a 'deregulated rather than unregulated system' (Roy, 2009b: 83).

Informal neighbourhoods are typically large in size and are often on the periphery of major cities in areas not subject to normal development pressures. They are often characterised by a lack of basic infrastructure and poor-quality housing, and the residents of these areas often have insecure land tenure, living with a constant threat of eviction (see, for example, the mass displacement caused by the demolition of *favelas* in Rio de Janeiro when Brazil was due to host the World Cup [de Souza, 2012]). Their growth is often the result of a mass movement of people from rural to urban areas, usually for economic reasons – a process that is often too rapid for local authorities to provide basic urban infrastructure, housing and services.

Scholars present different views of informal settlements. For example, Davis (2006) presents a rather apocalyptic view, highlighting the 'squalor and decay' of informal neighbourhoods, while Neuwirth (2005) focuses on the self-organisation of these places and on the self-determination and human agency created by informal areas.

Other accounts recognise the agency of dwellers *as well as* their direct need (see McFarlane, 2012; McGuirk, 2014; Roy & AlSayyad, 2004). This is mirrored in government policy around the world, which has begun to focus on the upgrading and legalisation of informal settlements as opposed to their demolition. These last accounts highlight how housing connects to wider community-building approaches, such as cultural practices (for example, through the employment of vernacular building traditions).

SUMMARY

- Housing is central to debates around social justice, health, well-being and community. Being without stable housing can affect your ability to get on in life or to live healthily and happily. It also plays a huge role in the microeconomy of the individual or family – the house is not now merely 'home' but is used as a financial collateral, a pension and inheritance, as well as being a social signifier. The social discourse around housing is often about the right to choose where you live and what kind of house you live in. Attached to this idea of choice is aspiration – the ability to move up the 'housing ladder' over a life span, to a better location or a bigger property. Yet, increasingly, for many low-income people around the world there is very little choice.

- The social stigma attached to social housing has provided the political impetus for various 'renewal' campaigns around the world – whether through demolition campaigns or state-led gentrification – meaning that there is a certain social violence attached to housing (and being without housing).

- State intervention, whether through welfare policies such as housing benefits or building new social homes, or through subsidising home buyers, builders or developers, is common in housing; yet there is an unevenness to this process around the world.

- While some countries have well-formed social housing policies, others lack any support at all for low-income groups, an issue that has led to widespread informal housing processes in the Global South, where people live in insanitary conditions at constant risk of demolition. Yet government policy can also actively create housing inequalities (such as a social housing shortage, due to the failure to replace homes bought through right-to-buy legislation or destroyed in demolition campaigns).

- High-profile struggles for socio-environmental justice have led to push backs against urban planning for growth. The rising community-led housing movement and housing activist movements for degrowth are approaches that seek to propose alternative solutions while at the same time opposing housing inequality.

FURTHER READING

Dorling, D. (2014) *All That Is Solid: The Great Housing Disaster*. London: Allen Lane.

Forrest, R., & Yip, N. M. (eds.) (2012) *Young People and Housing: Transitions, Trajectories and Generational Fractures*. Oxford: Routledge.

Jarvis, H., Cloke, J., & Kantor, P. (2009) *Cities and Gender*. Oxford: Routledge.

Marcuse, P., & Madden, D. (2016) *In Defense of Housing: The Politics of Crisis*. London: Verso.

Wealth and Poverty

Roger Burrows

The study of wealth and poverty is an interdisciplinary under-taking. This chapter shows how a geographical perspective can offer insights that add value to approaches that derive from economics, politics and sociology.

Overall, it would be fair to say that social scientists, social geographers among them, have tended to focus far more on the analysis of poverty than they have on wealth. This is entirely understandable given the widespread commitment that many have to issues of social justice and the alleviation of suffering (see Chapter 7 on justice). However, in recent years, as income and wealth inequalities have increased, it has come to be real-ised that without an adequate understanding of the *relationship* between wealth and poverty the veracity of research findings can be diminished. For this reason, many researchers have belatedly returned to the call made by the anthropologist Laura Nader in the 1970s to 'study up' (Nader, 1972) – to be as atten-tive to cultures of affluence and power as we are to cultures of poverty and powerlessness. This has led to a resurgence of interest in wealth, elites and power (Davis & Williams, 2017), especially the manner in which the actions of the rich and powerful come to structure the socio-spatial affordances con-fronted by the rest of us (Atkinson et al., 2017).

The recent work of economist Thomas Piketty (2014) has probably been the most important spur to this reframing of the debate, placing the issue within a far broader historical context than is the norm. He shows some of the structural reasons why income and wealth inequalities have been increasing since the 1980s and, especially, since 2008. We thus begin this chapter with a brief examination of his work.

We next examine an example of the impacts of the concentrations of income and wealth that he identifies on the built environment, taking the example of London as an emblematic case. This spatial reading of these processes is then extended in order to examine some of the different *methods* geographers have used to map out wealth and poverty more generally. If the arguments of social geographers are to be taken seriously, then it is useful to understand some of the technical foundations upon which their knowledge claims are made.

Three different examples are discussed from England and the UK: using single variables; combining many different variables together to generate a *ranking* of places from the 'most' to the least 'deprived'; and, finally, combining many different variables together in order to produce a more qualitative – what is called a geodemographic – classification of localities that attempts to describe spatial variations in *different types* of wealth and poverty.

TEXT BOX 22.1 | Selected Key Terms and Concepts about Wealth and Poverty

Income refers to the money received or earned on a continuous basis, as a return for work or investments. It is a flow of money.

Wealth is a stock of assets accumulated during the course of a life. Income and wealth tend to be correlated, but they are not the same thing. Some people with (currently) low incomes may already be wealthy, for example.

Poverty is one of the most contested concepts in all of the social sciences and can be operationalised in many different ways. However, in general it refers to a situation where the flow of income or stock of wealth available to a person or household is not sufficient for them to participate in the consumption practices and social activities that the majority of their peers perceive as necessary and legitimate.

Geodemographics is a form of statistical analysis that clusters together neighbourhoods that have similar cultural, demographic, economic and social attributes. Such classifications can provide a highly nuanced way of qualitatively differentiating between different types of wealth and poverty and how these manifest within different places.

THE ELEPHANT IN THE ROOM? THE CHANGING SHAPE OF GLOBAL INEQUALITIES

For much of the Global North, an association between increasing levels of economic growth and reducing levels of social inequality marked much of the last century; to be sure, major inequalities existed, but in general they seemed to weaken as economies grew in size. This pattern of association – what became known at the 'Kuznets curve' (Kuznets, 1955) – endured in many nations until at least the beginning of the 1980s. As Piketty (2014) has shown in his monumental study *Capital in the Twenty-First Century*, the reasons for this are now clear; the period between about 1918 and 1980 was one in which growth (g) in salaries and wages generally increased at a faster rate than returns (r) on capital investments: g > r. However, this relationship may well turn out to have been a 'historical blip'; the result of some pretty unusual circumstances – two World Wars, the Great Depression, the establishment of redistributive welfare states, the growth of the negotiating power of trade unions and so on. For Piketty, the combined global onslaught of processes of deregulation, privatisation, individualisation and so on from the mid-1970s onwards – often conceptualised together under the heading of neo-liberalism (Harvey, 2005) – has reversed this. As the twentieth century ended, the historical relation r > g, the one that had pertained prior to 1914, was reinstated and has continued to be maintained; the twenty-first century has, thus far, been marked by the inevitability of widening inequalities as the growth in income derived from capital investments has significantly outperformed income derived from salaries and wages.

This may all sound like a quite abstract, technical economic explanation for what has been happening to the global distribution of poverty and wealth, but the upshot of it is clear enough: a larger and larger share of global income and wealth is coming to be held by an ever smaller and smaller group of people.

There are now a number of visualisations that attempt to encapsulate what has been happening, but perhaps the most compelling is what has come to be known as the 'elephant chart'. Using World Bank data, the economists Lakner and Milanovic (2016) were the first to produce a visualisation showing just how each part of the world's income distribution had changed over the two decades between 1988 and 2008; it looked quite like the profile of an elephant with its trunk in the air! This analysis was then extended to cover a longer period, 1980 through to 2016, by Piketty and his colleagues and was unveiled in the World Inequality Report 2018 (World Inequality Lab, 2018) – the shape of the chart had changed somewhat, but the insights it provides are now a good deal more nuanced. It is reproduced here as Figure 22.1.

Over the thirty-six years covered by the chart, it is clear that real incomes have grown for all income groups, but they have done so in a far from uniform manner. The first thing to note is that those on the lowest incomes – those in the bottom 40 per cent of the global income distribution – have seen their real incomes increase by between 80 and 120 per cent. The bottom 50 per cent of the income distribution have captured some 12 per cent of the total growth in real incomes. This is largely due to the rise of the emerging economies in the Global South – China and India in particular. The

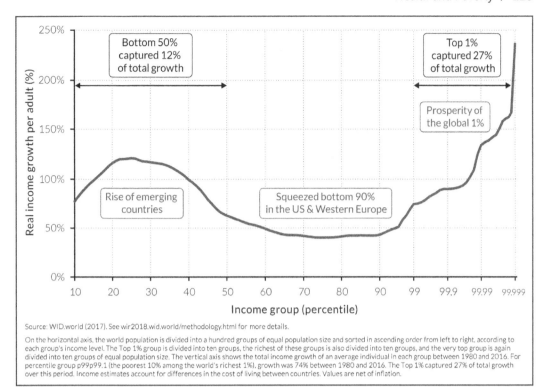

Source: WID.world (2017). See wir2018.wid.world/methodology.html for more details.

On the horizontal axis, the world population is divided into a hundred groups of equal population size and sorted in ascending order from left to right, according to each group's income level. The Top 1% group is divided into ten groups, the richest of these groups is also divided into ten groups, and the very top group is again divided into ten groups of equal population size. The vertical axis shows the total income growth of an average individual in each group between 1980 and 2016. For percentile group p99p99.1 (the poorest 10% among the world's richest 1%), growth was 74% between 1980 and 2016. The Top 1% captured 27% of total growth over this period. Income estimates account for differences in the cost of living between countries. Values are net of inflation.

FIGURE 22.1

Total income growth by percentile across all world regions 1980–2016. (Source: WID.world, 2017)

second thing to note is just how badly – relatively – most of those in the top 50 per cent of the global income distribution have fared; most of these people live in the United States and Western Europe, and most have seen their real incomes grow by 50 per cent or less. Third, and the most significant feature of the chart, is how those in the top 1 per cent of the global income distribution have seen dramatic increases in their real incomes: the top 1 per cent captured some 27 per cent of total income growth. However, closer inspection of the chart reveals that within this top 1 per cent it is the top 0.1 per cent, and especially the top 0.01 per cent, who have seen their incomes increase most significantly.

For Wilkinson and Pickett (2009), in their bestselling *The Spirit Level: Why More Equal Societies Almost Always Do Better*, it has been these changes in income and wealth *relativities* – rather than absolute deprivations per se – that have largely driven escalations in all manner of social pathologies in recent decades: crime, depression, drug abuse, ill health, murders and so on. Their – not uncontroversial – thesis is that such pathologies are strongly correlated with spatial *inequalities* rather than average levels of income and wealth. So, for example, poorer but more equal counties or regions tend, on average, to have better social outcomes than do those that are richer but more unequal.

GLOBAL SUPER-WEALTH

The 'pulling away' of a small number of global super-rich individuals has accelerated since the global financial crisis of 2008. Although one can quibble over the quality of the data and the appropriateness of different modes of operationalisation, the figures are now so shockingly stark that even if they were – by a very significant magnitude – in error, it would not alter the inescapable conclusion that patterns of global inequality (especially in the top half of the global income distribution) have not just widened but also done so on such a scale that some commentators have come to view it as a symptom of a fundamental structural fault in neoliberal capitalism (Streeck, 2016).

Any number of measures generates similar conclusions. Oxfam's reports from 2010 onwards (the most recent of which is Oxfam [2019]) demonstrate alarming concentrations of wealth. Whereas in 2010 the wealthiest 1 per cent of the global population possessed 44 per cent of global wealth, by 2017, and for the first time in history, they possessed well over half of it. Second, whereas in 2010 it was calculated that it would take the combined wealth of the richest 388 people in the world to be equivalent to the combined wealth of the poorest 50 per cent, by 2013 it was 92, by 2015 it was 61, and by 2017 it was just 26; to be clear, *the richest twenty-six people in the world possess as much wealth as the poorest 3.8 billion.*

There are other ways of trying to grasp the magnitude of this capture of global wealth. The financial services industry produces numerous reports, often couched in the language of the number of high-net-worth individuals (HNWIs) – people with one million dollars or more of 'investable' assets. The figures are telling. In 2008 there were estimated to be some 8.6 million such people distributed across the globe (Beaverstock & Hay, 2016: 5), but by 2017 this figure had more than doubled to 18.1 million. The geographical distribution of this population is highly concentrated: 5.285 million in the United States, 3.162 million in Japan, 1.365 million in Germany, 1.256 million in China, 629,000 in France, and an estimated 575,000 in the United Kingdom (compared to just 362,000 in 2008) (Capgemini, 2018).

In the UK this HNWI population resides mainly in London – over half a million of them live in a set of tightly circumscribed neighbourhoods (Burrows, Webber & Atkinson, 2017), the highest numbers being found in Belgravia, Chelsea, Hampstead, Paddington, South Kensington, Notting Hill, the West End, St Johns Wood and West Kensington. London has been, at least until recently, the city of choice for the global super-rich. The most recent 'rich list' produced by the *Sunday Times* (2018: 7) reveals that it contains the greatest number of resident (£) billionaires – ninety-three in 2017, compared to New York with sixty-six, San Francisco with sixty-four, Hong Kong with sixty-three and Moscow with fifty-five.

WEALTH AND THE BUILT ENVIRONMENT IN LONDON

All of this wealth sloshing around London has had myriad consequences for the built environment, of which perhaps the most materially evident is the appearance of a large number of 'super-high', 'super-prime' residential towers across the city. They are, of course, part of a global trend towards the construction of what social geographer Steve Graham (2015) has called the 'luxified skies'. The wealth that has not found its way into the changing sky-lines of the city, although sometimes less visible, has still had major impacts on the socio-spatial dynamics of the built environment. Over the last decade in particular, we have begun to witness an intensification of processes that were initially conceptualised as 'super-gentrification' – where early gentrifiers were 'replaced' (if not 'displaced') by people with much greater levels of wealth – but which have now reached a stage where even the 'gentry proper' – let alone 'ordinary elites' – can often no longer maintain a foothold in some streets where transnational plutocratic money/power has become culturally dominant (Burrows and Knowles, 2019).

Many properties have been transformed as super-affluent new-comers commission high-end designers to undertake often brutal structural conversions of older properties into 'state-of-the art' living spaces; maximising the size of all interior spaces and infusing them with exterior light has now become de rigueur, as have various design and technological 'solutions' to matters of privacy and security (Atkinson, 2019). However, in many areas of 'super-prime' London attractive to 'super-rich' elites, the nature of the original architecture combined with planning restrictions often makes it very difficult to extend properties laterally over existing terrain or to add additional floors on the top of properties. Thus, for some the only 'solution' has been to go 'down', and consequently residential basement developments in the wealthiest parts of London have also increased markedly in recent years (Baldwin, Holroyd & Burrows, 2019): central London has seen the construction of some 4,600 new residential basements – some of them huge – between 2007 and the end of 2017, which have a combined depth equivalent to the height of just over fifty Shards (the tallest building not just in London but also in the whole of the the EU).

As Minton (2017) shows, however, much of this plutocratic wealth sits cheek by jowl with some of London's poorest communities. One of the most shocking instances of this is in North Kensington, where the burnt-out shell of Grenfell Tower (Shildrick, 2018) sits within plain sight of basement developments – some with swimming pools – that have resulted in single-family houses being valued at well over the cost it has been estimated it would have taken to safely refurbish Grenfell's 120 flats (£11.3 million compared to the £9.7 million that was finally spent using substandard cladding). In other parts of wealthy London, poorer communities are being 'regenerated out' (Glucksberg, 2014) – decanted to poorer parts of London, or out of London all together – as social housing estates are demolished and replaced with more upmarket developments that few can afford to move back into. These processes, of what some see as 'state-led gentrification' (Watt, 2009), are changing the whole social makeup of the city (Minton, 2017). This clearly relates to issues of housing and social justice (see Chapter 7 on justice and Chapter 21 on housing).

MAPPING AND VISUALISING THE GEOGRAPHIES OF WEALTH AND POVERTY

The luxified skies and basements of London are, of course, just one – literally – concrete instantiation of the global concentration of wealth in the built environment. They are examples of how a distinctively geographical perspective can offer important insights to a field of study – that of economic inequalities – that is becoming ever more interdisciplinary (Savage, 2016).

The analysis of income, poverty and wealth can, of course, be undertaken at a broadly socio-demographic level of analysis wherein data is classified at the level of the individual, family or household and then aggregated across what are often essentially sociological variables such as age, educational qualifications, disability, housing tenure, race and ethnicity, social class and so on (Grusky, 2018) (see Part C on divisions). However, additional insights are offered when it is recognised that such variables are themselves highly variable across space, resulting in huge spatial variations in wealth and poverty at various geographical scales – the street, the neighbourhood, the broader locality, the region, the nation, the continent and, as we have already seen, globally (see Chapter 5 on scale). But more than this, there is now good evidence to show that interactions between particular variables are generative of additional, what are sometimes called 'neighbourhood effects', in which intersectional processes become manifest within particular *places*, producing levels of income and wealth inequalities (as well as other outcomes) over and above those which can be accounted for by the individual variables themselves (see Chapter 24 on education). In addition, it has become increasingly apparent that many of the *physical* qualities of places can also have an independent impact upon poverty and wealth. Pollution may invoke ill health, which may lead to lower incomes, for example (see Chapter 23 on health); distance from transport infrastructures may disadvantage those who may otherwise be able to gain higher-income employment; the natural aesthetics of particular locations may attract or repel people in a manner that may influence land, commercial and property values; and so on (Webber and Burrows, 2018).

The detailed mapping of poverty and wealth across place is now well established within social geography, having its origins in Charles Booth's 'Descriptive Map of London Poverty', first published in 1889; the cartographic innovations of the Chicago School of Sociology in the 1920s and 1930s; and the work of human ecologists in the 1950s (Webber and Burrows, 2018: 31–50), but the best means by which this is done is still open to much dispute (Dorling et al., 2007). There are, crudely, three different approaches: using single variables, combining many different variables together to generate an ordinal scale ('league table') *ranking* places from the 'most' to the least 'deprived' and combining many different variables together in order to produce a more qualitative nominal (or categorical) classification of localities that attempts to describe spatial variations in *different types* of wealth and poverty.

USING A SINGLE MEASURE

We might try and keep things simple and use just one measure and see how it varies across different spatial scales. This was recently done to great effect by using EU data on disposable household incomes (the amount of money a household has left for spending or saving after taxes and welfare benefits have taken effect). A visualisation of this process is shown in Figure 22.2.

Figure 22.2 shows quite a wide variation in average levels of disposable household income across the fourteen countries included in the analysis. The countries have been ranked in relation to these national averages, with Austria having the highest and Portugal the lowest, and the UK pretty much in the middle. What is then shown is the 'distance' from this national average of the 'richest' and 'poorest' regions *within* each country on this measure. In some countries the regional distribution of average disposable household income is slight – particularly in Austria, Ireland and Denmark; these are countries where regional variations in income are quite small. Compare this to other countries – such as Germany, France, Italy and, especially, the UK – and it is revealed that differences in national averages conceal some quite colossal differences in incomes between different parts of the country. The case of the UK is the most extreme, with huge regional differences noticeable especially in the huge concentrations of high incomes in central London. So even using a very simple single measure of, in this instance, household income, it is possible to describe analytically some otherwise obscured geographical variations in spatial inequalities.

FIGURE 22.2

The gap between average disposable household income in the richest and poorest region of the UK compared to similar figures in other EU countries. (Source: Peat, 2018)

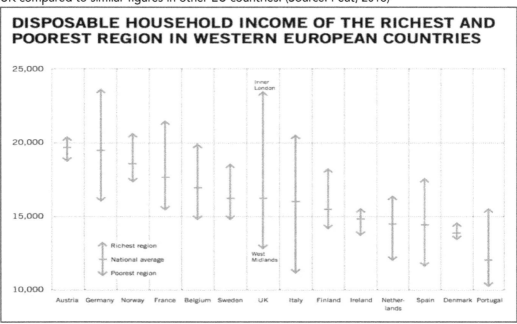

LEAGUE TABLES

A second approach – and one that is often favoured by policy makers and those with responsibility for the targeting of public resources – is to devise an index combining many different relevant variables in order to rank areas on a complex but essentially ordinal scale ('league table') of 'need'. In the context of England, the measure that does this is known as the indices of multiple deprivation (IMD) (Smith et al., 2015). The IMD has been through various iterations since 2000. In its most recent iteration, 2015, it takes a huge amount of data from various official sources across seven different domains – (1) income; (2) employment; (3) health and disability; (4) education, skills and training; (5) barriers to housing and services; (6) living environment; and (7) crime – and, through a complex set of statistical procedures, ranks each of the 32,844 small areas (based on a census geography) in England from the most to the least deprived. However, this does mean that two small neighbourhoods that are ranked at the same point on the scale might, in fact, be very different types of places, their equivalent location on this particular measure of multiple deprivation deriving from a very different combination of attributes.

GEODEMOGRAPHICS

A third approach tries to overcome this problem by developing a nuanced classification of places that are similar on a large number of different dimensions. What have come to be known as 'geodemographic classifications' were developed simultaneously in the United States and the UK in the early 1970s and are now widely used both in commerce and in local government. They are used to a lesser extent within academic research, although with the arrival of 'big data' – data that is simply a digital by-product of commercial, administrative, web or mobile activity – this seems to be changing somewhat (Webber and Burrows, 2018). A large number of variables – including income, debt and wealth data, but also demographic information, consumption habits, housing characteristics and so on (from both official and commercial sources) – are attached to an address (or a postcode) and are then subject to a form of statistical procedure called cluster analysis, which classifies each postcode into a set of exhaustive and mutually exclusive categories. What results are groups and types of postcodes that have similar distinctive characteristics; such an approach allows us to map out places – and at a very granular level – that are qualitatively alike ('ideal types'). It allows us to begin to examine the spatial distribution and juxtapositions of *different types* of wealth and poverty. Figure 22.3 – extracted from Webber and Burrows (2018: 120–21) – shows one of the most widely used geodemographic classifications, owned by Experian and widely used in both the commercial and the public sectors for purposes of marketing, targeting and planning. It is a system also used by the main UK political parties to target likely 'swing' voters.

Figures 22.4 and 22.5 show a selection of street scenes from two very different geodemographic groups. These are neighbourhoods that are both literally and metaphorically miles apart from each other. Figure 22.4 shows four are streets located in the 'alpha territories' – in London, Bath and Edinburgh. Figure 22.5 shows four streets all from the far less affluent 'industrial heritage' – streets located in Tyneside, Teesside, Doncaster and Preston.

One need not be convinced by such geodemographic classifications in order to recognise that there are significant qualitative geographical differences in the nature of wealth and poverty; such classifications can at least sensitise us to the distinctiveness of such differences. With

Mosaic Groups	% hhds	Mosaic Types	% hhds
A: Alpha Territory	3.5	A01: Global Power Brokers	0.3
		A02: Voices of Authority	1.2
		A03: Business Class	1.5
		A04: Serious Money	0.6
B: Professional Reward	8.2	B05: Mid-Career Climbers	2.3
		B06: Yesterday's Captains	1.8
		B07: Distinctive Success	0.5
		B08: Dormitory Villages	1.3
		B09: Escape to the Country	1.1
		B10: Parish Guardians	1.0
C: Rural Solitude	4.4	C11: Squires Among Locals	0.9
		C12: Country Loving Elders	1.3
		C13: Modern Agribusiness	1.4
		C14: Farming Today	0.5
		C15: Upland Struggle	0.3
D: Small Town Diversity	8.8	D16: Side Street Singles	1.2
		D17: Jacks of All Trades	2.0
		D18: Hardworking Families	2.6
		D19: Innate Conservatives	3.0
E: Active Retirement	4.3	E20: Golden Retirement	0.7
		E21: Bungalow Quietude	1.8
		E22: Beachcombers	0.6
		E23: Balcony Downsizers	1.3
F: Suburban Mindsets	11.2	F24: Garden Suburbia	2.1
		F25: Production Managers	2.6
		F26: Mid-Market Families	2.7
		F27: Shop Floor Affluence	2.7
		F28: Asian Attainment	1.0
G: Careers and Kids	5.8	G29: Footloose Managers	1.7
		G30: Soccer Mums and Dads	1.3
		G31: Domestic Comfort	1.1
		G32: Childcare Years	1.5
		G33: Military Dependents	0.2
H: New Homemakers	5.9	H34: Buy-to-Let Territory	1.8
		H35: Brownfield Pioneers	1.4
		H36: Foot on the Ladder	2.4
		H37: First to Move In	0.4

FIGURE 22.3

Mosaic neighbourhood groups and types, developed by Experian, 2009 version. (Source: Webber and Burrows, 2018: 120–21)

Mosaic Groups	% hhds	Mosaic Types	% hhds
I: Ex-Council Community	8.7	I38: Settled Ex-Tenants	2.1
		I39: Choice Right to Buy	1.7
		I40: Legacy of Labour	2.7
		I41: Stressed Borrowers	2.2
J: Claimant Cultures	5.2	J42: Worn-Out Workers	2.3
		J43: Streetwise Kids	1.1
		J44: New Parents in Need	1.8
K: Upper Floor Living	5.2	K45: Small Block Singles	1.8
		K46: Tenement Living	0.8
		K47: Deprived View	0.5
		K48: Multicultural Towers	1.1
		K49: Re-housed Migrants	1.0
L: Elderly Needs	6.0	L50: Pensioners in Blocks	1.3
		L51: Sheltered Seniors	1.1
		L52: Meals on Wheels	0.9
		L53: Low Spending Elders	2.7
M: Industrial Heritage	7.4	M54: Clocking Off	2.3
		M55: Backyard Regeneration	2.1
		M56: Small Wage Owners	3.1
N: Terraced Melting Pot	7.0	N57: Back-to-Back Basics	2.0
		N58: Asian Identities	0.9
		N59: Low-Key Starters	2.7
		N60: Global Fusion	1.4
O: Liberal Opinion	8.5	O61: Convivial Homeowners	1.7
		O62: Crash Pad Professionals	1.1
		O63: Urban Cool	1.1
		O64: Bright Young Things	1.5
		O65: Anti-Materialists	1.0
		O66: University Fringe	0.9
		O67: Study Buddies	1.1
Total Great Britain	100.0		100.0

FIGURE 22.3

Continued

reference to some of the geodemographic groups and types identified in Text Box 22.2, we will end this chapter by taking four examples of very different places – two of them 'wealthy' and two of them relatively 'poor' – and point towards some classic and more contemporary geographically inflected studies with which we might engage in order to get a better sense of the socio-spatial dynamics that underpin the making and reproduction of each. For more details and examples of other types of places, see the 'geodemographic travelogue' presented in Webber and Burrows (2018: 253–66).

Belsize Park Gardens, Hampstead, London, NW3 4LH

Rothesay Terrace, Edinburgh, EH3 7RY

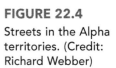
FIGURE 22.4
Streets in the Alpha territories. (Credit: Richard Webber)

Great Pulteney Street, Bath, BA2 4BP

Pelham Street, South Kensington, London, SW7 2NP

Cumberland Street, Wallsend, NE28 7SB

Albert Street, Mexborough, S64 9BT

FIGURE 22.5
Streets with industrial heritage. (Credit: Roger Burrows)

Coronation Street, Carlin How, Loftus, TS13 4DN

Elliott Street, Preston, PR1 7XN

TEXT BOX 22.2 | **Four Examples of Geodemographic Characterisations of Different Kinds of Wealth and Poverty, with Some Illustrative Studies**

1. London W8 is a prime example of what, in Figure 22.3, is labelled an alpha territory. Notting Hill Gate bounds W8 to the north, Holland Park to the west, Knightsbridge to the east and Cromwell Road to the south. Kensington High Street, which transects it, forms its main commercial artery. The almost twenty thousand adults who live in this neighbourhood are among the very wealthiest in the world. Over 60 per cent of the population is classified as being part of the alpha territory, the great bulk of them being 'global power brokers' – the neighbourhood type within the mosaic schema containing the very highest incomes in the UK. This is the very epicentre of the 'superrich' London we discussed in this chapter, where those living in the alpha territory are almost seventeen times more likely to be found than they are in the United Kingdom as a whole. The recent study by Burrows and Knowles (2019) is worth reading to better understand the nature and functioning of wealth here.

2. In contrast, London N1 is emblematic of what the geodemographic schema calls 'liberal opinion'. This is the location of archetypical liberal metropolitan wealth. London N1 covers the London borough of Islington, a key location in the history of urban studies. It was here that the concept of 'gentrification' was first developed by Ruth Glass (1964: xviii). It was here also a few years before the financial crash of 2008 that Butler and Lees (2006) claimed to be able to identify the emergence of what they termed 'super-gentrification' in Barnsbury, a specific part of Islington. Their data show that the 'traditional gentrifiers' of places such as Cloudesley Square, Lonsdale Square, Thornhill Square and Richmond Crescent (where Tony Blair and his family once lived) were slowly being replaced by far more affluent professionals working in the City of London.

3. The Isle of Sheppey in Kent, and the town of Sheerness in particular, is the location of Ray Pahl's *Divisions of Labour* (1984) and was recently the subject of a major revisiting (Crow and Ellis, 2017). *Divisions of Labour* was a study of 1980s small-town White working-class entrepreneurship and self-provisioning developed in the face of the economic realities of Thatcher's Britain. Today the upper and middle classes are still significantly underrepresented, and all of the neighbourhood types in the 'small-town diversity' group are overrepresented, those in the (now, within political discourse, emblematic) 'hardworking families' type especially so. The less affluent of those seeking active retirement are also overrepresented here, as are those of modest means living in terraced housing: 'back-to-back basics' and, especially, 'low-key starters'.

4. Sparkbrook in Birmingham was the location of the classic study *Race, Community and Conflict* by Rex and Moore (1967), which did much to popularise the concept of 'housing classes', and it remains an enduring contribution to the study of race and ethnicity. Here we now find a huge overrepresentation of those classified as living in the mosaic group 'terraced melting pot' – almost eleven times the prevalence compared to the country as a whole. In Sparkbrook and its environs we discover that some 80 per cent of adults live in the mosaic-type 'Asian identities'. Sparkbrook continues to be an important location if we want to understand the social dynamics of provincial neighbourhoods in which a significant proportion of the population are Muslims, the majority with origins in Pakistan and Bangladesh, living alongside other minority ethnic groups.

SUMMARY

- This chapter has tried to make a case for why the geographical study of poverty and wealth should be seen as two sides of the same coin. It is hard to understand one without the other at a time when the super-rich continue to pull away from all of us, whilst at the same time possessing the power to drive political and cultural agendas that are designed to undercut many of the domain assumptions of postwar welfare provision.

- There is a danger in making this case, however, as it tends to lead to a geographical focus on London and other global cities. It would be a pity if the excellent work of those concerned with the geographical analysis of poverty and welfare in the round (Milbourne, 2010), those working on rural poverty (Milbourne, 2004), those focused on the urban poverty of deindustrialised provincial cities (MacDonald, Shildrick & Furlong, 2014; Shildrick & MacDonald, 2013) and others did not also get big social geographical audiences.

- Some consideration of the methods employed to make geographical knowledge claims in relation to wealth and poverty are important. What sometimes appear to be quite dry and esoteric debates about measurement, classification, statistical methods and mapping technologies can often turn out to be crucial mediators of what is actually 'ground truth' (Pickles, 1995).

FURTHER READING

Burrows, R., Webber, R., & Atkinson, R. (2017) Welcome to 'Pikettyville'? Mapping London's alpha territories. *Sociological Review*, 65(2): 184–201.

Butler, T., & Lees, L. (2006) Super-gentrification in Barnsbury, London: Globalization and gentrifying global elites at the neighbourhood level. *Transactions of the Institute of British Geographers*, 31(4): 467–87.

Milbourne, P. (2010) The geographies of poverty and welfare. *Geography Compass*, 4(2): 158–71.

Shildrick, T. (2018) Lessons from Grenfell: Poverty propaganda, stigma and class power. *Sociological Review*, 66(4): 783–98.

Health

Clare Bambra and Alison Copeland

Today, North Americans live three years less than their counterparts in France or Sweden. People in the North of England live two years less, on average, than those in the South of England, and, in London, there is a seven-year drop in average life expectancy as you travel the seven stops along the Jubilee Tube line from Westminster to Canning Town (Figure 23.1) (Bambra, 2016). Why are there such inequalities in health across all geographical scales – between neighbourhoods, cities, regions and countries? Health geographers have traditionally explained these health divides in terms of the effects of *compositional* (who lives here?) and *contextual* (what is this place like?) factors. The compositional explanation asserts that the health of a given area, such as a town, region or country, is a result of the characteristics of the people who live there (individual-level demographic, behavioural and socioeconomic factors), whereas the contextual explanation argues that area-level health is also in part determined by the nature of the place itself in terms of its economic, social and physical environment.

More recently, it has been acknowledged that these two approaches are not mutually exclusive and that the health of places results from the interaction of people with the wider environment (Cummins et al., 2007). This chapter will therefore also examine the *relational* approach (which tries

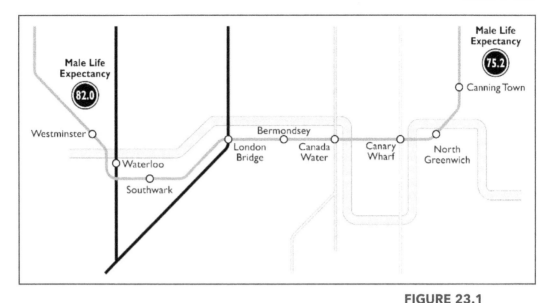

FIGURE 23.1

Life expectancy along the Jubilee Tube Line, London. (Source: Adapted from London Health Observatory, 2012)

to accommodate this interaction), as well as the *political economy* approach (which reconceptualises context, looking beyond the local and, instead, at the influence of national and international political and economic factors) (Bambra, 2016). We track the evolution of how geographers have conceptualised the relationship between place and health from an early focus on composition/context through to more recent relational and political economy approaches (Bambra, Smith & Pearce, 2019).

WHO LIVES HERE?
THE COMPOSITIONAL APPROACH

The compositional view argues that *who lives here* – primarily the health behaviours (smoking, alcohol, physical activity, diet, drugs) and socioeconomic (income, education, occupation) characteristics of the people living within a particular area (neighbourhood, city, region, country) – determines its health outcomes: that *poor people* result in *poor places*. Smoking, alcohol, physical activity, diet and drugs, the five so-called lifestyle factors or risky health behaviours, all influence health significantly. Smoking remains the most important preventable cause of mortality in the wealthy world and is causally linked to most major diseases, such as cancer and cardiovascular disease (Jarvis & Wardle, 2006). Likewise, excessive alcohol consumption is related to some cancers, as well as to other key risks such as high blood pressure. Alcohol-related deaths and diseases are on the increase. Poor diet and low exercise rates can lead to obesity, which is a major risk factor for poorer health and longevity. Drug abuse is an increasingly important determinant of death among the young (Bambra et al., 2010). People who do not smoke, have only moderate alcohol intake, consume a high amount of fruits and vegetables and engage regularly in physical activity will, on average, have a fourteen-year-higher life expectancy than individuals achieving no healthy behaviours (Khaw et al., 2008). So, on average, areas (countries, regions, cities, neighbourhoods) with higher rates of these unhealthy behaviours have worse health than others, all things being equal.

The socioeconomic status of the people living in an area is also of huge health significance. 'Socioeconomic status' is a term that refers to occupational class, income or educational level (Bambra, 2011; see also Chapter 15 on class). People with higher occupational status (e.g., professionals such as teachers or lawyers) have better health outcomes than nonprofessional workers (e.g., manual workers). By way of example, the data show that infant mortality rates are 16 per cent higher in children of routine and manual workers than of professional and managerial workers (Marmot, 2010). Having a higher income or being educated to degree level can also have a protective health effect, whereas having a lower income or no educational qualifications can have a negative health impact. The poorer someone is, the less likely they are to live in good-quality housing, have time and money for leisure activities, feel secure at home or work, have good-quality work or a job at all, or afford to eat healthy food – the social determinants of health (Marmot, 2010).

WHAT IS THIS PLACE LIKE?
THE CONTEXTUAL APPROACH

So, while the compositional view argues that it is *who lives here* that matters for area health – and that essentially *poor people make poor health* – the contextual approach instead highlights that *what this place is like* also matters for health. Health differs by place because it is also determined by the economic, social and physical environment of a *place*: *poor places lead to poor health*. Place mediates the way individuals experience social, economic and physical processes on their health: places can be salutogenic (health-promoting) or pathogenic (health-damaging) environments. Place acts as a health ecosystem. These place-based effects can also be seen as the *collective* effects of the social determinants of health. There are three contextual aspects to place that have traditionally been considered as important to health: economic, social and physical.

The compositional view takes into account the effects of individual socioeconomic position on health status. Area-level economics instead looks at the health effects of the local economic environment, independent of individual socioeconomic position, and the factors that influence health are often summarised as economic deprivation. They include area poverty rates, unemployment rates, wages and types of work and employment in the area. The mechanisms whereby the economic profile of a local area impacts on health are multiple. For example, it affects the nature of work that an individual can access in that place (regardless of their own socioeconomic position). It also impacts on the services available in a local area, as more affluent areas will attract more services (such as types of food available locally or the opportunities for physical activity) than more deprived areas, as businesses adapt to the consumer demands in each area (see below). Area-level economic factors such as poverty are a key predictor of health, including cardiovascular disease, all-cause mortality, limiting long-term illness and health-related behaviours (Macintyre, 2007).

Places also have social aspects that impact health. Opportunity structures are the socially constructed and patterned features of the area, which may promote health through the possibilities that they provide (Macintyre, Ellaway & Cummins, 2002). These include the services provided, publicly or privately, to support people in their daily lives, such as childcare, transport, food availability and access to a family physician or hospital, as well as the availability of health-promoting environments at home (e.g., good housing quality, access and affordability – see Chapter 21 on housing), work (good-quality work) and education (such as high-quality schools; see Chapter 24 on education). For example, local environments can shape our access to healthy – and unhealthy – goods and services, thus enhancing or reducing our opportunities to engage in healthy or unhealthy behaviours such as smoking, alcohol consumption, fruit and vegetable consumption and physical activity. One example is the obesogenic environment. The local food environment, such as the availability of healthy and unhealthy foods in the neighbourhood, as well as the opportunities for physical activity (Are there parks or gyms? Is the outside space safe and walkable?) are central components of the obesogenic environment. Research has shown that in some low-income areas there are food deserts, where there is a paucity of supermarkets and shops selling affordable fresh food alongside an abundance of convenience stores and fast-food outlets selling energy-dense junk food and ready-to-eat meals (Pearce et al., 2007; see also Chapter 34 on food and the more-than-human). Low-income neighbourhoods – particularly urban ones – may also inhibit the opportunities for physical activity. Associations have been found between the neighbourhood availability of fast food and obesity rates in a number of wealthy countries, including the United Kingdom, the United States and New Zealand (Pearce et al., 2007; Burgoine, Alvanides & Lake, 2011).

A second social aspect of place is collective social functioning. Collective social functioning and practices that are beneficial to health include high levels of social cohesion and social capital within the community. Social capital – 'the features of social organisation such as trust, norms and networks that can improve the efficiency of society by facilitating coordinated actions' (Putnam, 1993: 167) – has been put forward as a social mechanism through which place mediates the relationship between an individual's socio-economic status and health outcomes (Hawe & Shiell, 2000). Some studies have found that areas with higher levels of social capital have better health, such as lower mortality rates, self-rated health, mental health and health behaviours. More negative collective effects can also come from the reputation of an area (e.g., stigmatised places can result in feelings of alienation and worthlessness) or the history of an area (e.g., if there has been a history of racial oppression). Place attachment (an emotional bond that individuals or groups have with specific places), by contrast, can have a protective health effect (Gatrell & Elliot, 2009). Certain places become marginalised by gaining a spoiled identity and subsequently become stigmatised and discredited. This can be as a result of environment factors, such as air pollution or dirt, as well as from social stigma such as being labelled the obesity capital of Britain, as happened with Copeland in West Cumbria (North West England), or economic stigma such as low property prices (Bush, Moffatt & Dunn, 2001). The residents of stigmatised places can also be discredited by association with these place characteristics. A notable case of such place-based stigma is Love Canal, New York, the location of a toxic waste dump. Research has shown that such place-based stigma can result in psychosocial stress and associated ill health, alongside feelings of shame, on top of the physical health effects of air pollution, such as respiratory disease (Airey, 2003). Local attitudes (say, around smoking) can also influence health and health behaviours either negatively or positively (Thompson, Pearce & Barnett, 2007).

The physical environment is widely recognised as an important determinant of health and health inequalities (WHO, 2008). There is a sizeable literature on the positive health effects of access to green space, as well as the negative health effects of waste facilities, brownfield or contaminated land as well as air pollution (Bambra, 2016). A (in)famous example of the latter is the so-called Cancer Alley, the eighty-seven-mile stretch in the American state of Mississippi between Baton Rouge and New Orleans, the home of the largest petrochemicals site in the country (Markowitz & Rosner, 2003). In 2016, it was estimated that air pollution levels in London accounted for up to ten thousand unnecessary deaths per year (Walton et al., 2015).

Another example of how the physical environment of areas varies is in respect to land pollution. A study found that in the American city of Baltimore the mortality rates from cancer, lung cancer and respiratory diseases were significantly higher in neighbourhoods with larger amounts of brownfield land (Litt, Tran & Burke, 2002). Similarly, an English study of differences in exposure to brownfield land found that neighbourhoods with larger amounts of brownfield land have higher rates of poor health and limiting long-term illness (Bambra et al., 2014).

The health geography literature has also established the role of natural or green spaces as therapeutic or health-promoting landscapes (see Text Box 23.1). So, for example, studies have found that walking in natural rather than urban settings reduces stress levels and that people residing in green areas report less poor health than those with less green surroundings (Maas et al., 2005). The research also indicates that green space can impact health by attention restoration, stress reduction and the evocation of positive emotions (Abraham, Sommerhalder & Abel, 2010). An awareness of how such factors differ by place has led to the development of the concept of

TEXT BOX 23.1 | Real-World Theory: Therapeutic Landscapes

The term 'therapeutic landscapes' was introduced by Wil Gesler in 1992 to illustrate how some places or situations are considered healing – for example, mineral springs, such as in the spa town of Bath, or mountain retreats. He also suggested that other, less traditional landscapes could be considered healing, such as hospitals or native healers' huts. As Gesler (1992: 735) states, 'it appears that there must be environmental, individual, and societal factors that come together in the healing process in both traditional and nontraditional landscapes'. A number of health geographers have continued to research this theme, with Allison Williams' (2017) recent book *Therapeutic Landscapes* bringing together some of the leading scholars in this area. Often, the term is associated with increasing mental health and well-being. While mental health continues to carry a social stigma for many (Thornicroft et al., 2016; and see Chapter 12 on emotion), awareness of mental health issues and the need for emotional well-being have come to the forefront in recent years, with authors such as Hester Parr (2008) exploring their spatial context.

Using a case study approach, Sarah Curtis and colleagues (2007) used the theories around therapeutic landscapes to explore the design of a new psychiatric hospital in London. Interviews were undertaken with past service users, consultants, nurses and management to discuss aspects of the hospital design that they considered either detrimental or beneficial to mental health. The themes that emerged were the conflict between the need for privacy (of both service users and staff) versus the need for surveillance to ensure the safety of service users and staff, the need for a homely environment and contact with nature and the ability to integrate into a sustainable environment. As Curtis and colleagues (2007) note, while architects and planners often consider the physical environment in hospital design, the social environment, such as the need to be observed versus the need for privacy, is often ignored. This study was able to show a real-life example of how therapeutic landscape theory can inform the design of healing spaces.

'environmental deprivation', which is the extent of exposure to key characteristics of the physical environment that are either health promoting or health damaging (Pearce et al., 2010). Environmental deprivation is associated with all-cause mortality: mortality was lowest in areas with the least environmental deprivation and highest in those that are most environmentally deprived. The unequal sociospatial distribution of environmental deprivation has also led to commentators developing the concept of environmental justice. The fact that more deprived neighbourhoods are more likely to have air and land pollution and less likely to have green space can be seen as an aspect of social injustice (Pearce et al., 2010; see Chapter 33 on environmental justice).

POOR PEOPLE *AND* POOR PLACES: THE RELATIONAL APPROACH

The contextual and compositional explanations for how place relates to health are not mutually exclusive, and to separate them is an oversimplification that ignores the interactions between these two levels (Macintyre, Ellaway & Cummins, 2002). The characteristics of individuals are influenced by the characteristics of the area. For example, occupational class can be determined by the quality of the local schools and the availability of jobs in the local labour market, or the fact that children might not play outside due to having no private garden (a *compositional* resource) or no public parks or transport to get to them (a *contextual* resource) or because it might not be seen as appropriate for them to do so (*contextual* social functioning) (Macintyre, Ellaway & Cummins, 2002). Similarly, areas with more successful economies (e.g., more high-paid jobs) will have lower proportions of lower-socioeconomic-status residents.

Further, the collective resources model suggests that all residents, and particularly those on a low income, enjoy better health when they live in areas characterised by more and better social and economic collective resources. This may be especially important for those on low incomes, as they are usually more reliant on local services. Moreover, the health of poorer people may suffer more in deprived areas, where collective resources and social structures are limited, a concept known as deprivation amplification: the health effects of individual deprivation, such as lower socioeconomic status, can be *amplified* by area deprivation (Macintyre, 2007). Figure 23.2

FIGURE 23.2

Mean healthy lifestyle score across quintiles of neighbourhood deprivation and six categories of occupational social class. (Data from Lakshman et al., 2011)

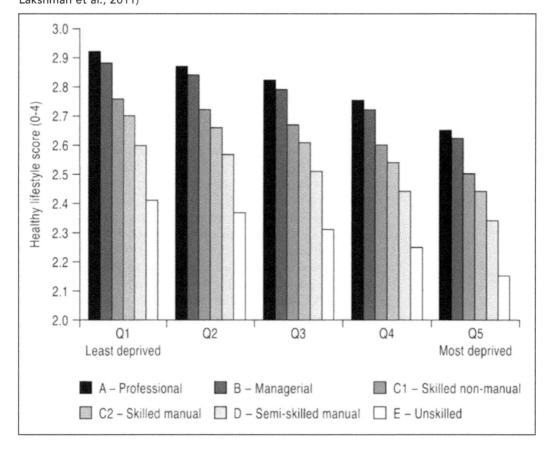

shows an example of these interaction effects. A healthy lifestyle score in a study in the east of England is affected by both individual occupation (compositional) and area-level deprivation (contextual): people from all occupational backgrounds fare worse in areas of higher deprivation than when living in more affluent areas (Lakshman et al., 2011).

Composition and context should not therefore be seen as separate or competing explanations but entwined. Both contribute to the complex relationship between health and place, an ecosystem made up of people, systems and structures. As Cummins and colleagues (2007: 1826) argue, 'there is a mutually reinforcing and reciprocal relationship between people and place', so a relational approach should be taken to understand how compositional and contextual factors interact to produce geographical inequalities in health. Table 23.1 provides an example of the relative role of compositional and contextual factors, both individually and collectively, in explaining health inequalities between the most and least deprived neighbourhoods of a case-study town, Stockton-on-Tees in the North East of England. Stockton has a seventeen-year gap in life expectancy for men and eleven years for women between its most and least deprived neighbourhoods. This is the largest gap in life expectancy within a single local authority in England. Table 23.1 shows the results of statistical modelling of household survey data that examines how much of the health gap in the town is explained by compositional and contextual factors and their interaction. The compositional factors used relate to individual-level socioeconomic factors (income, unemployment, etc.), psychosocial factors (loneliness, isolation, etc.) and behavioural factors (smoking, drinking, diet, exercise). The contextual data relate largely to the physical environment (noise, pollution, dirt, crime, safety, housing quality). Three measures of health are used: general well-being (EQ5D and EQVAS scales) and physical health (SF8PCS). Compositional factors account for by far the most of the gap: 47 per cent across all three of the health outcomes. Contextual factors account for between 3 per cent and 11 per cent. Of course, the different causes of health gaps often cluster together, as people who experience poor material factors often also experience poor psychosocial factors and poorer environments and are more likely to engage in less healthy behaviours. This interaction of compositional and contextual factors is also shown in Table 23.1, and it accounts for between 18 per cent and 30 per cent of the gap (Bhandari et al., 2017).

As often with statistical models, there is a certain proportion of the gap that remains unexplained, or the results may be skewed due to difficulties in the recruitment of participants or the artificially constructed boundary effects (see Text Box 23.2). However, this analysis shows that both contextual and compositional factors matter and that their interaction is an important cause of geographical inequalities in health, supporting a relational approach to health and place (Bhandari et al., 2017).

TABLE 23.1	Relative Role of Compositional and Contextual Factors in Explaining the Health Gap in Stockton-on-Tees (adapted from Bhandari et al., 2017)		
	Health Measure		
% Gap Explained	**Measure 1 (SF8PCS)**	**Measure 2 (EQ5D)**	**Measure 3 (EQVAS)**
Compositional	47%	47%	47%
Contextual	8%	11%	3%
Interactions	18%	30%	24%
Total explained	73%	88%	74%
Unexplained	27%	12%	26%

TEXT BOX 23.2 | Real-World Research: Researching Health

The Stockton study discussed in this chapter (and described fully in Bambra, Smith & Pearce, 2019) threw up a number of methodological 'real-world' challenges.

Multilevel models were used in the study (Mattheys et al., 2016). These are statistical models of factors that vary at more than one level (e.g., the individual and the community). In the Stockton study, the compositional (individual) health effects, such as lifestyle factors, were modelled within the contextual (area) health effects, such as deprivation. This approach, though, can lead to the *ecological fallacy* – where it is assumed that we can infer influences from the characteristics of the contained geographic area (such as an LSOA, or lower super output area) in which a person lives onto the people themselves (Robinson, 1950). In this case, it would assume that everyone living in a deprived neighbourhood is deprived.

Further, due to difficulties in recruiting a representative sample (due to different response rates by age and gender), the Stockton study sample was predominantly of older women (Akheter et al., 2018). So the findings cannot be generalised across the population of Stockton or, indeed, to other locations. Furthermore, LSOA geographical boundaries are artificially constructed, and people most often do not operate solely within those boundaries but will be influenced by the surrounding areas and beyond (known as the modifiable area unit problem [MAUP]) (Fotheringham & Wong, 1991). One way to mitigate for this is to use a moving average that allows attributes of the surrounding neighbourhoods (LSOAs) to be included in the model. In the Stockton study, to mitigate for the bias in the sample, efforts were taken to adjust for age, gender and any clustering of local area effects within the data (Bhandari et al., 2017).

This example shows that, even with the most rigorously designed study, care needs to be taken in how results are interpreted, given the interruption by 'real-world' issues in researchers' best-laid plans.

BEYOND THE INDIVIDUAL AND THE LOCAL: THE POLITICAL ECONOMY APPROACH

The political economy approach to explaining health divides focuses on the social, political and economic structures and relations that may be, and often are, outside the control of the individuals or the local areas that they affect (Krieger, 2003). Individual and collective social and economic factors such as housing, income and employment – indeed, many of the issues that dominate political life – are key determinants of health and well-being (Bambra, Fox & Scott-Samuel, 2005). Why some places and people are consistently privileged while others are consistently marginalised is a political choice. It is about where the power lies and in whose interests that power is exercised. Political choices can thereby be seen as the 'causes of the causes of the causes' of geographical inequalities in health (Bambra, 2016).

By way of example, we can examine the causes of stroke or heart disease (Bambra, 2016). The immediate *clinical cause* could be hypertension (high blood pressure). The *proximal cause* of the hypertension itself could be compositional lifestyle factors, such as poor diet, of which the *contextual cause* might be living in a low-income neighbourhood. The causes of the latter are political – low-income neighbourhoods exist because the political and economic system allows them to exist. Wages could be regulated so that they are higher (an example being the living wage) or food prices could be controlled/subsidised (e.g., in the United States, meat and corn oil receive government subsidies, not fruits and vegetables; likewise, in the European Union, farmers are encouraged to produce dairy), and neighbourhood food provision does not have to be left to the vagaries of the market (which leads to clustering of poor food availability in poor neighbourhoods).

In this sense, geographical patterns of health and disease are produced by the structures, values and priorities of political and economic systems (Krieger, 2003). Area-level health – be it local, regional or national – is determined, at least in part, by the wider political, social and economic system and the actions of the state- (government) and international-level actors (supranational government bodies such as the European Union, interstate trade agreements such as the Transatlantic Trade and Investment Partnership [TTIP], as well as the actions of large corporations): politics can make us sick – or healthy (Schrecker & Bambra, 2015) (see Chapter 5 on scale). Politics and the balance of power between key political groups – notably, labour and capital – determine the role of the state and other agencies in relation to health and whether there are collective interventions to improve health and reduce health inequalities, and also whether these interventions are individually, environmentally or structurally focused. In this way, politics (broadly understood) is the fundamental determinant of our health divides because it shapes the wider social, economic and physical environment and

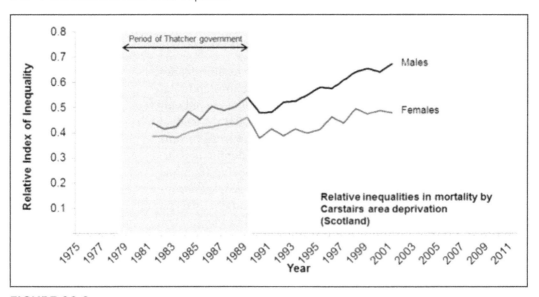

FIGURE 23.3

Geographical trends in health inequalities in Scotland 1981–2001 (by Carstairs-area deprivation).
(Source: Scott-Samuel et al., 2014)

the social and spatial distribution of salutogenic and pathogenic factors, both collectively and individually (Bambra, 2016).

An example of the influence of politics on health is seen in Figure 23.3, which shows the gap between the most and least deprived neighbourhoods and how this increased through the 1980s and 1990s. Collins and McCartney (2011) argue that this is a result of the Thatcher government's (1979–1990) neoliberal approach to the economy and society and that it constituted a political attack on the working class, and that Scotland (particularly Glasgow and the west of Scotland) became a particular target (Collins & McCartney, 2011). The Thatcher government radically altered the social settlement: mass unemployment became normalised via deindustrialisation at the same time that trade union and workers' rights were curtailed, there were significant reductions in welfare benefits leading to the intensification of poverty and wage compression, and vast reductions were seen in the availability of social housing (Scott-Samuel et al., 2014). While neoliberalism spread across many wealthy countries in the 1980s, the United Kingdom was exposed in a way that other European nations were not – in a rapid and intense manner that adversely affected health through unemployment, poverty, alienation and associated increases in risky health behaviours. For example, deindustrialisation was implemented as a 'shock doctrine', with very rapid loss of employment within a few years in the United Kingdom, while in other Western European countries it was phased in more gradually and often with more safety nets (such as employment services or inducements for new industry to come to the affected areas). A more recent example is the effects of austerity and the resulting reduction in welfare benefits and public services, affecting social geographies and health inequalities (Pearce, 2013).

SUMMARY

- To date, health geography has conventionally presented two main explanations for why there are such stark inequalities in health: compositional and contextual.

- More recently though, these approaches have been reconciled via the relational understanding of place and health. Further, a political economy approach has started to be taken up within the discipline so that the role of the wider macropolitical, economic and societal context is beginning to be examined.

- Inequalities in health can be seen at the local, national and global levels. These health divides have traditionally been explained in terms of the interaction of compositional (who lives here?) and contextual (what is this place like?) factors.

- Increasingly, though, the relationship between health and place is also understood to be influenced by national and international political and economic factors that operate outside the control of individuals and localities. This chapter examines how and why place matters for health at different geographical scales.

FURTHER READING

Bambra, C. (2016) *Health Divides: Where You Live Can Kill You.* Bristol: Policy Press.

Bambra, C., Smith, K., & Pearce, J. (2019) Scaling up: The politics of health and place. *Social Science & Medicine*, 232: 36–42.

Gatrell, A., & Elliot, S. (2009) *Geographies of Health: An Introduction.* London: Wiley.

Williams, A. (ed.) (2017) *Therapeutic Landscapes.* London: Routledge.

Education

Simon Tate

As Johanna Waters notes, early research into the geography of education was mainly conducted in the United Kingdom during the 1970s. It was concerned with identifying social and spatial inequalities in access to education and with highlighting the differences in educational attainment by pupils from different social backgrounds. Underpinning this research was the assumption that education is the key to social mobility but that educational opportunities are far from equal for working-class and middle-class children. Social geographers, with our interest in space and place, were in an excellent position to contribute to this sort of research because 'educational processes – from opportunities to outcomes – unfurl over space differently and relationally, with differential outcomes for individuals and groups' (Waters, 2018).

However, as Waters (2018) also notes, since around 2000 'geographies of education' (plural) have emerged from this early research to become a broader field of study that also addresses issues as diverse as how the education system reproduces class inequalities between generations (see, e.g., Goldthorpe, 2014) and the impact of neoliberal free markets on education (see, e.g., Pimlott-Wilson, 2017). While social geographers still have an important role to play, this work is increasingly interdisciplinary and international in focus, and it uses spatial variations in educational access and attainment to comment upon wider

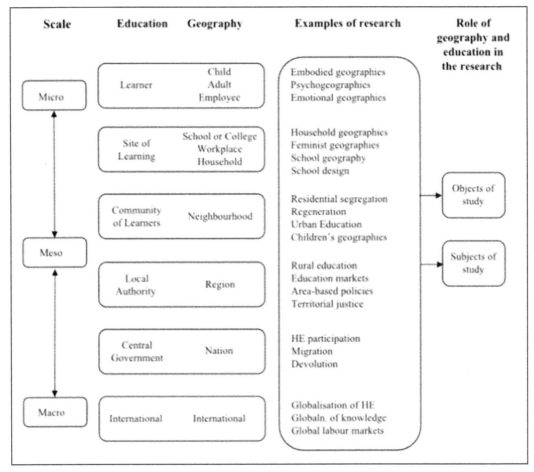

FIGURE 24.1

Towards a geography of education. (Source: Taylor, 2009: 657)

social, economic and political processes in the world (Thiem, 2009; Holloway et al., 2010). This newer body of research also defines education more broadly than the formal learning that takes place in schools, colleges and universities, and it employs another foundational concept in geography – scale – to provide a framework with which to systematically explore the relationship between geography and education (see Chapter 5 on scale). Helpfully, Chris Taylor offers Figure 24.1 to illustrate the range of issues and scales with which the geographies of education are currently concerned.

Given the increasing diversity of this body of work, this chapter illustrates how the geographical concepts of space and scale have been, and continue to be, applied in geographies of education research. In so doing, I argue that geography (as a subject) and we (as an academic community of social geographers) have a vital contribution to make to current debates about educational inequality and social mobility. I explore three contemporary educational issues. First, focusing on what Figure 24.1 refers to as the macro-scale, I explore the idea that there is a north–south divide between the quality of secondary schools in England. Second, at Taylor's meso-scale, I investigate the role of what Herbert and Thomas (1998) refer to as 'the neighbourhood effect' as an explanation of the differences in school access and attainment within UK regions. Finally, at the micro-scale, I explore the decision-making processes that affect the social and spatial transition from school to university for nontraditional students and explain the important role that social geographers have in mapping the social and spatial divides that these individual decisions can collectively produce. In so doing, all three sections of the chapter connect with other important themes in social geography (see Chapter 11 on the everyday, Chapter 15 on class and Chapter 20 on intersectionality).

A NORTH–SOUTH EDUCATIONAL DIVIDE BETWEEN ENGLISH SECONDARY SCHOOLS?

The idea of there being a north–south divide between the quality of secondary schools in England came to renewed prominence in 2015 when Sir Michael Wilshaw (who, at that time, was the Office for Standards in Education, Children's Services and Skills [Ofsted's] chief inspector) wrote in his annual report that we had 'nothing short of a divided nation after the age of 11' between schools in the North and Midlands and schools in the South of England (Ofsted, 2015: 9). The basis for Sir Michael's claim was that 79 per cent of schools in the South achieved a good or outstanding Ofsted report, compared with only 68 per cent in the North and Midlands (Ofsted, 2015). He also named sixteen weak local authorities, where fewer than 60 per cent of pupils attended good or outstanding schools and which had below-average attainment and progress at GCSE level. Of these, thirteen were in the North and Midlands: Barnsley, Blackpool, Bradford, Derbyshire, Doncaster, Hartlepool, Knowsley, Liverpool, Middlesbrough, Oldham, Salford, St Helens and Stoke-on-Trent. The other three were in the Isle of Wight, Swindon and South Gloucestershire. According to Jopling (2019), the idea that secondary schools in the North of England need to improve their performance has been reinforced since 2015 in the rhetoric around the government's Northern Powerhouse, an initiative launched in 2014 to increase economic productivity in the North of England (see, e.g., Children's Commissioner for England, 2018; Northern Powerhouse Partnership, 2018). Indeed, the idea of a north–south 'divide' in English education is a stereotype that now resonates in the media, government and wider society.

However, to what extent is the rhetoric of there being a north–south divide in English education an oversimplification? The rise of geographic information system (GIS) mapping in geography has enabled social geographers to make important contributions to answering this question. By mapping various educational statistics at a regional level, it has been possible for them to argue that English educational inequality is more complex. For example, as Figures 24.2 and 24.3 show, the perceived divide is at its worst when schools in the North East are compared to those in London: London schools outperformed those in the North East both in terms of the number of pupils attaining grades 9 to 4 in English and Maths GCSEs in 2018 and in the average points total per pupil studying A levels in 2018 (although the difference is less stark for A levels). This difference

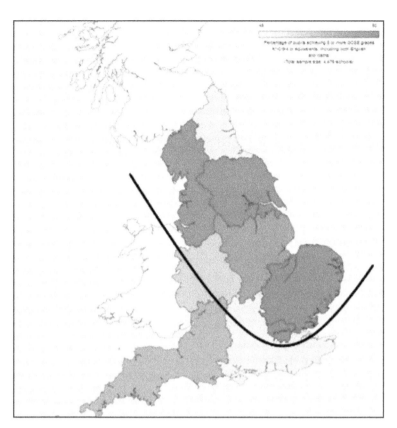

FIGURE 24.2
Map of the percentage of pupils in each English region gaining grades 9–4 in English and Maths GCSEs in 2018. (Source: SchoolDash / reproducable / Contains National Statistics data © Crown copyright and database right 2019)

FIGURE 24.3
Map of students' average points score in their best three A levels in 2018. (Source: SchoolDash / reproducable / Contains National Statistics data © Crown copyright and database right 2019)

can, in part, be attributed to the legacy of the London Challenge. The London Challenge was a school improvement programme launched by the United Kingdom's Labour Government in 2003 that was designed to create a step-change in the underperformance of London schools. It was initially aimed at secondary schools and was intended to run until 2008, although it was subsequently extended until 2011. A report for the Institute for Government in 2014 concluded that, 'during the period of the London Challenge, secondary school performance in London saw a dramatic improvement, and local authorities in inner London went from the worst performing to the best performing nationally' (Kidson & Norris, 2014: 2). Funding is also an important part of the explanation of why London schools perform well: Clifton, Round and Raikes (2016) estimate that in 2016 northern secondary schools received, on average, £1,300 less per student per year than secondary schools in London.

However, it is also clear from Figures 24.2 and 24.3 that, if there are broad patterns in educational attainment, they are very different depending on the statistics used to compare schools in the North with those in the South. For example, in Figure 24.3 the north–south 'divide' in A-level performance runs roughly along an imaginary line from the River Humber to the River Severn. In so doing, it broadly mirrors the more commonly spoken about north–south economic divide between places on either side of an imaginary line running from the Wash to the River Severn (see Figure 24.4). In contrast, in Figure 24.2 the 'divide' in GCSE performance broadly runs along

FIGURE 24.4

Map showing the levels of social deprivation in English regions in 2018, measured by the percentage of pupils entitled to free school meals. This is a common proxy, used for social deprivation in educational research. (Source: SchoolDash / reproducable / Contains National Statistics data © Crown copyright and database right 2019)

an imaginary line from the River Mersey to the River Thames. Whether this counts as a north–south divide at all is open to question as, for example, Figure 24.2 also shows higher levels of GCSE attainment in the North West than the South West. My own home region (the North East) is another interesting outlier: underperforming as a region compared to the rest of the North in GCSE results, yet outperforming the rest of the North in terms of A-level results.

These findings concur with those of Michael Jopling (2019), who points out that the north–south 'divide' in the quality of English secondary schools is not as significant as much of the rhetoric makes it seem at first. In addition, Jopling notes that there is no significant regional pattern in educational quality at primary-school level, with, for example, primary schools in the North East performing well while areas like West Berkshire lag behind. Finally, Jopling observes that the data used by Ofsted are often flawed as they do not take into account differences in school intakes, levels of economic disadvantage or school funding. Jopling's (2019) conclusion is that to understand educational inequality better we need to change the scale on which we focus, as our analysis 'will benefit from focusing more clearly on variations in performance within and across regions, rather than repeating generalised condemnations of regional underperformance' (Jopling, 2019: 40). As social geographers, we can respond to this call to change the scale on which we focus; one way to do this is through the neighbourhood effect on educational inequality in the United Kingdom, as I now discuss.

THE 'NEIGHBOURHOOD EFFECT' ON SCHOOL INEQUALITIES IN THE UNITED KINGDOM

Regarding the geographies of education at a meso-scale (Taylor, 2009), it is easy to assume that the only significant places that we need to consider are schools and colleges. It is equally easy to assume that our homes and the areas surrounding them are simply where we spend a significant amount of our leisure time. However, as social geographers, we recognise that the home is more than this – it is also a space of 'belonging and alienation, intimacy and violence, desire and fear . . . invested with meanings, emotions, experiences and relationships that lie at the heart of human life' (Blunt & Varley, 2004: 3). Consequently, the home is another important site in the meso-scale geographies of education that we need to examine alongside schools and colleges. When grouped together, school, college and home (and where they are located) make up what Herbert and Thomas (1998) refer to as 'the neighbourhood effect', which can have a powerful influence on educational outcomes: 'In addition to the influence of parents and home, children are affected by the values and codes of behaviour prevalent in the residential area in which they live [see Chapter 19 on age]. Neighbourhood values are likely to reinforce home values, and geographers have been interested in isolating a neighbourhood effect in education' (Herbert & Thomas, 1998: 202).

One way social geographers often begin to think about the link between education and 'the neighbourhood effect' is by considering the work of Pierre Bourdieu, who developed the concepts of cultural capital and social capital (see Chapter 15 on class). Bourdieu observed that cultural capital has three states: 'institutionalised' by our academic qualifications; 'embodied' in our personal characteristics, values and social skills; and 'objectified' in our personal possessions (Bourdieu, 1986). These are useful concepts to begin to understand the influence that the neighbourhood effect has upon pupils' educational aspirations and outcomes, as children enter the education system with different amounts of cultural capital. In other words, when we started our education, the playing field was not a level one: because of the environment in which we grew up, some of us had more advantages than others; in contrast, some of us will have had to work harder to overcome the relative disadvantages that we faced. These differences in cultural capital arise because parents, guardians and other family members both consciously and subconsciously influence their children through the transmission of cultural capital, passing on their beliefs and ideas between generations. Consequently, parents with a greater level of cultural capital have the 'skills, habits, and styles that are rewarded at the higher educational levels' (De Graaf, De Graaf & Kraaykamp, 2000: 93) and are able to provide the essential resources for their children to succeed. In contrast, parents with low cultural capital will find it harder do so. Johanna Waters (2006: 180) takes this analysis one stage further, arguing that 'The active accumulation of cultural capital represents the principle means by which the middle-class seeks to reproduce its social status across generations'. This is known as the social reproduction of the class system (see Chapter 28 on social reproduction).

Although Waters talks about the social reproduction of the middle class, it is important to note two things. First, Bourdieu does not make an assumption that those with more money are more likely to have more cultural capital. This is shown in his statement that '[the] most privileged sections of the dominant classes from the point of view of economic capital and power are not necessarily the most well-off in terms of cultural capital' (Bourdieu, 1977: 497). Instead, he argues that, regardless of socioeconomic background, when parents are engaged with (and invest in) the cultural capital of their children, this leads to improvements in their children's education. Second, Bourdieu's work is not deterministic. In other words, he is not arguing that those from socioeconomically disadvantaged backgrounds are destined to perform badly at school and that they will struggle to find a well-paid job and, therefore, will be impoverished. Upward social mobility is possible. For example, Siraj-Blatchford's (2010) research found that economically disadvantaged families often have high aspirations for their children and, because of this, create a positive home learning environment.

One question which arises from this is to what extent schools and colleges can compensate for a neighbourhood or home that lacks cultural or social capital. Here, the concept of 'fictive kin', a term coined by the anthropologist John Ogby, is key. In terms of education, fictive kin refers to anyone with no biological connection to a pupil but who may impact their educational attainment and aspirations: 'fictive kin relations . . . fill family-like roles and functions' (Braithwaite et al., 2010: 398; see also Tierney & Venegas, 2006). When a teacher or school attempts to compensate for the lack of support at home, they are fictively replacing family functions, taking on the role of biological family (i.e., the role of biological kin).

To illustrate this point further, let's look at an example of fictive kin operating in schools and colleges.

Bourdieu's idea of 'social capital' refers to our interpersonal networks and the social ties that create positive benefits for us as individuals. We gain social capital from teachers, friends, siblings, friends of our family, the groups with which we hang out in our neighbourhood and so on. Bourdieu argues that a person with 'a wealth of social capital infers the potential for economic and cultural capital connections' (Tierney & Venegas, 2006: 1689), whereas people with low social capital are also low in cultural capital. One way in which schools and colleges can attempt to raise the social and cultural capital of their pupils is by enhancing their social networks. Willis (1977) and Ball (1981) established that, broadly speaking, pupils tend to join proschool friendship groups or antischool friendship groups. They suggested that if a pupil is friends with proschool pupils, he or she is likely to have higher aspirations; conversely, those in antischool friendship groups have lower aspirations. Schools and colleges can encourage more of their pupils to join these 'proschool' friendship groups by manipulating the composition of their classes to enhance social networking. Looking at this through a geographical lens, the question becomes whether to divide both socially and spatially those with higher and lower levels of social and cultural capital. The argument in favour of mixed-ability classes is that pupils who are streamed according to their 'ability' into lower sets often lack the necessary social and cultural capital to do well in education. Instead, they reinforce or normalise each other's low expectations. Even those who are aspirational will struggle to flourish in that environment. In contrast, those in the higher-streamed sets, with more social and cultural capital, will push each other to do even better and to achieve even more. This has the potential to increase the disparities in educational outcomes between the two groups. In contrast, in mixed-ability classes there is the potential for these disparities to decrease as social and cultural capital is subconsciously transmitted through the new social networks that result. Consequently, the aspirations of those from the bottom sets are encouraged along, and up, by their social interactions with pupils who have higher levels of social and cultural capital. Nevertheless, whether pupils should be taught in mixed-ability classes or whether they should be placed in streamed classes according to their 'ability' is a controversial issue (Oakes & Guiton, 1995). At the heart of the debate lie issues of space, inclusivity and segregation, and so social geographers have an important role to play by bringing a spatial perspective to the meso level of the geographies of education.

THE SOCIO-SPATIAL DIVIDES IN HIGHER EDUCATION

Statistics from the House of Commons' Public Accounts Committee (2018) show that the percentage of students entering higher education from the lowest-participation areas of the United Kingdom (which strongly correlate to the areas of most social deprivation) is well below the percentage of students entering higher education from the highest-participation areas (25 per cent from the lowest-participation areas, compared to 59 per cent from the highest-participation areas). This is important in terms of social mobility, as the committee also notes that 'on average, graduates earn 42% more than non-graduates' (Public Accounts Committee, 2018: 8). Consequently, at Taylor's (2009) micro level of analysis, as social geographers we have an important role to play in exploring the decision-making processes that affect the transition from school to university for potential new students and to map the social and spatial divides that these individual decisions can collectively produce.

Of course, economic capital (i.e., ability to pay the cost) is an important factor in this decision-making process, as participation in higher education represents a significant financial commitment for students, with average student debt of £50,000 from a three-year degree course (Public Accounts Committee, 2018). However, a House of Commons Briefing Paper in 2018 concluded that there was 'no evidence that those from "lower" socioeconomic groups or (deprived) areas, with historically low levels of participation, have been adversely affected by tuition fees' (Bolton, 2018: 13). This begs the question: What other factors might also be important when potential new students are deciding whether to attend university and which university to go to? Consider Text Box 24.1 in thinking about this question.

In the process of widening participation to enable more nontraditional students to participate in higher education, many universities have been involved in outreach or access schemes – such as summer schools – which, once successfully completed, provide a reduced entry offer to potential new students. While on the surface this development looks positive (and, in many cases, it is), here, too, the Public Accounts Committee noted that geographical and social divides are emerging as 'not all universities are doing enough to support widening participation, and . . . some universities are doing more of the "heavy lifting" in relation to widening participation. Universities that are able to attract a lot of applicants because of their perceived prestige have less incentive to work hard to widen participation' (Public Accounts Committee, 2018: 10).

Once at university, as Holton and Riley (2013) observe, social divisions on campus can force some nontraditional students to withdraw both socially and academically from university life. More positively, research has also concluded that many nontraditional students find their own ways to integrate once at university (Barnes et al., 2011). Some become friends with students from similar socioeconomic backgrounds; some become friends with students from very different back-

TEXT BOX 24.1 | Real-World Research: Nontraditional Students' Transitions to University

In 2011, I conducted some research with Lauren Barnes, Amy Buckley and Peter Hopkins that aimed to discover what other factors are important when potential new students are deciding whether to attend university and which university to go to. In the research, we tried to identify the factors that influenced nontraditional students' decision-making about whether and where to study at university (Barnes et al., 2011). Christie (2007) defines nontraditional students as first-generation university attendees from working-class or minority backgrounds, and we found that within this group there were diverse reasons for choosing to continue to study at university. Here, Bourdieu's third concept, that of habitus, was also a useful tool for thinking through the issues. Habitus refers to the way our beliefs, values and expectations are influenced by where we grow up and the social surroundings we are exposed to on a daily basis: 'An individual's habitus consists of internalised, or "embodied", social structures that set the standards for the way in which he or she understand the world and "navigates" through life' (Almquist, Modin & Östberg, 2010: 33). In turn, our habitus influences our behavioural patterns, ambitions and everyday choices. It works alongside cultural capital to affect our everyday life and decisions.

For some of the students we spoke to as part of the research, their decision to attend university had been swayed by all of their friends going to university, their parents expecting them to go or their feeling that it was the taken-for-granted next step for them. These students tended to have higher levels of what Bourdieu refers to as cultural capital (Bourdieu, 1986). Others were influenced by external factors, which often included inspirational teachers encouraging them to study at university. In contrast, among those with lower levels of social capital, a lack of confidence about taking what was perceived as a 'leap into the unknown' was a recurring theme in our findings: for example, peers encouraging them not to apply to an 'elitist' university, as they would not 'fit in', and teachers reinforcing problematic stereotypes about particular Russell Group universities, which had a negative impact upon students' self-confidence and self-esteem. Consequently, nontraditional students tended to cluster in the post-1992 universities rather than in the Russell Group, creating a social and spatial divide. Indeed, Reay and colleagues (2001) argue that a sociospatial hierarchy has emerged in which the top tier of research-led institutions has an overwhelmingly White, middle-class student base.

grounds whom they otherwise would not have had the opportunity to meet. Geography students seem to have a particular advantage in this regard, as field courses at university are a particularly useful way of helping students get to know others in their year group. This points to the potential for higher education to be the catalyst for increased social and cultural capital, leading to increased social mobility.

In addition to cultural capital playing a role in informing the 'type' of university that is attractive to prospective nontraditional students, as social geographers we can inquire into the geography of where this group of students will attend university. Studies carried out in Liverpool (Holdsworth, 2006, 2009) and Edinburgh (Christie, 2007) show that many nontraditional students can feel restricted by their social 'immobility' and so end up attending their local university. Living at home in turn impacts their 'student experience'. As Holton and Riley (2013) conclude, while the experiences that students gain through higher education may create access to new opportunities, nontraditional students are too often tied to their home geographical location by family circumstances, meaning they cannot always take full advantage of such prospects: 'working-class students were saturated with a localism that was absent from the narratives of more economically privileged students' (Reay et al., 2001: 861).

In its evidence to the Public Accounts Committee, the Department for Education stated that reducing inequalities in educational provision in the United Kingdom was a 'huge priority' and that it was developing a Social Mobility Action Plan (Public Accounts Committee, 2018: 10). However, as we have seen, these issues are complicated, spatial, multiscalar and intersectional. Therefore, as Taylor (2009: 651) concludes, the contribution of social geographers to these debates going forward will remain 'pivotal' and 'significant'.

SUMMARY

- Geography (as a subject) and we (as an academic community of social geographers) have a vital contribution to make to current debates about educational inequality and social mobility at a variety of scales.
- The so-called north–south divide in the quality of English secondary schools is not as significant as much of the rhetoric makes it seem at first.
- Pierre Bourdieu developed the concepts of cultural capital and social capital, which can have a powerful influence on educational outcomes at the scale of neighbourhoods and individuals.
- Higher education can be the catalyst for increased social and cultural capital, leading to increased social mobility.

FURTHER READING

Christie, H. (2007) Higher education and spatial (im)mobility: Nontraditional students and living at home. *Environment and Planning A: Economy and Space*, 39: 2445–63.

Holton, M., & Riley, M. (2013) Student geographies: Exploring the diverse geographies of students and higher education. *Geography Compass*, 7(1): 61–74.

Jopling, M. (2019) Is there a north–south divide between schools in England? *Management in Education*, 33(1): 37–40.

Waters, J. L. (2006) Geographies of cultural capital: Education, international migration and family strategies between Hong Kong and Canada. *Transactions of the Institute of British Geographers*, 31(2): 179–92.

Policing the City

Elaine Campbell

Steve Narvaez Jara, a twenty-year-old aerospace student, cele-brated the New Year of 2018 at a party in Islington, London. Shortly after midnight, the energetic, aspirational Ecuadorean was brutally murdered and became the first of over seventy vic-tims stabbed to death in the capital in a single year. By Novem-ber 2018, recorded offences for knife-related violence across London boroughs had reached 14,721, representing an increase of 21 per cent over the previous year and marking its highest level since 2010 (Allen & Audickas, 2018: 21). At the time of writing this chapter, alarmist talk of a 'dramatic spike in knife crime' is triggering a moral panic about how London (and Lon-doners) are best kept safe, bolstered by overblown media claims that the UK capital has become a 'war zone' that is 'spiralling out of control'. This kind of commentary may be wide of the mark; yet it reminds us that, from time to time, a city's repu-tation pivots on its perceived capacity to be effectively policed. In other words, to talk of 'policing the city' not only says some-thing about the social value, meaning and status of the city – as dangerous, risky, disorderly, safe or violent, for example – but also raises complex questions about the myriad ways twenty-first-century cities can be, should be and *are* policed.

The history of modern Western policing – which dates from the beginning of the nineteenth century – runs in tandem with the formation of the nation-state, the advent of industrial capitalism, rural depopulation, mass urbanisation and the exponential growth of the city (Robinson & Scaglion, with Olivero, 1994) (see Chapter 10 on urban/rural). Structural transformations in the social, economic, political and cultural fabric of nascent, liberal-democratic societies raised new concerns about the stability of social order, the protection of private property and the quelling of what Lee described as 'an epoch of criminality' (1901: 203) (see Chapter 6 on social change). This set the conditions for establishing professional, bureaucratically organised police forces tasked with law enforcement, order maintenance and the spatial governance and control of shifting populations caught up in a maelstrom of rapid and uneven urban change. Social geographers Nick Fyfe (1991) and Steve Herbert (1997) have emphasised how modern policing involves the legitimate use of coercive force to restrict mobilities, enact and reinforce boundaries and control access into and out of specified and demarcated sites – as Fyfe notes, 'policing is an inherently *territorial* activity' (1991: 265; italics added).

The notion of policing as highly territorialised is reflected in the terms that we use to describe its organisational structure and operational deployments within the city – in the United Kingdom, for example, policing is spatially described as a scaled sequence of local beats, area commands and force areas. Indeed, ethnographies of urban police work tell us how police officers talk of city spaces as their 'ground': '[it] belongs to the police. . . . They possess it; it is their territory and members of the force from adjoining stations have no right of entry into or patrol of the ground' (Holdaway, 1983: 36). It is hard to accept the idea that the power to regulate, prohibit and enclose has no spatial reference point or that it cannot be located or locatable within a defined area or territory (Sack, 1980). However, if we take John Allen's (2004: 19) advice to be a little more 'spatially curious' in our analyses, this opens up the possibility of questioning not only the *whereabouts* of policing but also *what* we might mean by the city and how it can be policed.

This chapter takes up this challenge and explores different *kinds* of cities and the varied ways they are policed (see Table 25.1). Urban geographers have long since classified cities along key social, political, economic, technological and material dimensions and see this as a useful analytical tool (Bruce & Witt, 1971). In reality, of course, cities (and different approaches to policing) are dynamic entanglements of a wide array of socio-spatial configurations that jostle, intersect, overlap, coexist, compete and collide with one another. In this chapter, we will look closely at three city types: the neoliberal city, the global city and the vertical city.

TABLE 25.1	Key Concepts and Texts about Policing the City
Key Concepts	**Key Texts**
Neoliberal city	
Urban zonification	Lippert, R. K., & Walby, K. (eds.) (2013) *Policing Cities: Urban Securitization and Regulation in a 21st Century World*. London: Routledge.
Gated communities	Caldeira, T. (2000) *City Walls: Crime, Segregation and Citizenship in Sao Paolo*. Berkeley: University of California Press.
Consumerism	Hayward, K. J. (2004) *City Limits: Crime, Consumer Culture and the Urban Experience*. London: Glasshouse.
Militarisation	Graham, S. (2011) *Cities Under Siege: The New Military Urbanism*. London: Verso.
Global city	
Space of flows	Aas, K. F. (2007) *Globalization and Crime*. London: Sage.
Transnational policing	Bowling, B., & Sheptycki, J. W. E. (2012) *Global Policing*. London: Sage.
Plural policing	Jones, T., & Newburn, T. (eds.) (2006) *Plural Policing: A Comparative Perspective*. London: Routledge.
Vertical city	
Fortress architecture	Graham, S. (2016) *Vertical: The City from Satellites to Bunkers*. London: Verso.
Surveillance technologies	Haggerty, K. D., & Ericson, R. V. (eds.) (2006) *The New Politics of Surveillance and Visibility*. Toronto: Toronto University Press.
Digital policing	Wessels, B. (2007) *Inside the Digital Revolution: Policing and Changing Communication with the Public*. London: Routledge.

POLICING THE NEOLIBERAL CITY

Neoliberal cities are open for business. Sometimes they are referred to as progressive, consumerist or entrepreneurial (Lynch et al., 2013), and Brenner and Theodore (2002: 368) talk of such cities as becoming 'institutional laboratories for a variety of neoliberal policy experiments'. These include, on the one hand, the creation and promotion of enterprise zones, urban development corporations, gentrification schemes, public–private partnerships and place-marketing, and, on the other, an intensification of workfare programmes, decreased welfare spending and new strategies of social control, policing, risk-management and spatial governance (Herbert & Brown, 2006; Lynch et al., 2013). Taking all of these aspects together, neoliberal cities entrench social divisions and inequalities (see Part C on divisions) and do so in a variety of ways, not least through a diversification of policing methods and personnel, which find spatial expression in myriad exclusionary practices.

Consider, for example, Faranak Miraftab's (2012) research on urban regeneration through city improvement districts in Cape Town, South Africa. Here, she identifies patterns of 'zonification' based on old-style colonial practices of 'location creation' that alienate, dispossess and marginalise the urban poor, and in highly racialised ways. It is a state of affairs that is further explored by Paasche, Yarwood and Sidaway (2014: 1565), who note that private (nonstate) policing operatives working in these same city improvement districts have reterritorialised urban spaces by creating 'invisible boundaries', which displace not only 'undesirables' from certain (improved) areas but also the need for public (state) policing within them. Palmer, Warren and Miller (2012) and Palmer and Warren (2014) have similarly highlighted the proliferation of private policing and the introduction of a plethora of localised civil laws in the leisure spaces of the nighttime economy in Victoria, Australia. In an attempt to manage and regulate alcohol consumption in such spaces, and also to prevent alcohol-related harms, enhanced use of banning orders, the imposition of zonal controls and an increased use of surveillance technologies (such as ID scanning, Closed Circuit Television [CCTV] and body checks), they point out, have served to exclude antisocial populations, variously described as 'troublemakers, drunken thugs, hooligans, idiots, aggressive grog-fuelled yobbos and underage drinkers' (Palmer, Warren & Miller, 2012: 305) from licensed venues and entertainment outlets. As Lucy Zedner (2009) has observed, the redistribution of policing responsibilities across private-sector and public policing authorities has led to not only the spatial fragmentation of governance and law enforcement but also the emergence of an urban patchwork of security bubbles, quilts and corridors.

In the landmark text *Ecology of Fear*, Mike Davis (1998) writes of Los Angeles as a neoliberal city that is defined less by its meeting places and communal areas than by its walls and enclaves. The expansion of gated communities perfectly exemplifies this trend toward an increasingly divided urban world. Blakely and Snyder (1997) suggest three types of gated community predicated on lifestyle, prestige and security. The lifestyle model caters for a new leisure class and typically includes recreational and social amenities such as golf courses or country clubs; the prestige model offers high-income groups a premium location, aesthetically enhanced landscapes and luxury fixtures and fittings; the security model has less interest in promoting status than in creating a protected community and redefining the boundaries between 'rough' and 'respectable' neighbourhoods. It is this last model, in particular, that asks difficult questions about the policing of privatised residential spaces. In February 2012, Trayvon Martin, an African American high school student, was visiting relatives in the Retreat at Twin Lakes, a gated community in Sanford, Florida. On his way back from the shops, he was misrecognised as a trespasser, and Martin was confronted and challenged by the neighbourhood watch coordinator, George Zimmerman; in the altercation that ensued, Martin, who was unarmed, was fatally shot in the chest. Such incidents are far from rare and are indicative of systematic violence toward racialised bodies. As Marcia England (2008) notes, neoliberal strategies of neighbourhood responsibilisation – such as the Good Neighbor Agreements initiative that she researched in Seattle – foster socio-spatial relations of segregation and partition, re-create neighbourhoods 'as sites to be protected from "outside" infiltration' and mobilise 'geographies of citizenship' for some and 'geographies of nowhere' for others (2880) (see Chapter 7 on justice).

Urban and political geographers have been especially critical of the *militarisation* of policing practices in the context of the neoliberal city, though some argue that policing has always already been militarised and implicated in a socially divisive form of 'martial politics' (Howell, 2018). Mega-events, such as the Olympics, G8/G20 summits (see Figure 25.1), FIFA World Cups and European Football Championships (Fussey, 2015; Kitchen & Rygiel, 2014), weave together the demands of security and surveillance with those of business investment, cultural enterprise, cosmopolitanism, national reputation and economic regeneration. On such occasions, cities are transformed not only into showcase settings but also into 'battlespaces' and 'cities under siege' (Graham, 2011). Writing about the 2012 London Olympics, Fussey (2015) complains of a 'carceral archipelago' of security imprints across the capital, while Graham (2012) talks of 'lockdown London' and raises serious concerns about the deployment of surface-to-air missiles on the roofs of high-rise residential housing. It is little wonder that these kinds of policing and security deployments are regarded by urban geographers as 'the "home front" of new testing grounds for military weaponry and tactics of war' (Kitchen & Rygiel, 2014: 212).

FIGURE 25.1

G20 Summit 2010, Toronto, Canada. (Photograph by Chris Huggins. Creative Commons 2.0; found at Chris HugginsFlickr)

POLICING THE GLOBAL CITY

Globalisation, argues John Urry, is an unfinished process, 'which problematizes the fixed, given and static notions of social order' (2002: 59). Globalising processes have been aligned with two key transformations in the spatial organisation of society: first, time-space compression (Harvey, 1989) – the 'shrinking' of space and the shortening of time (see Chapter 4 on space and time); second, the advent of a networked society, 'a new society based upon knowledge, organised around networks and partly made up of flows' (Castells, 1996: 398). In a globalised world, the city takes on a renewed and yet profoundly altered importance and emerges as an economic and information hub and a base for the operations of transnational corporations, global financial and political institutions and international chains of consumers and producers. Indeed, since the early 2000s urban scholars have talked of the city as a space of flows rather than a space of places (Sassen, 2001). Policing the global city is thus less a matter of territorial control and the regulation of micro-locales and more about governing deterritorialised flows of capital, commodities, information and people, in the form of smuggling, terrorism, human trafficking, illegal immigration, money laundering and cybercrime.

One important manifestation of a shift away from localised, emplaced policing to an approach primarily geared to the interception and disruption of illicit circulations and mobilities is seen in relation to border control. In recent years, geographers, security analysts and criminologists have questioned the conventional view of the border as materially (and symbolically) positioned at the 'edge' of national space. This critical analytical work points to the shifting spatialities of contemporary bordering practices and recognises how the policing of the border relies on remote control, biometrics, smart technologies, digitised data capture and myriad preemptive, filtering, screening and scanning technologies (Amoore, 2006). The notion of a border as geographically fixed at the territorial frontiers of a political community is superseded by a sense of its 'everywhereness', its ubiquity, and as part of a continuum of policing practices that embeds border securities in the heart of the city – into 'the public spaces of the railway station, shopping mall and sports stadium' (Amoore, Marmura & Salter, 2008: 96). Cities, then, serve as hubs for the confiscation of illegal goods and commodities and the social sorting, legal categorisation and risk assessment of 'crimmigrant bodies' (Aas, 2011) to determine the grounds for their deportation, transfer or dispersal (see Chapter 26 on migration and diaspora).

As policing tasks become more spatially fluid and dispersed, the responsibilities for law enforcement also diffuse and proliferate across myriad policing actors. Policing scholars refer to this changed landscape as the advent of 'plural', 'networked' and 'transnational' policing (Rogers, 2017) and note how policing is now fragmented, decentred, multisited and multisectoral. The policing of cybercrime in general, and cyber-paedophilia in particular, does not merely reflect this trend but in many ways comes to exemplify it (see Chapter 31 on digital).

Consider the array of nonstate actors, agencies and authorities who act in responsibilised, preemptive, legally obligated and socially dispersed ways to regulate, monitor, report and disable suspicious online activity and inappropriate sexual communication with children – from internet service providers and software developers to parents and teachers, charitable organisations and social media providers (Campbell, 2016). At the same time, decentred policing arrangements respond to novel forms and spaces of paedophiliac offending, primarily facilitated by the proliferating use of social media platforms, the dark web and digital technologies, which blur any distinction between real and virtual paedophilia. While these technological advances can overwhelm traditional policing's crime-control capacities, they also generate new opportunities for the involvement of vigilant and concerned citizens, who are encouraged to participate and act preventively by installing protective software or promote the report of suspicious offline/online behaviour, or even to harness the power of crowdsourcing to assist police investigative work (Trottier, 2014).

In such circumstances, the idea of policing the city loses its spatial bearings and key reference points. Take, for example, the transnational policing initiative Operation Rescue (2008–2011); this was a three-year investigation of the global paedophile network 'boy lover.net' and was a coordinated operation involving the United Kingdom's Child Exploitation Online Protection Centre (CEOP), Europol, US Immigration and Customs and the police services of Australia, New Zealand, the Netherlands and Canada. The operation exposed seventy thousand members of this online site; it identified 670 suspected paedophiles aged seventeen to eighty-two years, and 184 arrests were made globally (Child Exploitation Online Protection Centre, 2011). Beyond the localised nature of arrests – taking place at homes, internet cafés, workplaces and, in one instance, a Scout camp – spatial governance and policing labour involves the interception, surveillance and disruption of a global market in child sexual abuse imagery. Policing the city recedes and gives way to the policing of transactional flows, networks of intercontinental and clandestine connectivity, fluid trajectories of monetary exchange and online/offline interactions.

POLICING THE VERTICAL CITY

'Securing the vertical space of cities of tomorrow would fundamentally entail more than traditional strategies for vertical patrols and neighbourhood watch. Strategies for intelligence, operational capabilities and community vigilance would need to adapt to meet the challenges. Intelligence-led policing would require a three-dimensional appreciation of

*the operating terrain, as crime hotspots, persons of interest
and anomalous activities, including hostile drones, might not
be horizontally limited to the streets'.*

—Rahman, 2017

In his commentary piece for Singapore's *Today*, Rahman draws
attention to the 'verticalisation' of contemporary cities. It is difficult
to miss the exponential growth of built environments, which rise
ever skywards from the city streets and descend below ground to
complex subterranea of sanctuary, utility and fortification (McNeill,
2005). Indeed, Steve Graham's (2016) work is in the vanguard of
a burgeoning and innovative scholarship that insists that we look
upwards and downwards, as well as across and through the urban
landscape, to better grasp its three-dimensional geographies. The
'vertical turn' in urban studies has several implications for thinking
about policing and the city and foregrounds myriad architectural,
infrastructural and technological innovations that have transformed
how cities are policed, kept under surveillance, visualised, protected
and rendered safe.

Architecturally, vertical analysts talk of the city as a space of 'splintering urbanism' (Graham & Marvin, 2001). They point, on the one
hand, to the organic growth of densely populated, self-constructed
favela settlements, precariously positioned on landslide-prone hill-
sides and colonised by the urban poor (Perlman, 2010), and, on the
other, to the spatial withdrawal of affluent households into new, elite,
high-rise towers, which offer 'luxury cocoons of über wealth and
fortress security' (Graham, 2016: 177) (see Chapter 21 on housing
and Chapter 22 on wealth and poverty). Other research has focused
on developments underground and pays attention to the growth
of so-called 'iceberg houses', 'billionaires' basements' and 'subterranean lairs' (Graham, 2016: 313), which form a labyrinth of super-
luxury, subsurface domestic fortifications. This kind of defensive
home ownership and residential security ushers in policing practices
of an increasingly capsular character (de Cauter, 2005), creating
a 'fortress city' (Low, 1997) formed of 'a highly fragmented, poly-
spherical patchwork of more or less hermetically enclosed and puri-
fied security spheres' (Klauser, 2010: 326). In many ways, plumbing
the heights and depths of the built environment has replicated and
intensified the socially segregative exclusions of the neoliberal city,
reproducing its spatial compartmentalisations on a vertical axis.

In addition to these architectural transformations, a number of
urban geographers have highlighted the infrastructural changes
needed to service contemporary cities. For example, Shapiro's (2016)
research on urban infrastructures emphasises an 'intermediate ver-
ticality' that mediates the panoptic visualisations of urban planners
and policing strategists and the messy realities of everyday life in
the city (see Chapter 11 on the everyday). He unpacks the idea of
'mezzanine strata' of urban space, suffused with 'a mangle of wires,
utility poles, and lamps; street signs, traffic lights, and billboards;
surveillance and third-story "kibitzers"' (Shapiro, 2016: 293). Paying

FIGURE 25.2

Digital city. (Photograph by ItNeverEnds Creative Commons 2.0; found at Pixabay)

particular attention to surveillance systems and the mezzanine-level hardware that supports them, Shapiro identifies a policing space that uses 'a critical mass of vigilance and visibility' (2016: 302) to moderate the informalities and discontinuities of 'eyes on the street' (Jacobs, 1961: 35) and the formalised intelligence-gathering techniques of policing authorities.

Yet more compelling than Shapiro's focus on mezzanine-level hardware are the digital infrastructures and technologies that support and facilitate the 'smart' city (Thorns, 2002). Sensors, satellites, radio masts, antennae, subsurface cables and fibre optics, tracking devices, drones and helicopters, 'thick with network connectivity', create an 'imperial infrastructure' (Holmes, 2004: 2), a dense web of surveillance that operates at all times, above and below the city streets. David Lyon describes this very well:

> From the road tolling system to the mobile phone call, the camera in the subway station to the bar-coded office door key, the loyalty programme in the store to the Internet usage checks at work, surveillance webs are thick in the city. . . . The aim is not necessarily to catch a glimpse of every actual event . . . so much as to anticipate actions to plan for eventuality. (2001: 54)

Despite this somewhat Orwellian prospectus, it is wise to remember that the digitalisation of policing and security comes with affordances as well as risks. Consider, for example, the Cairo-based initiative of HarassMap, an online, interactive platform for the anonymous reporting and mapping of incidents of sexual harassment in real time (Grove, 2015). This crowd-mapping technology entangles a 'networked assemblage of technological devices, including global positioning and imaging technologies, mobile phones, and Ushahidi software' (Grove, 2015: 346) with everyday experiences of sexual violences encountered on the Egyptian street. As Grove notes, this unique usage of a combination of digital technologies generates 'spaces in need of intervention' and produces 'a particular knowledge of targeting that resonates with other projects of securitization' (2015: 346). This kind of initiative could be said to democratise the policing function, empowering victims (of sexual violences, in this instance) to work proactively in reporting, making visible and mapping crime.

CONCLUSION

Policing the city is not a straightforward or 'obvious' proposition for social geographers. As this chapter has demonstrated, policing emerges at the intersections of social change and transformation, shifting paradigms of political economy and technological innovation and development. From the outset, policing has moved with the times, not only reconfiguring its core tasks and responsibilities but also reinventing its methodologies and scope. At the same time, the city does not stand still, organically and incrementally changing its nature and form in a continual process of accommodation, adaptation and regeneration. To talk of policing the city, we should, perhaps, start with a series of questions: What do we mean by policing? Who are the police? Where is policing to be found? What and who is policing for? And what kind of city is it, anyway? This chapter has explored three versions of the twenty-first-century city – neoliberal, global and vertical – each confronting different challenges and priorities and generating new risks and dangers. City 'types' do not exist in any pure form. In reality, cities (and approaches to policing) are continually in the making, never quite settled and stabilised as a singular *kind* of city, and always adapting to the dynamics and demographics of a changing world. At the end of the day, how we figure the urban and social geographies of governance and control is always a question of context. Put another way, *space matters* in our understanding of policing the city.

SUMMARY

- Policing is one of the defining elements of urban life, and a city's reputation rests on how well it is policed. Policing and the city are mutually implicated.
- Policing is an inherently territorial practice and is spatially organised to accommodate different types of city.
- Neoliberal cities prioritise the needs of business, enterprise and consumption. They are marked by policing approaches that aim to regulate, manage and control access to city spaces in ways that entrench social divisions and inequalities.

- Global cities act as economic and information hubs and prioritise the governance of flows, networks and mobilities. Policing is undertaken by many different actors and is fragmented across the private, public and not-for-profit sectors. This is sometimes referred to as 'plural policing'.

- Vertical cities feature myriad architectural, infrastructural and technological innovations. Policing practices require a three-dimensional appreciation of the city and take account of urban spaces that are both above and below ground.

- Policing the city always has to be explored in context to take account of social change and transformation, shifting paradigms of political economy and technological innovation and development.

FURTHER READING

Atkinson, R., & Blandy, S. (2016) *Domestic Fortress: Fear and the New Home Front*. Manchester: Manchester University Press.

Beckett, K., & Herbert, S. (2009) *Banished: The New Social Control in Urban America*. Oxford: Oxford University Press.

Campbell, E. (2016) Policing paedophilia: Assembling bodies, spaces and things. *Crime, Media, Culture*, 12(3): 345–65.

Isin, E. F. (ed.) (2013) *Democracy, Citizenship and the Global City*. London: Routledge.

Migration and Diaspora

Maddy Thompson and Robin Finlay

The migration of people and groups from one place to another is as long as the history of humanity. Migration and diaspora are therefore key areas of discussion, not just for social geographers but also for the wider societies in which we live. Recently, debates concerning who can freely migrate, who is forced to migrate and where they can move to have been rife in public debates worldwide, with 'immigration' increasingly becoming a key battleground in elections. This is in spite of the fact that in 2017, the United Nations showed that just 3.4 per cent, or 258 million, of the world's population were international migrants.

In this chapter, we begin by examining how social geographers theorise and understand migration, providing an overview to key theories developed by social geographers using the example of Philippine care migration, drawing attention to the relationship between gender and migration. We then document the contributions of social geographers to the development of the concept of diaspora, which describes the formation of a new community beyond the homeland. We explore the ideas of belonging and home and the formation of diaspora identities, focusing on the Moroccan diaspora in Granada, Spain.

MIGRATION AND MIGRANTS

At the most basic level, 'migration' refers to the movement of peo-ple(s) across space and time (see Chapter 4 on space and time) and the reshaping of places that occurs due to this movement. Social geographers initially studied migration under the auspices of 'population geography' in the 1950s (see Trewartha, 1953) but have since been key in developing critical discussions and concepts that advance migration research. Although social geographers are attuned to the cross-cutting political, economic and cultural factors that facilitate and hinder migration, their particular concern is with the relation with migration on societies, communities, households and individuals – the *societal* dimensions of migration.

A key concern is challenging standard classifications of migrants and certain stereotypes regarding who migrants are, thereby disrupt-ing and rethinking commonsense assumptions about the broader drivers of migration. For example, while it is generally assumed that migrants represent the world's most impoverished peoples, just 4 per cent of the world's migrants originate from low-income regions. As Thompson (2017: 81) reminds us, 'Most migrants are middle class, well-educated and able to afford the financial costs associated with migration'. Social geographers have been particularly adept in examining how migrants' status becomes complicated during and after migration in both their country of destination and their coun-try of origin. A migrant can be simultaneously middle and lower class – middle class in their country of origin, where they are able to afford luxuries, yet lower class in their country of destination, where they are marked as an 'other', tend to be employed in low-skill industries and often send remittances to family overseas, further weakening their status.

Whereas in the past scholars considered migration in terms of binaries, contemporary scholarship focuses on the dynamics and complexities of migration. We no longer think of migrants in binary terms of legal and illegal, asylum seeker/refugee and economic migrants, high and low skilled, forced and voluntary. Instead, we now recognise and explore the diversity and fluidity of migrant experiences and statuses, pay attention to processes and experiences of migration and give space to migrants who do not fit neatly into the above categories, or who fit in multiple and competing ones, such as spouses, children and grandparents.

For example, the migration of a skilled and qualified nurse from the Philippines to the United Kingdom on the surface appears to be legal, skilled, economic, voluntary migration. However, a social geographer would consider the societal context from which the nurse moved, the gendered politics involved in their migration and societal context in the destination they reach. In many cases, nurses in the Philippines feel that they have no choice but to migrate due to exploitation and a lack of employment opportunities in the Philippines. Others are pushed into migration by pressure of family members – their choice is not voluntary (Thompson, 2019). Additionally, despite qualifications, many migrant nurses in the United Kingdom undergo 'deskilling' through being underemployed (often as a health-care assistant) or, through losing their job, have 'illegal' status if their visa is invalidated (Batnitzky & McDowell, 2011). Finally, while the nurse may initially migrate alone, family members often follow, known as family reunification migration. Does a young child have decision-making capacity concerning migration? If an elderly parent or grandparent moves, is this migration for social well-being purposes rather than due to economic factors? Questions relating to the relations between issues of social reproduction (see Chapter 28 on social reproduction), family care and migration are key for social geographers, who often draw on feminist thought to examine divisions (see Part C on divisions).

THEORISING MIGRATION

With regard to theorising migration, social geographers have developed distinctly 'social' theories to account for increasingly complex and diversified forms of contemporary migration. It is useful to outline briefly mainstream migration theory to contextualise these developments. Initially, Lee's (1966) push–pull model, or the 'microeconomic' theory of migration, assumes that all migrants make rational and informed migration decisions and move to preferable economies. Conversely, macroeconomic approaches, favoured by Marxist and postcolonial scholars, argue that migration is a consequence of global inequality and capitalist expansion (see King, 2012b). People do not choose to migrate; rather, global structures of inequality, poverty and underdevelopment result in the world's periphery moving to the core. In both approaches, decisions to migrate are economically driven. Returning to our Filipino nurse, either she chooses to migrate based on a cost-benefit analysis of opportunities at home and overseas or she has no choice and is moved through the world by the forces of neoliberal and neocolonial capitalism. More recent research, however, including that undertaken by social geographers, takes seriously other dimensions of migration, recognising that households, considerations of cultural compatibility and social networks also influence decisions to migrate. Social geographers have developed many approaches, and three important ones are illustrated in Table 26.1.

By bringing attention to the social and cultural influences that contribute to migration, social geographers and other critical social scientists have diversified how we research and understand migration. Social geographers have also been key in advancing debates concerning gender and migration, further disrupting assumptions of migrants.

TABLE 26.1 | Theories of Migration

Theory	New Economics of Labour Migration (NELM)	Aspirations Approach	Networks
Overview	NELM follows push–pull thinking but argues migration is an economic strategy to increase *household* income. Migration diversifies the types and locations of work undertaken by family members, minimising the risks of illness, natural disasters or unemployment to households (Massey, 1990). The household becomes the scale of analysis rather than the individual.	Aspirations approaches recognise that migration decision-making is informed by popular culture and media representations of place. Individuals are more likely to move to places they actively desire than places with the best economic opportunities (Carling & Collins, 2018).	Networks approaches argue that although migration can initially be explained in economic terms, often the continuation of migration patterns cannot. Instead, migrant communities make certain destinations more attractive for aspiring migrants, providing them with a ready-made community (King, 2012b). Networks are central to discussions of diaspora.
Empirical example	Our Filipino nurse is likely the eldest woman sibling, as women Filipino migrants remit the most money. In South American rural settings, conversely, women are pushed into migration as they are deemed unsuitable for agricultural work (Lawson, 1998).	Thompson (2017) found that Filipino nurses with a keen interest in anime, video gaming or K-pop are likely to learn Nihongo and apply for positions in Japan or South Korea. Those drawn to Western pop culture desire and plan for migration to North America and the UK.	Religious institutions, cheap travel, foods, linguistic communities, cultural activities and family connections make places more attractive. Despite highly publicised abuses of Filipino nurses in Singapore, nurses continue drawing on networks to find employment there.

GENDER AND MIGRATION

Social geographers' contribution to disrupting and resisting existing assumptions and categories concerning migrants is most clear in the wider move to feminise migration research (Silvey, 2006). The need to feminise or account for the presence of women and the role of gender in migration is a relatively recent occurrence (see Chapter 16 on gender). Until the 1980s, it was largely assumed that women migrated only as dependents of men – as wives, mothers and children – and their migration experiences received little attention. During the 1980s and 1990s, feminist social geographers turned to analyse the numbers and experiences of women involved in migration (e.g., Lawson, 1998). This corresponded to the increasing numbers of women migrants globally as, by the early 1990s, roughly equal numbers of women and men migrated.

Since, there has been a concerted effort to study the importance of gender and migration rather than just women and migration. This means examining how migration is impacted by and impacts gender rather than just documenting the migrations of women. Text Box 26.1

describes the two overarching aspects of contemporary gender and migration research, and Figure 26.1 shows the highly gendered nature of migrant recruitment practices.

Social geographers and critical social scientists bring attention to who migrants are and break down the binary categories traditionally used to describe them. We now know that, despite enduring images of the young, economically active male migrant as the norm, women and men migrate in roughly equal numbers (United Nations, 2017). We know that migrants are typically middle class, and we understand that complexities of migrant agency are obscured by simple binaries of voluntary/forced, legal/illegal migration. More recently, there is a growing recognition that to fully understand the decision-making practices of migrants and their experiences of migrating and integrating into new societies an intersectional approach is required (see Bastia, 2014). An intersectional approach (see also Chapter 20 on intersectionality) examines how not just gender but also elements of identity, including religion, race, ethnicity, sexuality, disability, class and so on, influence migration experiences and decisions. The study of diaspora tackles some of these concerns.

DIASPORA

The increasing migration of people around the world has resulted in various concepts that seek to understand different phenomena related to the movement and resettlement of people. In social and cultural geography, the concept of diaspora has become increasingly popular, especially for scholars interested in the lived experience of migration. Diaspora studies draw on the notion of transnationalism, which refers to the relationships between sending and

TEXT BOX 26.1 | Gender and Migration Research

How migration constitutes gender: Topics of research include exploring whether gender identities remain intact, are challenged or become transformed through migration. For example, does migration empower or constrain our Filipino nurse's agency in relation to discrimination faced as a migrant and simultaneous economic independence gained from overseas employment (Salazar Parreñas, 2009)?

How gender constitutes migration: Topics of research include understanding how gender determines who migrates, why and to where, uncovering how gendered systems and inequalities produce and control the experiences of migrants (Nawyn, 2010). For example, the association of women with motherhood leads to the assumption that women are inherently caring and approachable and well suited to work in the services industry. Filipinos in particular are marketed as being 'natural' caregivers 'drawn' to nursing work (see Table 26.1).

FIGURE 26.1
Gendered migration recruitment practices. (Credit: Robin Finlay)

receiving places. Transnationalism is concerned with the material geographies of migration – the actual movements of peoples and things – as well as the imaginary geographies of migration – the movements of cultural and social ideas (Blunt, 2007). Prior to the 1980s, diaspora was restricted to descriptions of historical forced exile, specifically the exile of the Jews. However, with the increase of international migration in recent decades, diaspora has come to be associated with the general dispersal of people around the world and developed into a field of study (Karla, Kaur & Hutnyk, 2005). Examples of classic diasporas include the Jewish, Irish, Chinese, African and South Asian diasporas.

Diasporas are often considered groups of migrants or ancestors of migrants who share a common historic 'homeland'. Features of community, collective ethnic identity continuation, transnational connections and a shared orientation to a 'homeland' are generally considered to make a migrant diasporic (Grossman, 2018). Furthermore, diasporas are often seen as emblems of hybridity, where new forms of identity and belonging take shape through cross-cultural contact and mixing (Karla, Kaur & Hutnyk, 2005). The contribution of social geographies to the concept of diaspora, broadly speaking, is illustrating the centrality of space to the diaspora experience and critically examining how diasporas construct and perform place, home, belonging, identity and politics (Blunt, 2007). In this section, we examine two intersecting areas at the forefront of research in social geographies of diasporas: home, belonging and place-making; and diaspora identity formations.

TEXT BOX 26.2 | Real-World Research: Moroccan Diaspora Formations in Granada, Spain

A useful way to examine diaspora formations is through the place-making strategies of migrant communities. Finlay's (2015, 2019) research on the Moroccan diaspora in Granada, Spain, examines the place-making strategies of Moroccan migrants and illustrates the spatial nature of diaspora formations. His research demonstrates that, to form a diaspora, Moroccan migrants have accessed and transformed urban space in Granada, producing a visible Moroccan 'diaspora space' (Brah, 1996). Through religious, economic and cultural place-making strategies, a collective diasporic identity has been imbued into the area, creating a diasporic space of home and belonging. For example, the area incorporates oriental gift shops, Moroccan teashops, North African bakers and mosques (see Figure 26.2).

Finlay demonstrates that, for diasporas to initially take shape, favourable urban conditions that provide a foothold to the city are frequently required. In Granada, Moroccan migrants found a space that was underused and underregulated, allowing them to buy and rent properties at low cost with little interference from local government regulation. Moreover, a preexisting Muslim identity in the area made it relatively accommodating to a core identity of many Moroccan migrants. This shows that diasporas are formed by the place-making strategies of migrants, but they are also conditioned and shaped by the receiving cities' context and structures. Overall, Finlay's work illustrates the explicitly spatial nature of diaspora formations.

FIGURE 26.2
A teashop owned by
Moroccan migrants in
Granada, Spain. (Credit:
Robin Finlay)

Home, Belonging and Place-Making

Ideas of home for people in diaspora are often multiple and complex, with various places and cultures conveying a sense of home and belonging (see Chapter 21 on housing). There is usually a belonging to a 'faraway' homeland, a place of 'origin', *and* a belonging to the lived home in the place of settlement (Brah, 1996). Therefore, diaspora research is concerned with experiences and conditions in the place of settlement as well as the 'homeland' sending country.

A number of studies examine diaspora imaginations, relationships and connections with the 'homeland' space – for example, how the Greek diaspora of Germany imagine Greece as a homeland (Christou & King, 2010). Factors that can be important for diaspora connections with the homeland include history, stories, material culture, technology, food and childhood homecomings. Importantly, research demonstrates that in a diaspora there is a diversity of relations to the homeland, often shaped by issues such as identity, national/regional location, transnational trajectories and personal biographies.

Research also focuses on how diasporas make home anew and create a sense of belonging in the place of settlement. The process of homemaking is often spatial and involves producing and transforming places. Geographers are particularly interested in the place-making strategies of diasporas, examining how they imbue places with new meanings, cultures and identities. The city is considered the central location for the formation of diasporas (Finlay, 2015); thus most research on diaspora place-making is urban focused and examines the intersections of diaspora formations and city making. Text Box 26.2 provides a real-world example of diaspora formation. Yet achieving a sense of home and belonging is not a simple process for diasporas. The scale of place-making ranges from the home to the street, the neighbourhood and beyond. Government policies, politics of location and attitudes of the majority populace in the host culture also structure experiences of diaspora home, belonging and place-making. For example, Hall, King and Finlay (2017) illustrate how the enduring presence of racism and structural inequalities mean 'new' diasporas and migrants in Birmingham and Leicester in the United Kingdom frequently settle and make a home in marginalised city streets, where they have a level of autonomy and invisibility.

Diaspora Identity Formations

Like home and belonging, diaspora identity is typically seen as multiple and complex. At its crux, diaspora is a process of shared identity formation, where people in a diaspora share certain identity characteristics to feel part of a diasporic community. Research has traditionally prioritised ethnicity related to the 'homeland' in constructing the diaspora identity. Therefore, ethnic characteristics of the 'homeland', such as language, culture, history, food and ritual, are commonly seen as key characteristics for the formation of a diaspora identity.

Religion (see Chapter 14 on religion) is often another core feature of diaspora formations, with many scholars asserting the significance of religious belief in the formation and maintenance of diasporic identities. For example, for diasporas 'originating' in Muslim-majority societies, the role of the Islamic religion is considered especially important to the formation of a collective identity in diaspora (Aitchison & Hopkins, 2007). Given diaspora's frequent association with ethnic minority communities, race is another identity marker that is associated with diaspora identities (Alexander, 2010). As such, race, racialisation and racism (see Chapter 13 on race) are significant issues to consider when examining diaspora formations. Moreover, researchers have begun to look at the diversity of identities in diaspora communities, with issues such as gender, sexuality and class being explored (Campt & Thomas, 2008).

Journeys and connections with multiple places and cultures are core features of the diaspora experience, so diaspora identity is also shaped by the contact between different cultures and places, and this can produce identities that take on new formations. Since the 1990s, these processes of mixing and 'new' identity formations have received much attention in academic research, with geographers looking at how they take shape and intersect with place. The concept of hybridity is often used to describe diaspora identity formations, as it refers to the emergence of new cultural forms and identities from the mixing of two or more cultures (Karla, Kaur & Hutnyk, 2005). Forms of diasporic hybridity are found in language, food, music, dress and art. For example, Tex-Mex cuisine is neither completely Mexican nor Texan, but rather a 'hybrid' mixture that has developed through the encounters between Mexican migrants and Americans in the US–

Mexico borderland (Martynuska, 2017). Another example is how people's identification with nation-states often becomes hybridised through what some call hyphenated nationalities/ethnicities, such as British-Pakistani, Jamaican-British and Italian-American.

Hybrid identities are increasingly seen as a challenge to fixed and singular notions of identity, nation and belonging. Indeed, many scholars celebrate diaspora as a progressive process that can challenge racist discourses based on fixed and essential notions of identity and belonging. However, other scholars are more cautious about the progressive nature of diaspora, arguing that boundaries and fixed notions of identity are often reproduced by diasporas (Carter, 2005). Therefore, it is useful to see diaspora as a process that can take multiple forms of identity and belonging (Mavroudi, 2007). The role of the researcher is to explore how migrants engage and mobilise these different but overlapping diasporic processes over places and time.

SUMMARY

- Social geographers have made significant contributions to the field of migration studies, particularly through examining the lived experiences of migration and developing the concept of diaspora.
- Social geographers offer broader critiques to mainstream migration theories and categories, often by adopting a feminist lens. Migration processes are shown to be more complex and contested than traditional accounts suggest.
- The concept of diaspora allows us to reimagine notions of home, belonging, identity and place and further understand hybrid identities.

FURTHER READING

Blunt, A. (2007) Cultural geographies of migration: Mobility, transnationality, and diaspora. *Progress in Human Geography*, 3(5): 684–95.

Finlay, R. (2019) A diasporic right to the city: The production of a Moroccan diaspora space in Granada, Spain. *Social & Cultural Geography*, 20(6): 785–805.

Silvey, R. (2006) Geographies of gender and migration: Spatializing social difference. *International Migration Review*, 40(1): 64–81.

Thompson, M. (2017) Migration decision-making: A geographical imaginations approach. *Area*, 49(1): 77–84.

Encounter

Nathar Iqbal

This chapter explores the study of encounters across social geography. Encounters have become an increasingly popular issue for social geographers interested in social relations, identities and practices and how these both shape and are shaped by spaces, places and scales. Most of this literature is based on Western urban contexts and is linked to processes of globalisation and increasing patterns of diversity across different social identities and communities. Exploring the connections between them attends to the complexity of socio-spatial relations, which are ever more important to understand as the world becomes increasingly connected. At the outset, it is important to emphasise that encounters, as understood in social geography, are more than just issues of contact or interaction. Rather, the encounters that geographers are interested in relate to four concerns that Darling and Wilson (2016) outline, as seen in Table 27.1. A critical focus on encounters takes these concerns into account and sees them as distinct forms of relations (Wilson, 2017) shaped by space, time (see Chapter 4 on space and time) and broader contexts, and they are interrelated with how spaces and places are experienced and imagined. Given attendance to notions of difference and relationships between people, spaces and places, encounters are valuable for social geographic analysis and hold much currency in illuminating everyday negotiations of contemporary forms of difference.

TABLE 27.1	Four Concerns about Encounter (adapted from Wilson & Darling, 2016: table 1)

1. **Encounters are about difference.** How is difference made through encounters? How might difference be responded to and challenged? How do encounters reify difference?

2. Encounters might be fleeting/momentary but are **shaped by different and weaving temporalities.** How does the past shape present encounters? How might encounters with others/animals/things affect future experiences and feelings?

3. Encounters have the **potential to transform and destabilise difference and so can often be used in projects and politics of intervention.** What forms of encounters are designed and assigned value? What encounters do we presuppose as informing meaningful change?

4. Encounters are **fundamental in shaping space and subjectivity and vice versa.** Encounters occur in particular spaces and sites, but how do they become features that shape experiences of these? How are they vital to urban living? How are they and the spaces in which they occur negotiated?

Social geographers have largely focused on encounters of difference in urban contexts, informing the focus of the following section in which I explain why encounters resonate with debates about identities, difference and relationality, while also reflecting on encounters in terms of research methods (see Chapter 3 on researching social geographies). The first section reviews the emergence of encounters as a framework for studying difference and as a means by which to capture the diversity of place-making, scalar relationships, social difference and coexistence. I then explore encounters in my own work with LGBT people from Black and minority ethnic (BME) backgrounds and their experiences of using LGBT bars in Soho,

TABLE 27.2	Types of Encounter	
Types of Encounter	**Example**	**Reference**
Encounters of social difference	Multicultural encounters of race and Britishness in the everyday lives of British Bangladeshi women	Nayak (2017)
Human and animal encounters	Human-alligator relationships through tourism in Louisiana	Keul (2013)
Encounters with food	Chinese Muslim food practices in Guangzhou, China	Liu, Yang & Xue (2018)
Encounters with the environment	Emotional encounters with other ecologies in Dorset, England	Conradson (2007)
Encounters and materiality	Art and encounters in the context of artwork in Tower Hamlets, London	McNally (2019)
Religion and encounter	Sensuous geographies of religion in Accra, Ghana	de Witte (2016)
Research encounters	Insider and outsider categories and positionality	Mohammad (2001)

London, as well as in work with students from BME backgrounds at Newcastle University. I then offer some methodological considerations about the ways encounters can be explored by thinking about relations *in* qualitative research with people.

UNDERSTANDING ENCOUNTERS: DIFFERENCE, DIVERSITY AND RELATIONALITY

Interest in encounters stems from work in urban studies (see Chapter 10 on urban/rural). Simmel (1950) viewed encounters as fundamental for developing social connections, positive habits and perspectives associated with mediating difference and generating cooperation; this is about understanding encounters with those who are seen to be different, as well as their values and experiences. Later work similarly contributed to developing understandings of the richness and eclecticism of urban difference and sociality (Berman, 1982; Sennett, 1990). Also influential was Young's (1990) work on justice and difference, which underlined how contact with others in the city had the potential to moderate intolerance. In such accounts of urban life, encounters are concerned with difference. Wilson (2017: 452) notes that a simple definition of an encounter is 'a face-to-face meeting between adversaries or opposing forces'. Social geographers are well positioned to tease out the complexities of these relations and meetings of difference as they seek to develop understandings through an appreciation of the intersecting and broader social, spatial, political and historical contexts.

In relation to space, the principles outlined and the contributions that geographers can make become clearer. Massey (1995) viewed space not as a static entity upon which social processes played out but as a constellation of relations, networks and processes that highlights the complexity of the world we live in (see Chapter 1 on creating more social geographies). In this vein, a focus on the *relationality* of spaces attends to the multiple connections that make up space and place through a lens of simultaneity and interconnection. This means thinking about space, places and relations as in construction and flux rather than as preordained and fixed. The 'throwntogetherness' (Massey, 2005) of these connections, and therefore space, points to considerations of the diversity of relationships, their multiscalar processes and the dynamics of interactions and encounters that are produced within and through these, and how they shape relations of difference. Experiences of living with or encountering difference take place in different contexts, but the primary engagement for social geographers has been in exploring these in urban areas. This is largely because it is in these sites that increasing diversity manifests itself, and so negotiating difference becomes a feature of everyday urban life (Valentine & Waite, 2012). In urban Western contexts, which have been the primary places in which social geographers have explored encounters of difference, growing patterns of diversity across different social identities and how people negotiate these have stimulated geographers to uncover the dynamics of encounters of difference and how difference is made, imagined, felt and responded to.

A substantial thread of this work is generally hopeful about the potential for encounters to mediate negative responses or stances towards difference and diversity. Amin (2002) indicates that shared spaces such as sports clubs and libraries can help people to interact with others from different social groups and form new attachments or understandings through repeated encounters, increasing their familiarity and civil engagement. According to Amin (2002), such spaces are important because encounters of a fleeting nature, such as those associated with a city street or large shopping centre, are relatively insignificant for negotiating and developing positive attitudes towards difference because nothing substantial has been exchanged in these few moments. Through constant interaction, it is hoped that people develop connections and ways of negotiating difference through varied cultural transactions between people. Geographic work has explored encounters in a range of public and semipublic spaces, such as cafés (Laurier & Philo, 2006), schools (Hemming, 2011) and public transport (Wilson, 2011), highlighting the habits and engagements of people. These seek to outline how encounters might contribute to what Amin (2006) terms a sense of 'being-togetherness' and familiarity that spurs a positive sense of space and place. Such encounters can open up boundaries between social groups and foster compassion and understanding between them (Simonsen, 2008).

That being said, there is a healthy scepticism of the potential for everyday encounters of difference to challenge those relations of power, which are shaped by inequality and negative attitudes towards social diversity. There may be 'kindness and compassion' (Thrift, 2005) in negotiating difference in public spaces, but the extent to which encounters evolve into an appreciation of social difference in ways that challenge prejudice or develop long-term relations needs to be explored and understood (Clayton, 2009). As Valentine argues, regular or familiar civil encounters with people from different social backgrounds do not necessarily translate into positive attitudes about a given social group; tolerance is not a precursor to acceptance and celebration, so there is value in casting a critical eye over any romanticisation of encounters of difference. Valentine (2008: 325) therefore calls for more attention to be paid to 'meaningful contact . . . that actually changes values'. While sympathetic to Valentine's perspective, Wilson (2017: 460–61) critiques notions of 'actual values and belief' and 'meaningful' encounter. With respect to the former, this is because such a position implies that they 'are somehow separate and formed in isolation from encounters', and, in relation to the latter, it is because of 'how encounters are named, understood and identified as "meaningful"' and 'the danger of dismissing the different ways in which encounters are valued'. Different yet related perspectives and debates about encounters highlight the richness of not only the field but also the contested nature of encounters and the spaces of encounters themselves. Such thinking can be further clarified by providing some examples of geographic work on encounters.

Leitner's (2012) study with White residents of a town in Minnesota in the United States demonstrates the complex relationalities of identities, spaces and embodied experiences that intersect in moments of encounter. She highlights how these corrupt the politics and perceptions of belonging in the United States, making clear that, though encounters may happen in particular places and at particular times, these connect with other scales and the discourses surrounding these. Her respondents' encounters with immigrants were territorial, continually reinscribing the local town as belonging to White American residents while also marking the non-White body as 'dangerous' and out of place. Such encounters also evoked discourses and representations that spoke to the national scale, wherein being part of the nation required assimilation into normative values and customs of White America, disregarding the complicated histories and geographies of the United States. As she explains, 'spaces of encounters are not simply face-to-face embodied experiences, imbued with emotions, but also structural, and these are socially and spatially mediated' (Leitner, 2012: 833).

Encounters, therefore, cannot be reduced to static interpretations. Encounters of difference are also bound up in wider relations of power, as we saw in Leitner's work, and they can develop longer-term effects that may be either encouraging or undesirable (Wilson, 2017). Askins and Pain (2011), for example, explore how community art projects may develop transformative interactions between young refugees from African backgrounds and White British-born young people in North East England. Using a participatory approach and focusing on the materialities of interaction, they highlight how art objects can highlight and enact both similarities and differences and shape relations through renegotiations. They explain how using art materials 'shifted emphasis from discourse to doing, and tactile encounters with things were caught up in renegotiating Selves' (Askins & Pain, 2011: 814). The authors highlight the value of paying attention to how encounters occur through people *and* things, and also of understanding that, within community projects, conflicts and tensions can be useful to understand and explore. Such projects are seen to be more useful with respect to seeking to develop longer-term relations that challenge negative attitudes when implemented with local communities. Issues of how encounters 'scale up' from interpersonal interactions to wider societal impact and change are key concerns in the encounters literature (Askins, 2016; Darling & Wilson, 2016), and it is necessary to consider how the geographies of these influence broader politics of belonging and difference. These are inherently linked to the concerns in Table 27.1.

Developing debates on encounters, Hopkins (2014) contends that it is useful to consider relationality (see Chapter 1, summary), embodiment (thinking about the body in both a physical and a social/political sense) and emotions (see Chapter 12 on emotion) in understanding negotiations and the effects of encounters. In his work with young Sikh men in Scotland, he links their absence of scholarship to the positioning of these men as 'strangers' in the urban and national imaginary. In the context of heated debates about immigration, Scottish independence, citizenship and the racialisation of Islam that constructs Brown bodies as dangerous, participants describe various kinds of encounter and the various strategies that they adopt to help them to negotiate multicultural intimacies: educating people about Sikhism to counter incorrect associations with Islamist terrorism, tactically choosing what to wear and affiliating with the Scottish nation in ways that broaden the scope of Scottishness to a more inclusive form. These relational, emotional and embodied strategies enable them to contest their 'strangerhood', heeding the importance of understanding and acceptance beyond civil interactions and fleeting proximities. This approach aids thinking that can contribute to addressing relationships between geographic scales and their folding into moments of encounters, as well as their temporal dimensions.

In each of the above studies we see the importance of relational thinking in encounters when considering spaces, identities and difference and scale, as well as temporalities. Encounters are more than simply concerned with contact or meeting. Instead, because encounters are about difference and relationality, they are concerned with power relations as well as their broader contexts. As they are contextualised within different spaces, as well as producing spaces (and imaginations of these), encounters allow social geographers to consider the contemporaneity of complex forms of living in the twenty-first century, and they pose challenging as well as important and rich questions about the relationships between space, scale and people and, increasingly, about other types of encounters too, as seen in Table 27.2.

MULTICULTURAL ENCOUNTERS

Multicultural encounters are an important focus of research within social geographies of encounter. This work tends to focus on encounters between White people and ethnic minorities of diverse faiths. I now illustrate how I have looked at encounters in my own work in two projects, both of which focused upon multicultural encounters (see Text Boxes 27.1 and 27.2).

The examples from both projects demonstrate how encounters can consolidate varying power relations and understandings that reproduce difference and exclusion. While there were also examples that demonstrated how participants sought to negotiate these or educate out intolerance, the experiences of people in both projects showed the importance of relational and intersectional thinking in order to consider how people are seen to embody difference and discourses about these. Studying encounters of difference allows us to explore the complexity of these socio-spatial relationships.

TEXT BOX 27.1	Real-World Research: Encounters with Difference in Clubs and Pubs for LGBT BME People in London

I first explored encounters in research with LGBT people from BME backgrounds and some of their experiences of using LGBT bars and pubs in Soho, London. The participants in this study revealed common experiences of racism cloaked in sexual desire that link to the legacies of British colonialism and encounters of 'Otherness'. LGBT people from BME backgrounds can face challenging social, cultural and structural constraints that limit their abilities and desires to live 'openly' without prejudice and discrimination. They may have to contend with issues such as identifying as LGBT in their ethnic communities, racism in LGBT communities and spaces and the ills of homophobia and racism in wider society.

Many of the participants in this project detailed how sexual desires and fetishes that were noted in those whom they encountered on the scene were often set within and underlined by racial inequalities and hierarchies within these spaces:

> I think it's racist and that preference is racial when you go out and tell people that 'I like Asians or Blacks' and you want them because of that. (Junaid, British Pakistani)

> You still stand out and you're fetished because of that. . . . This old guy thought I was exotic and tried to cop off with me . . . and at times I've been rejected because of my skin colour. (Luke, British Black Caribbean)

Examples such as these and others that relied on stereotypes of ethnic minority bodies were common, particularly during dating, 'pulling' and sex. Other examples that clearly invoked race included assumptions about penis size, sexual roles and circumcision and revelations about never having 'slept with a Paki before' (Hani, British Pakistani). In these accounts, sexual desires for the bodies of my participants were predicated upon objectification of their 'Otherness'. Such experiences work to reinforce Whiteness and demonstrate the embodied relationalities of race, sexuality and desire. They are positioned as different and are reduced to the colour of their skin. While some may ask how expressing a desire or fetish for someone based upon their skin colour could be considered racist, by openly describing preferences for somebody through racially objectifying them, unequal relations of power are highlighted, replicated and reworked, and normalising such encounters can exclude and marginalise ethnic minorities. In these examples from Soho, participants narrated how their racialised sexualities challenged their perceptions of belonging within this specific area, in the LGBT community and in the country more generally. Encounters such as these tell us that negotiating difference and understanding how this is occurring in specific moments speak to complex relationships among those issues highlighted in earlier sections.

TEXT BOX 27.2 | Real-World Research: Multicultural Encounters at University

The other project that I include focused on how BME students experienced Newcastle University. It showed how forms of racism, such as racial stereotypes, cultural appropriation and racial microaggressions and misrepresentations, were common encounters. Here I focus on racial microaggressions linked to hair and speaking. A regular example that emerged in interviews was how Black students experienced encounters that involved questions about their hairstyles and other students touching their hair:

> One time a guy touched my hair and was like, 'Oh my God, it's like touching my dog'. I was like, 'Excuse me?' He was like, 'No, but I really love my dog'. (Jen, Mixed White and Black Caribbean)

> It's like you don't have a right to touch my hair. If you ask the question you have to accept there is a possibility I will refuse. Why ask that? I guess it's because of the nature of my background or I guess people just see me and think I am a black person first and then a person or woman later. (Melissa, Black Caribbean)

Such examples were absurdly frequent and uncomfortable, as were questions and assumptions about accents and English proficiency for British participants:

> I've had compliments on my English being good and I've been, like, 'Yes, really?' Okay, great, the only language I speak, really. (Siena, White Greek and Black African)

> I sound very, very Geordie and it is always quite amusing, because I will answer the phone and they hear the name and they hear the accent and they just think, 'Well I wouldn't have put those two together!' (Ayesha, British Pakistani)

Sue and colleagues (2007: 273) argue that racial microaggressions 'are so pervasive and automatic in daily conversations and interactions that they are often dismissed and glossed over as being innocent and innocuous'. Frequent interactions, such as those described in the above excerpts, demonstrate how encounters of difference may aggregate gradually to unmask perceptions of otherness that can regulate belonging and inclusion. Here the issue is how difference is being stressed or made in these encounters; touching the hair of Black students, or asking to, is clearly objectifying them, while surprise at their accent or English proficiency stresses a relationship that attributes these to White populations while misrecognising the identities and positions of British ethnic minorities.

POSITIONALITY IN RESEARCH ENCOUNTERS

I now turn to how you might consider encounters in your own work if you are engaging in qualitative research. Encounters can also be a useful point of reflection when *doing* research because they can, in themselves, shape the ways we view a given research topic. As research with people is generally interactive, geographers have become more mindful of the need to be self-aware of research conduct. England (1994) describes this as being 'critically reflexive', a process of self-conscious scrutiny of your position as a researcher and the power relations within the research process itself (see Chapter 3 on researching social geographies).

This idea emerged from feminist geography, which sought to critique the fallacy of an impartial and objective researcher. As we are all socially positioned, we have different identities, experiences, motivations, political perspectives and aspirations, and we bring these with us to our engagements with research participants. These factors influence our views, beliefs and opinions, and vice versa, and can facilitate unbalanced relations of power within research. Mohammad (2001) highlights how multiple positionalities shaped the research encounters in her work with Muslim Pakistani women in the United Kingdom (see Chapter 13 on race and Chapter 14 on religion). Due to her ethnic and religious background, she was cast as an 'insider' in the community she was working with; yet such a positioning can work to universalise what are complex categories/ positions and fix problematic assumptions that might, therefore, shape the knowledge that is produced.

Attending to and evaluating multiple positionalities within research encounters does not allow us to be rid of these power relations, but, at the very least, we can acknowledge them and modify aspects of our research where appropriate. There are always personal opinions and characteristics that shape research practice, so research is subjective; we all see the world differently, and this may influence what you do, how you engage with people and how you analyse, interpret and present data. For instance, thinking about the contemporary wider contexts of your research topic, as well as how you may be an insider or an outsider to the research participants, while also considering the complicated relationships of these where you may be simultaneously 'inside' or 'outside', is useful before any research encounter. Thinking about the research encounters themselves and being reflexive and honest about how these may have been shaped by different and multiple positions is useful when it comes to the analysis of an encounter and the data you gather. Thus, thinking about differences related to positionalities is part and parcel of being an ethical researcher, because we are being analytical about power relations, our standing within the research and the subjective nature of qualitative research being produced, thus thinking about how social positions condition research encounters and the research process iteratively.

CONCLUSION

Encounters enable social geographers to consider the richness of contemporary social relations. Studying these can offer a nuanced and intimate picture of how space and place are co-constitutively influenced by social, political and historical contexts, social practices and processes of differentiation; yet this specific or local space of encounter can simultaneously highlight multiscalar relationships that are important to understand. By evoking encounters as a useful issue for geographic research and thinking about intersectional forms and practices of identities and differences, debates about social cohesion, tolerance, acceptance and exclusions can be approached in a way that brings together and interrogates their multiple and conflicting relationships. While much of the extant research on encounters is based in urban contexts in the West, increasing the scope of encounters to include more voices from other parts of the world is progressively diversifying and expounding the richness of social encounters, as is work on different types of encounters. In an uncertain political and social climate of difference, the importance of understanding the heterogeneity of various groups and encounters will become ever more apparent and important for social geographers.

SUMMARY

- Encounters are about more than just contact or interaction. They can indicate social relations of difference that may be challenged, consolidated or negotiated in diverse ways.
- Encounters are about difference, are shaped by different temporalities, can transform relations and difference, and can shape space (and vice versa).
- Most research focuses on multicultural encounters and encounters with difference; there is also work about encounters with animals, food and the environment.
- It is helpful to consider how the specific spaces of encounters have relationships with other scales of geographic enquiry, while also thinking about their temporalities.

FURTHER READING

Askins, K. & Pain, R. (2011) Contact zones: Participation, materiality, and the messiness of interaction *Environment and Planning D: Society and Space*, 29(5): 803–21.

Leitner, H. (2012) Spaces of encounters: Immigration, race, class and the politics of belonging in small-town America. *Annals of the Association of American Geographers*, 102(4): 828–46.

Valentine, G. (2008) Living with difference: Reflections on geographies of encounter. *Progress in Human Geography*, 32(3): 323–37.

Wilson, H. (2017) On geography and encounter: Bodies, borders, and difference. *Progress in Human Geography*, 41(4): 451–71.

Social Reproduction

Al James

'At the most fundamental level, social reproduction is about how we live . . . the relationship between how we live at work and how we live outside of it'.
—Mitchell, Marston & Katz, 2003: 416

'The struggle for progressive social reproduction is a struggle for both resources and for control over time'.
—Bakker, 2007: 548

Social reproduction is a concept that has been progressively advanced since the 1960s by feminist scholars concerned with the varied social processes, material goods, institutions, agents and emotions involved in sustaining and reproducing individuals, families, communities and societies over time. At the heart of this concept is a focus on the relationship between paid labour and unpaid labour and the shifting, spatial and temporal boundaries between 'work' and 'home'. Scholars initially employed the concept of social reproduction to show how systems of capitalist production depend on the unpaid domestic labour of women. They argued that these activities should be given much greater appreciation and recognition in mainstream accounts of capitalist development, which instead position the home as somehow nonproductive and non–value producing (see Schwiter, Strauss & England, 2018). These value-producing activities include, for example, cleaning, ironing, child-bearing, shopping, food preparation and care for dependents. These are largely unwaged, nonmonetised and invisible forms of labour that take place behind closed doors within the home yet without which families, workforces, companies and nations would quickly grind to a halt. Over the last four decades, feminist geographers have shown how the establishment, operation and outcomes of social reproduction vary significantly across places. This vibrant body of work is, therefore, rooted in a broader conception of social reproduction that extends beyond the maintenance of the work-force to encompass collective and state-led activities, including the geographically uneven state provision of health care, education and childcare. Geographers have also developed a *global* lens of repro-ductive analysis, which connects the expansion of Western capital to global networks of social reproduction provided by migrant labour from the Global South.

In seeking to advance our geographical understanding of social reproduction, feminist scholars have consistently demonstrated how the majority burden of responsibility for activities of social repro-duction (or what Katz has memorably referred to as the 'fleshy, messy and indeterminate stuff of everyday life' [2001: 711]) con-tinues to be picked up by women (see also Chapter 16 on gender). Indeed, this stubborn pattern persists, despite the increased entry of women into the paid labour force in ever greater numbers since the 1970s. This has created new forms of hardship, as women struggle to juggle the competing activities of home, work and family (or what has become popularly known as 'work–life balance'). In seeking to reduce these pressures, social reproduction research has identified what employers and governments can do to help workers to bet-ter reconcile work and family through alternative types of working arrangements. Geographers have also demonstrated how employ-ers' provision of flexible work hours, spatial flexibility of work and employer assistance with childcare can also offer long-term compet-itive advantages for employers themselves (James, 2017) – and how work–life conflict is easier to manage in some places than others.

By seeking to make visible and revalourise the everyday activities of caring in the home, research into social reproduction disrupts a larger masculinist bias in economic theory. Such bias is evident in 'mainstream' conceptions of work, narrowly understood as some-thing that is done for a wage outside the home, visible in the pub-lic sphere, contractualised and typically done by a man! Concepts of social reproduction instead force a much broader and inclusive conceptualisation of 'work' and 'economy' to include that which is unpaid, done for love, completed behind closed doors in the home and regulated by family and kinship networks. In so doing, this work offers a powerful challenge to 'gender-blind, implicitly masculinist approaches across geography's subfields' (Winders & Smith, 2019: 877) and continues to inspire generations of undergraduate and graduate students to extend this work, to effect positive change and bring 'universal' economic theory 'down to earth and give it a pair of pants!' (Bordo, 1990: 137). There remains much to be done.

In seeking to enrol the next generation of students, this chapter offers a critical summary and introduction to social reproduction as a core concept in critical human geography, with some important components of the dynamic research agenda that it has generated. The chapter explores its meaning/s (what is it?), significance (why does it matter?), key sites and agents (where does it take place and who does it?), key drivers (what causes it?) and advances in under-standing (what have we learned?). The chapter takes issue with sub-disciplinary silos in human geography (see Chapter 1 for further critique), in which social reproduction as a sphere of activity has too long been assumed away as the 'exclusive' domain of feminist schol-ars. Social reproduction demands a much wider engagement across economic and social geographies, and the chapter connects to others on gender (Chapter 16), housing (Chapter 21), migration (Chapter 26), the everyday (Chapter 11) and health (Chapter 23).

THEORISING SOCIAL REPRODUCTION

At the broadest level, scholars of social reproduction are united in their collective focus on 'the varied processes involved in maintain-ing and reproducing individuals and societies over time' (Strauss, 2013: 182). Social reproduction might then best be understood as an 'umbrella concept', with different authors emphasising the biological reproduction of humans and the conditions and social constructions of motherhood and fatherhood; reproduction of the labour force, skills and expertise (through training, education and subsistence) as an input to firms' production processes in support of economic growth; and reproduction and provisioning of caring needs through which children, teenagers, adults and the elderly are sheltered, nur-tured and kept healthy – whether through private family and kin-ship networks, purchased through the private market or socialised through state supports (Bakker, 2007). Some influential definitions are included in Table 28.1 to illustrate this variety.

Different scholars also place different emphases on the major sites through which social reproduction takes place. In addition to the home, these range from workplace training to social housing, hospitals, schools, universities, social welfare programmes, childcare centres, playgrounds, parks, shops and farms (see Katz, 2001). This variety of conceptual emphases has emerged from the three broad schools of thought or 'ontologies' of social reproduction (scholars' fundamental conception of how they think reality is organised), suggested by Winders and Smith (2019).

'Work' Versus 'Home' as Separate Spheres

Discussions of social reproduction in the 1970s were inspired by the earlier writings by Karl Marx (*Capital* in 1867) and Friedrich Engels (*The Origin of the Family, Private Property and the State* in 1884), who

TABLE 28.1	Defining 'Social Reproduction'
Author/s	**Definition**
Laslett & Brenner (1989)	'The activities and attitudes, behaviours and emotions, responsibilities and relationships directly involved in the maintenance of life on a daily basis, and intergenerationally' (382).
Katz (2001)	'The material social practices through which people reproduce themselves on a daily and generational basis and through which the social relations and material bases of capitalism are renewed' (709).
Bakker (2007)	'The everyday activities of maintaining life and reproducing the next generation' (541).
Strauss & Meehan (2015)	'The interaction of paid labour and unpaid work in the reproduction of bodies, households, communities, societies and environments, and the ways in which these activities are organised to support – or undermine – human flourishing' (1).

were concerned with the reproduction of labour power for capitalist production (Katz, 2001). Workers go home at the end of each day to be fed, rested, clothed and nurtured to enable them to return to work the next day. Wages must therefore be socially determined to enable workers and their family dependents to engage in *recreation* – as literally the re-creation of labour power for the capitalist economy.

Conceptions of social reproduction within this framework are, therefore, rooted in a *categorical binary* between neatly demarcated realms of production (economic) in the public sphere of the factory and reproduction (noneconomic) in the private sphere of the household. This conception is strongly tied historically to a postwar Fordist model of mass production and a strong Keynesian welfare state, in which a (unionised) male breadwinner was supported by an unpaid female homemaker (Bakker, 2007).

Drawing on Marxist ideas, feminist geographers in the 1980s highlighted how women's oppression under the capitalist system could be understood as a function of the contradictory position of working-class women, whose domestic labour went unpaid despite its crucial role in sustaining production of goods and services in the public sphere (see McDowell, 1986; cf. McDowell & Massey, 1984). However, reading social reproduction as subservient only to the needs of capital is problematic. Other scholars have criticised the rootedness of these accounts in the experiences of White working-class women in cities in the Global North, whose particular experiences diverge from those of migrant working-class women in the same cities and beyond (e.g., Winders & Smith, 2019).

Work/Home as Distinct but Overlapping Spheres

The second conception of social reproduction expanded the analytical gaze beyond the household to include extended family, community, churches, libraries, shops, hospitals, agriculture, orphanages, alms-houses, charities, working social clubs and the welfare state (Katz, 2001). This approach responded to new socioeconomic realities in 'advanced' economies from the late 1980s onwards: a neoliberal rollback of the state, welfare reform, increased female labour-force participation and rise of multiple-earner and female-breadwinner households.

Rather than subordinate the sphere of social reproduction to the sphere of production, here both spheres are seen as *equivalent and interdependent*, overlapping in complex ways, and whose mutual relationship also varies over time, with key changes in the lifecourse of individuals and their families. These overlaps include, for example, the increased formal employment of women outside the home, the rise of teleworking among white-collar professional workers and the formal employment of low-waged workers in social reproduction in other people's homes (e.g., care for elderly, care for people with illness or disability, childcare, home care), which often generate class and racial divides between women. These overlaps are also theorised at the international scale, as a function of global care chains in which migrant workers from the Global South fulfil the social reproductive needs of higher-income households in the Global North.

Blurred Spheres ('Life's Work')

The third conception of social reproduction articulates a wholly blurred reality in which paid work and the rest of life are *fundamentally indistinguishable*. As first articulated by Mitchell, Marston and Katz (2003) under the banner of 'life's work', scholars have emphasised blurred distinctions between being 'at work' and 'off work', how people produce value in *all* domains of their lives and a complete breakdown of the (false) barriers between the social relations, spaces and practices of production and reproduction (see also Schwiter, Strauss & England, 2018). As part of this agenda, scholars have identified the increased marketisation of *all* spheres of human life under conditions of pervasive insecurity, in which responsibility for social reproduction has become privatised as states withdraw from social provisioning. This blurring is furthered by the rise of digital technologies, which means that the domains of work, home and leisure become indistinguishable.

An example is presented by Arlie Russell Hochschild, who has explored the purchase of social reproduction on the market – private childcare, domestic cleaning services, rent-a-grandma services and even outsourced ash-scattering and gravesite maintenance – or what Hochschild (2003, 2012) calls the 'commercialisation of intimate life'. Accordingly, capitalist market relations increasingly infiltrate social reproduction with the goal of reshaping all aspects of human life according to the market's criteria of efficiency and profitability (Bakker, 2007). The result is that some households and communities are placed in more precarious positions than others (Strauss & Meehan, 2015), as government investments in public social reproductive capacity through welfare provision, health care, education, public space and the environment are differently eroded in different places (Katz, 2001).

DOCUMENTING THE EVERYDAY REALITIES OF LIFE'S WORK

Drawing on these evolving conceptions of 'life's work', a growing body of research has demonstrated how contemporary geographies of social reproduction are rooted in, and reinforce, a distinctive set of social inequalities and injustices in which everyday activities of social reproduction are gendered, classed and racialised (Strauss, 2013). This work demonstrates that networks of social reproduction are not simply confined to the household, and that its activities are carried out more easily in some places than others.

One major strand of work has explored the unevenly gendered realities of social reproduction. As demonstrated by Susan Hanson and Geraldine Pratt (1995), employment opportunities closer to home have greater significance for women than men as they seek to reconcile work and family. They document the significant roles played by job hours and their flexibility; the proximity of work, home and day care; fit with partner's job and school schedules; and the gendered power relations within the household in constraining women's job search and mobility relative to men's. They highlight 'sequential scheduling strategies' of the 'second shift' within dual-career households (see Hochschild, 1997), in which couples arrange employment so that one adult is always at home to care for children, with consequent implications for the type and location of work.

Other research has explored the lived realities of household care and social reproduction in the wake of economic crisis and the geographically uneven impacts of austerity (the conditions that result from significant cuts to public expenditure, tax changes and welfare entitlements). Sarah Marie Hall (2015) examines the impacts of austerity on everyday family life in the United Kingdom. Her work reveals a range of interpersonal, intra- and intergenerational, gendered, reciprocal practices of borrowing, sharing, lending and consuming used by families to finance and sustain social reproduction in hard times for moral and material support. She found increasing reliance on food banks as a vital means of sustaining social reproduction and place-based variation in austerity hardship outcomes.

New class divisions in social reproduction are also evident through households' differential abilities to purchase childcare, as neoliberal states reduce their role and responsibility for its delivery. Parents are allegedly 'empowered' to exercise their consumer choice. Aisling Gallagher (2018) shows that this commodification of 'the business of care' in Western countries is generating profound inequalities between households, with significant geographical variation in how childcare markets are funded, structured and organised. This poses major difficulties for low-income households, not least given the decline in community and cooperative childcare provision. And while the purchase of childcare, prepared foods and domestic services might lessen the burden for some women, it increases it for others, such that gender divisions of labour are not fundamentally altered (Katz, 2001).

These gender inequalities exhibit an increasingly transnational and racialised dimension, as social reproduction in Western capitalist economies is enabled through low-paid migrant workers from the Global South. Underpinning these 'transnational care chains', female migrants care for their employers' children while continuing to mother their own – often left behind with relatives at a distance and across time zones (e.g., Madianou, 2012). In this way, gendered divisions of household labour have gone global; part of the struggle between the expansion and intensification of capital accumulation and the systems of social reproduction and everyday life required to sustain it in practice (see Bakker, 2007; Strauss, 2013).

A CRISIS OF SOCIAL REPRODUCTION?

As explored in the first half of this chapter, debates around social reproduction are certainly not new. Arguably, however, the contemporary moment presents new challenges, with conflicts between work, home and family heralded as 'the problem of our time'. Some scholars also warn of a major crisis of social reproduction looming, consequent from the triple whammy of (1) *new workplace realities* in which 'flexibility' means increased workloads, less predictable schedules and more unsocial hours as firms seek to minimise labour costs; (2) *changes in household structure* and complexity, through rises in female labour-force participation and dual-earner households, the decline of the extended family, increasing lone-parent households and greater elder-care responsibilities; and (3) *neoliberal rollback of social provisioning*. Neoliberal governments offer less support for social reproduction, transferring the burden of care down to the 'natural' level of home (Bakker & Gill, 2003), where women retain the major responsibility for it. The result is a complex, gendered, multivariable, exhausting juggling act between home and work (see James, 2017).

Referred to variously as 'the time squeeze', 'the time bind', 'time famine' and 'time scarcity', this situation reinforces mounting concerns around a 'care deficit' (Hochschild, 2003): the shortage of time and energy to invest in nurturing resilient, secure individuals, families, friendships and communities, at the same time as an increased *need* for care. As work increasingly occupies time previously set aside for other interests, studies report increased loneliness, eroding friendship support networks, negative impacts on parent–child relationships and a falling quality of life. Studies have also documented how work–life conflict can result in increased stress, negative effects on psychological and physical well-being and increased family tensions (e.g., Burchell, Lapido & Wilkinson, 2002; James, 2017). Thus, while neoliberal welfare state cutbacks have assumed an infinite capacity on the part of households to absorb the costs of reproduction and care (MacDonald, Phipps & Lethbridge, 2005), the reality exposes its limits.

The possibilities for reconciling life's work in practice vary widely between people and places. In other words, social reproduction is a profoundly spatial phenomenon (Winders & Smith, 2019) because of different levels of provision by employers, urban infrastructures of care and government patterns of welfare provision.

Employer Provision of Family-Friendly Working

Central to understanding these geographical differences in reconciling life's work are the major variations in employer provision of 'family-friendly working' or 'work–life balance' (WLB) arrangements. Employer-provided WLB arrangements are typically split across four categories in terms of those providing greater *temporal flexibility* (e.g., flex time, compressed working hours), greater *spatial flexibility* (e.g., teleworking from home), reduced *total work hours* and *employer assistance with childcare* (e.g., workplace crèche, childcare vouchers). Variations in provision reflect the scepticism at the so-called business case for WLB provision: many employers are unlikely to implement it unless they can identify 'bottom-line' economic advantages. There remains a relative dearth of empirical evidence, and WLB provision is often seen as a costly administrative burden that unfairly privileges a small subset of workers. This is exacerbated by the aftermath of the 'global' economic downturn.

Recent research has begun to fill this evidence gap, for example, James (2017) on high-tech professionals in the United Kingdom and Ireland, who juggle a wide range of family and personal life activities (childcare, volunteering, sports, youth leading, charity organising, homeschooling, animal care) with the highly variable time demands, international work team cooperation and need for instant customer response characteristic of high-tech work environments (see Text Box 28.1).

TEXT BOX 28.1 | **Real-World Research: Work–Life Advantage – Sustaining Workers, Sustaining Firms**

Research within feminist economic geography disrupts common employer perceptions around work–life balance provision as merely an administrative cost. Based on ten years of research with over 300 IT workers and 150 IT firms in the UK and Ireland, my work (James, 2017) demonstrates how, by making available a wider range of WLB arrangements, beneficial impacts on firms' innovative capacities and economic performance result. These advantages emerge as a function of increased worker engagement, enlarged firm access to external skills and expertise, and increased sustainability of worker learning.

The research shows that work–life provisions suitable for one class of employees may have little or no effect in reducing work–life conflict for another class. Moreover, the kinds of WLB provisions required by individuals are also changeable over time, in relation to major life events. Ultimately, this diversity points to the urgent need for more comprehensive suites of employer-provided work–life arrangements.

The research also highlights a crucial difference between employer provision of flexible working arrangements that challenge uneven gender divisions of unpaid labour (by encouraging men to take up a greater share of childcare) versus those that simply accept them (e.g., part-time working) and provide little benefit for stubborn gender inequalities of household reproductive labour.

FIGURE 28.1
Juggling work and life.
(Credit: Al James)

Work–Life City Limits and Urban Carescapes

Geographers have also explored how the means for reconciling life's work vary between cities with different urban geographies. The spatial fragmentation between housing, jobs, schools, transport systems, leisure and commodified caring services (elder-care facilities, child-care services, gyms, hair salons) is crucial to understanding the wider context in which decisions around social reproduction are made (England, 2010) – or what Helen Jarvis (2005: 141) has identified as the 'infrastructure of everyday life'. The coordination of everyday life within urban 'carescapes' involves the delicate coordination of multiple tasks of production and reproduction, undertaken by individual and collective actors and distributed across different (and often mismatched) spaces and times (Bowlby, 2012). Historically, for example, this included the Fordist demarcation of Western industrial cities into zones of capitalist industry, occupied primarily by men, set apart from suburban housing areas, occupied primarily by women engaged in unpaid labour. So the city form itself embodied distinctive ideas about the nonpermeability of spheres of production and social reproduction, as well as the gender order required for economic production. Fast-forward to the twenty-first century, and the urban present is much more complex for dual-earner households. Here, Perrons and colleagues (2006) highlight expanding travel-to-work areas, longer and more intense rush hours and growing congestion associated with school runs as some of the major everyday challenges that face workers, families, employers and service providers in reconciling social reproduction with waged work around daily activities that are often not in close proximity. These challenges are reinforced by suburban sprawl and the privatisation of public transport services. As such, the layout of cities represents much more than a benign stage on which life's work is played out and is itself constitutive of the complex geographies of work, home and family.

National Gendered Welfare Regimes

The terms in which debates around social reproduction are cast and acted upon vary nationally (Esping-Andersen, 1999), reflecting the many national traditions, cultures, institutional contexts and normative assumptions about gender roles (collectively understood as 'national welfare regimes'). At one end of the scale, Scandinavian national policy frameworks within the social democratic welfare tradition are best known for fostering more systemic and progressive possibilities for juggling work, home and family through legislation making it easier for women and men to combine paid work with the rest of life, government concerns to reduce working time for all and an explicit aim to degender parenthood and caring responsibilities. Developed in partnership among employers, the state and labour unions, a long period of generously paid parental leave, extensive publicly provided and state-subsidised childcare and cash benefits for children give support to Swedish workers. At the other end of the policy spectrum are English-speaking countries with liberal welfare regimes (including the United Kingdom, Ireland, the United States and Australia) where the problem of combining paid and unpaid work has instead largely been seen as a private affair (Lewis, 2009). Accordingly, families are expected to turn to the market, with employers encouraged to *voluntarily* provide more flexible working arrangements. The contradiction of life's work in neoliberal welfare regimes, then, is clear: just as women have been encouraged into paid work, the state-provided childcare that enabled them to do so has been rolled back. But, as research has shown, other models are possible!

Research is now emerging that documents a potential regendering of social reproduction in ways that might disrupt the problems outlined in this chapter. Recent studies suggest that increasing numbers of men now undertake significant caring responsibilities outside of paid work in response to shifting societal expectations around 'active fathering'; gender shifts in educational attainment; increased social acceptance of female-breadwinner households; shifting relative earnings; rising childcare costs; the increase in feminised service-sector employment, in which masculinity is seen as a disadvantage; and more progressive national policies promoting male uptake of care (see Boyer et al., 2017). In addition, recessionary labour market change and austerity welfare cuts have reshaped household decision-making around domestic labour. To be sure, numbers remain low, but the trend is encouraging. There is also evidence that these men are crafting new ways of doing social reproduction, distinct from their female counterparts (J. A. Smith, 2009).

SUMMARY

- Social reproduction is an umbrella concept focused on the relationship between paid labour and unpaid labour, shifting temporal and spatial boundaries between 'work' and 'home', and the varied social processes, material goods, institutions, agents and emotions involved in sustaining and reproducing individuals, families, communities and societies over time.
- Three broad schools of thought on social reproduction can be identified: distinct spheres ('work' versus 'home'), overlapping spheres (work/home) and blurred spheres ('life's work').
- The conditions and possibilities of social reproduction are geographically uneven in their distribution.
- Notwithstanding the efforts of some men 'going against the grain', women continue to bear most responsibility for everyday activities of social reproduction.
- Research by feminist scholars into social reproduction seeks to make visible and revalourise everyday activities of caring in the home, disrupting the masculinist bias in 'universal' economic theory.
- Some commentators identify a contemporary crisis of social reproduction, resulting from working longer and harder, increased female labour-force participation, increased household complexity, increased life expectancy and elder-care responsibilities and the neoliberal rollback of social welfare.

FURTHER READING

McDowell, L. M. (2004) Work, workfare, work/life balance and an ethic of care. *Progress in Human Geography*, 28(2): 145–63.

Mitchell, K., Marston, S., & Katz, C. (2003) Life's work: An introduction, review and critique. *Antipode*, 35(3): 414–42.

Strauss, K., & Meehan, K. (2015) New frontiers in life's work. In K. Meehan & K. Strauss (eds.), *Precarious Worlds: Contested Geographies of Social Reproduction*, pp. 1–22. Athens: University of Georgia Press.

Winders, J., & Smith, B. E. (2019) Social reproduction and capitalist production: A genealogy of dominant imaginaries. *Progress in Human Geography*, 43(5): 871–89.

Performance

Ruth Raynor

Figures is a mass sculptural durational performance created by Liz Crow in London in 2015 (http://wearefigures.co.uk, and see Figure 29.1). The piece foregrounds the human cost of austerity, which was implemented in the United Kingdom from 2010, contesting the extent to which this austerity was staged as necessary and inevitable. Liz created 650 sculptures from mud excavated from Bristol (her hometown) and taken to the banks of the River Thames. This represented the 650 constituencies affected by austerity. Later, 650 personal stories of hardship were told as part of the piece. The sculpting was an act of endurance. As a wheelchair user, Liz was carried to and from the shores of the Thames – in time with the tides – where she made the figures over eleven consecutive days and nights in all weathers. This emphasised human interdependence, the lost infrastructures of care and the unequal effects of austerity on debilitated bodies. The performance travelled through space and time as the figures were dried, burned and then returned to the sea in Bristol. Ahead of a national election, the activist art practice was a call for international action that represented, emotionally evoked and sought to intervene in the social life of austerity. The performance was encountered in a range of locations and at a range of times: on the banks of the Thames, in gallery spaces, on social media and blogs, in news items and on the website. Via these platforms, audio-recorded and written

FIGURE 29.1

Liz Crow, *Figures* mass-sculptural durational performance, 2015. (Source: Matthew Fessey – Roaring Girl Productions)

narratives were circulated widely too. Therefore, the performance expanded beyond the site and moment of 'happening'. The duration of the piece suggested austerity as an extended event and the weariness experienced by those living at the sharp end of austerity (Wilkinson & Ortega-Alcázar, 2019), who must repeatedly react to events which – like the tide – are out of their control. Through this practice, the artist, the sites in which this performance took place and the excavated mud all performed the 'restaging' (and restaging, and restaging) of austerity.

This example introduces how we will think about the place of 'performance' in social geography in the rest of the chapter. In recent years, the term has gained in popularity, but there are different concepts and methods associated with it. The first part of the chapter thinks about performance, and later performativity, as theories that explain how human behaviour is organised, how 'norms' are produced that close down possibilities and how resistance can be enacted through the very same mechanisms. These theories have also been engaged to further understand qualitative methods in social geographies. The next part of the chapter outlines work that analyses how performing-arts practices expand opportunities for making space and asks what feelings performances create. What do they tell us about different cultures, individuals and communities? Who is included and excluded in them and by them? How do they entrench or push back against norms and conventions? And finally, the performing arts themselves are drawn on to disseminate research in social geographies and as forms of methodological enquiry in their own right.

PERFORMANCE AND PERFORMATIVITY: THEORISATIONS OF THE SOCIAL PLACE AS A STAGE FOR PERFORMANCE IN EVERYDAY LIFE

Performance has been used as a metaphor for understanding everyday life in the social sciences and humanities. Early work in social geographies was grounded in the theorisations of Austin (1962), Garfinkel (1967) and Goffman (1959, 1963). Most notably, Erving Goffman's 'dramaturgical analysis' (1959) used the language of theatrical performance to explore social behaviour. In short, he suggested that 'front-stage' and 'backstage' behaviours differ according to commonly accepted rules and conventions. Simply put: When I am in the home, I behave differently from how I do when I am at work; I am different on my own from how I am with other people. I wear costumes, use props and alter my language choices in order to navigate the social world. These 'performances' emerge as a result of *encounter* between people and their localities (see Chapter 27). Therefore, performance names how judgements about other people are enacted, as well as the attempts to control these judgements.

Of course, relationships between front stage and backstage, locality and performance have changed a great deal in recent years, a shift mediated in part by digital technology and changes to working patterns. However, in the 1990s Goffman's theory was of particular interest to geographers because it emphasised relationships between human behaviour and *place*. Unsurprisingly, geographies of labour were some of the first to engage Goffman's theory (see Nash, 2000). For example, in 1994 Phil Crang reflected on his role as a waiter in a London restaurant, describing a 'skeleton' of conventions around which performances were tentatively negotiated. While Goffman 'suggests that the social role played by an individual is not a constant one, but dependent upon interactions in an encounter and the character of that particular encounter itself' (Crang, 1994: 686), here the restaurant is produced as a stable backdrop that framed a series of expectations about the actors' performance.

PERFORMATIVITY: COMPLEX AND UNSTABLE PERFORMANCES IN EVERYDAY LIFE

While Goffman's deployment of performance, referring to how people act in everyday life, was taken up by geographers interested in the impact of place on social behaviour, other social geographers were drawing on Judith Butler's (1990, 1993) theorisation of *performativity* to explore the effects of language and actions on the formation of identities (see Part C on divisions for a more detailed discussion of identity). Put simply, performativity (as *distinct* from performance) describes how what we say and do is influenced by already circulating (but unstable) languages and cultures. Words and thoughts are active. They inform behaviours, events and experiences and, as they do so, enforce norms or ideals. Power circulates in the construction of norms as the opportunities for other ways of doing or being are closed down. Specifically, the early work of Butler explored how gendered and sexual identities (see Chapters 16 and 17) are 'socially constructed'. But this does not mean that they are freely *chosen* (or performed); as she puts it, we do not wake up in the morning, go to the wardrobe and choose 'which gender to don that day' and then 'take it off again at night' (1993: x). However, neither does performativity refer to a deterministic model where everything is predecided by an overarching, already fixed social structure. That would leave no hope for change. Performativity offers a way of navigating between these very different ways of understanding the formation of identities. It does so, in part, by reversing the notion that gender and sexuality emerge as expressions of what we are. Instead, gender and sexuality are performed and reperformed via speech and acts that shape framings of possibility in everyday life.

Crucially, in Butler's analysis there is also room for slippage or subversion, and this means the intentional or nonintentional ways of becoming *other* than the socially prescribed or 'normative'. She used celebratory iterations of the hitherto derogatory 'queer(ness)' to work this through. In the 1990s, the significance of gender and sexuality in relation to the production and occupation of place began to be explored through Butler's concept of performativity. For example, McDowell and Court (1994) thought through the material effects of gender 'fictions' that were enacted on workers in London's financial district. Bell and colleagues' (1994) exploration of transgressive queer identities, lipstick lesbians and gay skinheads was also influential (see also Chapter 17). As Binnie later suggested, this field of work pointed to the understanding that 'space is not naturally authentically "straight" [nor gendered] but rather actively produced and (hetero) sexualized' (1997: 223). These approaches made an important contribution to the discipline by challenging heterosexual and masculinist ways of knowing, making *and* occupying place. However, Gregson and Rose (2000) argued that, at times, this work either intentionally or inadvertently reproduced a more fixed or stable account of space that was more closely aligned with Goffman than Butler's performativity. Drawing on research with community art practices in Scotland and car-boot sales in the northeast of England, they emphasised the 'performativity of space'. This meant holding onto Butler's identities as emergent, constructed and reconstructed, unstable and open to subversion. Taking this further, Gregson and Rose also considered how their own positions as researchers unfolded in normative and subversive ways. They foregrounded how practices of research 'got inside', informed and were informed by the author's own frames of possibility, and vice versa (we will return to this later).

Another criticism levelled at social geographies influenced by feminist and queer theories is that this work actually reproduces socially constructed binaries, like 'heterosexual' and 'homosexual', and in doing so performs the same fixity of identity (and space) that

Butler and others sought to deconstruct (see also Chapter 17). Just as Gregson and Rose (2000) thought performativity fell outside the explicit production of sexuality and gender, Oswin (2008) contested the limiting of queer theories to sexuality and gender studies and, further, found the reproduction of normative practices implicit in much of this work. This means that people and spaces are continually rendered either 'queer' or 'not queer' in sexualities research. This *reproduces* such identities through stable and binary logics: it gives the impression that everything is predecided by an overarching, already fixed social structure. Oswin drew together interventions from decolonial and intersectional scholars (see Chapter 20) in order to work this through. For example, referring to the oft-cited 'lipstick lesbians' and 'gay skinheads' (Bell et al., 1994), she noted 'the authors write that heterosexual or "real" skinheads are positioned against gay "style" skinheads. But why privilege the fascist heterosexual skinhead as "real" and the gay skinhead as "bad copy"? Why privilege heterosexual space as "real" and queer space as pretended, fake or copy?' (Bell et al., 1994: 37). This was an important argument at the time but, for Oswin (2008: 94), 'upon planting the radical flag of queerness, Bell et al. ignore the multifaceted nature of identity to deny the possibility that gay skinheads might also be fascists' and thus 'issues of race in [their] reconstruction of queer history' (citing Walker, 1995: 73).

The point that Oswin makes here is critical. She argues against 'queer space' and instead for a 'queer approach to space'. This means recognising that a politics of normativity refers not to particular identities but to the *processes* whereby normative assumptions and institutions are reproduced (after Duggan, 2003: 50). If research practices and cultures either intentionally or inadvertently reinforce the construction of stable identities or other taken-for-granted assumptions, then they are adopting a normative, not a queer, approach to the production of knowledge. Queering, then, is the act of 'operating beyond powers and controls that enforce normativity' (Browne, 2006: 889, in Oswin, 2008: 94). These *practices* should be applied with and beyond constructions of gender and sexuality and thought as/through intersectionally (see Chapter 20). For a good example of critical performance-based work that takes this proposition seriously in human geography, see McLean's (2017) article, which shows how community-based radical feminist and queer artistic practices were deployed to contest the appropriation of creativity in urban policy in Toronto, Canada. McLean's article is just one of many 'geographies of the performing arts' which give explicit critical attention to *how* space is constructed and sometimes contested through performing arts practices. For other analyses of the performing arts in human geography, see Simpson (2011) on the transformation of urban space via street performance and Rogers (2018), who, drawing on her own research on contemporary Cambodian dance practice, suggests that analysis of the performing arts can expand understanding of intercultural aesthetics, migrant mobilities and geopolitics.

PERFORMANCE AND THE PERFORMING ARTS IN SOCIAL RESEARCH PRACTICE

As Gregson and Rose (2000) and Oswin (2008) have differently demonstrated, theories of performance and performativity are not just useful for understanding what happens in social life. They also help us to understand social research and provide social geographers with a suite of methods to investigate and represent what happens in everyday life. As Latham argued, 'if social action can be viewed as performance, then it is also important to reframe the research process itself as a kind of performance' (2003: 1993). In part, he was drawing on work from Thrift and Dewsbury (2000), who argued that research outcomes in human geography were somehow flatter, or more deadened, than the lively subjects under investigation. Drawing upon studies of performance and the performing arts, they called for geographical research practices that may be 'fleshy and emotional', that may, in different ways, make the 'world come alive' (Thrift & Dewsbury, 2000: 422).

This intervention and the nonrepresentational theories (see Chapter 2) that it spoke to became part of a wider body of work, using performance as a metaphor for social research. Thrift and Dewsbury made a distinction between 'representations' and 'practices' to centre the lively, irreducible, excessive experiences of 'doing', using performing arts practice as an example. Nonrepresentational geographers do not seek to uncover 'meanings and values that apparently await discovery, interpretation, judgement and ultimate representation' (Lorimer, 2005: 84). Instead, a significant proportion of their work has become the immersion of the researcher in sites and practices so that they might *experience* particular phenomena, becoming attuned to what happens during the process of participation. This matters since, as McCormack (2008: 4) suggests, there is a long philosophical tradition 'in which experience and experiment are valourised as necessary elements of thinking'.

There is a subversive potential, then, in taking *practice* as the basis for experience and resisting the discursive reproduction of 'stable' identities. Further, there is subversive potential in the recognition that lived experiences may be affected by, *but also* exceed and escape, normative framings of possibility. Therefore, in much of this work participation becomes synonymous with a kind of proximity to the lively and embodied excesses of doing. For McCormack (2014), dance is a key site for complicating questions of representation because it is so difficult to replicate. Dance (and drawing) become just one possible 'field of variation in which to experiment with the question of how felt differences might register in thinking' (McCormack, 2014: 11). Increasingly, experiments in expressing 'what happens' through creative practice in research also take place in social and cultural geography, and the lines between doing and documenting research are intentionally blurred (e.g., see Macpherson & Bleasdale, 2012; Veal, 2016). Just as Crow's body, the mud, the tide and the shore performed and were excessive in her art, more recently theories and practices of performance extend beyond the human, and space is given to the affective capacities of 'nonhuman' environments, landscapes, materials, objects and animals, each of which have their part to play both in social research and in everyday life.

However, as attendance to relationships between affect and performing arts practices was beginning to flourish in cultural geographies, Nash (2000) gave a note of caution. She was wary of the risk that this approach to performance and practice would flatten the social struggles that I have described above for marginalised communities and individuals to make space and would, instead, favour 'the individualistic and universalizing sovereign subject' (2000: 664). She advocated for research 'which manages to combine the theoretical insights of theories of performativity with detailed attention to the political, economic and cultural geographies of specific "everyday practices"' (Nash, 2000: 664). Recent uses of performance in human geography have perhaps negotiated the challenges posed by adopting a 'queer' approach to space (as Oswin [2008] suggests), holding onto the contextual specificities of everyday practices (after Nash, 2000) *and* maintaining the singular, lively and fleshy excesses of bodies' doing in space (after Thrift & Dewsbury, 2000).

For example, Noxolo's (2015) work achieves this with African Caribbean dance as a form of mapping. For Noxolo, in popular culture Black bodies are often denied the opportunity to make space in European contexts. These are the effects of genres of colonialism, of historic and institutional forms of racism (see Chapter 13). The performance of African Caribbean dance as *cartography* (mapping), however, proclaims the rights of Black bodies to make, and become embedded in, the European places from which they have been hitherto marginalised; further, this takes place through the subversion of the *form* used for mapping, which shifts a colonial approach to making, fixing and owning space towards an affirmative form of immanent, lively and celebratory dance cartography. Dance is movement – and, through that movement, the making of space is not fixed but becomes fleshy, emotive and open-ended. In this way, the practice of dance documents the singularity of African Caribbean performers *and* pushes against performative processes of mapping, fixing space that impact Black bodies. So the dance facilitates a shared encounter that gets inside the body, that becomes an inclusive and affirmative act and that subverts colonial ways of organising people and space.

My own experimentation with performing arts (in this case, theatre making – see Text Box 29.1) for collaborative social research was by no means the first. Given an emphasis on action, inclusion and emotion, it is no surprise that, among a broad range of creative methods, social scientists, including social geographers, have deployed theatre practice for their participatory potentialities (Houston & Pulido, 2002; Nagar, 2002; Pratt & Kirby, 2003; Kaptani & Yuval-Davis, 2008).

TEXT BOX 29.1	Real-World Research: Participatory Theatre on Austerity

One of my own projects involved participative theatre making with a group of women at the sharp end of austerity in the United Kingdom (Raynor, 2017). This enacted a queer methodological *approach* to space. Rather than holding economically marginalised women up as villains, victims or heroes, the process enabled us to 'make strange', and then reflect on, the effects of political and discursive *practices* in austerity. Our shared experiences of 'doing' theatre games and exercises made space for an exploration of how 'powers and controls that enforced normativity' were shifting in austerity, as well as women's everyday acts of coping with and circumnavigating such controls. Through the doing and staging of a theatre play, women were not reduced (or, indeed, reducible) to a particular identity position. Instead, their singular, fleshy, lively and surprising excesses were centred. In one paper about the experience (Raynor, 2017), our attempts at 'dramatising austerity' were used as a metaphor (1) to show that we could never fully 'represent' women's singular everyday experiences in austerity, (2) to evoke some of the emotional and practical effects of austerity on these women and (3) to expand on the metaphor of performance by centring the significance of *form* (an approach to space) for understanding and communicating (writing and staging) women's experiences in everyday life.

For Cieri and McCauley (2007), the creation and presentation of theatre *is* a site of participatory action research (see Chapter 3). They describe a dialogic process whereby actor/collaborators and artist/researchers collected 'untold' stories about three charged historic events: the 1960s voting rights struggle in Mississippi, the mid-1970s school desegregation controversy in Boston and the 1969 Black Panther Party/Los Angeles Police department conflict. Researchers and community-based actors assembled transcripts into a narrative collage that was retold in performance. Here, embodied moments of 'retelling' about 'pain and grief, struggle and triumph' became cited as a reason for their resonance with audiences (Cieri & McCauley, 2007: 146). In this case, we see how theatre practice made the stories visceral to those who had not yet encountered them, through the liveliness of performance.

Most notably, in geography, Pratt and Johnston (2013) and Johnston and Pratt (2019) engage with *forum theatre* techniques in their research on migration and care. In this case, space is created for witnesses of a performance (of research materials) to engage with and discuss the issues at hand. Forum devices may also be used in attempts to inform local governance via 'legislative theatre' (Pratt & Johnston, 2007, after Boal, 2005/1998) and to enhance public engagement with neighbourhood planning (Cowie, 2017). In other cases, theatre practice is used to develop story collaboratively. This can be orientated towards action and advocacy for social change. For example, Pratt and Kirby (2003) show collaborators engaged in storytelling workshops (alongside other methods) in a project with nurses in union struggles over pay. For Pratt and Kirby (2003), theatre provided a 'safe space' where nurses could let their guard

FIGURE 29.2
Image from *DieHard Gateshead*, written by Ruth Raynor, produced by the Theatre of Moths. (Credit: Matt Jamie Photography, featuring Zoe Lambert and Jessica Johnson)

down about the practical and political pressures of the job. The space between reality and fiction enabled experimentation (Kershaw, 2000): 'ironically the fictional and farcical parts of the script allowed space to raise hard hitting and very specific criticisms of hospital administrators' (Pratt & Kirby, 2003: 19). Through these projects, we can see how performing arts practices have been deployed to disseminate social research and to co-create social research with collaborators in lively, emotional and fleshy ways.

To finish, let's look back to the piece by Liz Crow (see Figure 29.1) that was described at the start of this chapter and think about it through some of these ways of engaging with performance and the performing arts in social geographies:

1. An analysis of Crow's performance could be used to provide insight into lived experiences in austerity: this has the potential

to teach us something about social life at a particular time (post-2008 financial crisis) in a particular place (the United Kingdom).

2. Her intervention expands what it means to perform or 'do' something, from human to nonhuman actors, by including the mud, the tide and the shoreline in acts of burning, moulding, reading, moving.

3. This performance queered (made present and contestable) the shifting regulatory policies in austerity and their effects: through the reading of everyday narratives as the figures were burned, by foregrounding the unequal effects of austerity on disabled bodies and by evoking the exhaustion that accompanies 'doing' a response to the cuts, reforms and withdrawals of austerity.

This gives a sense of how you might engage with performance, performativity or the performing arts as an analytic or methodological tool in social geographies.

SUMMARY

- Performance has been deployed in social geographies as a metaphor for understanding what happens in everyday life as well as in social research.
- Performativity has been drawn on as a theory to understand the effects of language and acts on experiences and behaviours, while remaining open to their subversion and contestation, and to think about the indeterminacy and emergence of space.
- Recent attention has been turned to the notion of queering *approaches* to space, both in social research and through performing arts practice.
- The performing arts have been explored for their capacities to make space, and they have been practised and reflected on in experiments that seek to understand the effects of doing on thinking.
- The performing arts are an object of analysis that gives insights into social and cultural life.
- The performing arts are also developed as a participatory research practice and as a method for disseminating social research, inviting public dialogue and opening up pathways to action.

FURTHER READING

Gregson, N., & Rose, G. (2000) Taking Butler elsewhere: Performativities, spatialities and subjectivities. *Environment and Planning D: Society and Space*, 18(4): 433–52.

Johnston, C., & Pratt, G. (2019) *Migration in Performance: Crossing the Colonial Present.* London: Routledge.

Oswin, N. (2008) Critical geographies and the uses of sexuality: Deconstructing queer space. *Progress in Human Geography,* 32(1): 89–103.

Raynor, R. (2019) Speaking, feeling, mattering: Theatre as method and model for practice-based, collaborative research. *Progress in Human Geography,* 43(4): 691–710.

Rogers, A. (2018) Advancing the geographies of the performing arts: Intercultural aesthetics, migratory mobility and geopolitics. *Progress in Human Geography,* 42(4): 549–68.

Data
Niall Cunningham

Where do we locate 'data'? This is a key question for social geographers. There are few concepts so integral to the process of social research and so universal in their reach across an entire subdiscipline and, indeed, well beyond. We are in the most intensive and intensifying period of data accumulation that this planet has ever witnessed. Before we wake in the morning, a 'smart watch' may have been recording our heart rate throughout the night, ready to provide immediate feedback on the extent and satisfaction of our night's sleep. By the bed, a mobile phone jolts us from our rest with a medley of wake-up tunes in turn, suggested to us on the basis of predictive algorithms that our music-streaming site of choice has self-learned from our previous choices. A request to the 'smart speaker' turns on the lights and we step into our slippers, making our way to the bathroom across a hall, in which the temperature has been moderated by the 'smart thermostat' on the mobile phone that we already clutch in our hand and which is unlikely to leave our person for much of the entire day, if at all. Sleepily, we apply a squeeze of paste to the toothbrush and idly push it around our mouth for a few moments, only to be told in an instantaneous 'ping' via our smartphone app that we haven't spent long enough on our upper left molars this morning. We have not even had breakfast yet, and already our bodies have been mobilised in myriad processes of big data accumulation and analysis.

Data are so important to us as social geographers because they represent our way of knowing and thus, by extension, trying to understand and to represent the world around us. As social geographers, what interests us is how people interact with each other in space and the unequal relationships that are both cause and effect of those dynamics (see Chapter 1). Data are our empirical observations of the social world. Without data, all we have is conjecture and informed guesswork. The types of data we collect, the ways they are generated and the methods that are used to process and analyse them will inevitably lead to particular representations of the world (see Chapter 3). The decisions that must be made about what to include and what to exclude can result in only particular dimensions of an issue being foregrounded or, indeed, addressed at all. And at every point, therefore, there is human subjectivity informing those decisions and assumptions, meaning that the process of how we can and should gather data, and to what end, is never a neutral one.

It might seem strange then to locate data and data analysis as anything other than core or fundamental concerns of social geography, given just how overlooked, embodied and mundane our interactions with data are in our everyday lives. And yet data also appear in this book as an 'issue' – a topic for study in its own right – and there is very good reason for that. While we might often take these processes for granted, the ways data are generated, accumulated, stored, processed, sold, lost, analysed, presented and generally used are profoundly contentious. And while the scale, scope and speed of those processes of data accumulation may have accelerated, questions around the ethics of data have long been central to the concerns of social geographers, because those data shape how we frame and understand just what 'the social' is. This chapter will take an overview of data as an 'issue', locating our contemporary understanding of its power and potential within a longer-term historical context as well as with an eye to future developments.

THE HISTORIES OF DATA

Despite the technological focus in the opening paragraph, there is nothing new about data. One of the earliest surviving written sources in the United Kingdom are the Vindolanda Tablets (see Figure 30.1), which date from the first century CE, giving a fascinating insight into life on the northernmost frontier of the Roman Empire prior to the building of Hadrian's Wall (Bowman, 1994: 13). Such data are important because they provide information, the resource that enables us to know something of that past. The uncovering of such massive bodies of data presents great opportunities to shed light on ancient civilisations. Yet the fact that 'evidence of this kind and on this scale is quite simply unparalleled' (Bowman, 1994: 13) raises challenges regarding how to accurately represent such

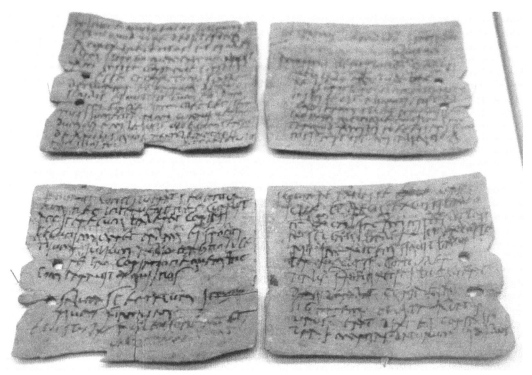

FIGURE 30.1

Roman writing tablet from the Vindolanda Roman fort of Hadrian's Wall, in Northumberland, first to second century AD. (Source: British Museum, CC BY-SA 3.0, https://creativecommons.org/licenses/by-sa/3.0)

material in ways that echo contemporary concerns around the harvesting of big data. What should we use? What should we leave out? How best can we analyse this? While there might be a scalar difference between such 'old' data and 'new' big datasets, which are infinitely extensible and continuously updated (Kitchin, 2014: 1–2), for social geographers with either historic or contemporary interests there are parallels. One is the difficulty of seeking to make sense of and represent meaning in massive datasets (Kitchin, 2013: 264). A second is the question of what methodologies and modes of representation to apply to materials, which can be in a huge variety of formats and encompass both subjective and seemingly objective forms of information. If we return to our example of the Vindolanda Tablets, that dataset contains an array of sources of valuable information, ranging from personal correspondence to enumerations of the military strength of various parts of the imperial frontier (VTO, 2003). These sorts of qualitative and quantitative data sources can be used to triangulate our understandings of the period (Hoggart, Davies & Lees, 2002) by allowing us to view people and events through different lenses. However, the use of various forms of data in this way can be both problematic and productive, because multiple underlying values and assumptions underpin their production. For Mason (2006: 20), this leads to tensions that are 'dialogic', because those underlying assumptions and prior questions can always be called into question, and, for her, this is a positive thing.

For a long time, tensions have existed between social geographers around the questions and assumptions that have formed the basis for various forms of data production. A powerful concept informing the thinking of many geographers around the role of data is Michel Foucault's notion of 'governmentality'. Foucault summarised this idea as the 'art of government' (Gordon, 1991: 3). It describes the means and modes by which states regulate the behaviour of their subject populations and attempt to manage those populations, in order that they might self-regulate their own behaviour, something he termed 'the conduct of conduct' (Lemke, 2002: 50–51).

For a population to be managed effectively in this way requires power. For Foucault, power was about force, but not necessarily in the sense of 'brute' force, as in the threat or use of physical violence or containment. Force was about the ability to direct power in particular ways and directions in order to make other states, as well as citizens within states, behave in desired ways (Elden, 2007). The exercise of power, for Foucault, was inseparable from – indeed, completely dependent upon – 'knowledge', hence his concept of 'power/knowledge' (Foucault, 1980). In order for a population to be controlled, it must first be known, and in his historical studies of statecraft Foucault saw the post-Enlightenment period of the late eighteenth and nineteenth centuries as the key period in which the state extended its knowledge of the population, through new instruments such as census enumerations and the systematic cartographic mapping of space (Huxley, 2007). These tools created new forms of data that favoured large-scale quantitative and geometric understandings of space and how it was constituted.

For these reasons, the idea of data cannot be understood in isolation from other key concepts, principally those of 'territory' and 'statistics'. Data provided a means by which a somewhat abstract and potentially dangerous or uncontrollable entity – the population – could be known by understanding it within a territorial space through mechanisms like the census. This knowledge thereby allowed the sovereign or state to allow that population a degree of freedom to circulate and to govern or discipline itself, within given constraints of law and order (Elden, 2007; Foucault, 2004). The historian Patrick Joyce (2003) has termed this the 'rule of freedom' and has demonstrated how the desire to know the rapidly industrialising city was limited not simply to the state itself. A new liberal civic culture was emerging in which a host of new philanthropic and lay scientific societies were trying to uncover 'the "laws" of the social' (Joyce, 2003), and the tool that enabled this was statistics.

It is still the case today that when big datasets like censuses or large-scale surveys are constructed they provide a wide variety of 'variables', each of which contains a distinctive attribute, perhaps relating to age, gender, employment status or self-assessed well-being, for example. When analysing those data, we might first look to make sense of the size and spread of the data, its distribution and how many individuals fall within particular categorisations, like ethnicity. Beyond that, we would then seek to understand relationships within those data. How does variable x relate to variable y? What is the change in the relationship between x and y when we consider (or control for) z? Perhaps the most important underpinning principle of data analysis is that of probability. The construction of 'objective' scientific facts is based on the ability to discount with a chosen degree of confidence the idea that randomness explains observed relationships between variables in a statistical model.

The power of statistics in the nineteenth century emerged as a means by which to impose order on the chaos of the universe and the complexity of social life, but also as a means by which to reject primitive ideas of determinism and predestination in the social world (Hacking, 1990: 1–11). So there are inherent contradictions in the post-Enlightenment development of statistics. At one level, the fundamental drive was progressive in seeking to know the world in ways that saw individual life outcomes not as the inevitable result of inherent individual deficiencies, but, at another level, statistical analyses in this period were heavily drawn on as a justification for selective population control and eugenics, most notably in the work of Thomas Malthus (1999/1798) and Francis Galton (1889). In the case of Galton, the major statistical tool that facilitated his analyses was multiple regression, in which a series of independent variables is used in a statistical model to predict a given dependent or outcome variable. The multiple regression model, sometimes in more complex and multilayered forms, still lies at the very heart of statistical analysis. Given these grim historical associations, we might understand why quantitative data and data analysis appear as an 'issue' (Barnes, 1998), but, as with any issue, it is by definition one that is contested. Hepple (2001) provides an important counterpoint on the origins of multiple regression, underlining its more progressive origins as a relevant methodology in human geography with roots independent of those biometric beginnings.

THE SOCIAL LIFE OF DATA: INTERVENING IN THE WORLD

A consideration of the broad historical contours of data and the powerful intellectual currents that have shaped the thinking of social geographers towards them has revealed why it is so important to think of data as an 'issue'. However, the example discussed in Text Box 30.1 brings the issue up to the present with a further reflection on researching social class from the author's own experience. As already noted in this book (see Chapter 15 on class), data themselves are inherently contentious, but then you may compound the problem by making those data relate to a research topic as sensitive and subjective as social class. Text Box 30.1 tells the story of a recent major investigation into social class, the BBC's Great British Class Survey (GBCS) experiment (BBC News, 2013; Jones, 2013), and, in particular, reflects on the power and implications of data, their capacity to have their own social lives and potential to intervene in the world (Beer & Burrows, 2013).

TEXT BOX 30.1 | Real-World Research: Measuring Social Class

The Great British Class Survey (GBCS) emerged out of a desire to understand the contemporary role and relevance of social class in the UK. Major social, economic and cultural shifts, ranging from deindustrialisation to the emergence of intersectional approaches which saw class experienced very differently from alternate racial and gender perspectives (Bottero, 2005), had altered traditional understandings of a tripartite 'working/middle/upper' class structure. Sociologists had long been arguing that measures based solely on occupational structure failed to reflect the shift in understandings of class away from *economy* and towards *culture* (Ray & Sayer, 1999). The GBCS notion of social class drew heavily on the French sociologist Pierre Bourdieu's influential work *Distinction* (1984). Bourdieu outlines class formation as the product of different 'capitals': 'social', 'cultural' and 'economic' – a complex interplay of numerous factors such as educational credentials, social networks, cultural activities and more orthodox stocks of financial capital.

The BBC hosted a survey on its website that invited the general public to respond to a wide range of questions which probed each of these areas in addition to other key attributes, such as age, gender and ethnicity. Between 2011 and 2013, 160,000 people participated. However, the data were skewed towards a younger and more affluent section of the British population than was representative of society as a whole. A smaller survey was then commissioned with a representative sample of just over one thousand people (Devine & Snee, 2015).

Analysis of the data resulted in a 'new model' of social class which radically upturned the traditional working/middle/upper class typology. Instead, it identified a complex structure of seven classes ranging from a 'precariat' to an 'elite', each with distinctive levels of social, economic and cultural capital that, with the exception of those groups clearly low or high for all of those measures, did not suggest a simple hierarchy (Savage et al., 2013).

The publication of these findings provoked extraordinary reactions among academics and the wider public. The advent of social media and digital technologies provided the means for people to engage with the research immediately and directly, pushing aside the traditional barriers and time delays to academic research dissemination. The unorthodox focus on social and cultural capital in the GBCS led to many witty and observant parodies on the data collection mechanism, such as that in Figure 30.2. Amusing as responses such as this may be, they underline the fundamental point that we were trying to make: in order to find such a parody funny, you must first accept that there is a social and cultural value attached to the everyday consumption and lifestyle choices that we make. It is the ability to know and navigate those differences that creates forms of what Bourdieu termed 'distinction'.

These data and the way they were interpreted also provided the basis for a wide variety of intellectual critiques and engagements. Some responses focused on the quality of the data and the problems of engaging a mass audience through new media forms (C. Mills, 2014), but they also revealed an inability or unwillingness to think of class in

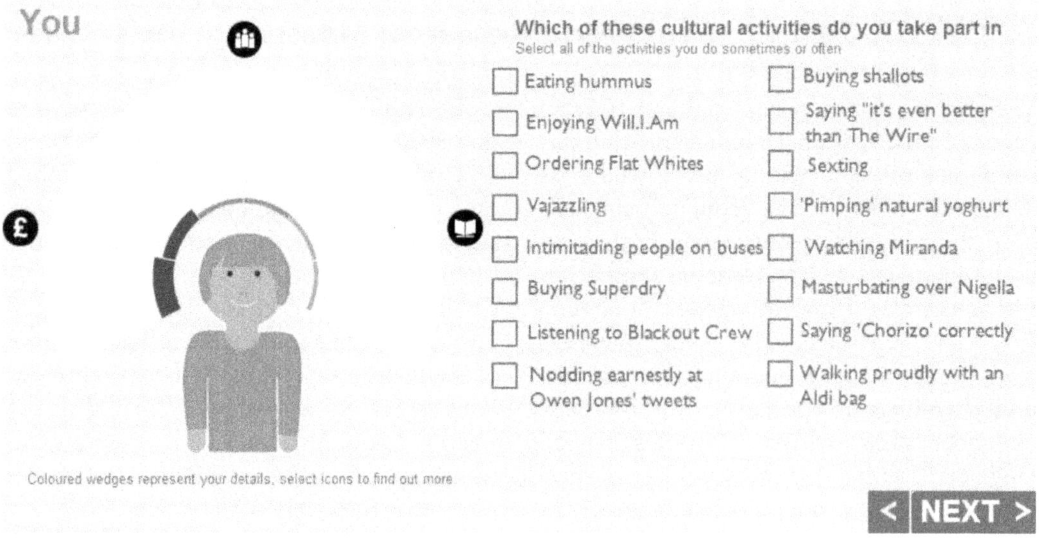

You

Which of these cultural activities do you take part in
Select all of the activities you do sometimes or often

☐ Eating hummus   ☐ Buying shallots

☐ Enjoying Will.I.Am   ☐ Saying "it's even better than The Wire"

☐ Ordering Flat Whites   ☐ Sexting

☐ Vajazzling   ☐ 'Pimping' natural yoghurt

☐ Intimidating people on buses ☐ Watching Miranda

☐ Buying Superdry   ☐ Masturbating over Nigella

☐ Listening to Blackout Crew   ☐ Saying 'Chorizo' correctly

☐ Nodding earnestly at   ☐ Walking proudly with an
Owen Jones' tweets   Aldi bag

Coloured wedges represent your details, select icons to find out more

< NEXT >

FIGURE 30.2
One example of a number of online parodies of the GBCS survey tool. (Source: @NewsManc, https://www.thepoke.co.uk/2013/04/04/the-best-of-the-bbc-class-calculator-spoofs/, accessed 25 June 2019)

terms beyond employment or wealth (Dorling, 2013). More substantively, authors raised questions that spoke to the implications of the data and the analytical constructions relating to them. If class is about more than occupation or wealth, it is also about more than describing class positions and is also the relations between them (Bradley, 2014). Furthermore, what are the ethical and political implications of these data definitions once they are let loose in the world (Tyler, 2015)? This is a profound ethical dilemma that the research team sought to deal with. By using data to rank people by a new metric such as cultural capital, are you reflecting the unseen realities of an unequal world, or are you actually constructing and reinforcing those divisions (Savage et al., 2015)? There is no perfect answer to this conundrum. The GBCS experiment highlighted the desire to move social science scholarship beyond the ivory towers of academia (Savage & Burrows, 2007) but also revealed the very real challenges in so doing.

THE FUTURE OF DATA

If data provide the state with the power to 'know' a population, and therefore to exercise power over it, in part through the ability to classify that population into different groups, the ability to categorise is therefore a 'political' act because it has the potential to create communities of belonging around selected types of identity (Hannah, 2001). There are positive aspects to this, in that labels of class, gender, ethnicity or otherwise can be adopted as tools of empowerment, and the data that flow from them can provide evidence of systematic inequalities that need addressing. However, they may also be divisive and can feed intergroup competition between conflicting identities, as has been noted in the Northern Ireland context, for example (Anderson & Shuttleworth, 1998). In Northern Ireland, which experienced sustained political violence in the late twentieth century between Catholic/nationalist, Protestant/unionist and state security forces, the census was often a focus of attention among both academics and the wider public, driving fears of encroachment and 'outbreeding' by one group or another but usually the Catholic minority. The census and the way it was interpreted often acted to entrench social divisions between different ethnic groups.

A Marxist analysis of race and racism would contend that the act and process of identifying and collecting data on different groups is designed to foster a form of 'false consciousness' between 'racialised' groupings who, in reality, have more in common than they do apart (Miles, 1989; Carter & Virdee, 2008). Whether we take a more generous or sceptical view of the role of the state in such data-generating processes, one thing is certain: from the moment that data are collected they are effectively out of date, typically becoming even more obsolete by the time they have been cleaned, analysed and cleared for release. Data are always effectively retrospective by the time we make sense of them. The emergence of 'big data' is changing that to some extent. The new forms of data and the technologies that produce them, like mobile phones, are such that they are not reliant upon or limited to massive, static surveys like the census, which capture a snapshot at a certain point in time, but are instead constantly in the process of accumulating and becoming something new (Kitchin, 2013). This idea may seem enticing, but it also presents massive challenges in how we think about data going forward. I will conclude this chapter by identifying three of these.

First, there is the sheer deluge of constantly updated datasets in a huge variety of forms, both structured and unstructured (like social media) and focused on the individual rather than the group. This has led some advocates to conclude that we no longer need to think in terms of statistical models (just like regression models) or big theories because we no longer need to generalise out from our data; everyone is somewhere in there (Anderson, 2008). As social geographers, this potentially poses a big challenge to us, as we are interested in trying to understand the ways people relate to and interact with one another in space. Theories and models provide us with road maps and means to interpret data that have been developed over centuries, in many cases drawing on accumulations of generations of human scholarship and intelligence. Dismissing this solely on the basis of the scalar seductions of big data seems dangerous, and perhaps new ways of theorising our data will emerge that balance empirical possibilities with enduring conceptual value (Kitchin, 2014: 5–7).

Secondly, data used to be something other than human, separate from ourselves. Increasingly, we are being provoked to think around the meshing of the human and nonhuman. The opening extract gave an insight into what this already looks like at an everyday level, but for many years now people have been trying to reconceptualise the relationship between the human self, technology and, by extension, data. One of the most influential people in this field is Katherine Hayles, who has spent much time studying what she terms the 'post-human' condition (1999). Hayles' view of the posthuman condition is one that privileges information (and thus data) over material-ity, and there are 'no real differences . . . between bodily existence and computer simulation' (1999: 2–3). So Hayles is identifying a world in which we have become so entwined in our daily lives with 'intelligent machines' that it is fundamentally changing not just our behaviours but also the very ways we think. She does not see this 'technogenesis' as either a good or a bad thing but simply the effect of another radical wave of new technology on what it means to be human or, indeed, posthuman (Hayles, 2012: 81).

The final challenge lies in the role of artificial intelligence (AI) and algorithms. If data analysis in the past was all about probability, the future is about the prediction of possibility (Amoore, 2013). AI can be thought of as a form of machine learning in which com-puters, having absorbed and analysed data, adapt their behaviour and suggestions in order to provide more effective solutions in the future. An example relevant to many university students is that of the plagiarism-detection software Turnitin, through which numer-ous pieces of coursework in the higher education sector are now sub-mitted. Turnitin is a private company that scans student submissions against a database of sources from across the internet and provides a similarity score, which universities use to help assess whether plagiarism has taken place. This database, which is the property of the company, is constantly being added to and revised through new submissions by students across the world and, in turn, forms the basis of its successful business model (Korn, 2019). Algorithms are the sets of rules by which data are analysed and either captured or classified in a particular way.

It might seem that algorithms provide a good means for dealing with issues like plagiarism, as they take a degree of decision-making for a difficult problem like plagiarism out of the hands of individuals and pass it to a machine that has no opinion or axe to grind. The prob-lem, however, is that algorithms do not operate in isolation from the social world in which they were created. We might make data plenti-ful and machine readable, but beyond that decisions must always be made about what counts, what does not and what analytical lens will be applied (Hildebrandt, 2013: 6). The algorithms that produce data do not operate free from theory or social influence, nor can those data ever 'speak for themselves' (Kitchin, 2014: 5). As social geographers, we need to be mindful of the potential of algorithms in addressing social problems (BBC News, 2013) and also of the power they have to reproduce or create new forms of inequality (Noble, 2018).

SUMMARY

- Data are central to social geographies. They are the means by which we can know and represent the world around us and the unequal relationships between people in space. When thinking about data, we cannot separate them from the ways they are analysed.

- Data have long been an 'idea' as well as a 'thing' (or 'things'). Social geographers have thought critically about the ways data have emerged over time and, particularly, how this relates to notions of power and territory. Data have been shaped very much by the historical experiences and political requirements that have given rise to them.

- Data have social lives. Once we create and analyse data, they can take on meanings that can be both concurred and contested. The analysis and interpretation of data are not an endpoint in themselves, and the implications of how we choose to represent our data can reverberate outward with unforeseen consequences.

- New and massive forms of data are providing great potential for social geographical research, but they are also raising deep questions. One of the fundamental challenges lies in how we conduct research in the future and how this relates to established bodies of empirical and conceptual knowledge. Another challenge lies in the effects that the everyday use of technology is having on human existence, to the extent that some theorists have considered us to be living in a 'posthuman' age. Finally, the emergence of AI and algorithms again offers great potential for social advances but also provides for the means to reinforce or produce new forms of inequality in the digital age.

FURTHER READING

Beer, D., & Burrows, R. (2013) Popular culture, digital archives and the new social life of data. *Theory, Culture and Society*, 30(4): 47–74.

Elden, S. (2007) Governmentality, calculation, territory. *Environment and Planning D: Society and Space*, 25: 562–80.

Kitchin, R. (2014) Big data, new epistemologies and paradigm shifts. *Big Data & Society*, 1(1): 1–12.

Noble, S. U. (2018) *Algorithms of Oppression*. New York: New York University Press.

Digital

Graeme Mearns and Carl Bonner-Thompson

IBM launched the personal computer in 1982. The Nintendo followed in 1985. By 1986, Listserv had introduced email. Global positioning systems (GPSs) were orbiting Earth in 1989. Microsoft Windows launched in 1990, the year of the World Wide Web. Text messaging was routinised in 1992. By 1998, people were 'Googling'. Facebook (2004), YouTube (2005), Twitter (2006), Instagram (2010) and other social media dominated the 'noughties'. Apple sold its first iPhone in 2007, FitBit launched in 2009 and 'tablet' sales overtook desktops in 2014. By 2018, Alexa had infiltrated thousands of homes and Apple became the world's first trillion-dollar company. This list of milestones gives a snapshot of transformations in tech that have occurred at the scale of the body, workplace and home over three decades.

Digital transformations have long concerned geography, but current hardware (laptops, GPS, smartphones) and software (statistical programmes, databases, geographic information systems) have become indispensable, while data generation, processing and analysis are unrecognisable from a few decades ago (Rose, 2016a). As various technologies are routinised in work, travel, consumption and other parts of daily life, they have impacted spatial phenomena, including economic relations, place governance and mapping. These transformations may be 'normal' for those born in the 1990s. Digital geographers work to understand these shifts from a spatial perspective.

The phrase 'digital geographies' was not used in social geography until the mid-2000s (Zook et al., 2004). Prior to this turn, the phrase lay in communications studies, computing, cultural theory, media studies and sociology (Berg, 2012). 'The digital' is used in this chapter following Ash, Kitchin and Leszczynski (2018), who highlight a range of approaches and methods spanning subdisciplines that allow the digital to serve as a research site that traverses topics rather than being a stand-alone field. Kitchin, Lauriault and Wilson (2017) contend that a broader definition is important, as the digitisation of once 'analogue' media, including newspapers and magazines, is changing how geography is done (research 'practice') and the types of topics under study ('objects') (DeLyser & Sui, 2013). The digital also hints at a concern with more than software, including socio-technical productions, artefacts and orderings, as well as discourses promoting and sustaining technology's reach and human uptake. Geographers are theorising these as a melding of software, data, people and places in work about 'cyberplaces', 'digiplaces', 'neogeography' and 'code/space' (Kitchin & Dodge, 2011). This chapter outlines the field's foundations, and it begins by tracing its origins.

TRACING STUDIES OF 'THE DIGITAL'

Three factors have motivated greater attention to the interrelationships between technology, people and place in social geography. First, a critique of research that rejected ideas of the internet as spaceless and placeless is summarised in Text Box 31.1. The latter pushed geographers to think beyond a narrow concern of what bodies could 'see' while challenging simplistic online/offline binaries (Crang, Crang & May, 1999). Second was the awareness that geography overly centred on happenings 'inside' technology, to the detriment of understanding what different user groups 'felt' when engaging with technology (Parr, 2002). Third was the recognition that, to understand the spaces constituted by people's uses of different technologies, there is a need to engage with theoretical and methodological approaches that pay attention to bidirectional links between bodies, emotions, devices and locations (Kinsley, 2013).

The concept of 'code/space' has been popularised to account for the complex ways that various software ('code') and hardware ('devices') impact perceptions, understandings and experiences of space, disorienting and reorienting bodies in certain settings (Harvard, 2013). Such a focus was not always so nuanced. The 1960s quantitative revolution undergirded early computer use to support statistical analyses (Haggett, 1965). Over time, these developed into more complex spatial modelling, geographical information systems (GISs) and remote-sensing techniques (Sui, 2013). These were critiqued by 1970s Marxist and humanistic geographers, and then again in the 1980s cultural turn (see Chapter 1 on creating more social geographies). The sharpest criticisms followed Harley's (1989) claim that maps never demarcate objective 'territories': maps are created by people. Therefore, they are shaped by how their cre-

TEXT BOX 31.1 | Virtual Geographies

The internet has a strong bearing on how the field of digital geographies has unfolded and has been theorised according to two phases of development. William Gibson's *Burning Chrome* (1982) and *Neuromancer* (1984) are usually cited as the science-fiction novels in which the term 'cyberspace' was first coined, implying a 'placeless terrain' of anonymous communication through which text occurred at distance from the human body. Some might theorise this early internet as Web 1.0. Such definitions seem incredibly far-fetched now but underpinned scholarly concerns with the geographies of cyberspace (Kitchin, 1998) and virtual geographies (Crang, Crang & May, 1999). The latter emphasised the coexistence of cyberspace and geographical space, depicting a real and stable internet rather than a relational and fluid one. Virtual geographies upended simplistic binaries (virtual/real, human/machine, online/offline) and challenged uneven power relations by suggesting that online and offline spaces do not simply overlap but inform one another, particularly useful in feminist theorisations of cyborg identities (Haraway, 2007). Both fields were important, but technology repertoires move on. Instagram, Facebook, Twitter and many other manifestations of Web 2.0 clarify that internet technologies are often used by people wishing to meet, propinquitously, muddying early thinking (Roth, 2014). The phrase 'Web 2.0' was coined in the mid-2000s to describe a second internet that involves the mainstreaming of private information posted to the public domain, a rhetoric of knowledge democratisation and 'prosumption', the blurring of the producer/consumer binary in content published online (Fuchs, 2011).

ators understand the world and, importantly, how they want the world to be understood.

Feminist geographers challenge 'objective' presentations of space, a factor in the growth of critical GIS and the repurposing of computational techniques that render counterhegemonic geographies visible. This work queried *whose* knowledges are produced by and for whom in deployments of technology to illustrate spatial orders (Haraway, 1988). Such questions are prominent again now in commentary on 'big data' (see Chapter 30 on data and Text Box 31.2). Nevertheless, digital sources have been shown to produce situated, reflexive, nonmasculinist and emotional knowledges rather than determinist ones. Participatory GIS, for instance, empowers groups that were once on the losing side of the digital divide, including women, ethnic minorities and LGBTQ people (Siebler, 2006).

SPACES AND PLACES

In tandem with the evolution of technology, understandings of space and place have been aided by interrogation of the connections between bodies and screens. Wharf (2018) suggests that digital environments influence how people imagine others elsewhere in the world. Social media dominate this commentary, but researchers are also examining the impacts of other technologies. For example, Rose (2016b) critiques the rollout of 'smart city' management systems,

TEXT BOX 31.2 | Real-World Research: Mapping Events with Antares

Big data are those previously unheard of in size, speed, variety and resolution, captured and analysed by computers (Kitchin, 2014). Many geographers are thinking through the difficulties of this interdisciplinary field as well as the approaches that may spark fresh insight or enable a revisiting of older questions (Leurs, 2017). For instance, Chohaney and Panozzo (2018) describe spatial patterns of marriage infidelity using data 'hacked' from the Ashley Madison website, while critiquing the outrage targeted at those whose personal data was made publicly available by the anonymous hacktivist group the Impact Team in August 2015. Elsewhere, Gong, Hassink and Maus (2017) comment on the emerging geographies of augmented reality (AR) with data from Pokémon Go, a 2016 smartphone game that blends online and offline worlds during play. Each of these researchers shows how big data can enable new insights into spatial understandings, illuminating patterns once not observable and allowing questions to be asked in a different way.

Describing efforts to extend the study of big data to urban processes and the geographies of sexualities through interdisciplinary collaboration involving computing scientists, mathematicians and geographers, Mearns and colleagues (2014) contend similarly while also articulating some of the challenges related to *doing* data-intensive geographies. Acknowledging that the utility of big data is derived from (geo)social media for the purposes of social research is a recent phenomenon, this team initially trialled Simmonds' (2016) Antares analytics software by collecting Twitter data authored in a collection of neighbourhoods known as Newcastle's West End. This pilot study was designed to determine how large-scale social media data might be leveraged at policy makers in areas where 'voices' can go unheard. A larger project used Antares to aid examination of online responses to the International Day against Homophobia, Transphobia and Biphobia (IDAHOBIT).

With a larger dataset having been captured about IDAHOBIT at a global scale, it was during this work that epistemological, methodological and ethical concerns about the analysis of social media data in scholarly research – as well as data production and circulations broadly – became clearer. On the one hand, the research team was able to see the travel of ideas and imagery pertaining to sexual and gender diversities in just about every country, as exemplified by Figure 31.1, providing a new means of accessing people for face-to-face research, collaboration and outreach. However, the team gained evidence of homophobic, transphobic, racist and misogynist content on Twitter, as well as evidence of people purposefully and unwittingly 'outing' the sexuality of others known locally. Particularly alarming is the fact that the Twitter commentary is often presented or interpreted as 'representative', especially in the press, but, as already clarified in this chapter, such data can *never* speak for an entire population but are partial.

Graham, Stephens and Hale (2015) posit similarly while also suggesting that big data 'shadows' privilege information from those deemed lucrative to advertisers. At its most extreme, this results in North–South polarities in the spatial basis of information, which mirrors and reproduces core economic peripheries. For instance, there are more Wiki articles on uninhabited Antarctica than on the African continent (Shelton, 2017). These uneven geographies are only beginning to be understood. Researchers are noting that, rather than a flattening of digital inequalities, these are intensifying, raising vital questions about how digitally mediated knowledge is produced, by whom and in whose interests. Consequently, bigger leanings towards such services – as in politics and decision-making – could reduce the power of vulnerable groups by leaving them (further) behind in political discourse.

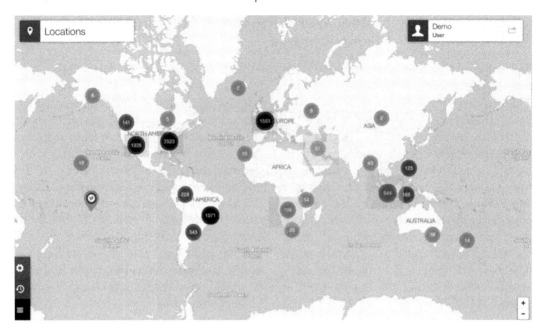

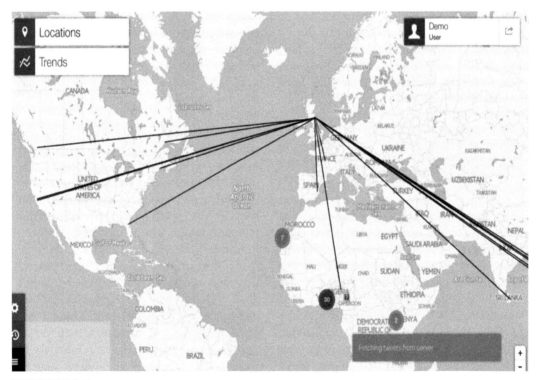

FIGURE 31.1

Map of location of tweets across the world. (Source: Screenshot of analysis backed with Antares data visualisation software [see Simmonds 2016 and Text Box 31.2]; retrieved July 19, 2018)

arguing that these contribute to a shared masculinist project rooted in a politics of market-led solutions to place governance.

Since the 1990s, some researchers have examined how the digital augments spatial relations. Initially, this work focused on how the internet was transforming economic, cultural, social and political geographies. Some adopted the determinist position of conceiving networked technologies as 'flattening' distance, rendering geography less relevant through instantaneous information transfer. Others suggest that, while digital technologies may contribute to space–time compression, geography remains critical as people use such services to meet others nearby and contribute to hybrid cultural productions, such as 'localised' podcast communities that now have global reach.

A political economy standpoint clarifies that the 'new' information economy transformed the spatial basis of employment, including a sizeable regional restructuring and creation of postindustrial landscapes. Geographers have underlined how urban hierarchies (like those of decision-making or wealth accumulation) have been strengthened by the agglomeration of information-rich businesses into cities that have 'wired' themselves for investment, pushing business cores into city peripheries or overseas where rents and labour costs are lower (Breathnach, 2000). Many systems involve real-time operational governance constitutive of the neoliberal city in which particular spaces become privatised. This can result in a 'splintered urbanism' of uneven development and creation of fragmentary infrastructures organised as much – if not more – for 'profile' than public good (Graham & Marvin, 2001).

DIGITAL DIVIDES

Digital divides were part of early geographical research on the internet. Geographers helped to highlight how access to the internet and interrelated technologies was spatially uneven. This was often inflected by gender, race, class, ability, nationality and location. However, in recent years the questions have become more complex than digital 'haves' and 'have-nots' and now concern *layers* of participation. Despite the penetration of manifold technologies into everyday spaces and places, access remains globally uneven while also being differentiated at sub/national levels (Kleine, 2013). For example, in telecommunications, some can afford top-end smartphones, while others are stuck using – or opt to stay with – cheaper devices. This impacts the services that people can use (North, Snyder & Bulfin, 2008). As smart cities spread and rely on information volunteered by users, such a classing hints at the uneven geographies that will unfold in underlying digital infrastructures, material forms, resources and sites of production and disposal, as in concentrations of 'e-waste' in the Global South (Lepawsky, 2015).

FOCI OF THE FIELD

Spaces and Places

Much research on the digital has been concerned with using big data to simulate urban processes and new applications like 'urban dashboards' that reshape how cities are planned by measuring citizens' interactions with different spaces. Amin and Thrift (2002: 125) note how 'nearly every urban practice is now mediated by code', a point clarified by Dodge and Kitchin's (2004) concept of 'code/space'. The latter motivates reflection on the mutually constitutive nature of software-space, highlighting that code/spaces are evoked through regulation and control of space and regimes of governmentality, such as networked surveillance and policing. Geographers tend to be highly critical of the possible negative ramifications of such endeavours, particularly in terms of equality and justice.

Looking to the continuing potentials of the internet for linking people and places in new ways, geographers can work to counter a potential hijacking of technology for restrictive or prohibitive regimes. The lasting liberatory potentials of such technologies are perhaps no more apparent than in Neve Shalom/Wāḥat as-Salām, a tightly knit village community of over three hundred people cofounded in 1969 by Israeli Jews and Arabs to demonstrate peace through cohabitation. Since 2001, community members have taken to social media to stimulate face-to-face interactions outside the village's working hours, while promoting peace to a wider public in Israel, Palestine and farther afield. Neve Shalom/Wāḥat as-Salām is colocated *and* networked, part of what Kahn and Kellner (2004: 88) describe as a 'planetary citizenry' that is using technologies to 'become informed, inform others and construct new social and political relations' and that is also place-specific in its functioning.

We can now see differently located citizen-subjects becoming entangled through purposeful and nonpurposeful interactions that unfold spatially in ways not possible just a couple of decades ago. Code/space is a useful concept for reflecting on how these new interrelationships offer individuals the possibility to multiply group belongings while 'tracing' these onto the spaces in which everyday lives play out (Sutko & de Souza e Silva, 2011). Such technologies do this in situ, on the move and in real time, augmenting a rafter of activities like shopping, navigating, sightseeing and protesting while altering knowledge politics by transforming expertise in the creators of spatial information and different epistemological strategies for asserting 'truth' (Elwood & Leszczynski, 2011).

Bodies, Emotions, Flesh

A more embodied approach to the digital focuses on human experience and emotion. Van Doorn (2011) examined the MySpace homepages of Dutch young people, positing that memories of shared experience become culturally available online, enabling discourses of genders and sexualities to unfold in nuanced ways. In turn, MySpace friendship groups recollect face-to-face encounters on one another's profiles using text messaging and photos. These postings become memory sources that are used to rearticulate understandings of gendered lives. In other words, 'fleshy' memories can be mediated and (re)made *through* the digital. However, this work does not account for the *feeling* body.

For Ash (2013), the software that brings mobile techologies into existence impacts on spatial experiences. He argues that 'atmospheres' mediated by technology produce new space-times. In other words, how spaces and places 'feel' is shaped by particular embodied understandings of a piece of technology. He uses the term 'technicity' to examine how embodied experiences of technology are impacted by intersections of human and nonhuman 'things'. The latter include sensory stimuli (sight, touch, sounds) in video games, wherein he uses Street Fighter IV to illuminate how bodily habits ('moves') usually need to be habituated for success in gaming. Similarly, Longhurst (2017) explores how screens can disorientate and reorientate bodies within places during Skype video calls. She attends to how the screen causes bodies to feel comfort or unease in such a way that blurs the relationship between the proximate and distant. Such moments, she suggests, help geographers in determining how different people live with technologies in a range of settings and based on one or more identities. Those who are comfortable with nudity over Skype, for instance, may well vary by gender and age. Additionally, Longhurst highlights how screens (containing moving images of bodies) become 'sticky' with emotions. Screens become central to how we feel, including towards family and friends not always nearby. Such analysis can help to expose how power emerges and is reproduced across bodies, screens and spaces.

MOVING FORWARD

Early engagement with the digital centred on applying preexisting approaches to 'new' material, spatial and technical realms of interaction like the internet (Ash, Kitchin & Leszczynski, 2018). 'Cyberspace' became a metaphor for connected objects – screens, servers and routers – joined to the body. It took time for feminist geographers to begin moving past concerns with what goes on behind the screen to examine the reorienting of embodied interactions and reorganisation of social and spatial relations between activities like work and family time (Valentine & Holloway, 2002). A related literature plots the material geographies of ubiquitous computing while wrestling with the social and cultural shifts brought forth by the internet of things, virtual assistants, smart watches and other 'wearables' (Lupton, 2015). Questions could address how these change our relationship with our bodies, especially fitness, body size and health (contested ideals in the social sciences). Addressing the inclusion/exclusion processes in respect of interactions with these emerging technologies remains a priority.

Social geographers are also among those who are developing a substantive theorisation of the politics of (big) data, algorithms and the sharing, platform and gig economies that are reliant upon these. What can be said of the spatial ramifications of Uber or geographical impacts of Airbnb, for example? Increased abilities to 'store, transmit and manipulate vast reserves of information have transformed places as well as the contours of privilege and disadvantage' (Sheppard et al., 1999: 798). Utopian and dystopian narratives of these changes – obvious in some press coverage – clarify the influence of heteronormativity and masculinism (see Chapter 17 on sexualities) in the design, development and marketing of many technologies and services (Datta, 2015). Those wishing to investigate digital geographies could benefit from staying attuned to how algorithms can participate in epistemologies that equate to 'definitive' evidence of spatial presence, movement and behaviour in what Crawford (2014) termed 'data-driven regimes of truth'. Such data are increasingly used to infer social, political and religious affiliations, as well as complicity in protests and predisposition towards certain activities. Such correlations are informed and reproduced by social and economic inequalities that must be resisted and challenged.

SUMMARY

- Digital geographers examine the spatial ramifications of hardware, software, multimedia (including new data) and technological infrastructures, as well as their impacts on identity, behaviours and discourse.
- Most research is user centred rather than examining the geographies of technology production.
- Simplistic accounts of a digital divide (those with and without access) have now become concerned with gradations of participation, for example, in the ability to afford or use high-end devices versus those restricted to entry-level equipment. Digital culture is not equal but classed.

FURTHER READING

Ash, J., Kitchin, R., & Leszczynski, A. (2016) Digital turn, digital geographies? *Progress in Human Geography*, 42(1): 25–43.

Ash, J., Kitchin, R., & Leszczynski, A. (2018) *Digital Geographies*. London: Sage.

Elwood, S., & Leszczynski, A. (2018) Feminist digital geographies. *Gender, Place & Culture*, 25(2): 1–16.

Graham, M., Stephens, M., & Hale, S. (2015) Featured graphic: Mapping the geoweb – a geography of Twitter. *Environment and Planning A: Economy and Space*, 45(1): 100–102.

Sustainability

Gareth Powells

Whether it is a global concern for our common future on Earth or a local concern for a 'piece of nature' such as a park, forest or river, understanding the relationships between society and environment is deep in the DNA of our discipline.

Within the broad body of research about the changing ways our human lives relate to and form part of the environment, one idea has become very well established since the late twentieth century in both geographic research and political discourse. That is the idea of sustainability, which is a term used to elucidate the reasons why a process or practice *can't* continue and also whether there is something about it which means it *shouldn't* continue. We can see these two ways to think about (un)sustainability in the example of burning fossil fuels to create electricity. First, burning fossil fuels is unsustainable because there is only a certain amount of oil, coal and gas to use. Once it is all burned, it will be gone. Hence relying on fossil fuels for energy is unsustainable as it is logically self-limiting; it *can't* be sustained. Second, it is also unsustainable because burning fossil fuels move carbon out of the ground (where it has been locked up in the fossil fuels) into the air (as carbon dioxide) at a rate that causes global warming. This *shouldn't* continue, because global warming is hugely environmentally, socially and economically damaging – so we must stop it to prevent us from doing great harm. At a more fundamental level, these questions can be asked of things as pervasive as capitalism. Can it sustain itself forever? Should it be allowed to endure?

Through the fossil fuel example, we can see that sustainability can be a matter of both logic and ethics. Furthermore, built into the concept of sustainability is an intrinsic tension between ways of living and the things that our lifestyles depend upon and deplete. If our children are to have the same chances to live well that we have enjoyed, then we must live in a way that can be sustained by not extracting resources from nature with such intensity that landscapes and ecosystems are unable to recover. In this sense, the goal is to achieve a constantly renegotiated balance, such that both nature and our lifestyles can be sustained over time; indeed, one of the major ways the term has been used is to signal our intergenerational responsibilities. Intergenerational justice has been a key feature of sustainability research and refers to the duties and responsibilities we have to future generations to give them the same life chances, opportunities and protections that we enjoy.

In this chapter, I first chart the emergence of sustainability, then turn to some of the central questions of sustainability, those of population and economic growth without limits. The next part of the chapter then specifically examines the social geographies of the coming era, the Anthropocene.

Throughout the chapter you are urged to consider that, through our research, our geographic practice and our own lives, we are always creating and sustaining some things and marginalising others. These choices about what to focus on in our research, what to buy, how to travel, who to be, what to stand up for, what to see in our data – these are all choices that matter (see also Chapter 3). In geographic research, then, sustainability is a question that provokes us. It is a challenge to which we must respond and a tool for critical questioning.

ORIGINS

The question of sustainability came into mainstream political and academic discourse in the late twentieth century in response to at least two developments. The first was that evidence of environmental damage – both local and distant – became very visible as the globalisation of industrial capitalism and communications technology meant that the negative impacts of the economy on the environment were, by the 1970s and 1980s, pervasive. Alongside a growing awareness of 'the environment' at a global scale, local cases of urban pollution and environmental damage did not escape critical attention. Indeed, they assembled around a new vocabulary of environmental injustice (the focus of Chapter 33).

Many consider the Earth Summit in Rio de Janeiro, Brazil, in 1992 to be a landmark moment in debates around nature–society–economy relationships. This was the United Nations Conference on Environment and Development (UNCED), and it created both a local agenda for action in the twenty-first century (Local Agenda 21), which was principally aimed at local and municipal governments, and a global framework to respond to climate change (the United Nations Framework Convention on Climate Change, the UNFCCC), by then established as the meta-threat to the planet and to its most dangerous inhabitants – us! At a local level, LA21 action has focused on issues like transport, housing and air quality, while at a global level there have been international agreements such as the Kyoto Protocol and, more recently, the Paris Agreement on green-house-gas emissions.

Geographers have made major contributions to understanding how climate change is being governed at multiple scales. Diana Liverman has played, and continues to play, a leading role in research on the human dimensions of global environmental change and the impacts of climate on society, and she has been an active contributor to global environmental governance (Liverman, 2018). At the urban scale, Harriet Bulkeley's work on how cities are adapting to climate change and the consequences for their citizens has been seminal in foregrounding the urban nature of climate justice and environmental governance (Bulkeley, 2013). Others have critically examined how geographies of race and gender are interwoven with questions of sustainability (see Chapters 16, 17 and 33).

Perhaps the most inescapable image of sustainability is that of a planet under siege from greenhouse gases and pollution, being stripped of its limited resources and, importantly, one that can no longer provide a safe space in which to sustain human flourishing. This is an important aspect of the sustainability concept: it is not only about protecting the environment for its own sake; questions of sustainability are also motivated by concern for humanity. This dual vulnerability has shaped how sustainability has developed as a discourse in academic and policy communities since its rise to prominence in the late twentieth century.

QUESTIONING POPULATION AND ECONOMIC GROWTH

Figure 32.1 powerfully communicates global population growth and fertility rates since the time of the Industrial Revolution in Europe. The explosion in population that was witnessed in the twentieth century, combined with the intensity of resource use since then, is perhaps the major reason for the emergence of sustainability as one of the major questions of our time. While many will wince as they observe the steep rise in population numbers, the rise and fall in the annual growth rate curve means that the global population is not expected to rise forever. Instead, most demographers agree that we are more likely to reach a steady state by 2100, albeit one with around eleven billion rather than the current seven billion mouths to feed.

This period since the Industrial Revolution in Europe, in which humans have taken control of the planet in terms of numbers and also due to our appetite and wastefulness (Whitehead, 2014), has been argued by Paul Crutzen (Crutzen, 2006) to be the start of a

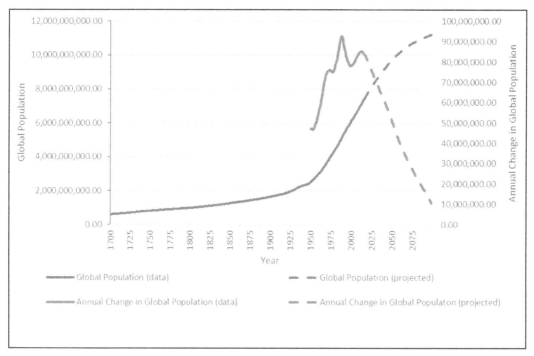

FIGURE 32.1

Global population growth since Industrial Revolution. (Source: Author's own, using data from Our World in Data [2019], Annual World Population Data; retrieved August 10, 2020, from https:// ourworldindata.org/ world-population -growth)

new epoch – the Anthropocene. In this view, we are no longer in the Holocene (the geological period since the last glacial period) but have entered a new period in the planet's history in which we are responsible for conditions on the planet (see also Chapter 33).

The Anthropocene has created new ways to think about, govern and study life in the twenty-first century. For some, the questions that matter are about the geographic injustices and differences in the way that communities will experience the Anthropocene – a condition created by previous generations in the Global North through deeply problematic processes of principally colonial, then neoliberal, industrial expansion. Indeed, the Anthropocene idea replenishes the well of critical energies to challenge the political ecology of the economy – that is, to expose the structural inequalities, vulnerabilities and risks that are inscribed into landscapes, seascapes, environments and cities. Political ecologists want to draw attention to the 'swirling political and economic relationships' that produce the environmental problems of the Anthropocene and that also frame solutions (Robbins, Hintz & Moore, 2014: preface).

For ecological modernists (such as Mol & Sonnenfeld, 2014), however, the Anthropocene represents a reality that can't be undone. Ecological modernisation scholars take a progressive approach to the challenge of how to live in the Anthropocene and ask new questions about the innovations – technological, cultural, political and economic – that are needed to create an ethical and sustainable twenty-first-century society.

Indeed, if we do not respond effectively to these challenges, then in a trillion or so years, when life on the planet will have been reborn many times over, as tectonic teeth eat up our dead cities and fossilise our waste, leaving a layer of sediment, future beings may point to this and say, 'Urgh, that must have been the Anthropocene!'

PUTTING ECONOMIC GROWTH IN ITS PLACE

Just as rapid population growth is not thought to be everlasting, concerns developed in the late 1960s and early 1970s that there may also be hard limits to economic growth. This was crystallised in the publication of *The Limits to Growth* by the Club of Rome (Meadows et al., 1972), an interdisciplinary group of economists and scientists commissioned to model population, industriali-sation, pollution, resource depletion and land availability over a one-hundred-year period. The authors are reported to have been overwhelmed by the magnitude of their findings, which predicted that the growth and globalisation of capitalist economy and society would overshoot planetary limits and that we would experience social and economic collapse.

The year 1972 may seem a long time ago to contemporary read-ers, but the Club of Rome's warnings bear a worrying resemblance to the recent sense of ecological crisis in governmental discourse and in grassroots protests. A tone of extreme urgency can be heard in the IPCC's (Intergovernmental Panel on Climate Change) 2018 announcement of the need for massive and radical action to mitigate the severity of climate change (IPCC, 2018), while in 2019 a new wave of environmental protests and strikes by young people in cities around the world may mark a new and more intensified period of desperate demands for environmental protection (see Figure 32.2).

FIGURE 32.2

Extinction Rebellion, London. (Source: Alexander Savin, licensed under CC BY 4.0)

Common to both top–down and bottom–up proclamations of crisis is a need to call into question the priority that has been given to economic growth. As recently as 2016, the UK government created an All Party Parliamentary Group on the Limits to Growth. Meanwhile, researchers like Tim Jackson and scholars working on the idea of degrowth (D'Alisa, Demaria & Kallis, 2014) are revisiting this basic question about how we might be able to grow in terms of quality of life and well-being yet without the need for economic or material growth (Jackson, 2016). European scholars such as Serge LaTouche (LaTouche, 2004) have argued that our focus should be on equality and justice within our economy rather than pursuing the impossibility of always squeezing more and more out of our finite planet. LaTouche refers to this as a switch in our thinking from efficiency to sufficiency, making the point that we have sufficient wealth already: it is just not very well used or very fairly distributed.

The sense that it might be time to move away from economic growth is slowly gaining popularity, even in more unlikely places such as the OECD (Boarini & D'Ercole, 2013), the European Commission (2018) and the IMF (LaGarde, 2013). This is for at least two reasons. First, gross domestic product (GDP) statistics are simply a bad measure of economic well-being. For example, GDP measures, and therefore values, the income that comes from the arms trade. If a country increases its exports of weapons of mass destruction, then its GDP is likely to grow. So GDP cannot distinguish between the qualities and characteristics of an economy that might be valued and those which are not. Second, GDP figures have masked the enormous inequalities between places and communities within a defined territory.

For some sustainability scholars, it is time to abandon GDP as a useful measure of how well a nation or region is doing. The argument for doing so is that GDP is, at best, a distraction and, at worst, an addiction that drives all kinds of unsustainable competitive compulsions to grow and grow. In this sense, the addiction to GDP growth harms us by hampering our ability to think and talk clearly about human well-being and the ways our ability to thrive, flourish and live well varies so dramatically between places. Alternative indicators are already well established. The genuine progress indicator (Lawn et al., 2013), for example, provides a global basis for comparative analysis of human progress in various places. It is much more helpful in revealing the extent or lack of human flourishing and prosperity, and it is free from the distractions of valuing things such as war and crime.

GEOGRAPHIES OF EVERYDAY SUSTAINABILITY

As well as challenging macro-scale ideas about growth and limits, qualitative geographers have responded to questions of sustainability with research into everyday lives. This research seeks to better understand and to show others the environmental implications of our daily activities. For some, the focus has been on our mental worlds of attitudes and identity, while others have focused on our practices or what we do. These are some of the primary ways to research the social geographies of sustainability. Doing so is vitally important if the question of our shared lives on the planet is under-stood to be a deeply human one.

Place Attachment

Responding to environmental risks such as climate change involves, among other things, significant changes to places and landscapes. As a result, some of the most emotionally charged aspects of any transition toward sustainability are the processes through which place attachments are challenged by new infrastructures and tech-nologies. These transformations affect communities the world over as, in particular, energy transitions take place (Bridge et al., 2013). Patrick Devine-Wright (2013) argues that attachments to places are emotional ties that will be affected by climate change in the form of floods, fires and altered weather patterns. Places will also be altered by things like flood defences, new farming practices and renewable energy technologies that form part of our response to global envi-ronmental change. In this sense, climate change, environmental deg-radation more generally and our sustainability-focused innovations threaten to disrupt our place attachments and thus our emotional lives through the trauma, grief and loss of cherished landscapes, livelihoods and social networks (Devine-Wright, 2013).

Nudgeographies

Geographers have recently become interested in the psychology of how we do and sometimes don't think about our environmental impacts, and how governments and businesses are becoming more active in 'nudging' us toward certain kinds of behaviour that are deemed (by them) to be more sustainable. Attempts to change our behaviour are not new; indeed, the home and the workplace have been spaces of environmental governance for many years, as individuals have been asked to 'do their bit' locally to contribute to wider envi-ronmental challenges. Recently, however, researchers such as Mark Whitehead and Jessica Pykett (Whitehead et al., 2019) and Louise Reid and Katherine Ellsworth-Krebs (Reid & Ellsworth-Krebs, 2018) have contributed to a growing field of neuro- or nudgeography, in which scholars are exploring the insight that much of everyday life is conducted and increasingly being shaped – and therefore, crucially, our environmental impacts are created – at the subconscious level. Geographers in this field are critically questioning how this insight is being used by governments and businesses in rather limited ways to change individual choices about how we commute (for example) by planting 'nudges' in our daily lives to encourage us to cycle or take the bus, without thinking more systematically about 'the potential for wider and more radical social change' (Barr & Prillwitz, 2014: 5).

From Behaviour to Practice

Geographers studying everyday life have also studied specific prac-tices, including our daily energy use at home (Powells et al., 2014) and our recycling of food and drinks packaging (Barr, 2017). Until recently, the environmental implications of daily life of consumers and citizens had been addressed by both policy makers and geographers through the lenses of individual choice, environmental citizenship and behaviour change, but in the last decade there has been a turn away from behaviour and toward practices. Recent contributions from around the world have connected researchers in geography with colleagues in other disciplines to develop a truly interdisciplinary field of research focused on the domestic spaces, workplaces and journeys of everyday life (Barr, Shaw & Coles, 2011; Macrorie, Foulds & Hargreaves, 2015; Shove, 2010; Walker, 2014).

There are two significant changes when comparing practice-based research to the psychological and attitudinal research introduced above. The first is that research on practices is much more interested in what we do rather than on what we think or say, and how materials, technologies and infrastructures are involved and shape our daily doings. This research, as a result, is much more detailed in its attention to the 'nitty-gritty' of daily life. The second change is that practice-based research is about 'we' not 'me'. Practice-oriented geographers are interested in the loosely socially shared things that we do, the ways they are reproduced through recursive socio-spatial and socio-technical processes and how everyday life changes (see Text Box 32.1).

TEXT BOX 32.1 | Social Practices of Laundry

Practices (like laundry practices, for example) are:

- 'Loosely socially shared' in that while individuals do them differently, social groups share similarities, to the extent that we can say, for example, that 'laundry' is laundry when we see it.

- 'Reproduced through recursive socio-spatial processes', in that each time we 'perform' each practice it may be slightly different to the last time – because it is impossible to hold the context in which you do your laundry and the performer (you) perfectly constant. The context and the performer change in many ways for all kinds of reasons, and this leads the practice to be altered slightly each time (see Chapter 29 on performance).

- Changing over the long term. Looking at the long-term change in our laundry practices over the last hundred years reveals the subtle but incredibly

powerful change mechanism created by shifting performances.

- Socio-spatial and socio-technical processes, which are in many ways contingent upon built environments, material cultures and infrastructures of homes, workplaces, cities and other places and spaces – the kinds of fabrics we wear, the kinds of detergents available, the kinds of appliances we use. Laundry practices are, then, *geographic* processes that are absolutely at the heart of the sustainability of our lives.

- Unnoticed on a day-to-day basis and not well captured by theories of behaviour change, attitudes or identity. Thinking about social practices as the things that use resources, and us as merely their performers, helps understand how in the long term daily life can change very significantly, which has major implications for pollution and resource use and hence for sustainability.

SUMMARY

- This chapter has introduced the concept of sustainability, shown how it helps us to see more clearly the tense relationships between everyday life and the environment, and encouraged us to question the idea of endless economic growth.
- It has also shown how the idea of sustainability is shaping our lives as we are nudged into new ways of living and how changes to our everyday practices can have long-term environmental impacts.
- Geographers are actively researching sustainability at all scales; from the home to the city to the national and the global. What this work shares is a purposeful curiosity about the kinds of lives that we might live, the (un)fairness of how different our lives are and what that means for the life chances of future generations who inherit the mess that we are making of our planet.

FURTHER READING

Castree, N., Demeritt, D., Liverman, D., & Rhoads, B. (eds.) (2009) *A Companion to Environmental Geography*. Chichester, UK: Wiley-Blackwell.

Robbins, P., Hintz, J., & Moore, S. A. (2014) *Environment and Society: A Critical Introduction*. Hoboken, NJ: John Wiley & Sons.

Whitehead, M. (2014) *Environmental Transformations: A Geography of the Anthropocene*. London: Routledge.

Environmental Justice

Joe Herbert

Environmental justice (EJ) can refer to a global social and political movement, a body of academic scholarship or a policy objective. For example, the concept and language of EJ has variously been drawn upon by grassroots Indigenous activists protecting their communities from fossil fuel extraction, academics undertaking theoretical considerations of how we might structure human relationships with the environment in a fair and equitable manner, and governments developing legislation to protect public access to a healthy and enjoyable environment. Because of the multiple dimensions of EJ, it is notoriously difficult to boil down to a single definition. What ties EJ together broadly, however, is a concern with the relationships between human experience of environment and social inequalities. Initially, EJ focused on uneven distribution of environmental goods and bads, which remains a fundamental component. However, a purely distributive notion of justice does not capture the spectrum of claims made in struggles for EJ. Importantly, EJ movements also seek to uncover and confront the uneven distribution of the *power* to influence environmental outcomes, which emerges along social divisions of race, class and gender (see Part C) as well as spatially between continents, nations, regions and neighbourhoods. In other words, the *justice* in EJ means moving beyond merely describing existing socio-environmental inequalities towards constructing political and ethical claims of what 'ought' to be (Walker, 2012) (see also Chapter 7 on justice). Issues of EJ should be of interest to social geographies, given its situation at the intersection of environment and society. The majority of this chapter focuses on two important areas of debate within EJ scholarship that underline this relevance: first, the multiple and diverse *spatialities* of EJ; and second, considerations of *scale*, using the example of the growing climate justice discourse. Social geographers are well positioned to play an (even more) active role in these discussions. Before embarking upon this deeper conceptual engagement with EJ, a useful place to start is with an overview of its development.

THE ORIGINS OF ENVIRONMENTAL JUSTICE

Part of what makes EJ a compelling concept is that it is as much activist led as academic. Unlike much theory, developed within the confines of academic institutions and subsequently applied to social realities, EJ has emerged from grassroots movements. The setting most commonly cited as representing the birth of the EJ movement is Warren County, North Carolina, in 1982, where the state government was proposing to deposit over six thousand lorry loads of toxic, contaminated soil (Agyeman, 2002). Not only was Warren County at this time one of the poorest in North Carolina, but its population was also 65 per cent African American (Schlosberg, 2007). A mass local opposition movement emerged, using nonviolent direct action to block the incoming lorries. The predominantly Black community was joined by many White residents, and mutual embracing of concerns among protestors created one of the first-ever alliances between civil rights and environmental activists (McGurty, 1997; Schlosberg, 2007). Accounts claim that around four hundred to five hundred demonstrators were arrested, which thrust the events into the forefront of the American nation's interest. Scholars, policy makers, civil society organisations and activists were prompted to conduct investigations into the locations of toxic waste facilities and the racial and socioeconomic profiles of the surrounding communities (Taylor, 2000). The resulting reports produced some of the earliest concrete evidence that people of colour and those of low income are disproportionately exposed to environmental hazards and also introduced the terms 'environmental racism' and 'environmental justice' (Agyeman et al., 2016). It was EJ that endured as a mobilising frame for a new social and political movement, emerging at the intersection of environmentalism and social justice, as it facilitated a broadening out from the initial focus on race in the United States in order to critique environmental discrimination along lines of class, gender and further axes that would emerge as the movement developed (Benford, 2005).

SPATIALITIES OF ENVIRONMENTAL JUSTICE

Though the explicit emergence of EJ is often cited as occurring in this regional US context, notions of EJ in reality extend much further back in time and across space.

Environmental Justice and the Global South

The EJ scholar Joan Martínez-Alier claims that 'the world environmental justice movement started long ago on a hundred dates and in a hundred places all over the world' (2002: 172). He describes how peasants and Indigenous peoples all over the world struggled against threats to their environments for centuries before the term 'environmental justice' appeared. Particularly in the Global South, Martínez-Alier notes, 'environmentalism of the poor' and 'popular environmentalism' are the labels more commonly adopted, though he presents these as analogous to notions of EJ that emerged in the Global North. The key point here is that the conceptual development of EJ has not been a one-way diffusion from the United States outwards (Rodríguez-Labajos et al., 2019; Agyeman et al., 2016). Rather, it continues to comprise a geographically and culturally diverse exchange of knowledge and practices. Some early contributions to the EJ paradigm from Global North contexts (predominantly the United States) have been outlined already. More recent developments have included increasing attention to injustices within urban environments, such as unequal access to high-quality food, energy supply and green space, as well as uneven resilience to climate change, across different neighbourhoods (see Anguelovski et al., 2018; Bulkeley, Edwards & Fuller, 2014). For example, Agyeman has advocated 'sharing cities' – where urban space and resources are reoriented around sharing cultures – as a means to combat both the huge ecological impact and uneven access to resources associated with modern cities (Agyeman et al., 2016; McLaren & Agyeman, 2015; see also Chapter 32 on sustainability). Meanwhile, influences from the Global South have included direct action by local communities struggling against the dispossession and destruction of their land and resources by transnational corporations and the state. Examples are resistance against extractive industries like mineral mining in India (Temper & Martínez-Alier, 2013) and agribusiness creating deforestation and export monocultures in Brazil (da Rocha et al., 2018). The EJAtlas is a useful online mapping project that has so far documented over 2,400 cases of environmental conflict around the world, reflecting the global reach of EJ considerations in contemporary times (see ejatlas.org; Temper et al., 2018).

Interpretations of Environmental Justice

The globalisation of the EJ discourse creates further fertile ground for social geographical contributions to the field. As ideas of EJ enter into new cultural and political spaces, there is a need for analysis that sheds light on how these diverse contexts reshape their own notions of EJ (Walker, 2009; Williams & Mawdsley, 2006). For example, geographers have studied how place attachment can play a vital role in EJ conflicts, such as in creating opposition to large-scale energy projects (Devine-Wright & Howes, 2010). However, geographers have also sounded caution that the place-specific reshaping of notions of EJ can be a subversive terrain and does not automatically generate unified struggles against environmental degradation (Holifield, Porter & Walker, 2009). Holifield, Porter and Walker (2009) illustrate this point with the example of Macias' (2008) study in which Hispano communities in New Mexico that were enacting an EJ frame ended up on the same side as the logging companies against White-dominated environmental organisations in a dispute over forest use. This raises the further important task of analysing how EJ movements around the world interpret 'justice' beyond Western liberal notions (Walker, 2009), given that justice and geography are co-constituted (Harvey, 1996). In other words, ideas of what constitutes EJ are shaped by the spaces in which they develop, and these notions of EJ in turn shape space also. Another consideration for geographers is expanding further upon traditional notions of space employed in EJ studies – in terms of linear proximity to environmental bads – in order to consider alternative conceptions. One illustration of the importance of this is provided by the global and diffuse contemporary processes of climate breakdown, which do not abide by artificial boundaries (Holifield, Porter & Walker, 2009). All of these tensions represent fertile ground for social geographical research, as contemporary ecological pressures bring EJ issues to the surface in new spaces and places.

SCALING ENVIRONMENTAL JUSTICE

Geographers have led the way in theorising EJ as a multiscalar concept (Cotton, 2018). In line with the US tradition, many early geographical contributions highlighted how grassroots movements against locally unwanted land uses simultaneously linked their struggles to broader contestations of environmental governance regimes (Towers, 2000; Kurtz, 2003). Alternatively, Marxist geographers warned that EJ conflicts have a tendency to descend into 'militant particularisms' (Harvey, 1996) and fail to highlight a systemic critique of capitalist political economy (Swyngedouw & Heynen, 2003). More recently, the growing intensity of capitalist globalisation – and, with it, climate change – in the twenty-first century has prompted evolving international configurations of EJ (Sikor & Newell, 2014). The EJ movement has not only expanded out from its original US- and race-based focus to study new territories and issues (including Indigenous, food and energy justice) but also scaled up from the community level to consider uneven power relations within and

FIGURE 33.1

'Mobilization for climate justice – "Stop" Chevron'. (Source: Creative Commons, https://www
.flickr.com/photos/forsevengenerations/albums/72157622582479986; licensed under CC BY
2.0, https://creativecommons.org/licenses/by/2.0/legalcode)

between nations. The proliferation of the concept of climate justice (CJ) has been one of the major outcomes of this process. After all, climate change can be conceptualised as the biggest EJ issue of all time (see Schlosberg & Collins, 2014).

Climate and Ecological Debt

CJ can be thought of as a branch and evolution of EJ that deals specifically with the intersection of climate change and social justice. Central to its conceptual foundations is an analysis of 'historical responsibility' for the current condition of our planetary environment, which recognises that wealthy nations of the Global North are responsible for the vast majority of the total historic atmospheric pollution. However, it is the world's most impoverished communities – largely concentrated in the Global South – that will suffer most severely from the devastating impacts of climate change. CJ movements argue therefore that the Global North holds a climate debt to the Global South, as well as a broader ecological debt extending beyond solely greenhouse-gas emissions. The roots of these debts can be traced back to colonialism (Gonzalez, 2015). Relationships of domination established through colonialism have allowed states of the North (like the United Kingdom) to embark upon rapid and ecologically destructive trajectories of 'development', predicated upon the intensive burning of fossil fuels, while violating the ability of (formerly) colonised states of the Global South to establish their own prosperity and well-being (Baptiste & Rhiney, 2016). There are multiple claims about how climate debts could be repaid. Warlenius (2018) has synthesised two core arguments. One method of repayment relates to the emissions debt, which describes the obligation of the Global North to repay its historical overuse of the carbon commons by reducing its emissions to levels below its share of the total sustainable amount, thus freeing up necessary 'sink capacity' for the Global South (Warlenius, 2018). The second method relates to the adaptation debt, which posits that the Global North should provide financial compensation to states in the Global South for them to develop the means to avert, and build resilience to, climate change. However, there are few signs that any such meaningful climate debt repayments will materialise.

Bleak Prospects for Climate Justice?

Evidently, these CJ claims represent, politically, a radical departure from the entrenched neoliberal framework that characterises international climate politics. It is unsurprising, then, that CJ discourses have struggled to permeate processes such as the United Nations Framework Convention on Climate Change (see Routledge, Cumbers & Driscoll Derickson, 2018; Okereke & Coventry, 2016). Additionally, there are deeply embedded socio-environmental materialities that obstruct progress towards CJ. For example, many heavily polluting production processes that arose in the Global North with the Industrial Revolution have now been outsourced to areas of the Global South due to the availability of cheaper labour and more lax environmental regulations, while the majority of profits and goods still return to Northern corporations and states (see Peng, Zhang & Sun, 2016; Grant & Oteng-Ababio, 2012). Accordingly, a huge proportion of the emissions created in countries such as India and China result from the production of cheap goods demanded by the Global North (Davis & Caldeira, 2010; Sovacool et al., 2017). These materialities problematise the convention in international climate diplomacy to attribute responsibility for greenhouse gas emissions in spatially bounded terms, with the nation-state the primary unit. It thus becomes extremely difficult to develop a conclusive framework detailing which actors should be brought to account for climate injustices and by what means. Nonetheless, CJ has taken up a position at the forefront of debates in the global EJ movement among activists and scholars. For example, the geographers Baptiste and Rhiney (2016) have highlighted the Caribbean experience of climate injustice resulting from centuries of colonial exploitation and its subordinate position within the global capitalist system. CJ is also one of the primary dimensions through which influences from the Global South have contributed to a conceptual expanding of EJ. Demonstrating this, prominent academic and activist groups in the Global North, such as the degrowth movement (see Demaria et al.,

2013; Martínez-Alier, 2012; see also Chapter 21 on housing) and NGOs such as Greenpeace have adopted notions of EJ and CJ from the South and Indigenous communities (Agyeman et al., 2016).

PROSPECTS FOR ENVIRONMENTAL JUSTICE IN SOCIAL GEOGRAPHIES

Walker and Bulkeley (2006) claim that 'the concept of environmental justice, from its earliest emergence in the civil rights politics of the United States, has always been intensely geographical' (655). This statement opens their editorial of a themed issue of the journal *Geoforum* entitled 'Geographies of Environmental Justice', indicative of the explosion of geographical research on EJ in the 2000s. However, as EJ debates remain thoroughly interdisciplinary, it is important to ask ourselves the question: why is it valuable to view issues of EJ through a social geographical lens? The previous sections have hopefully pointed to some answers by illustrating how EJ is bursting with considerations of space, place and scale, all key concepts within social geographies. In addition to these deeper theoretical convergences, there are also timely reasons to argue for a greater interaction of social geographers with issues of EJ, which this chapter will close with.

TEXT BOX 33.1 | **Real-World Research: Academic Activism and Environmental Justice Research**

Early research methods in environmental justice scholarship were almost exclusively quantitative. From the mid-1990s, this shifted to a more qualitative and interdisciplinary approach (Agyeman et al., 2016). Statistical studies in the late 1980s evidenced racial and class discrimination. However, in order to better understand the place-specificities of various conflicts and the relationships between people and their environment, more *embedded* research methods have become increasingly popular among scholars of environmental justice.

These have taken numerous forms. For example, Russell (2015) has described his use of 'militant ethnography' as eliminating all 'critical distance' between himself and his participants in researching the grassroots climate justice movement. Elsewhere, Reitan and Gibson (2012) have researched this movement through participatory action research, in which they embedded themselves in its networks as not just academics but also activists.

These embedded methods of academic-activist research take influence from feminist critiques of supposed researcher neutrality in the social sciences (see Harding, 2004, and Chapter 1). While such approaches can lead to immensely rich accounts of social realities, they also raise specific challenges. One is the prospect of overidentifying with subjects, which can invite claims from peers of political dogma and loss of academic rigour (Apoifis, 2017). There is no guaranteed way to avoid such scenarios. However, Lichterman (2002) reminds us that the mental and social distance created when we take moments to wear our 'researcher hat' more explicitly may be of benefit not just to our research but also to our participants. Nonetheless, as academic-activist research continues to proliferate alongside continuing political turmoil, further instructive accounts of how to apply such methods most effectively are likely to emerge (see also Chapter 3 on researching social geographies).

Social Geographies in the Anthropocene

Social geographies as a subdiscipline often leaves itself vulnerable to claims of anthropocentrism. Put simply, this refers to the representation of humanity as the most important entity or only holder of value in the universe. Perhaps the consequence of a relentless drive to understand the minutiae of human experience, it can be argued that social geographies often exhibits a relative neglect of humanity's coexistence and interrelationships with the other life forms and matter that constitute Earth's planetary biosphere, such as animals, ecosystems, plants and so on. This is particularly alarming, given that geographers often position the discipline as standing at the interface between the concepts of society and environment. Added to this, contemporary social geographies play out in an era of unprecedented ecological crisis, one that comprises social causes. Indeed, the Anthropocene is a now ubiquitous term, coined to reflect the notion that human activity has so fundamentally altered the Earth's atmosphere that it can be considered to have produced a new geological epoch (Crutzen & Stoermer, 2000). Given the severity of our ecological predicament, the more anthropocentric tendencies within social geographies at best perpetuate some degree of ignorance and at worst make scholars complicit in the hierarchical separation of humans from an othered 'nature', a mode of thinking that has contributed so significantly to the creation of the crisis we face (see also Chapter 32).

If the field of social geographies is to play any meaningful role in combating contemporary crises and bringing about both socially and environmentally just futures, it is vital that the incorporation of ecological perspectives in its scholarship is strengthened. By ecological, I mean approaches that develop our understanding of social geographical phenomena while acknowledging their situatedness and interdependency within a vast network of life, ecosystems and matter on Earth, from which humanity is neither detached nor 'above'.

To be clear, social geographies has never been devoid of such perspectives. On the contrary, one of its early pioneers, Élisée Reclus (1894), in developing his concept of a universal geography, argued that humanity was part of nature, becoming self-conscious, and so human and broader planetary flourishing could and must be reconciled. Contemporary work on developing and applying research approaches such as 'more-than-human geography' (Lorimer, 2012; see also Chapter 34), radical political ecologies (Springer, forthcoming; see also Text Box 33.2) and 'vegan geographies' (White, 2015) provide evidence that a movement towards more ecological perspectives in social geographies may be gaining momentum once again.

The Role of Environmental Justice

Given that they emerge at the intersection of environmental and social concerns, issues of EJ provide fertile ground for social geographers to contribute to the development of ecologically informed research approaches in the social sciences at a point in history where

TEXT BOX 33.2 | **Real-World Theory: Political Ecology for a 'More-Than-Human' Geography**

Political ecology is an analytical approach to the study of socio-environmental systems that makes explicit considerations of the wider relations of power within which they emerge. It contrasts with apolitical ecological approaches in that it moves from describing symptoms of environmental problems to actively critiquing the root causes and exploring alternative arrangements and action (Robbins, 2012). Though this description may sound confusingly similar to environmental justice itself, Holifield (2015) suggests that environmental justice should be thought of as a topic or concept that can be researched through many different approaches, one of which is political ecology.

In fact, political ecology had little contact with environmental justice during its early local-scale focus on the uneven distribution of environmental hazards. However, as environmental justice has scaled up and out, revealing considerations such as climate justice and linking local injustices into broader patterns of inequality, a wealth of research topics amenable to political ecology has emerged (Collard et al., 2018). In a description provided by Robbins, one can identify numerous factors that make political ecology a valuable lens through which to view contemporary issues of environmental justice:

[Political ecology] tends to reveal winners and losers, hidden costs, and the differential power that produces social and envi-

ronmental outcomes. As a result, political ecological research proceeds from central questions, such as: What causes regional forest loss? Who benefits from wildlife conservation efforts and who loses? What political movements have grown from local land use transitions? In answering, political ecologists follow a mode of explanation that evaluates the influence of variables acting at a number of scales, each nested within another, with local decisions influenced by regional polices, which are in turn directed by global politics and economics. (Robbins, 2012: 20)

The posthuman turn within geography has accelerated critiques of nature/society dualisms and highlighted humanity's place within networks also consisting of animals, plants, landscapes, technologies and objects, each exhibiting its own agency (Lorimer, 2012; Castree & Nash, 2006). However, scholarship under the banner of 'more-than-human' geography has rarely posed fundamental challenges to the structures and behaviours that are leading our planet towards ecological breakdown. Margulies and Bersaglio (2018) argue that political ecology, with its influences from postcolonial and feminist thought, is well positioned to 'sharpen the cutting edge' of more-than-human geography, creating a research approach that engages critically with the role of both humans and nonhumans in issues of environmental (in)justice.

this is so crucial. Yet they do not guarantee it. Even within early EJ debates, environmental damage was conceived of quite narrowly in terms of the inequalities it reflected between different social groups (Schlosberg & Collins, 2014). However, the acceleration of climate change and ecological breakdown in the twenty-first century has prompted a wholesale reconsideration among EJ scholars about the relationship between human and nonhuman, where a healthy and stable environment is now understood as a baseline that underpins *all* forms of justice (Schlosberg & Collins, 2014). Accordingly, prominent EJ scholars such as Schlosberg (2004) expand upon the concept of *environmental* justice (seen as justice among humans on environmental issues), arguing that we must talk alongside this about a further dimension of *ecological* justice (justice towards non-human nature – see Chapter 34). Only by acknowledging and valuing both of these dimensions of EJ can social geographers play a part in creating just and sustainable planetary futures.

SUMMARY

- Environmental justice is a plural concept that may represent a movement, a body of academic scholarship or a policy objective.

- The emergence of 'environmental justice' as a frame for a social and political movement originates in the blending of civil rights and environmental activism in the United States in the 1980s. However, the concept takes influences from all over the world (notably, Indigenous and peasant movements from the Global South).

- Environmental justice has expanded both geographically and conceptually, now encompassing not only local concerns around the uneven distribution of environmental hazards in minority ethnic and low-income communities but also an analysis of global socio-environmental power relations that reveal considerations such as climate justice.

- Environmental justice issues emerge at the intersection between society and environment and are imbued with substantial considerations of space, place and scale, thus making them of interest to social geographers.

- In the present era, where human impact on the planet is creating an increasingly severe crisis, it is vital for social geographers to employ research approaches that acknowledge human interdependency with the nonhuman world and society's ultimate embeddedness within ecological limits.

FURTHER READING

Agyeman, J., Schlosberg, D., Craven, L., & Matthews, C. (2016) Trends and directions in environmental justice: From inequity to everyday life, community, and just sustainabilities. *Annual Review of Environment and Resources*, 41: 321–40.

Holifield, R., Porter, M., & Walker, G. (2011) *Spaces of Environmental Justice*. Oxford: John Wiley & Sons.

Schlosberg, D. (2013) Theorising environmental justice: The expanding sphere of a discourse. *Environmental Politics*, 22(1): 37–55.

Temper, L., Demaria, F., Scheidel, A., Del Bene, D., & Martínez-Alier, J. (2018) The Global Environmental Justice Atlas (EJAtlas): Ecological distribution conflicts as forces for sustainability. *Sustainability Science*, 13(3): 573–84.

Walker, G. (2012) *Environmental Justice: Concepts, Evidence and Politics*. London: Routledge.

Food and More-Than-Human Geographies

Suzanne Hocknell

WHAT IS FOOD DOING IN A BOOK ON SOCIAL GEOGRAPHIES?

What comes to mind when you think of food and the social? Sunday lunch? Eid al-Fitr? Christmas dinner? Pizza with friends? Thanksgiving? A romantic picnic? From religious or secular celebrations to doing the coffee run, eating together – or *commensality* – is part of the oil of society. This chapter, though, is not just about commensality, although I will touch on that. Here, by exploring some of the ways research within food geographies investigates how bodies and relationships are 'made to matter, and not matter' (Evans & Miele, 2012) in *the doing* of food, I will consider the social geographies of food itself.

Food geographies – as a field distinct from agro-food studies – has been a vibrant area of research at least since the publication in 1997 of *Consuming Geographies* by Bell and Valentine. Food production, consumption and distribution are entangled with key issues of our times, from climate change to obesity to migration. Food geographers have brought together work in rural, urban, political, economic, feminist, postcolonial and more-than-human geographies to construct a distinct subfield that explores what food knowledges, practices and systems do, where and to whom.

Food is an intimately personal relationship. In the words of Bennett, 'food enters into what we become' (2007: 133). What we eat literally remakes our bodies and, in so doing, connects us to the animal, plant or fungal bodies from which that food came, the earth that sustained it, the microbial life that lives in and on it, the human labour within food webs and the economics of food systems. As such, the social geographies of food include nonhuman others; yet food production is often reported to be too animal based, too plantation based and too resource hungry to be sustainable, or too entwined with opaque, globalised networks to be fair (see Herman, Goodman & Sage, 2018). Meanwhile, food consumers are berated in the media for eating too much food to be healthy, or possibly not enough of the right sort, while those who cannot afford to consume must rely on the 'aid' of others. In this way, individual food consumption has become narrated as a responsibility of care for ourselves, our families, institutions (such as health services), nation, those that produce or become our food and the future of our planet.

Food is different from many other commodities in that it is a biological necessity. Nonetheless, the things that people ingest as food are not as straightforward as what is edible or nutritious. Although people are biological omnivores, there are significant social, cultural, religious and ethical differences in what is considered food, which are themselves knotted with the knowledge that food and the death of the eaten are intimately connected. Eaters judge and are judged through, and with, their food consumption and eating practices. See, for example, the media furore in the United Kingdom over the Greggs vegan sausage roll, which was launched in January 2019 (see Figure 34.1). Vegan sausage rolls are nothing new; they have been readily available in the United Kingdom for decades, but the tumult

FIGURE 34.1

Culture wars over the vegan sausage roll. (Source: Williams, 2019)

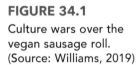

Veganism

Half-baked: what Greggs' vegan sausage roll says about Brexit Britain

It is not the first time culture wars have been fought over pastry and pork products. Is the launch of a vegan version the latest salvo or a chance for a divided country to heal itself?

Zoe Williams
@zoesqwilliams
Mon 7 Jan 2019 16.05 GMT

1,606   0

▲ A Greggs vegan sausage roll with a Quorn filling. Photograph: Christopher Furlong/Getty Images

I t is the controversy that nobody understands, while at the same time understanding it utterly: the Greggs vegan sausage roll. Launched on 3 January, presumably to coincide with Veganuary, it got off to a flying start thanks to the ire of Piers Morgan, who tweeted: "Nobody was waiting for a vegan bloody sausage, you PC-ravaged clowns." There is quite a lot packed into that tweet, if we want to go psychoanalytical on his ass: he at their appearance in the Newcastle-based fast-food chain Greggs is revealing of the entanglement of food with identity. The stuff of food – its *materiality* – is entangled with retail structures within social norms and hierarchies.

Food is essential for survival and ongoing health, but it is also entwined with a sense of self-identity, as well as multiple layers of community belonging. The way we each shop, cook and eat says something about the person we are, the person we would like to be and the society we would like to live in. In eating, tastes of home, both old and new, mingle with those of heritage and of belonging, hankerings for the 'exotic', appetites of aspiration and imaginaries of the future. Both public health campaigns and advertisements attempt to harness particular food materialities with emotional capacities as diverse as guilt, shame and fear, or pleasure, belonging and care. Yet, as with other forms of knowledge, the desires and possibilities of eaters are entangled with the geographies of power relations and practices. Manifold concerns and influences such as budget, time pressures, health, animal welfare or what the kids will eat interweave with food choices in complex ways. And although those food beliefs, decisions and practices shift over time (sometimes suddenly), they are often such a mundane, routine part of daily life that they go unnoticed and unchallenged.

In this chapter we will explore some of the approaches that geographers have used to understand how food choices are made and how these choices impact those entangled with the food at different nodes across and beyond food chains. The next section introduces two of the key methods used by geographers to understand such social geographies of food and explores their advantages and limitations. The third section details how the juggling of values in food choice is entangled with geographies of belonging and with power relations, structures and practices. The fourth section outlines the more-than-human social geographies hidden within the social norm of framing eating relations as consumption. Finally, we return to the question of what food is doing in a social geographies textbook.

RESEARCHING FOOD SYSTEMS

Researching Food Production

The 'follow the things' research method, developed by Cook (2004), starts with a deceptively simple question: 'Who made the things that we buy?' (see Figure 34.2). This work builds on Marxian theory that critiques the opaque nature of commodity production, by which Marx meant that commodities are a manifestation of social relationships, but these relations are *hidden* from consumers (Harvey, 2010). By following 'things' from their production through to consumption (or wastage), it is possible to explore the lives of the people and communities entangled with those things – people who might grow a crop, package a product, be dispossessed of land, work

FIGURE 34.2

Who makes what we buy? (Source: followthethings.com)

on a cargo ship, create a brand image or work on a supermarket checkout. These glimpses of the lives of others make visible the uneven impacts of the social, political and economic structures and processes that food connects us to.

'Follow the things'–type methods have been used to research gaps between regulations on paper and complex lived relationships in practice. By exposing links between, for example, poor welfare standards, maltreated workers and consumer safety, follow-the-things approaches enable us to understand more about the things we buy and evidence ways real-world positive interventions can be made.

Researching Food Choices

As outlined above, follow-the-things methods can do valuable work in evidencing and adding weight to campaigns for change in food systems. Yet, for consumers, the problem remains that they can only pick and choose from what is on offer for them to buy. For example, Guthman (2003) demonstrated that, in the United States, organic salad mixes are often grown in resource-intensive ways, depend on marginalised labour and led the way in the development of plastic packaging. When buying such salads, it is impossible for the consumer to prioritise organic inputs, resource use *and* workers' rights. This predicament is alluded to in one of the most frequently repeated food-related quotes in geography and beyond:

> The moral question is thus not, nor has it ever been: should one eat or not eat, eat this and not that, the living or the non-living, man or animal, but since one must eat in any case and since it is and tastes good to eat, and since there's no other definition of the good, how for goodness sake should one eat well? ... One never eats entirely on one's own: the rule underlying the statement, 'One must eat well'. It is a rule offering infinite hospitality. (Derrida, 1991: 115)

Infinite hospitality is, of course, impossible for any single individual to give. As can be seen in the Guthman example, consumers must prioritise some bodies and relationships to care about. In other words, to negotiate the constraints of consumer choice, eaters must on some level decide what foodstuffs are a 'best fit' to their sense of self and responsibility and perform that identity as best they can within the options available. When a consumer is obliged to choose in this bounded way, 'choice' cannot act positively on all of the relations within a food system. So, what to do?

A second key geographical approach to understanding food relations is through 'the visceral' and builds on the work of Probyn (2000). The viscera are 'the guts', and visceral geographies, rather than turning outwards to follow production–consumption supply chains to find the bodies and relationships entangled with them, turn inwards to explore the food tastes and gut reactions of 'situated bodies'. Visceral research begins with the understanding that there is no mind–body split. Rather, we are embodied minds and minded bodies *situated* within communities. See Text Box 34.1 for an example of how food tastes are not just a reaction of the mind *or* body but instead are knotted with multiply situated sociopolitical relations, beliefs, knowledges and identities.

| **TEXT BOX 34.1** | **Real-World Research: Food Tastes and Gut Reactions of Situated Bodies** |

In a project researching the geographies of margarine, Ruth, one of my research participants, described the experience of eating margarine as 'horrible', 'synthetic, really fake'. Yet, when asked about her childhood, she said, 'As a child . . . we had Flora [margarine], and I was fine with that'. Ruth's distaste for margarine was not a primary reaction to its flavour or because it had made her sick. In the intervening years something had shifted in how Ruth experienced the stuff of margarine against her lips and tongue. Digging deeper, it emerged that Ruth felt that butter resonated with the remembered rural landscapes of her childhood and her embodied knowledge of making it 'by just shaking [cream] in a bottle'. Ruth could not square margarine with this 'natural' imaginary, and so she came to experience it as a distasteful nonfood. Nonetheless, Ruth thought that she uses 'a lot of double think . . . [because] I'm aware of . . . the way the cows are treated and you know all of those ethical issues . . . [but] I can't afford to prioritise it and you know, and eat the way I want to eat'. Ruth's distaste for margarine was an involuntary gut reaction; yet it was not simply a 'yuck' response to the unfamiliar. Rather, it was entangled with her identity as an eater, her beliefs and knowledges about the world and her economic situation – with her situated body.

Commensality is at the heart of food relations, and thinking with the visceral aids the researcher in understanding how the ways someone shops, cooks and eats are intertwined with the person they would like to be and the society they would like to live in, as well as the society they do live in, and how they are situated within that society (see Chowbey, 2017). Attending to the visceral is a productive way both to unpack the social geographies of food and food relations in the now and to access the ways consumption and the values entangled with food can reinscribe or challenge social norms.

Researcher Beware: Strategic Ignorance

As explored above, both 'follow the things' and visceral research methods have been used by geographers to help make transparent some of the social geographies of food. In so doing, these approaches have shown how food practices are impacted by, and themselves impact, social relations. In my research, I have used both of these methods to explore how one product – margarine – is made, known and encountered (see Text Box 34.1). One of my industry participants, Max, a research and development manager for a supermarket 'own brand', mused that complete transparency in following the ingredients of margarine would 'require a book with every product'. Common-sense narratives might suggest that it is only right that consumers should have this knowledge so that they can make informed decisions about the food that they eat. Yet, thinking as geographers, we can see that if infinite hospitality is impossible for an individual to provide, then consumers can quickly become overwhelmed by such information. One way that this problem is managed is by consumer 'choice' becoming entangled with the stimulation of affect – see Text Box 34.2 for an example of this concept in action.

As QR codes linked to in-depth information about products become more common, it is important for geographers to research and critique the strategic ignorance (McGoey, 2012) perpetuated within the hierarchies and power relations of the doing of food. Even if a comprehensive product information book were to be produced, it would be embedded in social norms in which some things would be framed as important – worth knowing, worth doing something about – while others would not.

FOOD AND THE EVERYDAY SOCIAL

Framing Value

For those of us who have enough to eat, food is usually a mundane and routine part of daily life. However, what any one person chooses to eat is neither natural nor given. Food choice is embedded with personal desires and values that are themselves entangled with social and cultural norms. For example, whether the enticing green hues of an avocado or a garish sugar-glazed doughnut, a media trope at the time of writing is that insta-culture has led to consumers prioritising sur-

| **TEXT BOX 34.2** | **Real-World Research: The Stimulation of Affect** |

During fieldwork for my research into how margarine is made and understood, Erik, a research and development manager for a transnational corporation, showed me a transparent margarine tub that the company he works for had launched eighteen months earlier as a high-end alternative to the standard white margarine tubs. He explained:

> I really like what the guys are doing there. Just generally putting margarine in a transparent tub. We did a lot of work before we put margarine in a transparent tub . . . because, 'Is it going to get yellow? How is it going to behave? Will it be tasting good? Will it oxidise faster?' There was a lot of . . . but at the same time to me transparency is really a very strong message to consumers that instead of putting something in this ugly white plastic tub . . . you put it in transparent tub, so you actually can see what you buy. So in a way we are not hiding anything. . . . I would say it's probably about image, it's about perception, something which is difficult to affect. Naturalness. Yes, I think still margarine needs to be a bit more . . . maybe aggressive is not the right word, but more active in communicating what we are made from, how and . . . I think what's going on . . . to me, transparent tub was really a very important step in this direction. It's more breaking a psychological barrier. So we make it transparent. We show you what's inside.

This use of a transparent tub is an example of *the stimulation of affect*. The packaging is designed to shift the ways consumers respond to the product at an emotional level.

face values, *aesthetics*, over other food qualities. Yet, although insta-cultures may have shifted which aesthetics are valued, whether shiny red apples or the iconic Coca-Cola bottle, the visual has long been a large part of what shoppers have to go on when making food choices.

But why?

Like a toddler wanting ever more explanations of things that are 'just common sense' to grown-ups, it is important for geographers to dig below the surface of 'the obvious'. As with Erik's example of the transparent margarine tub in Text Box 34.2, why do food companies put so much time and money into the visual – the packaging and placing of products? What stories does the visual forefront about the foods we eat? And from what stories is our gaze reflected away? In other words, what are the social geographies embedded with, but hidden in, the ways foodstuffs are presented to consumers?

Aesthetics are, however, only one of many ways that consumers can and do judge value. As Ruth articulates in Text Box 34.1, tastes and distastes are shaped not just by sensory encounters with food but also by notions of the self being in accord with the ways a food stuff is framed (Hocknell, 2016; Hocknell & MacAllister, 2020). Further, it is not only individual foodstuffs that are subject to social norms in this way but also entire diets. As I write, veganism, after spending several decades as a predominantly subcultural choice, is having something of a moment in the UK mainstream. It is contended that vegan diets are healthier, more sustainable and more compassionate than diets that include animal products. This may be the case, and on the surface it certainly appears to be 'common sense'. Yet, applying a critical geographer's eye to new-wave veganism's focus on highly processed products that use imported and resource-hungry monocrops such as palm, soya, corn and sugar to replicate the flavours and textures of meat, fish and dairy, it can be argued that veganism has emerged in a form far removed from the low-impact, seasonal, hearty food of earlier incarnations. When researching food, it is important not to take 'commonsense' narratives for granted but to remain alert to the economic and social power relationships entangled with the ways food is framed, encountered and valued. It is important to keep asking the annoying 'why?' questions.

Situating Value

Another thing often valued in today's societies is time, or at least the perception of time saving. Convenience is a value, and entangled with convenience is an important argument that mid-twentieth-century changes in the ways food could be bought and prepared aided the societal shift to many more women working outside of the home. But we are now well into the twenty-first century, so perhaps it is time to release our inner toddler again to ask some questions about current incarnations of convenience food. Who exactly is convenience food convenient for in today's world? Take, for example, shop-bought hummus. Making hummus from tinned chickpeas is cheaper than buying ready-made hummus and takes about two minutes. Is this really inconvenient? Shop-bought hummus is packaged in plastic, needs refrigerating and has a short shelf life, and if it is not sold or eaten in this time frame, both the hummus and packaging become waste. Food waste is not particularly convenient for the environment; for the animals, plants or fungi whose bodies have become food; or for the people who struggle to afford enough to eat – it is a key issue of environmental justice (see Chapter 33). So who exactly is shop-bought hummus convenient for? What are the social geographies wrapped up with notions of convenience?

In 2013, the United Nations estimated that almost a third of all food that is produced is wasted (FAO, 2013: 6). This happens at all stages, from the field through transport and processing to the homes of consumers. The geographer Blake (2018a) has been exploring some of these questions in a two-pronged study that first follows food to understand more about how and why food becomes wasted and second engages with the visceral experiences of food-bank users to gain deeper understandings of the complex social geographies of 'waste' food redistribution programmes. Blake's inner toddler wanted to know not just why food becomes wasted but also why we think of perfectly edible food as waste. Why is food produced or sold by large corporations thought of as just 'food', food from a farmers market as 'alternative food' and food that has slipped out of both of those systems 'as "surplus food" or food waste'? Blake (2018b) asks what might shift in the social relations of food if we start to value this latter case as 'shared' or 'social' food.

Embodied Food Practices

An eater may wish to be healthy, or to care for the environment and the producers of their food, but they may also have financial constraints and still want to enjoy their food as an individual and as part of wider social relations. In trying to balance all those things through their consumption practices, eaters become caught in the trap of the impossibility of infinite hospitality. What any one person chooses to prioritise is therefore entangled with their own situation in that moment. For example, I love cooking. In my head at least, I also care a great deal about provenance and supporting local economies. Looking closely, though, what I *think* is not necessarily the same as what I actually *do*. On the way home from work late yesterday evening, I bought a reduced-price pizza from the massive twenty-four-hour transnational supermarket at the end of my street. I then added slices of Spanish organic red pepper from the farmers market; some British free-range, corn-fed chicken that had been reduced in a high-end supermarket, left over from my Sunday roast; and some kimchi'd chillies I had made a few months earlier. Putting aside that my Italian ex-housemate would be utterly horrified at what I had done to something as beautiful as pizza by fusing cuisines in this way, what is clear from this example is how my values and priorities slip and slide, as in leaving work late and desiring quick comfort food I have to think about which shops are still open and balance this with the budgeting imperative of what is reduced for quick sale, alongside values that prioritise animal welfare, local production or other concerns. When multiple situated knowledges are competing, they do not map straightforwardly onto practices.

But it is not just the eating individual who makes value judgements about food. Judgements are also made about their choices by others, in both personal and professional capacities (see Lee, 2012). Further, the appearance of eating bodies is assumed to say something about the inner self. Yet the abilities and desires of consumers to do bodywork are entangled with classed, gendered, racialised and cultural norms, judgements and opportunities. Geographers such as Colls and Evans (2009) have explored how debates around obesity differ according to social group. For example, the practices and knowledges framed by the establishment as working class become understood as a burden on society and in need of correction in ways that middle-class ones do not (see Chapter 15). Obese, curvaceous, cuddly, portly – all carry different social meanings. Value judgements (and their impacts) vary according to the situated positionality of both the viewed and the viewer. For Irigaray (2008), when such situated judgements align with social norms, they become 'common sense', and so their social construction (and the impacts of that construction) becomes invisible to us.

FOOD AND THE
MORE-THAN-HUMAN SOCIAL

To eat 'food is to eat its geography' (Coles, 2016: 257). The materialities of soil, water, weather, pesticides, labour, mycorrhizal fungi, earthworms, decomposing others, harvesting equipment, transport systems and preservatives fold with discourses, economies, technologies, places, systems and power relations with and in the stuff of food and the bodies of eaters. Together these materialities, in part, become flesh: 'One never eats entirely on one's own'. Yet it is the individual consumer who must choose where, amid all these relations, to direct their hospitality. But what if we disrupt the commonsense norm of the autonomous consumer? To help us to imagine this, let us for a moment think with microbes. Microbes live on and in everything and play key roles in creating our atmosphere and building our soils. Further, Dupre demonstrates that microbes carry out 'essential metabolic processes that we, in the narrow single-organism or single-genome sense, have never evolved for ourselves' (2012: 165). For example, without gut microbes, our abilities to digest food are extremely limited. So, if there is no singular subject, no 'me' in isolation from microbes, then this raises the question of where the self ends and the other begins. Thinking with microbes aids us in conceptualising ourselves not as autonomous individuals but as highly coordinated, co-evolved, multispecies systems, 'closer to the idea of an ecosystem than a state' (Ruddick, 2017: 128): as 'composite individuals' (Spinoza, 2002), whose subjectivities overspill our bags of skin.

Thinking of ourselves as composite individuals troubles commonsense consumer knowledges that hold that self and other, eater and eaten, are different kinds of things. These knowledges are co-constructed, normalised and maintained by practising consumption. Infinite hospitality is an impossibility for an individual to give, but decentring the singular individual reframes the question of 'who matters'. If we are no longer sure where the self ends and the other begins, then this situation obliges us to reconsider hospitality as collective, negotiated and more-than-human. To this end, Ruddick puts forward 'permaculture approaches' to food production as examples of hospitable practices, 'where *potentia* (the capacity inherent to things) and *potestas* (a system of their organisation) come into closer alignment, such that the system affects maximal thriving' (2017: 132). In other words, permaculture practitioners attempt to reframe hospitality from an impossible individual problem of who to care for to an opportunity to strengthen our commensal relations by co-creating resilient interconnections with diverse others (see Figure 34.3).

Home Permaculture Ethics

Earth Care

Provision for all life systems to continue and multiply.

Permaculture works with natural systems, rather than in competition with them. It uses methods that have minimal negative impact on the Earth's natural environment. In everyday life, this may involve buying local produce, eating in season, and cycling rather than driving. Its about choices we make, and how we manage the land. Its about opposing the destruction of wild habitats, and the poisoning of soil, water and atmosphere, and its about designing and creating healthy systems that meet our needs without damaging the planet.

People Care

Provision for people to access those resources necessary to their existence.

As a part of this planet, you matter! This is about ensuring the wellbeing of both individuals and communities. As individuals, we need to look after ourselves and each other so that as a community we can develop environmentally friendly lifestyles. In the poorest parts of the world, this is still about helping people to access enough food and clean water, within a safe society. In the rich world, it means redesigning our unsustainable systems and replacing them with sustainable ones. This could mean working together to provide efficient, accessible public transport, or to provide after-school clubs for kids. When people come together, friendships are formed and sustainability becomes possible.

Fair Share

By governing our own needs, living within limits and consciously co-creating, we can create surplus resources to further the other key permaculture ethics (Care for the Earth and Care for People).

Living within limits is not about limiting people's free movement, tight border controls and a one child policy. It is about conscious efforts to achieve a stable human inhabitation of the Earth, and respecting the genuine needs of other beings. Key social strategies include: access to family planning; helping people to meet their basic needs of clean water, nutrition, shelter, warmth, in addition to essential healthcare and education, including equal rights to education for girls.

The third ethic recognises that:
a) The Earth's resources are limited, and
b) These resources need to be shared by many beings.

Permaculture seeks to create and distribute life-giving resources fairly amongst people, animals and plants alike, not forgetting future generations who depend upon our conscious stewardship of the natural systems of the earth, which provide food, water and shelter.

FIGURE 34.3

Permaculture. (Permaculture Association, undated; Knowledge Base, https://knowledgebase.permaculture.org.uk/ethics)

SUMMARY

- This chapter opened with the question: What is food doing in a book on social geographies?

- In the second section, we investigated ways geographical methodologies have been employed to unveil how food practices are impacted by, and impact, social relations.

- In the third section, we learned that food geographies entail social relations with human and nonhuman others, and there remains much to learn about the social and cultural norms, structures and power relations entangled in what we eat, how we eat it and who we eat with, and the impact of these on health, communities, social justice and the environment.

- Building on this, in the fourth section, by exploring some of the ways the eating subject is not an autonomous consuming

individual but composite and relational, we began to see how this shift in understanding expands the question of care from a linear, moral one of how much hospitality is possible for any one individual to give to the holistic, ethical one of what any given hospitality does.

- In sum, the ways we as societies, cultures, communities and individuals *do* food are entangled with past and present social geographies and impact their possible futures.

FURTHER READING

Blake, M. (2018a) Enormous amounts of food are wasted during manufacture – here's where it occurs. *Conversation*, 5 September. https://theconversation.com/enormous-amounts-of-food -are-wasted-during-manufacturing-heres-where-it-occurs-1023 10

Blake, M. (2018b) Capitalism has coopted the language of food – costing the world millions of meals. *Conversation*, 1 February. https://theconversation.com/capitalism-has-co opted-the-language-of-food-costing-the-world-millions-of -meals-90780

Chowbey, P. (2017) How women use food to negotiate power in Pakistani and Indian households. *Conversation*, 8 November. https://theconversation.com/how-women-use-food-to -negotiate-power-in-pakistani-and-indian-households-77928

Herman, A., Goodman, M., & Sage, C. (2018) Six questions for food justice. *Local Environment*, 23(11): 1075–89.

Lee, J. (2012) A big fat fight: The case for fat activism. *Conversation*, 22 June. https://theconversation.com/a-big-fat-fight -the-case-for-fat-activism-7743

Williams, Z. (2019) Half-baked: What Greggs' vegan sausage roll says about Brexit Britain. *Guardian*, 7 January. https://www .theguardian.com/lifeandstyle/2019/jan/07/greggs-vegan -sausage-roll-brexit-britain-culture-wars

REFERENCES

Aas, K. F. (2011) 'Crimmigrant' bodies and bona fide travellers: Surveillance, citizenship and global governance. *Theoretical Criminology*, 15(3): 331–46.

Abbott, D. (2006) Disrupting the 'whiteness' of fieldwork in geography. *Singapore Journal of Tropical Geography*, 27(3): 326–41.

Abellán, J., Sequera, J., & Janoschka, M. (2012) Occupying the #Hotelmadrid: A laboratory for urban resistance. *Social Movement Studies*, 11: 320–26.

Abraham, A., Sommerhalder, K., & Abel, T. (2010) Landscape and well-being: A scoping study on the health-promoting impact of outdoor environments. *International Journal of Public Health*, 55(1): 59–69.

Adger, W. (2000) Social and ecological resilience: Are they related? *Progress in Human Geography*, 24(3): 347–64.

Adler, S., & Brenner, J. (1992) Gender and space: Lesbians and gay men in the city. *International Journal of Urban and Regional Research*, 16: 24–34.

Agyeman, J. (2002) Constructing environmental (in)justice: Transatlantic tales. *Environmental Politics*, 11(3): 31–53. https://doi.org/10.1080/714000627

Agyeman, J., Schlosberg, D., Craven, L., & Matthews, C. (2016) Trends and directions in environmental justice: From inequity to everyday life, community, and just sustainabilities. *Annual Review of Environment and Resources*, 41: 321–40. https://doi.org/10.1146/annurev-environ-110615-090052

Airey, L. (2003) 'Nae as nice a scheme as it used to be': Lay accounts of neighbourhood incivilities and well-being. *Health & Place*, 9(2): 129–37.

Aitchison, C., & Hopkins, P. (eds.) (2007) *Geographies of Muslim Identities: Diaspora, Gender & Belonging*. Aldershot, UK: Ashgate.

Aitken, S. (2001) *Geographies of Young People: The Morally Contested Space of Identity*. London: Routledge.

Aitken, S., & Valentine, G. (eds.) (2015) *Approaches to Human Geography*, 2nd ed. London: Sage.

Aitken, S., & Zonn, L. E. (eds.) (1994) *Place, Power, Situation and Spectacle: A Geography of Film*. Lanham, MD: Rowman & Littlefield.

Akhter, N., Bambra, C., Mattheys, K., Warren, J., & Kasim, A. (2018) Inequalities in mental health and well-being in a time of austerity: Longitudinal findings from the Stockton-on-Tees cohort study. *SSM Pop Health*, 6: 75–84. https://doi.org/10.1016/j.ssmph.2018.08.004

Alexander, C. (2010) Diaspora and hybridity. In P. H. Collins & J. Solomos (eds.), *The Sage Handbook of Race and Ethnic Studies*, pp. 487–507. London: Sage.

Allen, C. (2004) Bourdieu's habitus, social class and the spatial worlds of visually impaired children. *Urban Studies*, 41(3): 487–506.

Allen, C. (2010) *Islamophobia*. Farnham, UK: Ashgate.

Allen, G., & Audickas, L. (2018) *Knife Crime in England and Wales*. House of Commons Briefing Paper SN4304. http://researchbriefings.files.parliament.uk/documents/SN04304/SN04304.pdf

Allen, J. (2004) The whereabouts of power: Politics, government and space. *Geografiska Annaler*, 86B(1): 19–32.

Almquist, Y., Modin, B., & Östberg, V. (2010) Childhood social status in society and school: Implications for the transition to higher levels of education. *British Journal of Sociology of Education*, 31(1): 31–45.

Altman, D. (1997) Global gaze/global gays. *GLQ: A Journal of Lesbian and Gay Studies*, 3: 559–84.

Amin, A. (2002) Ethnicity and the multicultural city: Living with diversity. *Environment and Planning A: Economy and Space*, 34(6): 959–80.

Amin, A. (2006) The good city. *Urban Studies*, 43(5/6): 1009–23.

Amin, A., & Thrift, N. (2002) *Cities: Reimagining the Urban*. London: Wiley.

Amoore, L. (2006) Biometric borders: Governing mobilities in the war on terror. *Political Geography*, 25: 336–51.

Amoore, L. (2013) *The Politics of Possibility*. Durham, NC: Duke University Press.

Amoore, L., Marmura, S., & Salter, M. (2008) Editorial: Smart borders and mobilities: Spaces, zones, enclosures. *Surveillance and Society*, 5(2): 96–101.

Anderson, B. (2009) Affective atmospheres. *Emotion, Space and Society*, 2(2): 77–81.

Anderson, C. (2008) The end of theory: The data deluge makes the scientific method obsolete. *Wired*, 23 June. https://www.wired.com/2008/06/pb-theory/

Anderson, E., & McCormack, M. (2018) Inclusive masculinity theory: overview, reflection and refinement. *Journal of Gender Studies*, 27(5): 547–61.

Anderson, J., & Shuttleworth, I. (1998) Sectarian demography, territoriality and political development in Northern Ireland. *Political Geography*, 17(2): 187–208.

Anderson, K., & Smith, S. J. (2001) Editorial: Emotional geographies. *Transactions of the Institute of British Geographers*, 26(1): 7–10.

Anguelovski, I., Connolly, J. T., Masip, L., & Pearsall, H. (2018) Assessing green gentrification in historically disenfranchised neighborhoods: A longitudinal and spatial analysis of Barcelona. *Urban Geography*, 39(3): 458–91. https://doi.org/10.1080/02723638.2017.1349987

Ansell, N. (2009) Childhood and the politics of scale: Descaling children's geographies? *Progress in Human Geography*, 22(2): 190–209.

Anthias, F. (2001) New hybridities, old concepts: The limits of 'culture'. *Ethnic and Racial Studies*, 24(4): 619–41.

Antonsich, M. (2016) The 'everyday' of banal nationalism – ordinary people's views on Italy and Italian. *Political Geography*, 54: 32–42.

Antonsich, M., & Skey, M. (2017) Introduction: The persistence of banal nationalism. In M. Skey & M. Antonsich (eds.), *Everyday Nationhood: Theorising Culture, Identity and Belonging after Banal Nationalism*, pp. 1–13. London: Palgrave Macmillan.

Apoifis, N. (2017) Fieldwork in a furnace: Anarchists, anti-authoritarians and militant ethnography. *Qualitative Research*, 17(1): 3–19. https://doi.org/10.1177/1468794116652450

Arthurson, K., Darcy, M., & Rogers, D. (2014) Televised territorial stigma: How social housing tenants experience the fictional media representation of estates in Australia. *Environment and Planning A: Economy and Space*, 46: 1334–50.

Ash, J. (2013) Rethinking affective atmospheres: Technology, perturbation and space times of the non-human. *Geoforum*, 49: 20–28.

Ash, J., Kitchin, R., & Leszczynski, A. (2016) Digital turn, digital geographies? *Progress in Human Geography*, 42(1): 25–43.

Ash, J., Kitchin, R., & Leszczynski, A. (2018) *Digital Geographies*. London: Sage.

Ash, J., & Simpson, P. (2016) Geography and post-phenomenology. *Progress in Human Geography*, 40(1): 48–66.

Askins, K. (2009) 'That's just what I do': Placing emotion in academic activism. *Emotion, Space and Society*, 2(1): 4–13.

Askins, K. (2015) Being together: Everyday geographies and the quiet politics of belonging. *ACME: An International E-Journal for Critical Geographies*, 14(2): 461–69.

Askins, K. (2016) Emotional citizenry: Everyday geographies of befriending, belonging, and intercultural encounter. *Transactions of the Institute of British Geographers*, 41(4): 515–27.

Askins, K. (2018) Feminist geographies and participatory action research: Co-producing narratives with people and place. *Gender, Place & Culture*, 25(9): 1277–94.

Askins, K. (2019) Emotions. In *Antipode Editorial Collective* (eds.), *Keywords in Radical Geography*, pp. 107–12. Oxford: John Wiley & Sons.

Askins, K., & Pain, R. (2011) Contact zones: Participation, materiality, and the messiness of interaction. *Environment and Planning D: Society and Space*, 29(5): 803–21.

Atkinson, R. (2019) Necrotecture: Lifeless dwellings and London's super-rich. *International Journal of Urban and Regional Research*, 43(1): 2–13.

Atkinson, R., & Blandy, S. (2016) *Domestic Fortress: Fear and the New Home Front*. Manchester: Manchester University Press.

Atkinson, R., Burrows, R., Glucksberg, L., Kei-Ho, H., Knowles, C., & Rhodes, D. (2017) Minimum city? A critical assessment of some of the deeper impacts of the super-rich on urban life. In R. Forrest, B. Wissink & S. Yee Koh (eds.), *Cities and the Super-Rich: Real Estate, Elite Practices, and Urban Political Economies*, pp. 253–72. London: Palgrave.

Atkinson, W. (2007) Anthony Giddens as adversary of class analysis. *Sociology*, 41(3): 533–49.

Auge, M. (1995) Non-places. Introduction to *Anthropology of Supermodernity*, trans. J. Howe. London: Verso.

Austin, J. L. (1962) *How to Do Things with Words*. London: Clarendon Press.

Autonomous Geographies Collective. (2010) Beyond scholar activism: Making strategic interventions inside and outside the neoliberal university. *ACME: An International E-Journal for Critical Geographies*, 9(2): 245–75.

Bach, J. (2017) They come in peasants and leave citizens: Urban villages and the making of Shenzhen. In M. O'Donnell, W. Wong & J. Bach (eds.), *Learning from Shenzhen: China's Post-Mao Experiment from Special Zone to Model City*, pp. 138–70. Chicago: University of Chicago Press.

Bain, A. L., & Nash, C. (2007) The Toronto women's bathhouse raid: Querying queer identities in the courtroom. *Antipode*, 39(1): 17–34.

Bakker, I. (2007) Social reproduction and the constitution of a gendered political economy. *New Political Economy*, 12(4): 541–56.

Bakker, I., & Gill, S. (eds.) (2003) *Power, Production and Social Reproduction: Human In/security in the Global Political Economy*. Basingstoke, UK: Palgrave Macmillan.

Baldwin, S., Holroyd, E., & Burrows, R. (2019) Luxified troglodytism? Mapping the subterranean geographies of plutocratic London. *ARQ: Architectural Research Quarterly*, 23(3): 267–82.

Ball, S. (1981) *Beachside Comprehensive: A Case Study of Secondary Schooling*. Cambridge: Cambridge University Press.

Ball, S. J. (2003) *Class Strategies and the Education Market: The Middle Classes and Social Advantage*. London: Routledge Falmer.

Bambra, C. (2011) *Work, Worklessness, and the Political Economy of Health*. Oxford: Oxford University Press.

Bambra, C. (2016) *Health Divides: Where You Live Can Kill You*. Bristol: Policy Press.

Bambra, C. (ed.) (2019) *Health in Hard Times: Austerity and Health Inequalities*. Bristol: Policy Press.

Bambra, C., Fox, D., & Scott-Samuel, A. (2005) Towards a politics of health. *Health Promotion International*, 20(2): 187–93.

Bambra, C., Joyce, K., Bellis, M., Greatley, A., Greengross, S., Hughes, S., Lincoln, P., Lobstein, P., Naylor, P., Salay, R., Wiseman, M., & Maryon-Davis, A. (2010) Reducing health inequalities in priority public health conditions: Using rapid review to develop proposals for evidence-based policy. *Journal of Public Health*, 32(4): 496–505.

Bambra, C., Robertson, S., Kasim, A., Smith, J., Cairns-Nagi, J., Copeland, A., Finlay, N., & Johnson, K. (2014) Healthy land? An examination of the area-level association between brownfield land and morbidity and mortality in England. *Environment and Planning A: Economy and Space*, 46(2): 433–54.

Bambra, C., Smith, K., & Pearce, J. (2019) Scaling up: The politics of health and place. *Social Science and Medicine*, 232: 36–42.

Baptiste, A. K., & Rhiney, K. (2016) Climate justice and the Caribbean: An introduction. *Geoforum*, 73(July): 17–21. https://doi.org/10.1016/J.GEOFORUM.2016.04.008

Barker, A. J., & Pickerill, J. (2019) Doings with the land and sea: Decolonising geographies, Indigeneity, and enacting place-agency. *Progress in Human Geography*, 44(4): 640–62. https://doi.org/10.1177/0309132519839863

Barker, M. (1981) *The New Racism: Conservatives and the Ideology of the Tribe*. London: Junction Books.

Barnes, C. (2012) Understanding the social model of disability: Past, present and future. In N. Watson, A. Roulstone & C. Thomas (eds.), *Routledge Handbook of Disability Studies*, pp. 12–29. London: Routledge.

Barnes, L., Buckley, A., Hopkins, P., & Tate, S. (2011) The transition to and through university for non-traditional local students: Some observations for teachers. *Teaching Geography*, Summer: 70–71.

Barnes, T. (1998) A history of regression: Actors, networks, machines and numbers. *Environment and Planning A: Economy and Space*, 30: 203–23.

Barnett, C. (2018) Geography and the priority of injustice. *Annals of the American Association of Geographers*, 108: 317–26.

Barr, S. (2017) *Household Waste in Social Perspective: Values, Attitudes, Situation and Behaviour*. London: Routledge.

Barr, S., & Prillwitz, J. (2014) A smarter choice? Exploring the behaviour change agenda for environmentally sustainable mobility. *Environment & Planning C: Government Policy*, 32: 1–19. https://doi.org/10.1068/c1201

Barr, S., Shaw, G., & Coles, T. (2011) Sustainable lifestyles: Sites, practices, and policy. *Environment & Planning A: Economy and Space*, 43: 3011–29.

Bartolini, N., Robert, C., MacKian, S., & Pile, S. (2017) The place of the spirit: Modernity and the geographies of spirituality. *Progress in Human Geography*, 41(3): 338–54.

Bastia, T. (2014) Intersectionality, migration and development. *Progress in Development Studies*, 14(3): 237–48. https://doi.org/10.1177/1464993414521330

Bastian, M., Jones, O., Moore, N., & Roe, E. (eds.) (2017) *Participatory Research in More-Than-Human Worlds*. London: Routledge.

Bates, L. (2015) *Everyday Sexism*. London: Simon & Schuster.

Batnitzky, A., & McDowell, L. (2011) Migration, nursing, institutional discrimination and emotional/affective labour: Ethnicity and labour stratification in the UK national health service. *Social & Cultural Geography*, 12(2): 181–201. https://doi.org/10.1080/14649365.2011.545142

BBC News. (2011) The politics behind Nick Clegg's 'alarm clock Britain'. BBC News, 10 January. https://www.bbc.co.uk/news/uk-politics-12149705

BBC News. (2013) Huge survey reveals seven social classes in UK. 3 April. https://www.bbc.com/news/uk-22007058

BBC News. (2017) Paralympian tells of train toilet 'humiliation'. 3 January. https://www.bbc.co.uk/news/uk-england-essex-38495184

Beasley, C., Holmes, M., & Brook, H. (2015) Heterodoxy: Challenging orthodoxies about heterosexuality. *Sexualities*, 18(6): 681–97.

Beaumont, J., & Baker, C. (eds.) (2011) *Postsecular Cities: Space, Theory and Practice*. London: Continuum.

Beaverstock, J., & Hay, I. (2016) They've 'never had it so good': The rise and rise of the superrich and wealth inequality. In I. Hay & J. V. Beaverstock (eds.), *Handbook on Wealth and the Super-Rich*, pp. 1–17. Cheltenham, UK: Edward Elgar.

Beazley, H. (2015) Multiple identities, multiple realities: Children who migrate independently for work in Southeast Asia. *Children's Geographies*, 13(3): 296–309.

Beckett, K., & Herbert, S. (2009) *Banished: The New Social Control in Urban America*. Oxford: Oxford University Press.

Beckford, J. (2012) Public religions and the postsecular. *Journal for the Scientific Study of Religion*, 51(1): 1–19.

Beer, D., & Burrows, R. (2013) Popular culture, digital archives and the new social life of data. *Theory, Culture and Society*, 30(4): 47–74.

Bell, D. (1991) Insignificant others: Lesbian and gay geographies. *Area*, 23(4): 323–29.

Bell, D. (2009) Cultural studies and human geography. In N. Thrift & R. Kitchin (eds.), *International Encyclopedia of Human Geography*, pp. 437–41. Amsterdam: Elsevier.

Bell, D., & Binnie, J. (2000) *The Sexual Citizen: Queer Theory and Beyond*. Malden, MA: Polity Press.

Bell, D., & Binnie, J. (2004) Authenticating queer space: Citizenship, urbanism and governance. *Urban Studies*, 41(9): 1807–20.

Bell, D., Binnie, J., Cream, J., & Valentine, G. (1994) All hyped up and no place to go. *Gender, Place & Culture*, 1(1): 31–47.

Bell, D., & Valentine, G. (1995) *Mapping Desire: Geographies of Sexualities*. London: Routledge.

Bell, D., & Valentine, G. (1997) *Consuming Geographies: We Are Where We Eat*. London: Routledge.

Benford, R. (2005) The half-life of the environmental justice frame: Innovation, diffusion, and stagnation. In N. D. Pellow & R. J. Brulle (eds.), *Power, Justice, and the Environment: A Critical Appraisal of the*

Environmental Justice Movement, pp. 37–54. Cambridge, MA: MIT Press.

Ben-Naftali, O., Gross, A., & Michaeli, K. (2009) The illegality of the occupation regime: The fabric of law in occupied Palestinian territory. In A. Ophir, M. Givoni & S. Ḥanafî (eds.), *The Power of Inclusive Exclusion: Anatomy of Israeli Rule in the Occupied Palestinian Territories*, pp. 31–88. New York: Zone Books.

Bennett, A. (2000) *Popular Music and Youth Culture: Music, Identity and Place*. Basingstoke, UK: Macmillan.

Bennett, J. (2007) Edible matter. *New Left Review*, 45: 133–45.

Benwell, M. C. (2014a) From the banal to the blatant: Expressions of nationalism in secondary schools in Argentina and the Falkland Islands. *Geoforum*, 52: 51–60.

Benwell, M. C. (2014b) Considering nationality and performativity: Undertaking research across the geopolitical divide in the Falkland Islands and Argentina. *Area*, 46: 163–69.

Benwell, M. C. (2017) Argentine territorial nationalism in the South Atlantic and Antarctica. In K. Dodds, A. D. Hemmings & P. Roberts (eds.), *Handbook on the Politics of Antarctica*, pp. 540–54. Cheltenham, UK: Edward Elgar.

Benwell, M. C., & Dodds, K. (2011) Argentine territorial nationalism revisited: The Malvinas/Falklands dispute and geographies of everyday nationalism. *Political Geography*, 30: 441–49.

Benwell, M. C., & Hopkins, P. (2016) *Children, Young People and Critical Geopolitics*. Aldershot, UK: Ashgate.

Benwell, M. C., Núñez, A., & Amigo, C. (2019) Flagging the nations: Citizen's active engagements with everyday nationalism in Patagonia, Chile. *Area*, 51(4): 719–27. doi:10.1111/area.12517

Berg, L. D. (2013) Hegemonic geographies and their 'others': Towards an interlocking approach to emplacing geographical knowledges. *Dialogues in Human Geography*, 3(2): 200–204.

Berg, L. D., & Longhurst, R. (2003) Placing masculinities and geography. *Gender, Place & Culture*, 10(4): 351–60.

Berg, M. (2012) Checking in at the urban playground: Digital geographies and electronic *flâneurs*. In F. Communello (ed.), *Networked Sociability and Individualism: Technology for Personal and Professional Relationships*, pp. 169–94. Hershey, PA: IGI Global.

Berman, M. (1982) *All That Is Solid Melts into the Air: The Experience of Modernity*. London: Verso.

Bhandari, R., Akhter, N., Warren, J., Kasim, A., & Bambra, C. (2017) Geographical inequalities in general and physical health in a time of austerity: Baseline findings from the Stockton-on-Tees cohort study. *Health & Place*, 48: 111–22.

Bilge, S. (2013) Intersectionality undone: Saving intersectionality from feminist intersectionality studies. *Du Bois Review: Social Science Research on Race*, 10(2): 402–24.

Billig, M. (1995) *Banal Nationalism*. London: Sage.

Binnie, J. (1997) Coming out of geography: Towards a queer epistemology? *Environment and Planning D: Society and Space*, 15(2): 223–37.

Binnie, J. (2004) *The Globalization of Sexuality*. London: Sage.

Binnie, J. (2007) Sexuality, the erotic and geography: Epistemology, methodology and pedagogy. In L. Browne, J. Lim & G. Brown (eds.), *Geographies of Sexualities: Theory, Practices and Politics*, pp. 29–38. Aldershot, UK: Ashgate.

Binnie, J., & Skeggs, B. (2004) Cosmopolitan knowledge and the production of sexualised space: Manchester's gay village. *Sociological Review*, 52(1): 39–61.

Binnie, J., & Valentine, G. (1999) Geographies of sexuality – A review of progress. *Progress in Human Geography*, 23(2): 175–87.

Bissell, D. (2019) Social & Cultural Geography at 20 years: Looking back, thinking forward. *Social & Cultural Geography*, 20(1): 1–3.

Blake, M. (2018a) Enormous amounts of food are wasted during manufacture – here's where it occurs. *Conversation*, 5 September. https://theconversation.com/enormous-amounts-of-food-are-wasted-during-manufacturing-heres-where-it-occurs-102310

Blake, M. (2018b) Capitalism has coopted the language of food – costing the world millions of meals. *Conversation*, 1 February. https://theconversation.com/capitalism-has-coopted

-the-language-of-food-costing-the-world
-millions-of-meals-90780

Blakely, E. J., & Synder, M. G. (1997) *'Fortress America': Gated Communities in the United States*. Washington, DC: Brookings Institute Press.

Blazek, M., & Kraftl, P. (2015) *Children's Emotions in Policy and Practice.* London: Palgrave Macmillan.

Blewett, J., & Hanlon, N. (2016) Disablement as inveterate condition: Living with habitual ableism in Prince George, British Columbia. *Canadian Geographer – Geographe Canadien*, 60(1): 46–55.

Blomley, N. K., Delaney, D., & Ford, R. T. (2001) *The Legal Geographies Reader: Law, Power, and Space*. Malden, MA: Wiley-Blackwell.

Bluestone, B., Stevenson, M. H., & Williams, R. (2008) *The Urban Experience: Economics, Society, and Public Policy*. Oxford: Oxford University Press.

Blunt, A. (2003) Collective memory and productive nostalgia: Anglo-Indian homemaking at McCluskieganj. *Environment and Planning D: Society and Space*, 21(6): 717–38.

Blunt, A. (2007) Cultural geographies of migration: Mobility, transnationality, and diaspora. *Progress in Human Geography*, 3(5): 684–95.

Blunt, A., & Varley, A. (2004) Geographies of home. *Cultural Geographies*, 11(1): 3–6.

Blunt, A., & Wills, J. (2000) *Dissident Geographies: An Introduction to Radical Ideas and Practice*. Harlow, UK: Prentice-Hall.

Boal, A. (2005/1998) *Legislative Theatre: Using Performance to Make Politics*. London: Routledge.

Boarini, R., & D'Ercole, M. M. (2013) Going beyond GDP: An OECD Perspective. *Fiscal Studies*, 34: 289–314.

Bock-Luna, B. (2007) *The Past in Exile: Serbian Long-Distance Nationalism and Identity in the Wake of the Third Balkan War*. Berlin: LIT Verlag.

Bolton, P. (2018) Tuition fee statistics. House of Commons briefing paper 917, 19 February. researchbriefings.files.parliament.uk/documents/SN00917/SN00917.pdf

Bondi, L. (1991) Gender divisions and gentrification: A critique. *Transactions of the Institute of British Geographers*, 16: 190–98.

Bondi, L. (2005) Making connections and thinking through emotions: Between geography and psychotherapy. *Transactions of the Institute of British Geographers*, 30(4): 433–48.

Bondi, L. (2013) Research and therapy: Generating meaning and feeling gaps. *Qualitative Inquiry*, 19(1): 9–19.

Bondi, L., Davidson, J., & Smith, M. (2005) Introduction: Geography's emotional turn. In J. Davidson, L. Bondi & M. Smith (eds.), *Emotional Geographies*, pp. 1–16. Aldershot, UK: Ashgate.

Bondi, L., & Domosh, M. (1982) Other figures in other places: On feminism, postmodernism and geography. *Environment and Planning D: Society and Space*, 10(2): 199–213.

Bonner-Thompson, C. (2017) The meat market: Production and regulation of masculinities on the Grindr grid in Newcastle upon Tyne, UK. *Gender, Place & Culture*, 24(11): 1611–25.

Bonnett, A. (2015) *The Geography of Nostalgia*. London: Routledge.

Bonnett, A. (2016) Whiteness and the West. In C. Dwyer & C. Bressey (eds.), *New Geographies of Race and Racism*, pp. 31–42. Aldershot, UK: Ashgate.

Bordo, S. (1990) Feminism, postmodernism, and gender scepticism. In L. Nicholson (ed.), *Feminism/Postmodernism*, pp. 133–56. London: Routledge.

Boring, A., Ottoboni, K., & Stark, P. B. (2016) Student evaluations of teaching (mostly) do not measure teaching effectiveness. *ScienceOpen Research*, 1: 1–11.

Botterill, K., Hopkins, P., Sanghera, G., & Arshad, R. (2016) Securing disunion: Young people's nationalism, identities and (in)securities in the campaign for an independent Scotland. *Political Geography*, 55: 124–34.

Bottero, W. (2005) *Stratification: Social Division and Inequality*. Abingdon, UK: Routledge.

Bourdieu, P. (1977) Cultural reproduction and social reproduction. In J. Karabel & A. H. Halsey (eds.), *Power and Ideology in Education*. New York: Oxford University Press.

Bourdieu, P. (1984) *Distinction: A Social Critique of the Judgment of Taste.* London: Routledge & Kegan Paul.

Bourdieu, P. (1986) The forms of capital. In J. Richardson (ed.), *Handbook of Theory and Research for the Sociology of Education*, pp. 241–58. Westport, CT: Greenwood.

Bourdieu, P., & Nice, R. (1977) *Outline of a Theory of Practice.* Cambridge: Cambridge University Press.

Bowen, J. R. (2007) *Why the French Don't Like Headscarves: Islam, the State, and Public Space.* Princeton, NJ: Princeton University Press.

Bowlby, S. (2012) Recognising the time-space dimensions of care: Caringscapes and carescapes. *Environment and Planning A: Economy and Space*, 44: 2101–18.

Bowlby, S., & McDowell, L. (1987) The feminist challenge to social geography. In M. Pacione (ed.), *Social Geography: Progress and Prospect*, pp. 295–323. London: Croom Helm.

Bowman, A. K. (1994) *Life and Letters on the Roman Frontier: Vindolanda and Its People.* New York: Routledge.

Boyer, K., Dermott, E., James, A., & MacLeavy, J. (2017) Regendering care in the aftermath of recession? *Dialogues in Human Geography*, 7(1): 56–73.

Bradley, H. (2014) Class descriptors or class relations? Thoughts towards a critique of Savage et al. *Sociology*, 48(3): 429–36.

Brah, A. (1996) *Cartographies of Diaspora: Contesting Identities.* Hoboken, NJ: Taylor & Francis.

Braithwaite, D. O., Bath, B. W., Baxter, L. A., DiVerniero, R., Hammonds, J. R., Hosek, A. M., Willer, E. K., & Wolf, B. M. (2010) Constructing family: A typology of voluntary kin. *Journal of Social and Personal Relationships*, 27: 388–408.

Breathnach, P. (2000) Globalisation, information technology and the emergence of niche transnational cities: The growth of the call centre sector in Dublin. *Geoforum*, 31: 477–85.

Brenner, N., & Theodore, N. (2002) Cities and the geographies of actually existing neoliberalism. *Antipode*, 34(3): 349–79.

Brickell, K. (2012) 'Mapping' and 'doing' critical geographies of home. *Progress in Human Geography*, 36(2): 225–44.

Bridge, G., Bouzarovski, S., Bradshaw, M., & Eyre, N. (2013) Geographies of energy transition: Space, place and the low-carbon economy. *Energy Policy*, 53: 331–40.

Brown, G. (2008) Urban (homo)sexualities: Ordinary cities and ordinary sexualities. *Geography Compass*, 2(4): 1215–31.

Brown, G. (2012) Homonormativity: A metropolitan concept that denigrates ordinary gay lives. *Journal of Homosexuality*, 59: 1065–72.

Brown, G., & Browne, K. (2016) *The Routledge Research Companion to Geographies of Sex and Sexualities.* London: Routledge.

Brown, K. (2014) Global environmental change I: A social turn for resilience? *Progress in Human Geography*, 38(1): 107–17.

Browne, K. (2006) Challenging queer geographies. *Antipode*, 38: 885–93.

Browne, K., & Ferreira, E. (2015) *Lesbian Geographies: Gender, Place and Power.* Farnham, UK: Ashgate.

Browne, K., Nash, C. J., & Hines, S. (2010) Introduction: Towards trans geographies. *Gender Place & Culture*, 17(5): 573–77.

Bruce, G. D., & Witt, R. E. (1971) Developing empirically derived city typologies: An application of cluster analysis. *Sociological Quarterly*, 12(2): 238–46.

Buffel, T., Phillipson, C., & Scharf, T. (2013) Experiences of neighbourhood exclusion and inclusion among older people living in deprived inner-city areas in Belgium and England. *Ageing & Society*, 33: 89–109.

Bulkeley, H. (2013) *Cities and Climate Change.* London: Routledge. https://doi.org/10.4324/9780203077207

Bulkeley, H., Edwards, G. A. S., & Fuller, S. (2014) Contesting climate justice in the city: Examining politics and practice in urban climate change experiments. *Global Environmental Change*, 25 (March): 31–40. https://doi.org/10.1016/J.GLOENVCHA.2014.01.009

Bunge, W., Jr. (1969) *The First Years of the Detroit Geographical Expedition: A Personal Report. field notes*, discussion paper no. 1: 1–59.

Bunge, W. (1971) *Fitzgerald: Geography of a Revolution.* Cambridge, MA: Schenkman.

Burchell, B. J., Ladipo D., & Wilkinson, F. (eds.) (2002) *Job Insecurity and Work Intensification*. London: Routledge.

Burgoine, T., Alvanides, S., & Lake, A. (2011) Assessing the obesogenic environment of north east England. *Health & Place*, 17(3): 738–47.

Burman, A. (2014) 'Now we are *Indígenas*': Hegemony and Indigeneity in the Bolivian Andes. *Latin American and Caribbean Ethnic Studies*, 9: 247–71. https://doi.org/10.1080/17442222.2014.959775

Burrows, R., & Knowles, C. (2019) The haves and the have yachts: Socio-spatial struggles in London between the merely wealthy and the super-rich. *Cultural Politics*, 15(1): 90–105.

Burrows, R., Webber, R., & Atkinson, R. (2017) Welcome to 'Pikettyville'? Mapping London's alpha territories. *Sociological Review*, 65(2): 184–201.

Bush, J., Moffatt, S., & Dunn, C. (2001) 'Even the birds round here cough': Stigma, air pollution and health in Teesside. *Health & Place*, 7(1): 47–56.

Butler, J. (1990) *Gender Trouble: Feminism and the Subversion of Identity*. New York: Routledge.

Butler, J. (1993) *Bodies That Matter: On the Discursive Limits of 'Sex'*. New York: Routledge.

Butler, M. L. (2018) 'Guardians of the Indian image': Controlling representations of Indigenous cultures in television. *American Indian Quarterly*, 42(1): 1–42.

Butler, T., & Lees, L. (2006) Super-gentrification in Barnsbury, London: Globalization and gentrifying global elites at the neighbourhood level. *Transactions of the Institute of British Geographers*, 31(4): 467–87.

Buttimer, A. (1976) Grasping the dynamism of the lifeworld. *Annals of the Association of American Geographers*, 66(2): 277–92.

Cahill, C. (2007a) Doing research with young people: Participatory research and the rituals of collective work. *Children's Geographies*, 5(3): 297–312.

Cahill, C. (2007b) The personal is political: Developing new subjectivities through participatory action research. *Gender, Place & Culture*, 14(3): 267–92.

Cahill, C., Cerecer, D., Quijada, A., Reyna Rivarola, A. R., Hernández Zamudio, J.,

& Alvarez Gutiérrez, L. (2019) 'Caution, we have power': Resisting the 'school-to-sweatshop pipeline' through participatory artistic praxes and critical care. *Gender and Education*, 31(5): 576–89. doi:10.1080/09540253.2019.1582207

Campbell, E. (2016) Policing paedophilia: Assembling bodies, spaces and things. *Crime, Media, Culture*, 12(3): 345–65.

Campt, T., & Thomas, D. (2008) Gendering diasporas: Transnational feminism, diaspora and its hegemonies. *Feminist Review*, 90(1): 1–8.

Canessa, A. (2007) Who is Indigenous? Self-identification, Indigeneity, and claims to justice in contemporary Bolivia. *Urban Anthropology*, 36(3): 195–237.

Canessa, A. (2014) Conflict, claim and contradiction in the new 'Indigenous' state of Bolivia. *Critique of Anthropology*, 34: 153–73. https://doi.org/10.1177/0308275X13519275

Cantle Report. (2001) *Report of the Community Cohesion Review Team*. Institute of Community Cohesion, led by Ted Cantle, Home Office.

Capgemini. (2018) *World Wealth Report 2018*. https://www.capgemini.com/ch-de/wp-content/uploads/sites/26/2018/06/Capgemini-World-Wealth-Report-19.pdf

Carling, J., & Collins, F. (2018) Aspiration, desire and drivers of migration. *Journal of Ethnic and Migration Studies*, 44(6): 909–26. https://doi.org/10.1080/1369183X.2017.1384134

Carter, B., & Virdee, S. (2008) Racism and the sociological imagination. *British Journal of Sociology*, 59(4): 661–79.

Carter, S. (2005) The geopolitics of diaspora. *Area*, 37(1): 54–63. https://doi.org/10.1111/j.1475-4762.2005.00601.x

Casey, M. (2010) Multiple identities, multiple realities: Lesbian, gay and queer lives in the North East of England. In L. Moon (ed.), *Counselling Ideologies: Queer Challenges to Heteronormativity*, pp. 143–65. London: Taylor & Francis.

Castells, M. (1983) *The City and the Grassroots*. London: Edward Arnold.

Castells, M. (1996) *The Rise of the Network Society*. Oxford: Blackwell.

Castree, N., Demeritt, D., Liverman, D., & Rhoads, B. (eds.) (2009) *A Companion to Environmental Geography*. Chichester, UK: Wiley-Blackwell.

Castree, N., & Nash, C. (2006) Editorial: Posthuman geographies. *Social & Cultural Geography*, 7(4): 501–4. https://doi.org/10.1080/14649360600825620

Catney, G. (2016) The changing geographies of ethnic diversity in England and Wales, 1991–2011. *Population, Space and Place*, 22(8): 750–76.

Cavanagh, S. L. (2010) *Queering Bathrooms: Gender, Sexuality, and the Hygienic Imagination*. Toronto: University of Toronto Press.

Chakrabortty, A. (2017) Over 170 years after Engels, Britain is still a country that murders its poor. *The Guardian*, 25.

Chatterton, P., Featherstone, D., & Routledge, P. (2013) Articulating climate justice in Copenhagen: Antagonism, the commons, and solidarity. *Antipode*, 45(3): 602–20.

Chatterton, P., & Hollands, R. (2003) *Urban Nightscapes: Youth Cultures, Pleasure Spaces and Corporate Power*. London: Routledge.

Chen, B., Liu, D., & Lu, M. (2017) City size, migration, and urban inequality in the People's Republic of China. ADBI Working Paper 723. Tokyo: Asian Development Bank Institute. https://www.adb.org/publications/city-size-migration-and-urban-inequality-prc

Child Exploitation and Online Protection Centre. (2011) Hundreds of suspects tracked in international child abuse investigation. Press release, 16 March.

Children's Commissioner for England. (2018) *Growing Up North*. London: Children's Commissioner for England. http://www.childrenscommissioner.gov.uk/wp-content/uploads/2018/03/Growing-Up-North-March-2018-1.pdf

Chohaney, M. L., & Panozzo, K. A. (2018) Infidelity and the internet: The geography of Ashley Madison usership in the United States. *Geographical Review*, 108(1): 69–91.

Chouinard, V. (1999) Life at the margins: Disabled women's explorations of ableist spaces. In E. K. Teather (ed.), *Embodied Geographies: Spaces, Bodies and Rites of Passage*, pp. 142–56. London: Routledge.

Chouinard, V., Hall, E., & Wilton, R. (eds.) (2010) *Towards Enabling Geographies: 'Disabled' Bodies and Minds in Society and Space*. Farnham, UK: Ashgate.

Chowbey, P. (2017) How women use food to negotiate power in Pakistani and Indian households. *Conversation*, 8 November. https://theconversation.com/how-women-use-food-to-negotiate-power-in-pakistani-and-indian-households-77928

Christie, H. (2007) Higher education and spatial (im)mobility: Nontraditional students and living at home. *Environment and Planning A: Economy and Space*, 39: 2445–63.

Christou, A., & King, R. (2010) Imagining 'home': Diasporic landscape of the Greek-German second generation. *Geoforum*, 41(4): 638–46. https://doi.org/10.1016/j.geoforum.2010.03.001

Cieri, M., & McCauley, R. (2007) Participatory theatre: Creating a source for staging an example in the USA. In S. Kindon, R. Pain & M. Kesby (eds.), *Participatory Action Research Approaches and Methods: Connecting People, Participation and Place*, pp. 141–49. Abingdon, UK: Routledge.

Clayton, J. (2009) Thinking spatially: Towards an everyday understanding of inter-ethnic relations. *Social & Cultural Geography*, 10(4): 481–98.

Clayton, J. (2013) Geography and everyday life. In B. Warf (ed.), *Oxford Bibliographies in Geography*. New York: Oxford University Press. doi:10.1093/OBO/9780199874002-0095

Clement, V. (2019) Beyond the sham of the emancipatory Enlightenment: Rethinking the relationship of Indigenous epistemologies, knowledges, and geography through decolonizing paths. *Progress in Human Geography*, 43: 276–94.

Clifton, J., Round, A., & Raikes, L. (2016) Northern schools: Putting education at the heart of the Northern Powerhouse. Manchester: IPPR North. https://www.ippr.org/files/publications/pdf/northern-schools_May2016.pdf

Cloke, P. J. (1977) An index of rurality for England and Wales. *Regional Studies*, 11: 31–46.

Cloke, P. J. (1978) Changing patterns of urbanisation in rural areas of England and

Wales, 1961–1971. *Regional Studies*, 12: 603–17.

Cloke, P., Cook, I., Crang, P., Goodwin, M., Painter, J., & Philo, C. (2012) *Practising Human Geography*. London: Sage.

Cloke, P., Crang, P., & Goodwin, M. (2014) *Introducing Human Geographies*. London: Routledge.

Cloke, P., May, J., & Johnsen, S. (2010) *Swept Up Lives? Re-envisioning the Homeless City*. Oxford: Wiley-Blackwell.

Closs Stephens, A. (2013) *The Persistence of Nationalism: From Imagined Communities to Urban Assemblages*. London: Routledge.

Cockayne, D. G., & Richardson, L. (2017) Queering code/space: The co-production of socio-sexual codes and digital technologies. *Gender, Place & Culture*, 24(11): 1642–58.

Cohen, P. (1993) *Home Rules: Some Reflections on Racism and Nationalism in Everyday Life*. London: University of East London.

Coleman-Fountain, E. (2014) *Understanding Narrative Identity through Lesbian and Gay Youth*. Basingstoke, UK: Palgrave Macmillan.

Coles, B. (2016) Ingesting places: Embodied geographies of coffee. In E.-J. Abbots & A. Lavis (eds.), *Why We Eat, How We Eat*: *Contemporary Encounters between Foods and Bodies*, pp. 255–70. Abingdon, UK: Ashgate.

Collard, R.-C., Harris, L. M., Heynen, N., & Mehta, L. (2018) The antinomies of nature and space. *Environment and Planning E: Nature and Space*, 1(1–2): 3–24. https://doi.org/10.1177/2514848618777162

Collins, C., & McCartney, G. (2011) The impact of neoliberal political attack on health: The case of the Scottish effect. *International Journal of Health Services*, 41(3): 501–26.

Collins, P. H. (1990) *Black Feminist Thought: Knowledge, Consciousness, and the Politics of Empowerment*. London: Harper Collins Academic.

Collins, P. H., & Bilge, S. (2016) *Intersectionality*. Cambridge: Polity Press.

Colls, R., & Evans, B. (2009) Introduction: Questioning obesity politics. *Antipode*, 41(5): 1011–20.

Combahee River Collective. (1982/2019) A black feminist statement. In G. T. Hull, P. B. Scott & B. Smith (eds.), *All the Women Are White, All the Blacks Are Men, But Some of Us Are Brave*, pp. 13–22. Old Westbury, NY: Feminist Press.

Commission on Co-operative and Mutual Housing (CCMH). (2009) *Bringing Democracy Home*. West Bromwich: CCMH.

Connell, R. W. (1995) *Masculinities*. Cambridge: Polity Press.

Connell, R. W., & Messerschmidt, J. R. (2005) Hegemonic masculinity: Rethinking the Concept. *Gender and Society*, 19(6): 829–59.

Conradson, D. (2003) Landscape, care and the relational self: Therapeutic encounters in rural England. *Health & Place*, 11(4): 337–48.

Conradson, D. (2007) Freedom, space and perspective: Moving encounters with other ecologies. In J. Davidson, L. Bondi & M. Smith (eds.), *Emotional Geographies*, pp. 103–16. Aldershot, UK: Ashgate.

Constable, N. (2009) Migrant workers and the many states of protest in Hong Kong. *Critical Asian Studies*, 41(1): 143–64.

Cook, I. (2004) Follow the thing: Papaya. *Antipode*, 36(4): 642–64.

Cooper, A. J. (1988) *A Voice from the South*. Oxford: Oxford University Press.

Copp, J. (1972) Rural sociology and rural development. *Rural Sociology*, 37: 515–33.

Copus, A., & Hopkins, J. (2017) Outline conceptual framework and definition of the Scottish Sparsely Populated Area (SPA). RESAS RD 3.4.1, Demographic change in remote areas, Working Paper 1 (Objective 1.1). Aberdeen: James Hutton Institute.

Cosgrove, D. (2001) *Apollo's Eye: A Cartographic Genealogy of the Earth in the Western Imagination*. Baltimore, MD: Johns Hopkins University Press.

Cote, A., & Nightingale, A. (2012) Resilience thinking meets social theory: Situating social change in socio-ecological systems (SES) research. *Progress in Human Geography*, 36(4): 475–89.

Cotton, M. (2018) Environmental justice as scalar parity: Lessons from nuclear waste management. *Social Justice Research*, Open Access: 1–22. https://doi.org/10.1007/s11211-018-0311-z

Country, B., Wright, S., Suchet-Pearson, S., Lloyd, K., Burarrwanga, L., Ganambarr, R., Ganambarr-Stubbs, M., Ganambarr, B., Maymuru, D., & Sweeney, J. (2016) Co-becoming Bawaka: Towards a relational understanding of place/space. *Progress in Human Geography*, 40: 455–75. https://doi.org/10.1177/0309132515589437

Cowie, P. (2017) Performing planning: Understanding community participation in planning through theatre. *Town Planning Review*, 88(4): 401–421.

Cox, K. R. (1998) Spaces of dependence, spaces of engagement and the politics of scale; or, looking for local politics. *Political Geography*, 17(1): 1–23.

Crang, M., Crang, P., & May, J. (1999) *Virtual Geographies: Bodies, Spaces, Relations.* London: Routledge.

Crang, P. (1994) It's showtime: On the geographies of workplace display in a restaurant in South East England. *Environment and Planning D: Society and Space*, 12: 675–704.

Cranston, S., & Lloyd, J. (2018) Bursting the bubble: Spatializing safety for privileged migrant women in Singapore. *Antipode*, 51(2): 478–96.

Crawford, K. (2014) When Fitbit is the expert witness. *Atlantic*, 19 November. https://www.theatlantic.com/technology/archive/2014/11/when-fitbit-is-the-expert-witness/382936/?single_page=true

Crawford, K., Gray, M. L., & Miltner, K. (2014) Critiquing big data: Politics, ethics, epistemology. *International Journal of Communication*, 8(1): 1663–72.

Crawley, H. (2007) *When Is a Child Not a Child? Asylum, Age Disputes and the Process of Age Assessment.* Immigration Law Practitioners' Association (ILPA). https://pureportal.coventry.ac.uk/en/publications/when-is-a-child-not-a-child-asylum-age-disputes-and-the-process-o

Cream, J. (1995) Re-solving riddles: The sexed body. In D. Bell & G. Valentine (eds.), *Mapping Desire: Geographies of Sexualities*, pp. 31–40. London: Routledge.

Creasey, S. (2018) Calling the male Harriet Harmans: Why equality in politics benefits men as well as women. *New Statesman*, 19 July. https://www.newstatesman.com/politics/feminism/2018/07/stella-creasy-equality-politics-feminism-benefits-women-male-harriet-harmans

Crenshaw, K. (1989) Demarginalizing the intersections of race and sex: A black feminist critique of antidiscrimination doctrine, feminist theory and antiracist politics. *University of Chicago Legal Forum*, 1: 139–67.

Crenshaw, K. (1991) Mapping the margins: Intersectionality, identity politics, and violence against women of color. *Stanford Law Review*, 43(6): 1241–99.

Cresswell, T. (1996) *In Place/Out of Place.* Minneapolis: University of Minnesota Press.

Cross, M., & Keith, M. (2013) Racism and the postmodern city. In M. Cross & M. Keith (eds.), *Racism, the City and the State*, pp. 8–37. Abingdon, UK: Routledge.

Crow, G., & Ellis, J. (2017) *Revisiting* Divisions of Labour. Manchester: Manchester University Press.

Crutzen, P. J. (2006) The Anthropocene. In E. Ehlers & T. Krafft (eds.), *Earth System Science in the Anthropocene*, pp. 13–18. Berlin: Springer.

Crutzen, P. J., & Stoermer, E. (2000) The 'Anthropocene'. *Global Change Newsletters*, 41: 17–18. http://www.igbp.net/download/18.316f18321323470177580001401/1376383088452/NL41.pdf

Cummins, S., Curtis, S., Diez-Roux, A., & Macintyre, S. (2007) Understanding and representing 'place' in health research: A relational approach. *Social Science & Medicine*, 65(9): 1825–38.

Curtis, S., Gesler, W., Fabian, K., Francis, S., & Priebe, S. (2007) Therapeutic landscapes in hospital design: A qualitative assessment by staff and service users of the design of a new mental health inpatient unit. *Environment & Planning C: Government Policy*, 25: 591–610. https://doi.org/10.1068/c1312r

D'Alisa, G., Demaria, F., & Kallis, G. (eds.) (2014) *Degrowth: A Vocabulary for a New Era.* Oxford: Routledge.

Daniels, P., Bradshaw, M., Shaw, D., Sidaway, J., & Hall, T. (2016) *An Introduction to Human Geography.* Harlow, UK: Pearson.

Darling, D., & Wilson, H. (2016) *Encountering the City: Urban Encounters from Accra to New York.* Abingdon, UK: Routledge.

da Rocha, D. F., Firpo Porto, M., Pacheco, T., & Leroy, J. P. (2018) The map of conflicts related to environmental injustice and health in Brazil. *Sustainability Science*, 13(3):

709–19. https://doi.org/10.1007/s11625-017-0494-5

Datta, A. (2015) 100 smart cities, 100 utopias. *Dialogues in Human Geography*, 5(1): 49–53.

Datta, A., Hopkins, P., Johnston, L., Olson, E., & Silva, J. M. (2019) *The Routledge International Handbook of Gender and Feminist Geographies*. London: Routledge.

Datta, K., McIllwaine, C., Herbert, J., Evans, Y., May, J., & Wills, J. (2009) Men on the move: Narratives of migration and work among low-paid migrant men in London. *Social & Cultural Geography*, 10(1): 853–74.

Davidson, J. (2003) *Phobic Geographies: The Phenomenology and Spatiality of Identity*. Aldershot, UK: Ashgate.

Davidson, J., Bondi, L., & Smith, M. (2005) *Emotional Geographies*. Aldershot, UK: Ashgate.

Davies, A. (2011) (Un)just geographies? Review of Dorling's *Injustice* and Soja's *Seeking Spatial Justice*. *Geographical Journal*, 177(4): 380–84.

Davis, A., & Williams, K. (2017) Elites and power after financialization. *Theory, Culture & Society*, 34(5–6): 3–26.

Davis, A. Y. (1981) *Women, Race, and Class*. New York: Random House.

Davis, M. (1998) *Ecology of Fear: Los Angeles and the Imagination of Disaster*. New York: Metropolitan Books.

Davis, M. (2006) *Planet of Slums*. London: Verso.

Davis, M. (2008) Indigenous struggles in standard-setting: The United Nations Declaration on the Rights of Indigenous Peoples commentary. *Melbourne Journal International Law*, 9: 439–71.

Davis, S. J., & Caldeira, K. (2010) Consumption-based accounting of CO_2 emissions. *PNAS*, 107(12): 5687–92. https://doi.org/10.1073/pnas.0906974107

de Cauter, L. (2005) *The Capsular Civilization: On the City in the Age of Fear (Reflect No. 3)*. Rotterdam: Nai.

De Certeau, M. (1984) *The Practice of Everyday Life*. Berkeley: University of California Press.

Deckha, N. (2003) Insurgent urbanism in a railway quarter: Scalar citizenship at King's Cross, London. *ACME: An International E-Journal for Critical Geographies*, 2(1): 33–56.

DEFRA (Department for Environment, Food and Rural Affairs). (2008) *A Framework for Pro-environmental Behaviours*. London: Stationery Office.

De Graaf, N. D., De Graaf, P. M., & Kraaykamp, G. (2000) Parental cultural capital and educational attainment in the Netherlands: A refinement of the cultural capital perspective. *Sociology of Education*, 73(2): 92–111.

de la Cadena, M., & Starn, O. (2007) *Indigenous Experience Today*. Oxford: Berg.

Del Casino, V. (2009) *Social Geography: A Critical Introduction*. Chichester, UK: Wiley-Blackwell.

de Leeuw, S., & Hunt, S. (2018) Unsettling decolonizing geographies. *Geography Compass*, 12: e12376. https://doi.org/10.1111/gec3.12376

Deleuze, G., & Foucault, M. (1980) Intellectuals and power. In M. Foucault, *Language, Counter-Memory, Practice: Selected Essays and Interviews*, pp. 205–17. Ithaca, NY: Cornell University Press.

De Lima, P. (2012) Moving beyond class and status – Intersectionality and place/space as a framework for understanding social divisions? Paper presented to QUCAN/TARRN annual meeting, Inverness, Scotland.

DeLyser, D., & Sui, D. (2013) Crossing the qualitative-quantitative divide II: Inventive approaches to big data, mobile methods and rhythmanalysis. *Progress in Human Geography*, 37(1): 293–305.

Demaria, F., Schneider, F., Sekulova, F., & Martínez-Alier, J. (2013) What is degrowth? From an activist slogan to a social movement. *Environmental Values*, 22(2): 191–215. https://doi.org/10.3197/096327113X13581561725194

Demeritt, D. (2002). What is the 'social construction of nature'? A typology and sympathetic critique. *Progress in Human Geography*, 26(6): 767–90.

Derickson, K. (2017) Urban geography II: Urban geography in the age of Ferguson. *Progress in Human Geography*, 41(2): 230–44.

Derrida, J. (1991) Eating well, or the calculation of the subject: An interview. In E. Cadava, P. Connor & J.-L. Nancy (eds.), *Who Comes After the Subject?*, pp. 96–119. London: Routledge.

de Souza, M. L. (2012) *Panem et circenses* versus the right to the city (centre) in Rio de Janeiro: A short report. *City*, 16(5): 563–72.

Devine, F., & Snee, H. (2015) Doing the Great British Class Survey. *Sociological Review*, 63(2): 240–58.

Devine-Wright, P. (2013) Think global, act local? The relevance of place attachments and place identities in a climate changed world. *Global Environmental Change*, 23: 61–69. https://doi.org/10.1016/j.gloenvcha.2012 .08.003

Devine-Wright, P., & Howes, Y. (2010) Disruption to place attachment and the protection of restorative environments: A wind energy case study. *Journal of Environmental Psychology*, 30(3): 271–80. https://doi.org/10.1016/J.JENVP.2010.01.008

de Witte, M. (2016) Encountering religion through Accra's urban soundscape. In J. Darling & H. Wilson (eds.), *Encountering the City: Urban Encounters from Accra to New York*, pp. 133–50. Abingdon, UK: Routledge.

Doan, P. (2010) The tyranny of gendered spaces – Reflections from beyond the gender dichotomy. *Gender, Place & Culture*, 17(5): 635–54.

Dodge, M., & Kitchin, R. (2004) Flying through code/space: The real virtuality of air travel. *Environment and Planning A: Economy and Space*, 26(2): 195–211.

Dorling, D. (2013) What class are you? *Statistics Views*, 11 April. http://www.statisticsviews .com/details/feature/4582421/What-Class -Are-You.html

Dorling, D. (2014a) *Inequality and the 1%*. London: Verso.

Dorling, D. (2014b) *All That Is Solid: The Great Housing Disaster*. London: Allen Lane.

Dorling, D. (2017) *The Equality Effect*. Oxford: New Internationalist.

Dorling, D. (2018) *Peak Inequality: Britain's Ticking Timebomb*. Bristol: Policy Press.

Dorling, D., Rigby, J., Wheeler, B., Ballas, D., Thomas, B., Fahmy, E., Gordon, D., & Lupton, R. (2007) *Poverty, Wealth and Place in Britain, 1968 to 2005*. Bristol: Policy Press.

Dove, M. R. (2006) Indigenous people and environmental politics. *Annual Review of Anthropology*, 35: 191–208. https://doi. org/10.1146/annurev.anthro.35.081705 .123235

Dreher, T. (2017) The uncanny doubles of queer politics: Sexual citizenship in the era of same-sex marriage victories. *Sexualities*, 20(1–2): 176–95.

Duffy, M., Waitt, G., Gorman-Murray, A., & Gibson, C. (2011) Bodily rhythms: Corporeal capacities to engage with festival spaces. *Emotion, Space and Society*, 4(1): 17–24.

Duffy, M., Waitt, G., & Harada, T. (2016) Making sense of sound: Visceral sonic mapping as a research tool. *Emotions, Space and Society*, 20(1): 49–57.

Duggan, L. (2002) The new homonormativity: The sexual politics of neoliberalism. In R. Castronovo & D. D. Nelson (eds.), *Materializing Democracy: Toward a Revitalized Cultural Politics*, pp. 175–94. Durham, NC: Duke University Press.

Duggan, L. (2003) *The Twilight of Equality? Neoliberalism, Cultural Politics and the Attack on Democracy*. Boston: Beacon Press.

Dunn, K. (2004) Islam in Sydney: Contesting the discourse of absence. *Australian Geographer*, 25(3): 333–53.

Dunn, K. (2005) Repetitive and troubling discourses of nationalism in the local politics of mosque development in Sydney, Australia. *Environment and Planning D: Society and Space*, 23: 29–50.

Dupre, J. (2012) *Processes of Life: Essays in the Philosophy of Biology*. Oxford: Oxford University Press.

Dwyer, C. (1999) Veiled meanings: Young British Muslim women and the negotiation of differences. *Gender, Place & Culture*, 6(1): 5–26.

Dwyer, C. (2015) Photographing faith in Suburbia. *Cultural Geographies*, 22(3): 531–38.

Dwyer, C., & Bressey, C. (2008) *New Geographies of Race and Racism*. London: Routledge.

Dwyer, C., Shah, B., & Sanghera, G. (2008) From cricket lover to terror suspect – Challenging representations of young British Muslim men. *Gender, Place & Culture*, 15(2): 117–36.

Dyck, I. (2005) Feminist geography, the 'everyday', and local–global relations: Hidden spaces of place-making. *Canadian Geographer – Le Géographe canadien*, 49(3): 233–43.

Dyer, R. (1988) White. *Screen*, 29(4): 44–65.

Edensor, T. (2002) *National Identity, Popular Culture and Everyday Life.* Oxford: Berg.

Edensor, T. (2011) Commuter: Mobility, rhythm and commuting. In T. Cresswell & P. Merriman (eds.), *Geographies of Mobilities: Practices, Spaces, Subjects,* pp. 189–204. Farnham, UK: Ashgate.

Edensor, T. (ed.) (2016) *Geographies of Rhythm.* London: Routledge.

Edensor, T., & Millington, S. (2009) Illuminations, class identities and the contested landscapes of Christmas. *Sociology,* 43(1): 103–21.

Ehrkamp, P., & Nagel, C. (2012) Immigration, places of worship and the politics of citizenship in the US South. *Transactions of the Institute of British Geographers,* 37(4): 624–38.

Elden, S. (2007) Governmentality, calculation, territory. *Environment and Planning D: Society and Space,* 25: 562–80.

Elwood, S., Lawson, V., & Sheppard, E. (2016) Geographical relational poverty studies. *Progress in Human Geography,* 41(6): 745–65.

Elwood, S., & Leszczynski, A. (2011) Privacy, reconsidered: New representations, data practices and the geoweb. *Geoforum,* 42(1): 6–15.

Elwood, S., & Leszczynski, A. (2018) Feminist digital geographies. *Gender, Place & Culture,* 25(2): 1–16.

Engels, F. (1872/1997) *The Housing Question.* Moscow: Progress.

England, K. (1994) Getting personal: Reflexivity, positionality and feminist research. *Professional Geographer,* 46: 80–89.

England, K. (2010) Home, work and the shifting geographies of care. *Ethics, Place and Environment,* 13(2): 131–50.

England, M. (2008) When 'good neighbours' go bad: Territorial geographies of neighbourhood associations. *Environment and Planning A: Economy and Space,* 40: 2879–94.

Equality Act. (2010) London: Stationery Office. http://www.legislation.gov.uk/ukpga/2010/15/contents

Escárcega, S. (2010) Authenticating strategic essentialisms: The politics of Indigenousness at the United Nations. *Cultural Dynamics,* 22: 3–28. https://doi.org/10.1177/0921374010366780

Esping-Andersen, G. (1999) *Social Foundations of Postindustrial Economies.* Oxford: Oxford University Press.

European Commission. (2018) *Beyond GDP.* https://ec.europa.eu/newsroom/env/newsletter-specific-archive-issue.cfm?newsletter_service_id=300&pdf=true

Evans, A., & Miele, M. (2012) Between food and flesh: How animals are made to matter (and not matter) within food consumption practices. *Environment and Planning D: Society and Space,* 30: 298–314.

Evans, B. (2008) Geographies of youth/young people. *Geography Compass,* 2(5): 1659–80.

Evans, R. (2011) 'We are managing our own lives . . .': Life transition and care in sibling-headed households affected by AIDS in Tanzania and Uganda. *Area,* 43(4): 384–96.

Falah, G.-W., & Nagel, C. (2005) *Geographies of Muslim Women: Gender, Religion, and Space.* New York: Guidford Press.

FAO. (2013) *Food Wastage Footprint: Impacts on Natural Resources.* http://www.fao.org/3/i3347e/i3347e.pdf

Farbotko, C., Stratford, E., & Lazrus, H. (2016) Climate migrants and new identities? The geopolitics of embracing or rejecting mobility. *Social & Cultural Geography,* 17(4): 533–52.

Fawcett Society. (2017) *Close the Gender Gap.* https://www.fawcettsociety.org.uk/close-gender-pay-gap

Feldman, A. (2002) Making space at the nations' table: Mapping the transformative geographies of the international Indigenous peoples' movement. *Social Movement Studies,* 1: 31–46. https://doi.org/10.1080/14742830120118882

Ferreira, E., & Salvador, R. (2015) Lesbian collaborative web mapping: Disrupting heteronormativity in Portugal. *Gender, Place & Culture,* 22(7): 954–70.

Fincher, R., & Iveson, K. (2012) Justice and injustice in the city. *Geographical Research,* 50(3): 231–41.

Finlay, R. (2015) Narratives of belonging: The Moroccan diaspora in Granada, Spain. In A. Christou & E. Mavroudi (eds.), *Dismantling Diasporas: Rethinking the Geographies of Diasporic Identity, Connection and Development,* pp. 43–55. Farnham, UK: Ashgate.

Finlay, R. (2019) A diasporic right to the city: The production of a Moroccan diaspora space in Granada, Spain. *Social & Cultural Geography*, 20(6): 785–805.

Finlay, R., & Hopkins, P. (2020) Resistance and marginalisation: Islamophobia and the political participation of young Muslims in Scotland. *Social & Cultural Geography,* 21(4): 546–68. https://doi.org/10.1080/14649365.2019.1573436

Flowerdew, R., & Martin, D. (2005) *Methods in Human Geography: A Guide for Students Doing a Research Project.* Harlow, UK: Longman.

Forrest, R., & Yip, N. M. (eds.) (2012) *Young People and Housing: Transitions, Trajectories and Generational Fractures.* Oxford: Routledge.

Fotheringham, A. S., & Wong, D. W. S. (1991) The modifiable areal unit problem in multivariate statistical analysis. *Environment & Planning A: Economy and Space*, 23: 1025–44. https://doi.org/10.1068/a231025

Foucault, M. (1980) *Power/Knowledge: Selected Interviews and Other Writings 1972–1977*, ed. Colin Gordon. New York: Pantheon Press.

Foucault, M. (2004) *Security, Territory, Population: Lectures at the Collège de France 1977–78,* trans. Graham Burchell. London: Palgrave Macmillan.

Frantz, K., & Howitt, R. (2012) Geography for and with Indigenous peoples: Indigenous geographies as challenge and invitation. *GeoJournal*, 77: 727–31. https://doi.org/10.1007/s10708-010-9378-2

Freire, P. (1972) *Pedagogy of the Oppressed.* Harmondsworth, UK: Penguin.

Freund, P. (2001) Bodies, disability and spaces: The social model and disabling spatial organisations. *Disability & Society*, 16(5): 689–706.

Fritzsche, P. (2002) How nostalgia narrates modernity. In P. Fritzsche & A. Confino (eds.), *The Work of Memory: New Directions in the Study of German Society and Culture*, pp. 62–85. Champaign: University of Illinois Press.

Fuchs, C. (2011) New media, Web 2.0 and surveillance. *Sociology Compass*, 5: 134–47.

Fuglerud, O. (1999) *Life on the Outside: The Tamil Diaspora and Long-Distance Nationalism.* London: Pluto.

Fuller, D., & Kitchin, R. (eds.) (2004) *Radical Theory/Critical Praxis: Making a Difference beyond the Academy?* Kelowna, BC: Praxis E-Series.

Fussey, P. (2015) Command control and contestation: Negotiating security at the London 2012 Olympics. *Geographic Journal*, 181(1): 212–23.

Fyfe, N. (1991) The police, space and society: The geography of policing. *Progress in Human Geography*, 15(3): 249–67.

Fyfe, N. (2006) *Images of the Street: Planning Identity and Control in Public Space.* London: Routledge.

Fyfe, N., & Kenny, J. (2005) *The Urban Geography Reader.* New York: Routledge.

Gaertner, S. L., & Dovidio, J. F. (1986) *The Aversive Form of Racism.* San Diego, CA: Academic Press.

Gaete-Reyes, M. (2015) Citizenship and the embodied practice of wheelchair use. *Geoforum*, 64: 351–61.

Gale, R. (2007) The place of Islam in the geography of religion: Trends and Intersections. *Geography Compass*, 1(5): 1015–36.

Gale, R. (2013) Religious residential segregation and internal migration: The British Muslim case. *Environment and Planning A: Economy and Space*, 45(4): 872–91.

Gallagher, A. (2018) The business of care: Marketization and the new geographies of childcare. *Progress in Human Geography*, 42(5): 706–22.

Galton, F. (1889) *Natural Inheritance.* London: Macmillan.

Gandy, M. (2017) Urban atmospheres. *Cultural Geographies*, 24(3): 353–74.

Gao, Q., Duo, Y., & Zhu, H. (2018) Secularisation and resistant politics of sacred space in Guangzhou's ancestral temple, China. *Area*, 51(3): 570–77. doi:10.1111/area.12512

Gao, Q., Qian, J., & Yuan, Z. (2018) Multi-scaled secularization or postsecular present? Christianity and migrant workers in Shenzhen, China. *Cultural Geographies*, 25(4): 553–70.

Garcia-Ramon, M. D. (2003) Globalization and international geography: The questions of languages and scholarly traditions. *Progress in Human Geography*, 27(1): 1–5.

Garfinkel, H. (1967) *Studies in Ethnomethodology*. Englewood Cliffs, NJ: Prentice-Hall.

Garland-Thomson, R. (2011) Misfits: A feminist materialist disability concept. *Hypatia: A Journal of Feminist Philosophy*, 26(3): 591–609.

Gatrell, A., & Elliot, S. (2009) *Geographies of Health: An Introduction*. London: Wiley.

Gesler, W. M. (1992) Therapeutic landscapes: Medical issues in light of the new cultural geography. *Social Science & Medicine*, 34: 735–46. https://doi.org/10.1016/0277-9536(92)90360-3

Gibson, C. C., Ostrom, E., & Ahn, T.-K. (2000) The concept of scale and the human dimensions of global change: A survey. *Ecological Economics*, 32(2): 217–39.

Gieseking, J. J., & Mangold, W. (2014) *The People, Place and Space Reader*. New York: Routledge.

Gillespie, K., & Collard, R. (eds.) (2015) *Critical Animal Geographies: Politics, Intersections and Hierarchies in a Multispecies World*. Abingdon, UK: Routledge.

Gillespie, K., & Collard, R. (eds.) (2017) *Critical Animal Geographies: Politics, Intersections and Hierarchies in a Multispecies World*, 3rd ed. Abingdon, UK: Routledge.

Gilmore, R. (2007) *Golden Gulag: Prisons, Surplus, Crisis, and Opposition in Globalizing California*. Berkeley: University of California Press.

Glass, R. (1964) Aspects of change. In R. Glass et al. (eds.), *London: Aspects of Change*, pp. xiii–xlii. London: MacGibbon & Kee.

Gleeson, B. J. (1996) A geography for disabled people? *Transactions of the Institute of British Geographers*, 21(2): 387–96.

Gleeson, B. (1999) *Geographies of Disability*. London: Routledge.

Glick, J. (2008) Gentrification and the racialized geography of home equity. *Urban Affairs Review*, 44(2): 280–95.

Gløersen, E., Dubois, A., Copus, A., & Schürmann, C. (2006) Northern peripheral, sparsely populated regions in the European Union. Nordregio Report 2006: 2, Stockholm. http://norden.diva-portal.org/smash/get/diva2:700429/FULLTEXT01.pdf

Glucksberg, L. (2014) We was regenerated out: Regeneration, recycling and de-valuing communities. *Valuation Studies*, 2(2): 97–118.

Goffman, E. (1959) *The Presentation of Self in Everyday Life*. Garden City, NY: Doubleday.

Goffman, E. (1963) *Stigma: Notes on the Management of Spoiled Identity*. Englewood Cliffs, NJ: Prentice-Hall.

Gökarıksel, B. (2012) The intimate politics of secularism and the headscarf: The mall, the neighbourhood, and the public square in Istanbul. *Gender, Place & Culture*, 19(1): 1–20.

Gökarıksel, B., & Smith, S. (2017) Intersectional feminism beyond US flag hijab and pussy hats in Trump's America. *Gender, Place & Culture*, 24(5): 628–44.

Goldthorpe, J. H. (2014) The role of education in intergenerational social mobility: Problems from empirical research in sociology and some theoretical pointers from economics. *Rationality and Society*, 26(3): 265–89.

Gong, H., Hassink, R., & Maus, G. (2017) What does *Pokémon Go* teach us about geography? *Geographica Helvetica*, 72: 227–30.

Gonzalez, C. G. (2015) Environmental justice, human rights, and the Global South. *Santa Clara Journal of International Law*, 13: 151–95. https://digitalcommons.law.scu.edu/scujil/vol13/iss1/8/

González, S. (2006) Scalar narratives in Bilbao: A cultural politics of scales approach to the study of urban policy. *International Journal of Urban and Regional Research*, 30(4): 836–57.

Goode, J. P. (2017) Humming along: Public and private patriotism in Putin's Russia. In M. Skey & M. Antonsich (eds.), *Everyday Nationhood: Theorising Culture, Identity and Belonging after* Banal Nationalism, pp. 121–46. London: Palgrave Macmillan.

Goodley, D. (2001) Learning difficulties: The social model of disability and impairment: Challenging epistemologies. *Disability & Society*, 16(2): 207–31.

Gordon, C. (1991) Governmental rationality: An introduction. In G. Burchell, C. Gordon & P. Miller (eds.), *The Foucault Effect: Studies in Governmentality*, pp. 1–52. Chicago: University of Chicago Press.

Gorman-Murray, A., & Hopkins, P. (2014) *Masculinities and Place*. Farnham, UK: Ashgate.

Grabham, E. (2007) Citizen bodies, intersex citizenship. *Sexualities*, 10(1): 29–48.

Graham, M., Stephens, M., & Hale, S. (2015) Featured graphic: Mapping the geoweb – a geography of Twitter. *Environment and Planning A: Economy and Space*, 45(1): 100–102.

Graham, S. (2011) *Cities Under Siege: The New Military Urbanism*. London: Verso.

Graham, S. (2012) Olympics 2012 security: welcome to lockdown London. *City*, 16: 446–51.

Graham, S. (2015) Luxified skies: How vertical urban housing became an elite preserve. *City*, 19(5): 618–45.

Graham, S. (2016) *Vertical: The City from Satellites to Bunkers*. London: Verso.

Graham, S., & Marvin, S. (2001) *Splintering Urbanism: Networked Infrastructures, Technological Mobilities and the Urban Condition*. London: Routledge.

Grant, R., & Oteng-Ababio, M. (2012) Mapping the invisible and real 'African' economy: Urban e-waste circuitry. *Urban Geography*, 33(1): 1–21. https://doi.org/10.2747/0272-3638.33.1.1

Gregory, D. (1994) *Geographical Imaginations*. Cambridge, MA: Blackwell.

Gregory, R., Johnston, J. T., Pratt, G., Watts, M., & Whatmore, S. (2000) *Dictionary of Human Geography*. Oxford: Wiley-Blackwell.

Gregson, N. (1986) On duality and dualism: The case of structuration and time geography. *Progress in Human Geography*, 10(2): 184–205.

Gregson, N., & Rose, G. (2000) Taking Butler elsewhere: Performativities, spatialities and subjectivities. *Environment and Planning D: Society and Space*, 18(4): 433–52.

Grossman, J. (2018) Toward a definition of diaspora. *Ethnic and Racial Studies*, 42(8): 1263–82. https://doi.org/10.1080/01419870.2018.1550261

Grove, N. S. (2015) The cartographic ambiguities of HarassMap: Crowdmapping security and sexual violence in Egypt. *Security Dialogue*, 46(4): 345–64.

Grusky, D. B. (2018) *Social Stratification: Class, Race, and Gender in Sociological Perspective*. London: Routledge.

Gunaratnam, Y. (2003) *Researching 'Race' and Ethnicity: Methods, Knowledge and Power*. London: Sage.

Guthman, J. (2003) Fast food/organic food: Reflexive tastes and the making of 'yuppie chow'. *Social & Cultural Geography*, 4: 45–58.

Haboud, M. (2009) Ecuador Amazónico. In S. Inge (ed.), *Atlas sociolingüístico de pueblos indígenas en América Latina*, pp. 333–59. Cochabamba, Bolivia: FUNPROEIB Andes.

Hacking, I. (1990) *The Taming of Chance*. Cambridge: Cambridge University Press.

Hägerstrand, T. (1970) What about people in regional science. *Papers in Regional Science*, 24(1): 6–21.

Hägerstrand, T. (1982) Diorama, path and project. *Tijdschrift voor Economisch en Sociologisch Geografie*, 73(6): 323–39.

Hägerstrand, T. (2006) Foreword. In A. Buttimer & T. Mels (eds.), *By Northern Lights*, pp. xi–xiv. Aldershot, UK: Ashgate.

Haggett, P. (1965) *Locational Analysis in Human Geography*. London: Edward Arnold.

Hajjar, L. (2005) *Courting Conflict: The Israeli Military Court System in the West Bank and Gaza*. Berkeley: University of California Press.

Halfacree, K. (1993) Locality and social representation: Space, discourse and alternative definitions of the rural. *Journal of Rural Studies*, 9(1): 23–37.

Hall, E. (2005) The entangled geographies of social exclusion/inclusion for people with learning disabilities. *Health and Place*, 11(2): 107–15.

Hall, E., & Wilton, R. (2017) Towards a relational geography of disability. *Progress in Human Geography*, 41(6): 727–44.

Hall, S. (1983) Teaching race. *Early Child Development and Care*, 10(4): 259–74.

Hall, S., King, J., & Finlay, T. (2017) Migrant infrastructure: Transaction economies in Birmingham and Leicester, UK. *Urban Studies*, 54(6): 1311–27. https://doi.org/10.1177/0042098016634586

Hall, S. M. (2015) Everyday family experiences of the financial crisis: Getting by in the recent economic recession. *Journal of Economic Geography*, 16(2): 305–30.

Hall, S. M. (2018) Everyday austerity: Towards relational geographies of family, friendship and intimacy. *Progress in Human Geography*, 43(5): 769–89.

Hancock, A. M. (2016) *Intersectionality: An Intellectual History*. Oxford: Oxford University Press.

Hannah, M. (2001) Sampling and the politics of representation in the US Census 2000. *Environment and Planning D: Society and Space*, 19: 515–34.

Hansen, N., & Philo, C. (2007) The normality of doing things differently: Bodies, spaces and disability geography. *Tijdschifit voor Economische en Sociale Geografie*, 98(4): 493–506.

Hanson, S., & Pratt, G. (1995) *Gender, Work and Space*. London: Routledge.

Haraway, D. (1988) Situated knowledges: The science question in feminism and the privilege of partial perspective. *Feminist Studies*, 14(3): 575–99.

Haraway, D. (2007) *When Species Meet*. Minneapolis: University of Minnesota Press.

Harding, A., & Blokland, T. (2014) *Urban Theory: A Critical Introduction to Power, Cities and Urbanism in the 21st Century*. London: Sage.

Harding, S. G. (2004) *The Feminist Standpoint Theory Reader: Intellectual and Political Controversies*. New York: Routledge.

Harley, J. B. (1989) Deconstructing the map. *Cartographica*, 26(1): 1–20.

Harper, S. (2005) *Ageing Societies*. London: Hodder.

Harper, S., & Laws, G. (1995) Rethinking the geography of ageing. *Progress in Human Geography*, 19: 199–221.

Harvard, S. (2013) *The Mediatization of Culture and Society*. London: Routledge.

Harvey, D. (1973) *Social Justice and the City*. Baltimore, MD: Johns Hopkins University Press.

Harvey, D. (1989) *The Condition of Postmodernity: An Inquiry into the Origins of Cultural Change*. Oxford: Blackwell.

Harvey, D. (1996) *Justice, Nature and the Geography of Difference*. Cambridge, MA: Blackwell.

Harvey, D. (2005) *A Brief History of Neoliberalism*. Oxford: Oxford University Press.

Harvey, D. (2010) *A Companion to Marx's Capital*. London: Verso.

Hawe, P., & Shiell, A. (2000) Social capital and health promotion: A review. *Social Science & Medicine*, 51(6): 871–85.

Hay, I. (2016) *Qualitative Research Methods in Human Geography*. Oxford: Oxford University Press.

Hayles, N. K. (1999) *How We Became Posthuman*. Chicago: University of Chicago Press.

Hayles, N. K. (2012) *How We Think*. Chicago: University of Chicago Press.

Hemming, P. (2007) Renegotiating the primary school: Children's emotional geographies of sport, exercise and active play. *Children's Geographies*, 5(4): 353–71.

Hemming, P. (2011) Meaningful encounters? Religion and social cohesion in the English primary school. *Social & Cultural Geography*, 12(1): 63–81.

Henderson, S., Holland, J., McGrellis, S., Sharpe, S., & Thomson, R. (2007) *Inventing Adulthoods: A Biographical Approach to Youth Transitions*. London: Sage.

Hepple, L. W. (2001) Multiple regression and spatial policy analysis: George Udny Yule and the origins of statistical social science. *Environment and Planning D: Society and Space*, 19: 385–407.

Herbert, D. T., & Thomas, C. J. (1998) School performance, league tables and social geography. *Applied Geography*, 18(3): 199–223.

Herbert, S. (1997) Territoriality and the police. *Professional Geographer*, 49(1): 86–94.

Herbert, S., & Brown, E. (2006) Conceptions of space and crime in the punitive neoliberal city. *Antipode*, 38(4): 755–77.

Herman, A., Goodman, M., & Sage, C. (2018) Six questions for food justice. *Local Environment*, 23(11): 1075–89.

Hildebrandt, M. (2013) Slaves to big data. Or are we? Keynote address to 9th Annual Conference on Internet, Law & Politics, 25 June. https://works.bepress.com/mireille_hildebrandt/52/

Hitchen, E. (2019) The affective life of austerity: Uncanny atmospheres and paranoid temporalities. *Social & Cultural Geography*, online. https://doi.org/10.1080/14649365.2019.1574884

Hochschild, A. R. (1997) *The Time Bind: When Work Becomes Home and Home Becomes Work*. New York: Henry Holt.

Hochschild, A. R. (2003) *The Commercialisation of Intimate Life*. Berkeley: University of California Press.

Hochschild, A. R. (2012) *The Outsourced Self*. New York: Metropolitan Books.

Hockey, J., & James, A. (2003) *Social Identities across the Life Course*. New York: Palgrave Macmillan.

Hocknell, S. (2016) Chewing the fat: Unpacking distasteful encounters. *Gastronomica*, 16(3): 13–18.

Hocknell, S., & MacAllister, L. (2020) A sticky situation? Fatty distaste and the embodied performances of class. In E. Falconer (ed.), *Space, Taste and Affect: Atmospheres That Shape How We Eat*. London: Routledge.

Hodkinson, S. (2012) The new urban enclosures. *City*, 16(5): 500–518.

Hoggart, K. (1990) Let's do away with rural. *Journal of Rural Studies*, 6: 245–57.

Hoggart, K., Davies, A., & Lees, L. (2002) *Researching Human Geography*. London: Arnold.

Holdaway, S. (1983) *Inside the British Police: A Force at Work*. Oxford: Basil Blackwell.

Holdsworth, C. (2006) 'Don't you think you're missing out, living at home?': Student experiences and residential transitions. *Sociological Review*, 54: 495–519.

Holdsworth, C. (2009) Between two worlds: Local students in higher education and 'scouse'/student identities. *Population, Space and Place*, 15: 225–37.

Holdsworth, C. (2010) Why volunteer? Understanding motivations for student volunteering. *British Journal of Educational Studies*, 58(4): 421–37.

Holdsworth, C., & Morgan, D. (2005) *Transitions in Context: Leaving Home, Independence and Adulthood*. Berkshire, UK: Open University Press.

Holifield, R. (2015) Environmental justice and political ecology. In T. Perreault, G. Bridge & J. McCarthy (eds.), *The Routledge Handbook of Political Ecology*, pp. 585–97. Oxford: Routledge.

Holifield, R., Porter, M., & Walker, G. (2009) Introduction: Spaces of environmental justice: Frameworks for critical engagement. *Antipode*, 41(4): 591–612. https://doi.org/10.1111/j.1467-8330.2009.00690.x

Holifield, R., Porter, M., & Walker, G. (2011) *Spaces of Environmental Justice*. Oxford: John Wiley & Sons.

Hollibaugh, A., & Weiss, M. (2015) Queer precarity and the myth of gay affluence. *New Labor Forum*, 24(3): 18–27.

Holloway, J. (2003) Make believe: Spiritual practice, embodiment and sacred space. *Environment and Planning A: Economy and Space*, 35(11): 1961–74.

Holloway, L., & Hubbard, P. (2001) *People and Place: The Extraordinary Geographies of Everyday Life*. Harlow, UK: Prentice-Hall.

Holloway, S. L., Hubbard, P., Jöns, H., & Pimlott-Wilson, H. (2010) Geographies of education and the significance of children, youth and families. *Progress in Human Geography*, 34(5): 583–600.

Holloway, S. L., & Valentine, G. (2000) *Children's Geographies: Playing, Living, Learning*. London: Routledge.

Holmes, B. (2004) Drifting through the grid: Psychogeography and imperial infrastructure. https://www.scribd.com/document/57872191/Brian-Holmes-Drifting-Through-the-Grid

Holt, L. (2004) Children with mind-body differences: Performing disability in primary school classrooms. *Children's Geographies*, 2(2): 219–36.

Holt, L. (2007) Children's sociospatial (re)production of disability within primary school playgrounds. *Environment and Planning D: Society and Space*, 25(5): 783–802.

Holt, L. (2010) Young people's embodied social capital and performing disability. *Children's Geographies*, 8(1): 25–37.

Holt, L., Bowlby, S., & Lea, J. (2017) Everyone knows me. . . . I sort of like move about: The friendships and encounters of young people with special educational needs in different school settings. *Environment and Planning A: Economy and Space*, 49(6): 1361–78.

Holton, M., & Riley, M. (2013) Student geographies: Exploring the diverse geographies of students and higher education. *Geography Compass*, 7(1): 61–74.

Holton, M., & Riley, M. (2016) Student geographies and homemaking: Personal belonging(s) and identities. *Social & Cultural Geography*, 17(5): 623–45.

hooks, b. (1981) *Ain't I a Woman: Black Women and Feminism.* New York: Routledge.

Hopkins, P. (2006a) Youthful Muslim masculinities: Gender and generational relations. *Transactions of the Institute of British Geographers,* 31(3): 337–52.

Hopkins, P. (2006b) Youth transitions and going to university: The perceptions of students attending a geography summer school access programme. *Area,* 38(3): 240–47.

Hopkins, P. (2007a) 'Blue squares', 'proper' Muslims and transnational networks: Narratives of national and religious identities amongst young Muslim men living in Scotland. *Ethnicities,* 7(1): 61–81.

Hopkins, P. (2007b) Global events, national politics, local lives: Young Muslim men in Scotland. *Environment and Planning A: Economy and Space,* 39: 1119–33.

Hopkins, P. (2007c) Young people, masculinities, religion and race: New social geographies. *Progress in Human Geography,* 10(8): 811–19.

Hopkins, P. (2009) Women, men, positionalities and emotion: Doing feminist geographies of religion. *ACME: An International E-journal for Critical Geographies,* 8(1): 1–17.

Hopkins, P. (2010) *Young People, Place and Identity.* London: Routledge.

Hopkins, P. (2011) Multiple, marginalised, passé or politically engaged? Some reflections on the current place of social geographies. *Social & Cultural Geography,* 12(6) 533–38.

Hopkins, P. (2014) Managing strangerhood: Young Sikh men's strategies. *Environment and Planning A: Economy and Space,* 46(7): 1572–85.

Hopkins, P. (2015) Young people and the Scottish independence referendum. *Political Geography,* 46: 91–92.

Hopkins, P. (2016) Gendering Islamophobia, racism and white supremacy: Gendered violence against those who look Muslim. *Dialogues in Human Geography,* 8(2): 186–89.

Hopkins, P. (ed.) (2017) *Scotland's Muslims: Society, Politics and Identity.* Edinburgh: Edinburgh University Press.

Hopkins, P. (2019) Social geography I: Intersectionality. *Progress in Human Geography,* 43(5): 937–47. https://doi.org/10.1177/0309132517743677

Hopkins, P., Botterill, K., Sanghera, G., & Arshad, R. (2017) Encountering misrecognition: Being mistaken for being Muslim. *Annals of the American Association of Geographers,* 107(4): 934–48.

Hopkins, P., & Gale, R. (eds.) (2009) *Muslims in Britain: Race, Place and Identities.* Edinburgh: Edinburgh University Press.

Hopkins, P., & Gorman-Murray, A. (2019) Masculinities and geography, moving forward: Men's bodies, emotions and spiritualities. *Gender, Place & Culture,* 26(3): 301–14.

Hopkins, P., & Noble, G. (2009) Masculinities in place: Situated identities, relations and intersectionality. *Social & Cultural Geography,* 10(8): 811–19.

Hopkins, P., Olson. E., Pain, R., & Vincett, G. (2011) Mapping intergenerationalities in the formation of young people's religious identities. *Transactions of the Institute of British Geographers,* 36(2): 314–27.

Hopkins, P., & Pain, R. (2007) Geographies of age: Thinking relationally. *Area,* 39(3): 287–94.

Hopkins, P., Todd, L., & Newcastle Occupation. (2012) Occupying Newcastle University: Student resistance to government spending cuts in England. *Geographical Journal,* 18(2): 104–9.

Horschelmann, K., & Van Blerk, L. (2011) *Children, Youth and the City.* London: Routledge.

Horton, J., & Kraftl, P. (2005) For more-than-usefulness: Six overlapping points about children's geographies. *Children's Geographies,* 3: 131–43.

Horton, J., & Kraftl, P. (2013) *Cultural Geographies: An Introduction.* London: Routledge.

Houston, D., & Pulido, L. (2002) The work of performativity: Staging social justice at the University of Southern California. *Environment and Planning D: Society and Space,* 20(4): 401–24.

Hovorka, A. J. (2015) The *Gender, Place and Culture* Jan Monk Distinguished Annual Lecture: Feminism and animals: Exploring interspecies relations through intersectionality, performativity and standpoint. *Gender, Place & Culture,* 22(1): 1–19.

Howell, A. (2018) Forget 'militarization': race, disability and the 'martial politics' of the police and of the university. *International Feminist Journal of Politics*, 20(2): 117–36.

Howitt, R. (1998) Scale as relation: Musical metaphors of geographical scale. *Area*, 30(1): 49–58.

Howitt, R., & Stevens, S. (2010) Cross-cultural research: Ethics, methods, and relationships. In I. Hay (ed.), *Qualitative Research Methods in Human Geography*. Oxford: Oxford University Press.

Hubbard, P. (2008) Here, there, everywhere: The ubiquitous geographies of heteronormativity. *Geography Compass*, 2(3): 640–58.

Hubbard, P. (2013) Kissing is not a universal right: Sexuality, law and the scales of citizenship. *Geoforum*, 49: 224–32.

Huxley, M. (2007) Geographies of governmentality. In J. W. Crampton & S. Elden (eds.), *Space, Knowledge and Power: Foucault and Geography*, pp. 185–204. Aldershot, UK: Ashgate.

Hyams, M. (2004) Hearing girls' silences: Thoughts on the politics and practices of a feminist method of group discussion. *Gender, Place & Culture*, 11(1): 105–19.

Imrie, R. (1996) *Disability and the City*. London: Chapman.

Imrie, R. (2012a) Universalism, universal design and equitable access to the built environment. *Disability and Rehabilitation*, 34(10): 873–82.

Imrie, R. (2012b) Auto-disabilities: The case of shared space environments. *Environment and Planning A: Economy and Space*, 44(9): 2260–77.

Imrie, R., & Edwards, C. (2007) The geographies of disability: Reflections on the development of a sub-discipline. *Geography Compass*, 1(3): 623–40.

IPCC. (2018) *Special Report 15 on Global Warming of 1.5°C*. Intergovernmental Panel on Climate Change.

Irigaray, L. (2008) *Sharing the World*. London: Continuum.

Isin, E. F. (ed.) (2013) *Democracy, Citizenship and the Global City*. London: Routledge.

Jackson, P. (1981) Phenomenology and social geography. *Area*, 13(4): 299–305.

Jackson, P. (1994) Black male: Advertising and the cultural politics of masculinity. *Gender, Place & Culture*, 1(1): 49–59.

Jackson, T. (2016) *Prosperity without Growth: Foundations for the Economy of Tomorrow*. London: Routledge.

Jacobs, J. (1961) *The Death and Life of Great American Cities*. New York: Random House.

Jacobs, M. D. (2005) Maternal colonialism: White women and Indigenous child removal in the American West and Australia, 1880–1940. *Western Historical Quarterly*, 36: 453–76. https://doi.org/10.2307/25443236

James, A. (2017) *Work-Life Advantage: Sustaining Regional Learning and Innovation*. Oxford: Wiley-Blackwell.

James, A., Jenks, C., & Prout, A. (2001) *Theorizing Childhood*. Cambridge: Polity Press.

Jarvis, H. (1999) The tangled webs we weave: Household strategies to co-ordinate home and work. *Work, Employment and Society*, 13(2): 225–47.

Jarvis, H. (2005) *Work/Life City Limits*. Basingstoke, UK: Palgrave Macmillan.

Jarvis, H. (2017) Sharing, togetherness and intentional degrowth. *Progress in Human Geography*, 43(2): 256–75.

Jarvis, H., Cloke, J., & Kantor, P. (2009) *Cities and Gender*. Oxford: Routledge.

Jarvis, M., & Wardle, J. (2006) Social patterning of individual health behaviours: The case of cigarette smoking. In M. Marmot & R. Wilkinson (eds.), *The Social Determinants of Health*, pp. 224–37. Oxford: Oxford University Press.

Jeffrey, A. (2016) Geography of justice. *Oxford Bibliography*. http://www.oxfordbibliographies.com/view/document/obo-9780199874002/obo-9780199874002-0055.xml

Jensen, L. (2006) New immigrant settlements in rural America: Problems, prospects and policies. *Reports on Rural America*, 1(3).

Johansen, E. (2008) Imaging the global and the rural: Rural cosmopolitanism in Sharon Butala's *The Garden of Eden* and Amitav Ghosh's *The Hungry Tide*. *Postcolonial Text*, 4(3): 1–18.

Johnson, J. T., Cant, G., Howitt, R., & Peters, E. (2007) Creating anti-colonial geographies: Embracing Indigenous peoples knowledges and rights. *Geographical Research*, 45: 117–20. https://doi.org/10.1111/j.1745-5871.2007.00441.x

Johnson, M. (2011) Reconciliation, Indigeneity, and postcolonial nationhood in settler states. *Postcolonial Studies*, 14: 187–201. https://doi.org/10.1080/13688790.2011.563457

Johnston, C., & Pratt, G. (2019) *Migration in Performance: Crossing the Colonial Present.* London: Routledge.

Johnston, L. (2007) Mobilising pride/shame: Lesbians, tourism and parades. *Social & Cultural Geography*, 8(1) 29–45.

Johnston, L. (2015) Gender and sexuality I: Genderqueer geographies? *Progress in Human Geography*, 50(5): 668–78.

Johnston, L. (2018a) *Transforming Gender, Sex, and Place: Gender Variant Geographies.* London: Routledge.

Johnston, L. (2018b) Gender and sexuality III: Precarious places. *Progress in Human Geography*, 42(6): 928–36. doi:10.1177/0309132517731256

Johnston, R. J., Gregory, D., Pratt, G., & Watts, M. (2000) *Dictionary of Human Geography.* Oxford: Blackwell.

Jonas, A. E. G., McCann, E., & Thomas, M. (2015) *Urban Geography: A Critical Introduction.* Oxford: John Wiley & Sons.

Jones, C. (2015) Frames of law: Targeting advice and operational law in the Israeli military. *Environment and Planning D: Society and Space*, 33(4): 676–96.

Jones, E., & Eyles, J. (1977) *An Introduction to Social Geography.* Oxford: Oxford University Press.

Jones, S. (2013) Great British Class Survey finds seven social classes in the UK. *Guardian*, 3 April. https://www.theguardian.com/society/2013/apr/03/great-british-class-survey-seven

Jopling, M. (2019) Is there a north–south divide between schools in England? *Management in Education*, 33(1): 37–40.

Jou, S.-C., Clark, E., & Chen, H.-W. (2016) Gentrification and revanchist urbanism in Taipei? *Urban Studies*, 53(3): 560–76.

Joyce, P. (2003) *The Rule of Freedom: Liberalism and the Modern City.* London: Verso.

Jupp, E., Pykett, J., & Smith, F. M. (eds.) (2017) *Emotional States: Sites and Spaces of Affective Governance.* London: Routledge.

Kahn, R., & Kellner, D. (2004) New media and internet activism: From the Battle of Seattle to blogging. *New Media and Society*, 6: 87–95.

Kaptani, E., & Yuval-Davis, N. (2008) Participatory theatre as a research methodology: Identity, performance and social action among refugees. *Sociological Research Online*, 13(5).

Karla, V. S., Kaur, R., & Hutnyk, J. (2005) *Diaspora and Hybridity.* London: Sage.

Karp, D. A., Stone, G. P., & Yoels, W. C. (1991) *Being Urban: A Sociology of City Life*, 2nd ed. New York: Praeger.

Kärrholm, M. (2009) To the rhythm of shopping: On synchronisation in urban landscapes of consumption. *Social & Cultural Geography*, 10(4): 421–40.

Katz, C. (2001) Vagabond capitalism and the necessity of social reproduction. *Antipode*, 33(4): 709–28.

Katz, C. (2004) *Growing up Global: Economic Restructuring and Children's Everyday Lives.* Minneapolis: University of Minnesota Press.

Kenna, T. (2011) Studentification in Ireland? Analysing the impacts of students and student accommodation on Cork City. *Irish Geography*, 22(2–3): 191–213.

Kershaw, B. (2000) Performance, community and culture. In L. Goodman & J. De Gay (eds.), *The Routledge Reader in Politics and Performance*, pp. 136–42. London: Routledge.

Kesby, M. (2000) Participatory diagramming as a means to improve communication about sex in rural Zimbabwe: A pilot study. *Social Science and Medicine*, 50(12): 1723–41.

Kesby, M. (2007) Methodological insights on and from *Children's Geographies*. *Children's Geographies*, 5(3): 193–205.

Keul, A. (2013) Embodied encounters between humans and gators. *Social & Cultural Geography*, 14(8): 930–53.

Khaw, K., Wareham, N., Bingham, S., Welch, A., Luben, R., & Day, N. (2008) Combined impact of health behaviours and mortality in men and women: The EPIC-Norfolk prospective population study. *Plos Medicine*, 5(3): 39–47.

Kidson, M., & Norris, E. (2014) Implementing the London Challenge. https://www.instituteforgovernment.org.uk/sites/default/files/publications/Implementing%20the%20London%20Challenge%20-%20final_0.pdf

Kindon, S. (2003) Participatory video in geographic research: A feminist way of looking? *Area*, 35(2): 142–53.

Kindon, S., Pain, R., & Kesby, M. (2007) *Connecting People, Participation and Place: Participatory Action Research Approaches and Methods*. London: Routledge.

King, M. L. (1963) Letter from a Birmingham jail. 16 April. Martin Luther King, Jr. Research and Education Institute, Stanford University. https://kinginstitute.stanford.edu/king-papers/documents/letter-birmingham-jail

King, R. (2012a) Geography and migration studies: Retrospect and prospect. *Population, Space and Place,* 18(2): 134–53.

King, R. (2012b) Theories and typologies of migration: An overview and a primer. Working Paper. Malmö University. https://www.mah.se/upload/Forskningscentrum/MIM/WB/WB%203.12.pdf

Kinsley, S. (2013) Beyond the screen: Methods of investigating geographies of life 'online'. *Geography Compass*, 7(8): 540–55.

Kirby, V. (1992) Addressing essentialism differently: Some thoughts on the corpo-real. Occasional Paper Series, 4. University of Waikato, Department of Women's Studies.

Kitchen, V., & Rygiel, R. (2014) Privatizing security, securitizing policing: The case of the G20 in Toronto, Canada. *International Political Sociology,* 8: 201–17.

Kitchin, R. (1998) Towards geographies of cyberspace. *Progress in Human Geography*, 22: 385–406.

Kitchin, R. (2007) *Mapping Worlds: International Perspectives on Social and Cultural Geographies*. London: Taylor & Francis.

Kitchin, R. (2013) Big data and human geography: Opportunities, challenges and risks. *Dialogues in Human Geography*, 3(3): 262–67.

Kitchin, R. (2014) Big data, new epistemologies and paradigm shifts. *Big Data & Society*, 1(1): 1–12.

Kitchin, R., & Dodge, M. (2011) *Code/Space: Software and Everyday Life*. Cambridge, MA: MIT Press.

Kitchin, R., Lauriault, T. P., & Wilson, M. W. (2017) *Understanding Spatial Media*. London: Sage.

Kitossa, T. (2000) Same difference: Biocentric imperialism and the assault on Indigenous culture and hunting. *Environments*, 28: 23–36.

Klauser, F. (2010) Splintering spheres of security: Peter Sloterdijk and the contemporary fortress city. *Environment and Planning D: Society and Space*, 28(2): 326–40.

Kleine, D. (2013) *Technologies of Choice? ICTs, Development and the Capabilities Approach*. Cambridge, MA: MIT Press.

Knox, P., & McCarthy, L. (2012) *Urbanization: An Introduction to Urban Geography*, 3rd ed. Cambridge: Pearson.

Knox, P., & McCarthy, L. (2014) *Urbanization: An Introduction to Urban Geography*, new international ed. Cambridge: Pearson.

Knox, P., & Pinch, S. (2009) *Urban Social Geography: An Introduction*. London: Routledge.

Kobayashi, A. (1994) Coloring the field: Gender, 'race', and the politics of fieldwork. *Professional Geographer*, 45(1): 73–80.

Kobayashi, A. (2010) GPC ten years on: Is self-reflexivity enough? *Gender, Place & Culture*, 10(4): 345–49.

Kobayashi, A., & Peake, L. (1994) Unnatural discourse: 'Race' and gender in geography. *Gender, Place & Culture*, 1(2): 225–43.

Kobayashi, A., & Peake, L. (2000) Racism out of place: Thoughts on whiteness and an antiracist geography in the new millennium. *Annals of the Association of American Geographers*, 90(2): 392–402.

Koefoed, L., & Simonsen, K. (2011) 'The stranger', the city and the nation: On the possibilities of identification and belonging. *European Urban and Regional Studies*, 18(4): 343–57.

Kong, L. (1990) Geography and religion: Trends and prospects. *Progress in Human Geography*, 14: 355–71.

Kong, L. (1999) Cemeteries and columbaria, memorials and mausoleums: Narrative and interpretation in the study of deathscapes in geography. *Australian Geographical Studies*, 37(1): 1–10.

Kong, L. (2001) Mapping 'new' geographies of religion: Politics and poetics in modernity. *Progress in Human Geography*, 25: 211–33.

Kong, L. (2010) Global shifts, theoretical shifts: Changing geographies of religion. *Progress in Human Geography*, 34(6): 755–76.

Korn, M. (2019) Advance publications to buy plagiarism-scanning company Turnitin for nearly $1.75 billion. *Wall Street Journal*, 6 March. https://www.wsj.com/articles/advance-publications-nearing-deal-to-buy-plagiarism-scanning-company-turnitin-for-1-75-billion-11551887268

Krieger, N. (2003) Theories for social epidemiology in the twenty-first century: An ecosocial perspective. In R. Hofrichter (ed.), *Health and Social Justice: Politics, Ideology, and Inequity in the Distribution of Disease – a Public Health Reader*, pp. 428–50. San Francisco: Jossey-Bass.

Krivokapic-Skoko, B., Reid, C., & Collins, J. (2018) Rural cosmopolitanism in Australia. *Journal of Rural Studies*, 64: 153–63. doi:10.1016/j.jrurstud.2018.01.014

Kulpa, R., & Silva, J. M. (2016) Decolonizing queer epistemologies: Section introduction. In G. Brown & K. Browne (eds.), *The Routledge Research Companion to Geographies of Sex and Sexualities*, pp. 139–42. London: Routledge.

Kurtz, H. E. (2003) Scale frames and counter-scale frames: Constructing the problem of environmental injustice. *Political Geography*, 22 (8): 887–916. https://doi.org/10.1016/J.POLGEO.2003.09.001

Kusters, A. (2017) When transport becomes a destination: Deaf spaces and networks on the Mumbai suburban trains. *Journal of Cultural Geography*, 34(2): 170–93.

Kuznets, S. (1955) Economic growth and income inequality. *American Economic Review*, 45(March): 1–28.

LaGarde, C. (2013) A new global economy for a new generation. Speech given in Davos, Switzerland, 23 January.

Lakner, C., & Milanovic, B. (2016) Global income distribution: From the fall of the Berlin Wall to the Great Recession. *World Bank Economic Review*, 30(2): 203–32.

Lakshman, R., McConville, A., How, S., Flowers, J., Wareham, N., & Cosford, P. (2011) Association between area-level socioeconomic deprivation and a cluster of behavioural risk factors: Cross-sectional, population-based study. *Journal of Public Health*, 33(2): 234–45.

Laslett, B., & Brenner, J. (1989) Gender and social reproduction: Historical perspectives. *Annual Review of Sociology*, 15: 381–404.

Latham, A. (2003) Research, performance, and doing human geography: Some reflections on the diary-photograph, diary-interview method. *Environment and Planning A: Economy and Space*, 35(11): 1993–2017.

LaTouche, S. (2004) Degrowth economics. *Monde Diplomatique*, 11.

Latour, B. (1993) *We Have Never Been Modern*. Cambridge, MA: Harvard University Press.

Laurier, E. (2009) Ethnomethodology/ethno methodological geographies. In N. Thrift & R. Kitchin (eds.), *International Encyclopedia of Human Geography*, pp. 632–37. Amsterdam: Elsevier.

Laurier, E., & Philo, C. (2006) Possible geographies: A passing encounter in a café. *Area*, 38(4): 353–63.

Lawn, P., Kubiszewski, I., Costanza, R., Franco, C., Talberth, J., Jackson, T., & Aylmer, C. (2013) Beyond GDP: Measuring and achieving global genuine progress. *Ecological Economics*, 93: 57–68. https://doi.org/10.1016/j.ecolecon.2013.04.019

Lawrence, R., & Adams, M. (2005) First Nations and the politics of Indigeneity: Australian perspectives on Indigenous peoples, resource management and global rights. *Australian Geographer*, 36: 257–65. https://doi.org/10.1080/00049180500150035

Laws, G. (1995) Theorizing ageism: Lessons from feminism and postmodernism. *Gerontologist*, 35: 112–18.

Lawson, V. A. (1998) Hierarchical households and gendered migration in Latin America: Feminist extensions to migration research. *Progress in Human Geography*, 22(1): 39–53.

Lea, J. (2008) Retreating to nature: Rethinking 'therapeutic landscapes'. *Area*, 40(1): 90–98.

Lea, J., Cadman, L., & Philo, C. (2015) Changing the habits of a lifetime? Mindfulness meditation and habitual geographies. *Cultural Geographies*, 22(1): 49–65.

Lee, E. S. (1966) A theory of migration. *Demography*, 3(1): 47–57. doi:10.2307/2060063

Lee, J. (2012) A big fat fight: The case for fat activism. *Conversation*, 22 June. https://

theconversation.com/a-big-fat-fight-the
-case-for-fat-activism-7743

Lee, W. L. M. (1901) *A History of Police in England*. London: Methuen.

Lees, L., Slater, T., & Wyly, E. (2013) *Gentrification*. London: Routledge.

Lefebvre, H. (1992/1974) *The Production of Space*, trans. D. N. Smith. Oxford: Basil Blackwell.

Lefebvre, H. (2004) *Rhythmanalysis: Space, Time and Everyday Life*, trans. S. Elden & G. Moore. London: Continuum.

LeGates, R., & Stout, S. (2011) *The City Reader*, 5th ed. New York: Routledge.

Leib, J. (2011) Identity, banal nationalism, contestation, and North American license plates. *Geographical Review*, 101: 37–52.

Leitner, H. (2012) Spaces of encounters: Immigration, race, class and the politics of belonging in small-town America. *Annals of the Association of American Geographers*, 102(4): 828–46.

Lemke, T. (2002) Foucault, governmentality, and critique. *Rethinking Marxism*, 14(3): 49–64.

Lennox, C., & Waites, M. (2013) *Human Rights, Sexual Orientation and Gender Identity in the Commonwealth: Struggles for Decriminalisation and Change*. Human Rights Consortium, Institute of Commonwealth Studies, School of Advanced Study, University of London.

Lepawsky, J. (2015) The changing geography of global trade in electronic discards: Time to think the e-waste problem. *Geographical Journal*, 181(2): 147–59.

Leurs, K. (2017) Feminist data studies: Using digital methods for ethical, reflexive and situated socio-cultural research. *Feminist Review*, 115: 130–54.

Lewis, J. (2009) *Work-Family Balance, Gender and Policy*. Cheltenham, UK: Edward Elgar.

Ley, D. (1983) *A Social Geography of the City*. New York: Harper and Row.

Ley, D. (2008) The immigrant church as urban service hub. *Urban Studies*, 45(10): 2057–74.

Leyshon, M. (2008) 'We're stuck in the corner': Young women, embodiment and drinking in the countryside. *Drugs: Education, Prevention and Policy*, 15(3): 267–89.

Lichterman, P. (2002) Seeing structure happen: Theory-driven participant observation. In B. Klandermans & S. Staggenborg (eds.), *Methods of Social Movement Research*, pp. 118–45. Minneapolis: University of Minnesota Press.

Limb, M., & Dwyer, C. (2001) *Qualitative Methodologies for Geographers: Issues and Debates*. London: Hodder Arnold.

Listerborn, C. (2015) Geographies of the veil: Violent encounters in urban public spaces in Malmö, Sweden. *Social & Cultural Geography*, 16(1): 95–115.

Litt, J., Tran, N., & Burke, T. (2002) Examining urban brownfields through the public health macroscope. *Environmental Health Perspectives*, 110(2): 183–93.

Little, J. (2014) Society-space. In P. Cloke, P. Crang & M. Goodwin (eds.), *Introducing Human Geographies*, pp. 23–36. London: Routledge.

Liu, C., Yang, R., & Xue, D. (2018) Chinese Muslims' daily food practices and their geographies of encounter in urban Guangzhou. *Social & Cultural Geography*, online first. https://doi.org/10.1080/14649365.2018.1550583

Liu, Y., Li, Z., & Liu, Y. (2015) Growth of rural migrant enclaves in Guangzhou, China: Agency, everyday practice and social mobility. *Urban Studies*, 52(16): 3086–3105.

Liverman, D. M. (2018) Geographic perspectives on development goals: Constructive engagements and critical perspectives on the MDGs and the SDGs. *Dialogues in Human Geography*, 8: 168–85. https://doi.org/10.1177/2043820618780787

Logan, J. (1988) Fiscal and developmental crises in black suburbs. In S. Cummings (ed.), *Business Elites and Urban Development*, pp. 333–56. Albany: State University of New York Press.

London Health Observatory. (2012) *Health Inequalities Overview*. London: London Health Observatory.

Longhurst, R. (1994) The geography closest in – The body . . . the politics of pregnability. *Australian Geographical Studies*, 32(2): 214–23.

Longhurst, R. (2000) 'Corporeographies' of pregnancy: 'Bikini babes'. *Environment and Planning D: Society and Space*, 18: 453–72.

Longhurst, R. (2001) *Bodies: Exploring Fluid Boundaries*. London: Routledge.

Longhurst, R. (2004) *Bodies: Exploring Fluid Boundaries*. Hoboken, NY: Taylor & Francis.

Longhurst, R. (2005) Fat bodies: Developing geographical research agendas. *Progress in Human Geography*, 29: 247–59.

Longhurst, R. (2011) Becoming smaller: Autobiographical spaces of weight loss. *Antipode*, 44(3): 871–88.

Longhurst, R. (2017) *Skype: Bodies, Screens, Space*. London: Routledge.

Longhurst, R., & Johnston, L. (2014) Bodies, Gender, Place & Culture: 21 years on. *Gender, Place & Culture*, 21(3): 267–78.

Lopez Pila, E. (2014) 'We don't lie and cheat like the Collas do': Highland–lowland regionalist tensions and Indigenous identity politics in Amazonian Bolivia. *Critique of Anthropology*, 34: 429–49. https://doi.org/10.1177/0308275 X14543393

Lorimer, H. (2005) Cultural geography: The busyness of being 'more-than-representational'. *Progress in Human Geography*, 29(1): 83–94.

Lorimer, H. (2013) Human/non-human. In P. J. Cloke, P. Crang & M. Goodwin (eds.), *Introducing Human Geographies*, pp. 37–50. Oxford: Routledge.

Lorimer, J. (2012) Multinatural geographies for the Anthropocene. *Progress in Human Geography*, 36(5): 593–612. https://doi.org/ 10.1177/0309132511435352

Low, S. M. (1997) Urban fear: building the fortress city. *City and Society*, 9(1): 53–71.

Lubitow, A., Rainer, J., & Bassett, L. (2017) Exclusion and vulnerability on public transit: Experiences of transit dependent riders in Portland, Oregon. *Mobilities*, 12(6): 924–37.

Lugones, M. (2007) Heterosexualism and the colonial/modern gender system. *Hypatia*, 22(1): 186–219.

Lugones, M. (2010) Toward a decolonial feminism. *Hypatia*, 25(4): 742–59.

Lupton, D. (2015) Quantified sex: A critical analysis of sexual and reproductive self-tracking using apps. *Culture, Health and Sexuality*, 17(4): 440–53.

Lynch, M., Omori, M., Roussell, A., & Valasik, M. (2013) Policing the 'progressive' city: The racialized geography of drug law enforcement. *Theoretical Criminology*, 17(3): 335–57.

Lyon, D. (2001) *Surveillance Society: Monitoring Everyday Life*. Milton Keynes, UK: Open University Press.

Lyons, H. (2019) Assembling the nation: Spatialising young, religious American's affective experiences of the nation, fear and danger in the everyday. PhD thesis, Newcastle University.

Maas, J., Verheij, R., de Vries, S., Spreeuwenberg, P., & Groenewegen, P. (2005) Green space, urbanity, and health: How strong is the relation? *European Journal of Public Health*, 60(7): 587–92.

MacDonald, M., Phipps, S., & Lethbridge, L. (2005) Taking its toll: The influence of paid and unpaid work on women's well-being. *Feminist Economics*, 11(1): 63–94.

MacDonald, R., Shildrick, T., & Furlong, A. (2014) 'Benefit Street' and the myth of workless communities. *Sociological Research Online*, 19(3): 1–6.

Macias, T. (2008) Conflict over forest resources in northern New Mexico: Rethinking cultural activism as a strategy for environmental justice. *Social Science Journal*, 45(1): 61–75. https://doi.org/10.1016/J.SOSCIJ.2007.12.006

Macintyre, S. (2007) Deprivation amplification revisited; or, is it always true that poorer places have poorer access to resources for healthy diets and physical activity? *International Journal of Behavioral Nutrition and Physical Activity*, 4(32): 1–7.

Macintyre, S., Ellaway, A., & Cummins, S. (2002) Place effects on health: How can we conceptualise, operationalise and measure them? *Social Science & Medicine*, 55(1): 125–39.

MacKinnon, D. (2011) Reconstructing scale: Towards a new scalar politics. *Progress in Human Geography*, 35(1): 21–36.

MacLeod, G. (2018) The Grenfell Tower atrocity: Exposing urban worlds of inequality, injustice, and an impaired democracy. *City*, 22(4): 460–89.

Macpherson, H. (2008) I don't know why they call it the Lake District they might as well call it the rock district! The workings of humour and laughter in research with members of visually impaired walking groups. *Environment and Planning D: Society and Space*, 26(6): 1080–95.

Macpherson, H., & Bleasdale, M. (2012) Journeys in ink: re-presenting the spaces of inclusive arts practice. *Cultural Geographies*, 19(4): 523–34.

Macrorie, R., Foulds, C., & Hargreaves, T. (2015) Governing and governed by practices: Exploring governance interventions in low-carbon housing policy and practice. In Y. Strengers & C. Maller (eds.), *Social Practices, Intervention and Sustainability: Beyond Behaviour Change*, pp. 95–111. London: Taylor & Francis.

Maddrell, A. (2009) A place for grief and belief: The Witness Cairn, Isle of Whithorn, Galloway, Scotland. *Social & Cultural Geography*, 10(6): 675–93.

Maddrell, A. (2011) *Complex Locations: Women's Geographical Work in the UK 1950–1970*. Oxford: Wiley-Blackwell.

Maddrell, A., & Sidaway, J. (eds.) (2010) *Deathscapes: New Spaces for Death, Dying and Bereavement*. Farnham, UK: Ashgate.

Maddrell, A., Strauss, K., Thomas, N. J., & Wyse, S. (2016) Mind the gap: Gender disparities still to be addressed in UK higher education geography. *Area*, 48(1): 48–56.

Madianou, M. (2012) Migration and the accentuated ambivalence of motherhood: The role of ICTs in Filipino transnational families. *Global Networks*, 12(3): 277–95.

Maestri, G., & Hughes, S. M. (2017) Contested spaces of citizenship: Camps, borders and urban encounters. *Citizenship Studies*, 21(6): 625–39.

Maharawal, M. (2018) The anti-eviction mapping project: Counter mapping and oral history toward Bay Area housing justice. *Annals of the American Association of Geographers*, 108(2): 380–89.

Mahtani, M. (2006) Challenging the ivory tower: Proposing anti-racist geographies within the academy. *Gender, Place & Culture*, 13(1): 21–25.

Mahtani, M. (2014) Toxic geographies: Absences in critical race thought and practice in social and cultural geography. *Social & Cultural Geography*, 15(4): 359–67.

Maliepaard, E. (2015) Bisexual spaces: Exploring geographies of bisexualities. *ACME: An International E-Journal for Critical Geographies*, 14(1): 217–34.

Malpass, P. (2005) *Housing and the Welfare State. The Development of Housing Policy in Britain*. Basingstoke, UK: Palgrave Macmillan.

Malthus, T. (1999/1798) *An Essay on the Principe of Population*. Oxford: Oxford University Press.

Manzo, K. (2008) Imaging humanitarianism: NGO identity and the iconography of childhood. *Antipode*, 40(4): 623–57.

Marcuse, P., & Madden, D. (2016) *In Defense of Housing: The Politics of Crisis*. London: Verso.

Margulies, J. D., & Bersaglio, B. (2018) Furthering post-human political ecologies. *Geoforum*, 94(August): 103–6. https://doi.org/10.1016/J.GEOFORUM.2018.03.017

Maria, S. J., & Jorge, V. P. (2014) Geographies of sexualities in Brazil: Between national invisibility and subordinate inclusion in postcolonial networks of knowledge production. *Geography Compass*, 8(10): 767–77.

Markowitz, G., & Rosner, D. (2003) *Deceit and Denial: The Deadly Politics of Industrial Pollution*. Berkeley: University of California Press.

Marmot, M. (2010) *Fair Society Health Lives: The Marmot Review*. London: University College.

Marston, S. A. (2000) The social construction of scale. *Progress in Human Geography*, 24(2): 219–42.

Marston, S., Jones, J., & Woodward, K. (2005) Human geography without scale. *Transactions of the Institute of British Geographers*, 30: 416–32.

Martínez-Alier, J. (2002) *The Environmentalism of the Poor*. Cheltenham, UK: Edward Elgar.

Martínez-Alier, J. (2012) Environmental justice and economic degrowth: An alliance between two movements. *Capitalism Nature Socialism*, 23(1): 51–73. https://doi.org/10.1080/10455752.2011.648839

Martynuska, M. (2017) Cultural hybridity in the USA exemplified by Tex-Mex cuisine. *International Review of Social Research*, 7(2): 90–98. https://doi.org/10.1515/irsr-2017-0011

Mason, J. (2006) Mixing methods in a qualitatively driven way. *Qualitative Research*, 6(1): 9–25.

Massey, D. (1990) Social structure, household strategies, and the cumulative causation of migration. *Population Index*, 56(1): 563–26. doi:10.2307/3644186

Massey, D. (1991a) A global sense of place. *Marxism Today*, 9 June.

Massey, D. (1991b) Flexible sexism. *Environment and Planning D: Society and Space*, 9: 31–57.

Massey, D. (1994/2013) *Space, Place and Gender*. London: Wiley-Blackwell.

Massey, D. (1995) The conceptualization of place. In D. Massey & P. Jess (eds.), *A Place in the World?*, pp. 45–86. Milton Keynes, UK: Open University Press.

Massey, D. (2005) *For Space*. London: Sage.

Massey, D., & Allen, J. (eds.) (1984) *Geography Matters*. Cambridge: Cambridge University Press.

Massey, D., Human Geography Research Group, Bond, S., & Featherstone, D. (2009) The possibilities of a politics of place beyond place? A conversation with Doreen Massey. *Scottish Geographical Journal*, 125(3–4): 401–20.

Matthews, H., & Limb, M. (1999) Defining an agenda for the geography of children: Review and prospect. *Progress in Human Geography*, 23(1): 61–90.

Matthews, H., Limb, M., & Taylor, M. (1999) Reclaiming the street: The discourse of curfew. *Environment and Planning A: Economy and Space*, 31(10): 1713–30.

Mattheys, K., Bambra, C., Akhter, N., Warren, J., & Kasim, A. (2016) Inequalities in mental health in a time of austerity: Baseline findings from the Stockton-on-Tees Cohort Study. *SSM Population Health*, 2: 350–59.

Mavroudi, E. (2007) Diaspora as process: (De)constructing boundaries. *Geography Compass*, 1(3): 467–79. https://doi.org/10.1111/j.1749-8198.2007.00033.x

May, J., Wills, J., Datta, K., Evans, Y., Herbert, J., & McIlwain, C. (2007) Keeping London working: Global cities, the British state and London's new migrant division of labour. *Transactions of the Institute of British Geographers*, 32: 151–67.

Mayhew, H. (1985) *London Labour and the London Poor*. Middlesex, UK: Penguin.

McAreavey, R. (2012) Resistance or resilience? Tracing the pathway of recent arrivals to a 'new' rural destination. *Sociologia Ruralis*, 52(4): 488–507.

McAreavey, R. (2017) *New Immigration Destinations: Migrating to Rural and Peripheral Areas*. London: Routledge.

McAreavey, R., & Krivokapic-Skoko, B. (2019) In or out? Understanding how social and symbolic boundaries influence the economic integration of transnational migrants in non-metropolitan economies. *Sociologia Ruralis*, online first. https://doi.org/10.1111/soru.12236

McCormack, D. P. (2008) Thinking spaces for research-creation. *Inflexions*, 1(1): 1–6.

McCormack, D. P. (2014) *Refrains for Moving Bodies: Experience and Experiments in Affective Spaces*. London: Duke.

McDowell, L. M. (1983) Towards an understanding of the gender division of urban space. *Environment and Planning D: Society and Space*, 1(1): 59–72.

McDowell, L. M. (1986) Beyond patriarchy: A class-based explanation of women's subordination. *Antipode*, 18(3): 311–21.

McDowell, L. M. (1997) *Capital Culture: Gender at Work in the City*. Oxford: Blackwell.

McDowell, L. M. (1999) *Gender, Identity and Place: Understanding Feminist Geographies*. Minneapolis: University of Minnesota Press.

McDowell, L. M. (2003) *Redundant Masculinities? Employment Change and White Working-Class Youth*. Oxford: Blackwell.

McDowell, L. M. (2004) Work, workfare, work/life balance and an ethic of care. *Progress in Human Geography*, 28(2): 145–63.

McDowell, L. M., & Court, G. (1994) Performing work: Bodily representations in merchant banks. *Environment and Planning D: Society and Space*, 12(6): 727–50.

McDowell, L. M., & Massey, D. (1984) A woman's place? In D. Massey & J. Allen (eds.), *Geography Matters*, pp. 128–47. Cambridge: Cambridge University Press.

McDowell, L. M., & Peake, L. (1990) Women in British geography revisited: Or the same old story. *Journal of Geography in Higher Education*, 14(1): 19–30.

McFarlane, C. (2012) Rethinking informality: Politics, crisis, and the city. *Planning Theory and Practice*, 13(1): 89–108.

McGoey, L. (2012) Strategic unknowns: Towards a sociology of ignorance. *Economy and Society*, 41: 1–16.

McGuirk, J. (2014) *Radical Cities: Across Latin America in Search of a New Architecture.* London: Verso.

McGurty, E. M. (1997) From NIMBY to civil rights: The origins of the environmental justice movement. *Environmental History*, 2(3): 301–23. https://www.jstor.org/stable/3985352

McKittrick, K. (2011) On plantations, prisons, and a black sense of place. *Social & Cultural Geography*, 12(8): 947–63.

McLaren, D., & Agyeman, J. (2015) *Sharing Cities: A Case for Truly Smart and Sustainable Cities.* Cambridge, MA: MIT Press.

McLean, H. (2017) Hos in the garden: Staging and resisting neoliberal creativity. *Environment and Planning D: Society and Space*, 35(1): 38–56.

McNally, D. (2019) 'I am Tower Hamlets': Enchanted encounters and the limit to art's connectivity. *Social & Cultural Geography*, 20(2): 198–221.

McNeill, D. (2005) Skyscraper geography. *Progress in Human Geography*, 29(1): 41–55.

Meadows, D. H., Meadows, D. L., Randers, J., & Behrens, W. W., III. (1972) *The Limits to Growth: A Report to the Club of Rome.* http://www.donellameadows.org/wp-content/userfiles/Limits-to-Growth-digital-scan-version.pdf

Mearns, G., Simmonds, R., Richardson, M., Turner, P., Watson, P., & Missier, P. (2014) Tweet my street: A cross-disciplinary collaboration for the analysis of local Twitter data. *Future Internet*, 6(2): 378–96.

Meer, N., Nayak, A., & Pande, R. (2015) Special issue: The matter of race. *Sociological Research Online*, 20(3): 1–5.

Merriman, P., & Jones, R. (2017) Nations, materialities and affects. *Progress in Human Geography*, 41: 600–617.

Meth, P. (2003) Entries and omissions: Using solicited diaries in geographical research. *Area*, 35(2): 195–205.

Milbourne, P. (2004) *Rural Poverty: Marginalisation and Exclusion in Britain and the United States.* London: Routledge.

Milbourne, P. (2010) The geographies of poverty and welfare. *Geography Compass*, 4(2): 158–71.

Miles, R. (1989) *Racism.* London: Routledge.

Militz, E. (2017) On affect, dancing and national bodies. In M. Skey & M. Antonsich (eds.), *Everyday Nationhood: Theorising Culture, Identity and Belonging after* Banal Nationalism, pp. 177–96. London: Palgrave Macmillan.

Miller, D. (2003) *Political Philosophy: A Very Short Introduction.* Oxford: Oxford University Press.

Mills, C. (2014) The Great British class fiasco: A comment on Savage et al. *Sociology*, 48(3): 437–44.

Mills, S. (2014) Geographies of education, volunteering and the lifecourse: The Woodcraft Folk in Britain (1925–1975). *Cultural Geographies*, 23(1): 103–19.

Mills, S. (2016) Jives, jeans and Jewishness? Moral geographies, atmospheres and the politics of mixing at the Jewish Lads' Brigade & Club 1954–1969. *Environment and Planning D: Society and Space*, 34(6): 1098–1112.

Mills, S., & Waite, C. (2017) Brands of youth citizenship and the politics of scale: National Citizen Service in the United Kingdom. *Political Geography*, 56: 66–76.

Minton, A. (2017) *Big Capital: Who Is London For?* London: Penguin.

Miraftab, F. (2012) Colonial present: Legacies of the past in contemporary urban practices in Cape Town, South Africa. *Journal of Planning History*, 11: 283–307.

Misgav, C., & Johnston, L. (2014) Dirty dancing: The (non)fluid embodied geographies of a queer nightclub in Tel Aviv. *Social & Cultural Geography*, 15(7): 730–46.

Mitchell, D. (1997) The annihilation of space by law: The roots and implications of anti-homeless laws in the United States. *Antipode*, 29(3): 303–35.

Mitchell, D. (2003) *The Right to the City: Social Justice and the Fight for Public Space.* New York: Guilford Press.

Mitchell, K., Marston, S., & Katz, C. (2003) Life's work: An introduction, review and critique. *Antipode*, 35(3): 414–42.

Mitchell, K., Marston, S., & Katz, C. (eds.) (2004) *Life's Work: Geographies of Social Reproduction.* Oxford: Blackwell.

Modood, T., Berthoud, R., Lakey, J., Nazroo, J., Smith, P., Virdee, S., & Beishons, S. (eds.) (1997) *Ethnic Minorities in Britain: Diversity and Disadvantage*. London: Policy Studies Institute.

Mohammad, R. (2001) 'Insiders' and/or 'outsiders': Positionality, theory and praxis. In M. Limb & C. Dwyer (eds.), *Qualitative Methodologies for Geographers: Issues and Debates*, pp. 101–17. London: Arnold.

Mol, A. P. J., & Sonnenfeld, D. A. (2014) *Ecological Modernisation around the World: Perspectives and Critical Debates*. London: Routledge.

Mollett, S. (2017) Irreconcilable differences? A postcolonial intersectional reading of gender, development and human rights in Latin America. *Gender, Place & Culture*, 24(1): 1–17.

Mollett, S., & Faria, C. (2013) Messing with feminist political ecology. *Geoforum*, 45: 116–25.

Mollett, S., & Faria, C. (2018) The spatialities of intersectional thinking: Fashioning feminist geographic futures. *Gender, Place & Culture*, 25(4): 565–77.

Moore, A. (2008) Rethinking scale as a geographical category: From analysis to practice. *Progress in Human Geography*, 32(2): 203–25.

Moran, J. (2005) *Reading the Everyday*. London: Routledge.

Moran, J. (2008) *Queuing for Beginners: The Story of Daily Life from Breakfast to Bedtime*. London: Profile Books.

Morin, K. M., & Guelke, J. K. (2007) *Women, Religion and Space: Global Perspectives on Gender and Faith*. Syracuse, NY: Syracuse University Press.

Moss, P., Falconer Al-Hindi, K., & Kawabata, H. (2002) *Feminist Geography in Practice: Research and Methods*. Malden, MA: Wiley-Blackwell.

Mott, C., & Cockayne, D. (2017) Citation matters: Mobilizing the politics of citation toward a practice of 'conscientious engagement'. *Gender, Place & Culture*, 24(7): 954–73.

Mountz, A., Bonds, A., Mansfield, B., Loyd, J., Hyndman, J., Walton-Roberts, M., Basu, R., Whitson, R., Hawkins, R., Hamilton, T., & Curran, W. (2015) For slow scholarship: A feminist politics of resistance through collective action in the neoliberal university.

ACME: An International E-Journal for Critical Geographies, 14(4): 1235–59.

mrs c. kinpaisby-hill. (2011) Participatory praxis and social justice: Towards more fully social geographies. In V. Del Casino, M. E. Thomas, P. Cloke & R. Panell (eds.), *A Companion to Social Geography*, pp. 214–34. Oxford: Blackwell.

Muehlebach, A. (2001) 'Making place' at the United Nations: Indigenous cultural politics at the UN working group on Indigenous populations. *Cultural Anthropology*, 16(3): 415–48.

Murji, K., & Solomos, J. (eds.) (2005) *Racialization: Studies in Theory and Practice*. Oxford: Oxford University Press.

Nader, L. (1972) Up the anthropologist: Perspectives gained from 'studying up'. In D. Hymes (ed.), *Reinventing Anthropology*, pp. 284–311. New York: Random House.

Nagar, R. (2002) Women's theater and the redefinitions of public, private, and politics in North India. *ACME: An International E-Journal for Critical Geographies*, 1: 55–72.

Nagar, R., & Geiger, S. (2007) Reflexivity and positionality in feminist fieldwork revisited. In A. Tickell, E. Sheppard & J. Peck (eds.), *Politics and Practice in Economic Geography*, pp. 267–78. London: Sage.

Nagel, C., & Staeheli, L. (2006) Topographies of home and citizenship: Arab-American activists in the United States. *Environment and Planning A*, 38(9): 1599–1614.

Nagel, C., & Staeheli, L. (2008) Integration and the negotiation and 'here' and 'there': The case of British Arab activists. *Social & Cultural Geography*, 9(4): 415–30.

Nagy, R. (2008) Transitional justice as global project: Critical reflections. *Third World Quarterly*, 29(2): 275–89.

Najib, K., & Hopkins, P. (2019) Veiled Muslim women's strategies in response to Islamophobia in Paris. *Political Geography*, 73: 103–11. https://doi.org/10.1016/j. polgeo.2019.05.005

Najib, K., & Hopkins, P. (2020) Where does Islamophobia take place and who is involved? Reflections from Paris and London. *Social & Cultural Geography*, 21(4): 458–78. doi:10.10 80/14649365.2018.1563800

Najib, K., & Teeple Hopkins, C. (2020) Introduction. Special issue: Geographies of

Islamophobia. *Social & Cultural Geography*, 21(4): 449–57.

Nash, C. (2000) Performativity in practice: Some recent work in cultural geography. *Progress in Human Geography*, 24(4): 653–64.

Nash, C., & Gorman-Murray, A. (2014) LGBT neighbourhoods and 'new mobilities': Towards understanding transformations in sexual and gendered urban landscapes. *International Journal of Urban and Regional Research*, 38(3): 756–72.

Nash, C. J. (2010) Trans geographies, embodiment and experience. *Gender, Place & Culture*, 17(5): 579–95.

Nash, C. J., & Bain, A. (2007) Pussies declawed: Unpacking the politics of a queer women's bathhouse raid. In G. Brown, K. Browne & J. Lim (eds.), *Geographies of Sexuality: Theory, Practice and Politics*, pp. 159–68. Surrey, UK: Ashgate.

Nash, C. J., Gorman-Murray, A., & Browne, K. (2019) Geographies of intransigence: Freedom of speech and heteroactivist resistances in Canada, Great Britain and Australia. *Social & Cultural Geography*: 1–21.

National Council on Disability. (2006) The Impact of Hurricanes Katrina and Rita on people with disabilities: A look back and remaining challenges. https://www.ncd.gov/publications/2006/Aug072006

Nawyn, S. J. (2010) Gender and migration: Integrating feminist theory into migration studies. *Sociology Compass*, 4(9): 749–65. https://doi.org/10.1111/j.1751-9020.2010.00318.x

Nayak, A. (2003) Last of the 'real Geordies'? White masculinities and the subcultural response to deindustrialisation. *Environment and Planning D: Society and Space*, 21(1): 7–25.

Nayak, A. (2006a) After race: Ethnography, race and post-race theory. *Ethnic and Racial Studies*, 29(3): 411–30.

Nayak, A. (2006b) Displaced masculinities: Chavs, youth and class in the post-industrial city. *Sociology*, 40(5): 813–31.

Nayak, A. (2017) Purging the nation: Race, conviviality and embodied encounters in the lives of British Bangladeshi Muslim young women. *Transactions of the Institute of British Geographers*, 42(2): 289–302.

Nayak, A., & Jeffrey, A. (2011) *Geographical Thought: An Introduction to Ideas in Human Geography*. London: Routledge.

Nayak, A., & Kehily, M. J. (2014) Chavs, chavettes and pramface girls: Teenage mothers, marginalised young men and the management of stigma. *Journal of Youth Studies*, 17(10): 1330–45.

Naylor, S., & Ryan, J. (2002) The mosque in the suburbs: Negotiating religion and ethnicity in south London. *Social & Cultural Geography*, 3(1): 39–60.

Neal, S., & Agyeman, J. (eds.) (2006) *The New Countryside?: Ethnicity, Nation and Exclusion in Contemporary Rural Britain*. Bristol: Policy Press.

Nelson, A., & Schneider, F. (eds.) (2019) *Housing for Degrowth: Principles, Models, Challenges and Opportunities*. London: Routledge.

Neuwirth, R. (2005) *Shadow Cities: A Billion Squatters, a New Urban World*. New York: Routledge.

Newman, J. (2017) Rationality, responsibility and rage: The contested politics of emotion governance. In E. Jupp, J. Pykett & F. M. Smith (eds.), *Emotional States: Sites and Spaces of Affective Governance*. London: Routledge.

Noble, B. J. (2002) Seeing double, thinking twice: The Toronto drag kings and (re-) articulations of masculinity. *Journal of Homosexuality*, 43(3–4): 251–61.

Noble, S. U. (2018) *Algorithms of Oppression*. New York: New York University Press.

North, S., Snyder, I., & Bulfin, S. (2008) Digital tastes: Social class and young people's technology use. *Information, Communication and Society*, 11(7): 895–911.

Northern Powerhouse Partnership. (2018) Educating the north: Driving ambition across the Powerhouse. http://www.northernpower housepartnership.co.uk/publications/educat ing-the-north-driving-ambition-across-the -powerhouse

Noxolo, P. (2015) Moving maps: African-Caribbean dance as embodied mapping. In S. Barboar, D. Howard, T. Lacroix & J. Misrahi-Barak (eds.), *Diasporas, Cultures of Mobilities, 'Race'*, vol. 2, *Diaspora, Memory and Intimacy*. Montpellier: Presses Universitaires de la Méditerranée.

Noxolo, P. (2017) Introduction: Decolonising geographical knowledge in a colonised and re-colonising postcolonial world. *Area*, 49(3): 317–19.

Oakes, J., & Guiton, G. (1995) Matching: The dynamics of high school tracking decisions. *American Educational Research Journal*, 32(1): 3–33.

Oberhauser, A. M., Fluri, J. L., Whiston, R., & Mollett, S. (2018) *Feminist Spaces: Gender and Geography in a Global Context*. London: Routledge.

OECD. (2011) Regional typology. https://www.oecd.org/cfe/regional-policy/OECD_regional_typology_ Nov2012.pdf

OECD. (2016) OECD regional outlook 2016: Productive regions for inclusive societies. http://www.oecd.org/regional/oecd-regional-outlook-2016-9789264260245-en.htm

Ofsted. (2015) *The Annual Report of Her Majesty's Chief Inspector of Education, Children's Services and Skills 2014/15*. London: Ofsted.

Okereke, C., & Coventry, P. (2016) Climate justice and the international regime: Before, during, and after Paris. *Wiley Interdisciplinary Reviews: Climate Change*, 7(6): 834–51. https://doi.org/10.1002/wcc.419

Oliver, C., Blythe, M., & Roe, J. (2018) Negotiating sameness and difference in geographies of older age. *Area*, 50(4): 444–51. https://doi.org/10.1111/area.12429

Olson, E. (2006) Development, transnational religion, and the power of ideas in the High Provinces of Cusco, Peru. *Environment and Planning A: Economy and Space*, 38: 885–902.

Oswin, N. (2008) Critical geographies and the uses of sexuality: Deconstructing queer space. *Progress in Human Geography*, 32(1): 89–103.

Oxfam. (2019) *Public Good or Private Wealth?* https://oxfam.app.box.com/s/f9meuz1jrd9e1xrkrq59e37tpoppqup0/file/385579400762

Paasche, T. F., Yarwood, R., & Sidaway, D. (2014) Territorial tactics: The socio-spatial significance of private policing strategies in Cape Town. *Urban Studies*, 51(8): 1559–75.

Pacione, M. (2009) *Urban Geography: A Global Perspective*, 3rd ed. London: Routledge.

Pahl, R. (1966) The rural–urban continuum. *Sociologia Ruralis*, 6(3–4): 299–329.

Pahl, R. (1984) *Divisions of Labour*. London: Blackwell.

Pain, R. (1991) Space, sexual violence and social control: Integrating geographical and feminist analyses of women's fear of crime. *Progress in Human Geography*, 15(4): 415–31.

Pain, R. (2001) Gender, race, age and fear in the city. *Urban Studies*, 38(5–6): 899–913. https://doi.org/10.1080/00420980120046590

Pain, R. (2003) Social geography: On action-orientated research. *Progress in Human Geography*, 27(5): 677–85.

Pain, R. (2006) Paranoid parenting? Rematerialising risk and fear for children. *Social & Cultural Geography*, 7(2): 221–43.

Pain, R. (2014a) Everyday terrorism: Connecting domestic violence and global terrorism. *Progress in Human Geography*, 38: 531–50.

Pain, R. (2014b) Seismologies of emotion: Fear and activism during domestic violence. *Social & Cultural Geography*, 15(2): 127–50.

Pain, R. (2019) Chronic urban trauma: The slow violence of housing dispossession. *Urban Studies*, 56(2): 385–400.

Pain, R. (2020) Geotrauma: Violence, place and repossession. *Progress in Human Geography*.

Pain, R., & Bailey, C. (2004) British social and cultural geography. *Social & Cultural Geography*, 5(2): 319–29.

Pain, R., Barke, M., Gough, J., Fuller, D., MacFarlane, R., & Mowl, G. (2001) *Introducing Social Geographies*. London: Arnold.

Pain, R., & Hopkins, P. (2010) Social geographies of age and ageism: Landscapes, lifecourse and justice. In S. J. Smith, R. Pain, S. Marston & J. P. Jones (eds.), *Sage Handbook of Social Geographies*, pp. 78–88. London: Sage.

Pain, R., Kesby, M., & Askins, K. (2011) Geographies of impact: Power, participation and potential. *Area*, 43(2): 183–88.

Pain, R., Mowl, G., & Talbot, C. (2000) Difference and the negotiation of 'old age'. *Environment and Planning D: Society and Space*, 18(3): 377–94.

Painter, J. (2000) Pierre Bourdieu. In M. Crang and N. Thrift (eds.), *Thinking Space*, pp. 239–59. London: Taylor & Francis.

Palmer, D., & Warren, I. (2014) The pursuit of exclusion through banning. *Australian and New Zealand Journal of Criminology*, 47(3): 429–46.

Palmer, D., Warren, I., & Miller, P. (2012) ID scanning, the media, and the politics of urban surveillance in an Australian regional city. *Surveillance and Society*, 9(3): 293–309.

Palmiste, C. (2008) Forcible removals: The case of Australian Aboriginal and Native American children. *AlterNative: An International Journal of Indigenous Peoples*, 4: 75–88. https://doi.org/10.1177/11771801 0800400206

Panelli, R. (2004) *Social Geographies: From Difference to Action*. London: Sage.

Panelli, R. (2008) Social geographies: Encounters with Indigenous and more-than-White/Anglo geographies. *Progress in Human Geography*, 32(6): 801–11.

Panelli, R., Hubbard, P., Coombes, P., & Suchet-Pearson, S. (2009) De-centring white ruralities: Ethnic diversity, racialisation and Indigenous countrysides. *Journal of Rural Studies*, 25(4): 355–64.

Pappé, I. (2007) *The Ethnic Cleansing of Palestine*. Oxford: Oneworld.

Parisi, D., Lichter, D. T., & Taquino, M. C. (2011) Multi-scale residential segregation: Black exceptionalism and America's changing color line. *Social Forces*, 89: 829–52.

Park, R., Burgess, E., & McKenzie, R. (1925) *The City*. Chicago: University of Chicago Press.

Parker, S. (2015) *Urban Theory and the Urban Experience*, 2nd ed. London: Routledge.

Parnell, S., & Robinson, J. (2012) (Re)theorizing cities from the Global South: Looking beyond neoliberalism. *Urban Geography*, 33(4): 593–617.

Parr, H. (2002) New body geographies: The embodied spaces of health and medical information on the Internet. *Environment and Planning D: Society and Space*, 20(1): 73–95.

Parr, H. (2008) *Mental Health and Social Space: Towards Inclusionary Geographies?* Oxford: Blackwell.

Pateman, T. (2011) Rural and urban areas: Comparing lives using rural/urban classifications. *Regional Trends*, 43(1): 11–86.

Peach, C. (2002) Social geography: New religions and ethnoburbs – contrasts with cultural geography. *Progress in Human Geography*, 26(2): 252–60.

Peach, C. (2006a) Muslims in the 2001 Census of England and Wales: Gender and economic disadvantage. *Ethnic and Racial Studies*, 29(4): 629–55.

Peach, C. (2006b) Islam, ethnicity and South Asian religions in the London 2001 census. *Transactions of the Institute of British Geographers*, 31(3): 353–70.

Peach, C., Robinson, V., & Smith, S. (1981) *Ethnic Segregation in Cities*. London: Croom Helm.

Peake, L. (2010) Gender, race, sexuality. In S. J. Smith, R. Pain, S. Marston & J. P. Jones (eds.), *Sage Handbook of Social Geographies*, pp. 55–77. London: Sage.

Peake, L. (2016) Classics in human geography: David Bell & Gill Valentine's *Mapping Desire: Geographies of Sexualities* (London: Routledge). *Progress in Human Geography*, 40(4): 574–78.

Peake, L., & Kobayashi, A. (2002) Policies and practices for an antiracist geography at the millennium. *Professional Geographer*, 54(1): 50–61.

Pearce, J. (2013) Introduction commentary: Financial crisis, austerity policies, and geographical inequalities in health. *Environment and Planning A: Economy and Space*, 45(9): 2030–45.

Pearce, J., Blakely, T., Witten, K., & Bartie, P. (2007) Neighborhood deprivation and access to fast-food retailing – A national study. *American Journal of Preventive Medicine*, 32(5): 375–82.

Pearce, J., Richardson, E., Mitchell, R., & Shortt, N. (2010) Environmental justice and health: The implications of the socio-spatial distribution of multiple environmental deprivation for health inequalities in the United Kingdom. *Transactions of the Institute of British Geographers*, 35(4): 522–39.

Peat, J. (2018) The UK has 9 out of the 10 poorest regions in northern Europe. *The London Economic*. https://www.thelondon economic.com/news/the-uk-has-9-out -of-the-10-poorest-regions-in-northern -europe/06/06/

Peng, S., Zhang, W., & Sun, C. (2016) 'Environmental load displacement' from the north to the south: A consumption-based perspective with a focus on China. *Ecological Economics*, 128(August): 147–58. https://doi.org/10.1016/J.ECOLECON.2016.04.020

Perkins, H., & Thorns, D. C. (2011) *Place, Identity and Everyday Life in a Globalizing World*. Basingstoke, UK: Palgrave Macmillan.

Perlman, J. (2010) *Favela: Four Decades of Living on the Edge in Rio de Janeiro*. Oxford: Oxford University Press.

Perrons, D. (2004) *Globalization and Social Change: People and Places in a Divided World*. London: Routledge.

Perrons, D., Fagan, C., McDowell, L., & Ward, K. (eds.) (2006) *Gender Divisions and Working Time in the New Economy*. Cheltenham, UK: Edward Elgar.

Phillips, D. (2006) Parallel lives? Challenging discourses of British Muslim self-segregation. *Environment and Planning D: Society and Space*, 24(1): 25–40.

Philo, C. (1992) Neglected rural geographies: A review. *Journal of Rural Studies*, 8(2): 193–207.

Pickerill, J., & Krinsky, J. (2012) Why does Occupy matter? *Social Movement Studies*, 11(3–4): 279–87.

Pickles, J. (1995) *Ground Truth: The Social Implications of Geographical Information Systems*. New York: Guilford Press.

Piketty, T. (2014) *Capital in the Twenty-First Century*. Cambridge, MA: Harvard University Press.

Pimlott-Wilson, H. (2017) Individualising the future: The emotional geographies of neoliberal governance in young peoples' aspirations. *Area*, 49(3): 288–95.

Pink, S. (2009) Urban social movements and small places. *City*, 13(4): 451–65.

Podmore, J. (2013) Critical commentary: Sexualities landscapes beyond homonormativity. *Geoforum*, 49(1): 263–67.

Popke, J. (2011) Latino migration and neoliberalism in the US South: Notes toward a rural cosmopolitanism. *Southeastern Geographer*, 51: 242–59.

Postero, N. (2010) Morales's MAS government: Building Indigenous popular hegemony in Bolivia. *Latin American*

Perspectives, 37: 18–34. https://doi.org/10.1177/0094582X10364031

Postero, N. (2013) Introduction: Negotiating Indigeneity. *Latin American and Caribbean Ethnic Studies*, 8: 107–21. https://doi.org/10.1080/17442222.2013.810013

Powells, G., Bulkeley, H., Bell, S., & Judson, E. (2014) Peak electricity demand and the flexibility of everyday life. *Geoforum*, 55: 43–52. https://doi.org/10.1016/j.geoforum.2014.04.014

Power, A., & Bartlett, R. (2018) 'I shouldn't be living there because I am a sponger': Negotiating everyday geographies by people with learning disabilities. *Disability & Society*, 33(4): 562–78.

Pratt, G. (2012) *Families Apart: Migrating Mothers and the Conflicts of Labor and Love*. Minneapolis: University of Minnesota Press.

Pratt, G., & Johnston, C. (2007) Turning theatre into law, and other spaces of politics. *Cultural Geographies*, 14(1): 92–113.

Pratt, G., & Johnston, C. (2013) Staging testimony in Nanay. *Geographical Review*, 103(2): 288–303.

Pratt, G., & Johnston, C. (2014) Filipina domestic workers, violent insecurity, testimonial theatre and transnational ambivalence. *Area*, 46(4): 358–60.

Pratt, G., & Kirby, E. (2003) Performing nursing: The BC Nurses' Union theatre project. *ACME: An International E-Journal for Critical Human Geographies*, 2: 14–32.

Pratt, G., & Rosner, V. (2012) *The Global and the Intimate: Feminism in Our Time*. New York: Columbia University Press.

Probyn, E. (2000) *Carnal Appetites: Food, Sex, Identities*. New York: Routledge.

Pruitt, L. R. (2009) Latina/os, locality and law in the rural South. *Harvard Latino Law Review*, 12: 140–69.

Public Accounts Committee. (2018) *The Higher Education Market: 45th Report of Session (2017–19)*. London: Stationery Office.

Punch, S. (2003) Childhoods in the majority world: Miniature adults or tribal children? *Sociology*, 37(2): 277–95.

Putnam, R. (1993) *Making Democracy Work: Civic Traditions in Modern Italy*. Princeton, NJ: Princeton University Press.

Pyer, M., & Tucker, F. (2017) 'With us, we, like, physically can't': Transport, mobility and the leisure experiences of teenage wheelchair users. *Mobilities*, 12(1): 36–52.

Radcliffe, S., & Westwood, S. (1996) *Remaking the Nation: Place, Identity and Politics in Latin America*. London: Routledge.

Radcliffe, S. A. (2017a) Geography and Indigeneity I: Indigeneity, coloniality and knowledge. *Progress in Human Geography*, 41: 220–29. https://doi.org/10.1177/0309132515612952

Radcliffe, S. A. (2017b) Decolonising geographical knowledges. *Transactions of the Institute of British Geographers*, 42: 329–33.

Radcliffe, S. A. (2018) Geography and Indigeneity II: Critical geographies of Indigenous bodily politics. *Progress in Human Geography*, 42: 436–45. https://doi.org/10.1177/0309132517691631

Raento, P., & Brunn, S. D. (2005) Visualizing Finland: Postage stamps as political messengers. *Geografiska Annaler: Series B, Human Geography*, 87: 145–64.

Rahman, M. F. A. (2017) Securing the vertical space of cities. Today Online, 1 March. http://www.todayonline.com/commentary/securing-vertical-space-cities

Raju, S. (2002) We are different, but can we talk? *Gender, Place & Culture: A Journal of Feminist Geography*, 9(2): 173–77.

Ray, L., & Sayer, A. (1999) Introduction. In L. Ray & A. Sayer (eds.), *Culture and Economy after the Cultural Turn*, pp. 1–24. London: Sage.

Raynor, R. (2017) Dramatising austerity: Holding a story together (and why it falls apart . . .). *Cultural Geographies*, 24(2): 193–212.

Raynor, R. (2019) Speaking, feeling, mattering: Theatre as method and model for practice-based, collaborative, research. *Progress in Human Geography*, 43(4): 691–710.

Reay, D., Crozier, G., & James, D. (2011) *White Middle-Class Identities and Urban Schooling*. Basingstoke, UK: Palgrave Macmillan.

Reay, D., Davies, J., David, M., & Ball, S. J. (2001) Choices of degree or degrees of choice? Class, 'race' and the higher education choice process. *Sociology*, 35: 855–74.

Reclus, E. (1894) *The Earth and Its Inhabitants: The Universal Geography*. London: J. S. Virtue.

Regidor, E. (2004) Measures of health inequalities: Part 2. *Journal of Epidemiology and Community Health*, 58(3): 900–903.

Reid, L., & Ellsworth-Krebs, K. (2018) Nudge(ography) and practice theories: Contemporary sites of behavioural science and post-structuralist approaches in geography? *Progress in Human Geography*, 43(2): 295–313. https://doi.org/10.1177/0309132517750773

Reitan, R., & Gibson, S. (2012) Climate change or social change? Environmental and leftist praxis and participatory action research. *Globalizations*, 9(3): 395–410. https://doi.org/10.1080/14747731.2012.680735

Relph, E. (1970) An inquiry into the relations between phenomenology and geography. *Canadian Geographer*, 14: 193–201.

Relph, E. (1981a) *Place and Placelessness*. London: Sage.

Relph, E. (1981b) *Rational Landscapes and Humanistic Geography*. London: Croom Helm.

Rex, J., & Moore, R. (1967) *Race, Community and Conflict: A Study of Sparkbrook*. Oxford: Oxford University Press.

Reynolds, K., Block, D., & Bradley, K. (2018) Food justice scholar-activism and activist-scholarship. *ACME: An International Journal for Critical Geographies*, 17(4): 988–98.

Reynolds, K., & Cohen, N. (2016) *Beyond the Kale: Urban Agriculture and Social Justice Activism in New York City*. Athens: University of Georgia Press.

Rhodes, J., & Brown, L. (2019) The rise and fall of the 'inner city': Race, space and urban policy in postwar England. *Journal of Ethnic and Migration Studies*, 45(17): 3243–59. doi:10.1080/1369183X.2018.1480999

Richardson, M. J. (2018) Occupy Hong Kong? *Gweilo* citizenship and social justice. *Annals of the American Association of Geographers*, 108(2): 486–98.

Richardson, T. (ed.) (2016) *Inside Out: Contemporary British Psychogeography*. London: Rowman & Littlefield.

Robbins, P. (2012) *Political Ecology: A Critical Introduction*. Hoboken, NJ: John Wiley & Sons.

Robbins, P., Hintz, J., & Moore, S. A. (2014) *Environment and Society: A Critical Introduction.* Hoboken, NJ: John Wiley & Sons.

Robinson, C. D., & Scaglion, R., with Olivero, J. M. (1994) *Police in Contradiction: The Evolution of the Police Function in Society.* Westport, CT: Greenwood Press.

Robinson, J. (2016) Thinking cities through elsewhere: Comparative tactics for a more global urban studies. *Progress in Human Geography*, 40(1): 3–29.

Robinson, W. S. (1950) Ecological correlations and the behavior of individuals. *American Sociological Review*, 15: 351–57. https://doi .org/10.2307/2087176

Rodó-de-Zárate, M. (2016) Feminist and queer epistemologies beyond the academia and the Anglophone world: Political intersectionality and transfeminism in the Catalan context. In G. Brown & K. Browne (eds.), *The Routledge Research Companion to Geographies of Sex and Sexualities*, pp. 155–64. London: Routledge.

Rodríguez-Labajos, B., Yánez, I., Bond, P., Greyl, L., Munguti, S., Ojo, G., & Overbeek, W. (2019) Not so natural an alliance? Degrowth and environmental justice movements in the global south. *Ecological Economics*, 157(March): 175–84. https://doi .org/10.1016/J.ECOLECON.2018.11.007

Rogers, A. (2018) Advancing the geographies of the performing arts: Intercultural aesthetics, migratory mobility and geopolitics. *Progress in Human Geography*, 42(4): 549–68.

Rogers, C. (2017) *Plural Policing: Theory and Practice.* Bristol, UK: Policy Press.

Rose, G. (1993) *Feminism and Geography: The Limits of Geographical Knowledge.* Cambridge: Polity Press.

Rose, G. (2004) 'Everyone's cuddled up and it just looks really nice': An emotional geography of some mums and their family photos. *Social & Cultural Geography*, 5(4): 549–64.

Rose, G. (2016a) Rethinking the geographies of cultural 'objects' through digital technologies. *Progress in Human Geography*, 40(3): 334–51.

Rose, G. (2016b) Posthuman agency in the digitally mediated city: Exteriorization, individuation, reinvention. *Methods, Models and GIS*, 107(4): 779–93.

Roser, M., Ritchie, H., & Ortiz-Ospina, E. (2019) World population growth. Our World in Data. https://ourworldindata.org/world-population-growth#population-size-vs-population-growth-rate

Ross, N. J. (2007) 'My journey to school . . .': Foregrounding the meaning of school journeys and children's engagements and interactions in their everyday localities. *Children's Geographies*, 5(4): 373–91.

Roth, Y. (2014) Locating the "Scruff Guy": Theorizing body and space in gay geosocial media. *International Journal of Communication*, 8: 2113–33.

Routledge, P., & Cumbers, A. (2009) *Global Justice Networks: Geographies of Transnational Solidarity.* Manchester: Manchester University Press.

Routledge, P., Cumbers, A., & Driscoll Derickson, K. (2018) States of just transition: Realising climate justice through and against the state. *Geoforum*, 88(January): 78–86. https://doi.org/10.1016/J.GEOFORUM.2017 .11.015

Rowles, G. D., & Bernard, M. (2012) *Environmental Gerontology: Making Meaningful Places in Old Age.* New York: Springer.

Roy, A. (2005) Urban informality: Toward an epistemology of planning. *Journal of the American Planning Association*, 71(2): 147–58.

Roy, A. (2009a) Strangely familiar: Planning and the worlds of insurgence and informality. *Planning Theory*, 8(1): 7–11.

Roy, A. (2009b) Why India cannot plan its cities: Informality, insurgence and the idiom of urbanization. *Planning Theory*, 8: 76–87.

Roy, A. (2016) Who's afraid of postcolonial theory? *International Journal of Urban and Regional Research*, 40(1): 200–209.

Roy, A., & AlSayyad, N. (eds.) (2004) *Urban Informality in the Era of Globalization: A Transnational Perspective.* Lanham, MD: Lexington Books.

Ruddick, S. (1996) Constructing difference in public spaces: Race, class, and gender as interlocking systems. *Urban Geography*, 17(2): 132–51.

Ruddick, S. (2017) Rethinking the subject, reimagining worlds. *Dialogues in Human Geography*, 7(2): 118–39.

Runnymede Trust. (1997) *Islamophobia: A Challenge for Us All*. London: Runnymede Trust.

Russell, B. (2015) Beyond activism/academia: Militant research and the radical climate and climate justice movement(s). *Area*, 47(3): 222–29. https://doi.org/10.1111/area.12086

Ryan, F. (2018) 'It's horrifically painful': The disabled women forced into unnecessary surgery. *Guardian*, 6 August. https://www.theguardian.com/society/2018/aug/06/disabled-women-surgery-catheter-accessible-toilets

Ryan, S. (2005) Busy behaviour in the Land of the Golden M: Going out with learning disabled children in public places. *Journal of Applied Research in Intellectual Disabilities*, 18(1): 65–74.

Sabsay, L. (2012) The emergence of the other sexual citizen: Orientalism and the modernisation of sexuality. *Citizenship Studies*, 16(5–6): 605–62.

Sack, R. D. (1980) *Conceptions of Space in Social Thought*. London: Macmillan.

Sadurski, W. (1984) Social justice and legal justice. *Law and Philosophy*, 3(3): 329–54.

Saegert, S. (2016) Rereading 'The Housing Question' in light of the foreclosure crisis. *ACME: An International E-Journal for Critical Geographies*, 15(3): 659–78.

Said, E. (1986) The burdens of interpretation and the question of Palestine. *Journal of Palestine Studies*, 16(1): 29–37.

Said, E. (1992) *The Question of Palestine*. New York: Vintage Books.

Salazar Parreñas, R. (2009) Inserting feminism in transnational migration studies. *Migration Online*, May. http://lastradainternational.org/lsidocs/RParrenas_InsertingFeminisminTransnationalMigrationStudies.pdf

Saldanha, A. (2004) Vision and viscosity in Goa's psychedelic trance scene. *ACME: An International E-Journal for Critical Geographies*, 4(2): 172–93.

Saldanha, A. (2006) Reontologising race: The machinic geography of phenotype. *Environment and Planning D: Society and Space*, 24(1): 9–24.

Sandberg, L., & Tollefsen, A. (2010) Talking about fear of violence in public space: Female and male narratives about threatening situations in Umea, Sweden. *Social & Cultural Geography*, 11(1): 1–15.

Sassen, S. (2001) *The Global City: New York, London, Tokyo*, 2nd ed. Princeton, NJ: Princeton University Press.

Savage, M. (2016) Are we seeing a new inequality paradigm in social science? *Impact of Social Sciences Blog*, 3 June. https://blogs.lse.ac.uk/politicsandpolicy/are-we-seeing-a-new-inequality-paradigm-in-social-science/

Savage, M., & Burrows, R. (2007) The coming crisis of empirical sociology. *Sociology*, 41(5): 885–99.

Savage, M., Cunningham, N., Devine, F., Friedman, S., Laurison, F., McKenzie, L., Miles, A., Snee, H., & Wakeling, P. (2015) *Social Class in the 21st Century*. London: Penguin.

Savage, M., Devine, F., Cunningham, N., Taylor, M., Li, Y., Hjellbrekke, J., Le Roux, B., Friedman, S., & Miles, A. (2013) A new model of social class? Findings from the BBC's Great British class survey experiment. *Sociology*, 47(2): 219–50.

Sayer, A. (2010) *Method in Social Science*, rev. 2nd ed. London: Routledge.

Sayre, N. F. (2009) Scale. In N. Castree, D. Demeritt, D. Liverman & B. Rhoads (eds.), *A Companion to Environmental Geography*, pp. 95–108. Chichester, UK: Wiley-Blackwell.

Sayyid, S., & Vakil, A. (2010) *Thinking through Islamophobia: Global Perspectives*. London: Hurst.

Schlosberg, D. (2004) Reconceiving environmental justice: Global movements and political theories. *Environmental Politics*, 13(3): 517–40. https://doi.org/10.1080/0964401042000229025

Schlosberg, D. (2007) *Defining Environmental Justice: Theories, Movements and Nature*. Oxford: Oxford University Press.

Schlosberg, D. (2013) Theorising environmental justice: The expanding sphere of a discourse. *Environmental Politics*, 22(1): 37–55.

Schlosberg, D., & Collins, L. B. (2014) From environmental to climate justice: Climate change and the discourse of environmental justice. *Wiley Interdisciplinary Reviews: Climate Change*, 5(3): 359–74. https://doi.org/10.1002/wcc.275

Schnell, I. (2016) Glocal spatial lifestyle in Tel Aviv. *Geography Research Forum*, 24: 58–76.

Schrecker, T., & Bambra, C. (2015) *How Politics Makes Us Sick: Neoliberal Epidemics*. London: Palgrave Macmillan.

Schwanen, T., Hardill, I., & Lucas, S. (2012) Spatialities of ageing: The co-construction and co-evolution of old age and space. *Geoforum*, 43: 1291–95.

Schwiter, K., Strauss, K., & England, K. (2018) At home with the boss: Migrant live-in caregivers, social reproduction and constrained agency in the UK, Canada, Austria and Switzerland. *Transactions of the Institute of British Geographers*, 43: 462–76.

Scott, J. C. (1985) *Weapons of the Weak: Everyday Forms of Peasant Resistance*. London: Yale University Press.

Scott-Samuel, A., Bambra, C., Collins, C., Hunter, D., McCartney, G., & Smith, K. (2014) The impact of Thatcherism on health and well-being in Britain. *International Journal of Health Services*, 44(1): 53–71.

Scourfield, J., Dicks, B., Drakeford, M., & Davies, A. (2006) *Children, Place and Identity: Nation and Locality in Middle Childhood*. London: Routledge.

Scriven, R. (2014) Geographies of pilgrimage: Meaningful movements and embodied mobilities. *Geography Compass*, 8(4): 249–61.

Searle, B. A., & Smith, S. J. (eds.) (2010) *The Blackwell Companion to the Economics of Housing: The Housing Wealth of Nations*. Oxford: Wiley-Blackwell.

Selby, J., Dahi, O., Fröhlich, C., & Hulme, M. (2017) Climate change and the Syrian civil war revisited. *Political Geography*, 60: 232–44.

Sennett, R. (1990) *The Conscience of the Eye: The Design and Social Life of Cities*. London: Faber & Faber.

Shabazz, R. (2015) *Spatializing Blackness: Architectures of Confinement and Black Masculinity in Chicago*. Chicago: University of Illinois Press.

Shapiro, A. (2016) The mezzanine. *Space and Culture*, 19(4): 292–307.

Sharma, S. (2012) 'The church is . . . my family': Exploring the interrelationship between familial and religious practices and spaces. *Environment and Planning A: Economy and Space*, 44(4): 816–31.

Sharma, S., & Guest, M. (2013) Navigating religion between university and home: Christian students' experiences in English universities. *Social & Cultural Geography*, 14(1): 59–79.

Sharp, J. P., Routledge, P., Philo, C., & Paddison, R. (1999) *Entanglements of Power: Geographies of Domination/Resistance*. London: Routledge.

Shaw, R. (2014) Beyond night-time economy: Affective atmospheres of the urban night. *Geoforum*, 51: 87–95.

Shaw, R. (2015) 'Alive after five': Constructing the neoliberal night in Newcastle upon Tyne. *Urban Studies*, 52(3): 456–70.

Shaw, W. (2001) Way of whiteness: Negotiating settlement agendas in (post)colonial inner-Sydney. PhD dissertation, University of Melbourne.

Shaw, W. (2007) *Cities of Whiteness*. Oxford: Blackwell.

Shelton, T. (2017) Spatialities of data: Mapping social media 'beyond the geotag'. *Geojournal*, 82(4): 721–34.

Sheppard, E., Couclelis, H., Graham, S., Harrington, J. W., & Onsrud, H. (1999) Geographies of the information society. *International Journal of Geographical Information Science*, 13(8): 797–823.

Shevsky, E., & Williams, M. (1949) *The Social Areas of Los Angeles: Analysis and Typology*. Berkeley: University of California Press.

Shildrick, T. (2018) Lessons from Grenfell: Poverty propaganda, stigma and class power. *Sociological Review*, 66(4): 783–98.

Shildrick, T., & MacDonald, R. (2013) Poverty talk: How people experiencing poverty deny their poverty and why they blame the poor. *Sociological Review*, 61(2): 285–303.

Shortall, S., & Alston, M. (2016) To rural proof or not to rural proof: A comparative analysis. *Politics & Policy*, 44(2): 35–55.

Shove, E. (2009) Everyday practice and the production and consumption of time. In E. Shove, F. Trentmann & R. Wilk (eds.), *Time, Consumption and Everyday Life: Practice, Materiality and Culture*, pp. 17–35. Oxford: Berg.

Shove, E. (2010) Beyond the ABC: Climate change policy and theories of social change. *Environment and Planning A: Economy and Space*, 42(6): 1273–85.

Siebler, R. (2006) Public participation geographic information systems: A literature review and framework. *Annals of the Association of American Geographers*, 96: 491–507.

Sikor, T., & Newell, P. (2014) Globalizing environmental justice? *Geoforum*, 54(July): 151–57. https://doi.org/10.1016/J.GEOFORUM.2014.04.009

Silvey, R. (2006) Geographies of gender and migration: Spatializing social difference. *International Migration Review*, 40(1): 64–81.

Simmel, G. (1950) The metropolis and mental life. In K. Wolff & G. Simmel (eds.), *The Sociology of Georg Simmel*, pp. 409–24. Detroit: Free Press.

Simmonds, R. (2016) Antares: A scalable, efficient platform for stream, historic, combined and geospatial querying. PhD dissertation, Newcastle University.

Simonsen, K. (2008) Place as encounters: Practice, conjunction and co-existence. In J. Baerenholdt & B. Granas (eds.), *Mobility and Place: Enacting Northern European Peripheries*, pp. 13–27. Aldershot, UK: Ashgate.

Simpson, P. (2011) Street performance and the city: Public space, sociality, and intervening in the everyday. *Space and Culture*, 14(4): 415–30.

Siraj-Blatchford, I. (2010) Learning in the home and at school: How working-class children 'succeed against the odds'. *British Educational Research Journal*, 36(3): 463–82.

Skeggs, B. (1997) *Formations of Class and Gender: Becoming Respectable*. London: Sage.

Skelton, T., & Valentine, G. (1998) *Cool Places: Geographies of Youth Cultures*. London: Routledge.

Skinner, M. W., Cloutier, D., & Andrews, G. J. (2015) Geographies of ageing: Progress and possibilities after two decades of change. *Progress in Human Geography*, 39(6): 776–99.

Smith, A. D. (1998) *Nationalism and Modernism*. London: Routledge.

Smith, D. (2016) *Disability in the United Kingdom 2016*. Cambridge: Papworth Trust.

Smith, D. M. (1974) Who gets what where, and how: A welfare focus for human geography. *Geography*, 59(4): 289–97.

Smith, D. M. (2000) Social justice revisited. *Environment and Planning A: Economy and Space*, 32(7): 1149–62. https://doi.org/10.1068/a3258

Smith, D. P. (2009) 'Student geographies', urban restructuring, and the expansion of higher education. *Environment and Planning A: Economy and Space*, 41: 1795–1804.

Smith, D. P., & Mills, S. (2019) The 'youth-fullness' of youth geographies: 'Coming of age'? *Children's Geographies*, 17(1): 1–8.

Smith, J. A. (2009) *The Daddy Shift: How Stay-at-Home Dads, Breadwinning Moms, and Shared Parenting Are Transforming the American Family*. Boston: Beacon Press.

Smith, L. T. (2007) *Decolonizing Methodologies: Research and Indigenous Peoples*. New York: Zed Books.

Smith, N. (1984) *Uneven Development: Nature, Capital and the Production of Space*. Oxford: Blackwell.

Smith, N. (1987) Gentrification and the rent gap. *Annals of the Association of American Geographers*, 77(3): 462–65.

Smith, N. (1992) Geography, difference and the politics of scale. In J. Doherty, E. Graham & M. Malek (eds.), *Postmodernism and the Social Sciences*, pp. 57–79. London: Palgrave Macmillan.

Smith, S. J. (1986) *Crime, Space and Society*. Cambridge: Cambridge University Press.

Smith, S. J. (1999) Society-space. In P. Cloke, P. Crang & M. Goodwin (eds.), *Introducing Human Geographies*, pp. 212–23. London: Arnold.

Smith, S. J., Pain, R., Marston, S., & Jones, J. P. (2010) *Sage Handbook of Social Geographies*. London: Sage.

Smith, T., Noble, M., Noble, S., Wright, G., McLennan, D., & Plunkett, E. (2015) *The English Indices of Deprivation 2015: Research Report*. London: Department for Communities and Local Government.

Soja, E. W. (1980) The socio-spatial dialectic. *Annals of the Association of American Geographers*, 70(2): 207–25.

Soja, E., & Miguel Kanai, J. (2007) The urbanization of the world. In R. Burdett & D. Sudjic (eds.), *The Endless City*, pp. 54–69. London: Phaidon.

Sovacool, B. K., Burke, M., Baker, L., Kumar Kotikalapudi, C., & Wlokasm, H. (2017) New frontiers and conceptual frameworks for energy justice. *Energy Policy*, 105(June):

677–91. https://doi.org/10.1016/J.ENPOL .2017.03.005

Sparke, M. (2009) Nationalism. In D. Gregory, R. Johnston, G. Pratt, M. J. Watts & S. Whatmore (eds.), *The Dictionary of Human Geography*, pp. 488–90. Chichester, UK: Wiley-Blackwell.

Spinoza, B. (1677/2001) *Ethics*. London: Wordsworth Editions.

Spinoza, B. (2002) *Spinoza: Complete works*, trans. Samuel Shirley. Indianapolis: Hackett.

Springer, S. (forthcoming) Total liberation ecology: Integral anarchism, anthroparchy, and the violence of indifference. In S. Springer (ed.), *Undoing Human Supremacy*. Oakland, CA: PM Press.

Spyrou, S., & Christou, M. (eds.) (2014) *Children and Borders*. Basingstoke, UK: Palgrave Macmillan.

Srinivasan, K. (2019) Remaking more-than-human society: Thought experiments on street dogs as 'nature'. *Transactions of the Institute of British Geographers*, 44(2): 376–91.

Stanton, M. (2000) The rack and the web: The other city. In L. Lokko (ed.), *White Paper, Black Marks: Architecture, Race, Culture*, pp. 114–45. London: Athlone.

Steadman Jones, G. (1992) *Outcast London: A Study of the Relationship between Classes in Victorian Society*. Middlesex: Penguin.

Stewart, K. (1988) Nostalgia – A polemic. *Cultural Anthropology*, 3(3): 227–41.

Story, M. F. (1998) Maximizing usability: The prinicples of universal design. *Assistive Technology*, 10: 4–12.

Stratford, E., & Low, N. (2015) Young islanders, the meteorological imagination, and the art of geopolitical engagement. *Children's Geographies*, 13(2): 164–80.

Strauss, K. (2013) Unfree again: Social reproduction, flexible labour markets and the resurgence of gang labour in the UK. *Antipode*, 45(1): 180–97.

Strauss, K., & Meehan, K. (2015) New frontiers in life's work. In K. Meehan & K. Strauss (eds.), *Precarious Worlds: Contested Geographies of Social Reproduction*, pp. 1–22. Athens: University of Georgia Press.

Streeck, W. (2016) *How Will Capitalism End? Essays on a Failing System*. London: Penguin.

Stryker, S., & Whittle, S. (eds.) (2006) *The Transgender Studies Reader*. London: Taylor & Francis.

Stump, R. (2008) *The Geography of Religion: Faith, Place and Space*. Lanham, MD: Rowman & Littlefield.

Sue, D. W., Capodilupo, C. M., Torino, G. C., Bucceri, J. M., Holder, A. M. B., Nadal, K. L., & Esquilin, M. (2007) Racial microaggressions in everyday life: Implications for clinical practice. *American Psychologist*, 62(4): 271–86.

Sui, D. Z. (2013) GIS and urban studies: Positivism, post-positivism and beyond. *Urban Geography*, 15(3): 258–78.

Sultana, F. (2007) Reflexivity, positionality and participatory ethics: Negotiating fieldwork dilemmas in international research. *ACME: An International E-Journal for Critical Geographies*, 6(3): 374–85.

Sultana, F. (2009) Fluid lives: Subjectivities, gender and water in rural Bangladesh. *Gender, Place & Culture*, 16(4): 427–44.

Sultany, N. (2007) *The Legacy of Justice*, Aharon Barak: A critical review. *Harvard International Law Journal Online*, 48: 83–92.

Sumartojo, S. (2017) Making sense of everyday nationhood: Traces in the experiential world. In M. Skey & M. Antonsich (eds.), *Everyday Nationhood: Theorising Culture, Identity and Belonging after* Banal Nationalism, pp. 197–214. London: Palgrave Macmillan.

Sunday Times. (2018) Rich list 2018: The UK's richest people who made fortunes from the internet. 13 May. https://www.thetimes.co.uk/ article/sunday-times-rich-list-2018-richest-people-tech-5rczhlx2c

Sutko, D. M., & de Souza e Silva, A. S. (2011) Location-aware mobile media and urban sociability. *New Media and Society*, 13(5): 807–23.

Swyngedouw, E. (1997) Neither global nor local: 'Glocalization' and the politics of scale. In K. Cox (ed.), *Spaces of Globalization: Reasserting the Power of the Local*, pp. 137–66. New York: Guilford Press.

Swyngedouw, E. (2007) Technonatural revolutions: The scalar politics of Franco's hydrosocial dream for Spain, 1939–1975.

Transactions of the Institute of British Geographers, 32(1): 9–28.

Swyngedouw, E., & Heynen, N. C. (2003) Urban political ecology, justice and the politics of scale. *Antipode*, 35(5): 898–918. https://doi .org/10.1111/j.1467-8330.2003.00364.x

Tamas, S. (2011) *Life after Leaving: The Remains of Spousal Abuse.* Walnut Creek, CA: Left Coast Press.

Tan, Q. H. (2012) Flirtatious geographies: Clubs as spaces for the performance of affective heterosexualities. *Gender, Place & Culture*, 20(6): 718–36.

Tarrant, A. (2013) Grandfathering as spatio-temporal practice: Conceptualizing performances of ageing masculinities in contemporary familial carescapes. *Social & Cultural Geography*, 14(2): 192–210.

Taylor, C. (2009) Towards a geography of education. *Oxford Review of Education*, 35(5): 651–69.

Taylor, D. E. (2000) The rise of the environmental justice paradigm: Injustice framing and the social construction of environmental discourses. *American Behavioral Scientist*, 43(4): 508–80. https://doi .org/10.1177%2F0002764200043004003

Taylor, P. J. (1982) A materialist framework for political geography. *Transactions of the Institute of British Geographers*, 7(1): 15–34.

Tell MAMA. (2017) *A Constructed Threat: Identity, Prejudice and the Impact of Anti-Muslim Hatred.* Tell MAMA Annual Report 2016. London: Tell MAMA.

Tell MAMA. (2018) *Beyond the Incident: Outcomes for Victims of Anti-Muslim Prejudice.* Tell MAMA Annual Report 2017. London: Tell MAMA.

Temper, L., Demaria, F., Scheidel, A., Del Bene, D., & Martínez-Alier, J. (2018) The Global Environmental Justice Atlas (EJAtlas): Ecological distribution conflicts as forces for sustainability. *Sustainability Science*, 13(3): 573–84. https://doi.org/10.1007/s11625-018 -0563-4

Temper, L., & Martínez-Alier, J. (2013) The God of the Mountain and Godavarman: Net present value, Indigenous territorial rights and sacredness in a bauxite mining conflict in India. *Ecological Economics*, 96 (December): 79–87. https://doi.org/10.1016/ J.ECOLECON.2013.09.011

Thiem, C. H. (2009) Thinking through education: The geographies of contemporary educational restructuring. *Progress in Human Geography*, 33(2): 154–73.

Thien, D. (2005) After or beyond feeling? A consideration of affect and emotion in geography. *Area*, 37(4): 450–54.

Thomas, C. (1999) *Female Forms: Experiencing and Understanding Disability.* Buckingham, UK: Open University Press.

Thompson, L., Pearce, J., & Barnett, R. (2007) Moralising geographies: Stigma, smoking islands and responsible subjects. *Area*, 39(4): 508–17.

Thompson, M. (2017) Migration decision-making: A geographical imaginations approach. *Area*, 49(1): 77–84.

Thompson, M. (2019) Everything changes to stay the same: Persistent global health inequalities amidst new therapeutic opportunities and mobilities for Filipino nurses. *Mobilities*, 14(1): 38–53. https://doi.or g/10.1080/17450101.2018.1518841

Thornicroft, G., Mehta, N., Clement, S., Evans-Lacko, S., Doherty, M., Rose, D., Koschorke, M., Shidhaye, R., O'Reilly, C., & Henderson, C. (2016) Evidence for effective interventions to reduce mental-health-related stigma and discrimination. *Lancet* 387: 1123–32. https:// doi.org/10.1016/S0140-6736(15)00298-6

Thorns, D. (2002) *The Transformation of Cities: Urban Theory and Urban Life.* Basingstoke, UK: Palgrave.

Thrift, N. (1997) The still point. In S. Pile & M. Keith (eds.), *Geographies of Resistance*, pp. 124–51. London: Routledge.

Thrift, N. (2005) But malice afterthought: Cities and the natural history of hatred. *Transactions of the Institute of British Geographers*, 30(2): 133–50.

Thrift, N., & Dewsbury, J.-D. (2000) Dead geographies and how to make them live. *Environment and Planning D: Society and Space*, 18: 411–32.

Tierney, W. G., & Venegas, K. M. (2006) Fictive kin and social capital: The role of peer groups in applying and paying for college. *American Behavioural Scientist*, 49(12): 1687–1702.

Till, J. (2014) Scarcity and agency. *Journal of Architectural Education*, 68(1): 9–11.

Timar, J. (2004) More than 'Anglo-American', it is 'Western': Hegemony in geography from a Hungarian perspective. *Geoforum*, 35(5): 533–38.

Timms, C. (2017) In Britain, it's not just the train toilets that disabled people can't get into. *Guardian*, 5 January. https://www.theguardian.com/commentisfree/2017/jan/05/train-toilets-disabled-people-anne-wafula-strike

Tishkoff, S. A., & Kidd, K. K. (2004) Implications of biogeography of human populations for 'race' and medicine. *Nature Genetics*, 36(11s): S21–S27.

Tivers, J. (1978) How the other half lives: The geographical study of women. *Area*, 10: 302–6.

Tolia-Kelly, D. (2010) The geographies of cultural geography I: Identities, bodies and race. *Progress in Human Geography*, 34(3): 358–67.

Tolia-Kelly, D. P. (2011) Narrating the postcolonial landscape: Archaeologies of race at Hadrian's Wall. *Transactions of the Institute of British Geographers*, 36(1): 71–88.

Tönnies, F. (2002) *Community and Society: Gemeinschaft und Gesellschaft*, trans. & ed. Charles Price Loomis. New York: Courier Dover.

Torres, R., Popke, M., Jeffrey, E., & Hapke, H. M. (2006) The South's silent bargain: Rural restructuring, Latino labor and the ambiguities of migrant experience. In H. A. Smith & O. J. Furuseth (eds.), *Latinos in the New South*, pp. 37–68. Burlington, VT: Ashgate.

Towers, G. (2000) Applying the political geography of scale: Grassroots strategies and environmental justice. *Professional Geographer*, 52(1): 23–36. https://doi.org/10.1111/0033-0124.00202org/10.1111/0033-0124.00202

Trewartha, G. T. (1953) A case for population geography. *Annals of the Association of American Geographers*, 43(2): 71–97. doi:10.1080/00045605309352106

Trottier, D. (2014) Crowdsourcing CCRV surveillance on the internet. *Information, Communication and Society*, 17(5): 609–26.

Trudeau, D., & McMorran, C. (2011) The geographies of marginalization. In V. Del Casino, M. E. Thomas, P. Cloke & R. Panelli (eds.), *A Companion to Social Geography*, pp. 437–53. Oxford: Blackwell.

Turan, Z. (2011) Material memories of the Ottoman Empire: Armenian and Greek objects of legacy. In K. Phillips & G. Reyes (eds.), *Global Memoryscapes: Contesting Remembrance in a Transnational Age*, pp. 173–94. Tuscaloosa: University of Alabama Press.

Tyler, I. (2015) Classificatory struggles: Class, culture and inequality in neoliberal times. *Sociological Review*, 63(2): 493–511.

UNFPA. (2017) World population trends. 29 August. https://www.unfpa.org/world-population-trends

United Nations. (2017) Highlights. In *International Migration Report 2017* (ST/ESA/SER.A/404). https://www.un.org/en/development/desa/population/migration/publications/migrationreport/docs/MigrationReport2017_Highlights.pdf

UPIAS. (1976) *Fundamental Principles of Disability*. London: Union of the Physically Impaired Against Segregation.

Urry, J. (2002) The global complexities of September 11th. *Theory, Culture and Society*, 19(4): 57–69.

Valdivia, G. (2005) On Indigeneity, change, and representation in the north-eastern Ecuadorian Amazon. *Environment and Planning A: Economy and Space*, 37: 285–303. https://doi.org/10.1068/a36182

Valentine, G. (1989) The geography of women's fear. *Area*, 21(4): 385–90.

Valentine, G. (1993) (Hetero)Sexing space: Lesbian perception and experiences of everyday spaces. *Environment and Planning D: Society and Space*, 11(4): 284–413.

Valentine, G. (2001) *Social Geographies: Space and Society*. London: Routledge.

Valentine, G. (2004) *Public Space and the Culture of Childhood*. Aldershot, UK: Ashgate.

Valentine, G. (2007) Theorizing and researching intersectionality: A challenge for feminist geography. *Professional Geographer*, 59(1): 10–21.

Valentine, G. (2008) Living with difference: Reflections on geographies of encounter. *Progress in Human Geography*, 32(3): 323–37.

Valentine, G., & Holloway, S. (2002) Cyberkids? Exploring children's identities and social networks in on-line and off-line worlds. *Annals of the Association of American Geographers*, 92(2): 302–19.

Valentine, G., & Skelton, T. (2003) Finding oneself, losing oneself: The lesbian and gay scene as a paradoxical space. *International Journal of Urban and Regional Research*, 27(4): 849–66.

Valentine, G., Vanderbeck, R. M., Sadgrove, J., Andersson, J., & Ward, K. (2016) Transnational religious networks: Sexuality and the changing power geometries of the Anglican community. *Transactions of the Institute of British Geographers*, 38(1): 50–64.

Valentine, G., & Waite, L. (2012) Negotiating difference through everyday encounters: The case of sexual orientation and religion and belief. *Antipode*, 44(2): 474–92.

Valins, O. (2003) Defending identities or segregating communities? Faith-based schooling and the UK Jewish community. *Geoforum*, 34(2): 235–47.

Van Blerk, L. (2008) Poverty, migration and sex work: Youth transitions in Ethiopia. *Area*, 40(2): 245–53.

Van Blerk, L. (2013) New street geographies: The impact of urban governance on the mobilities of Cape Town's street youth. *Urban Studies*, 50(3): 556–73.

Vanderbeck, R. M. (2008) Reaching critical mass? Theory, politics, and the culture of debate in children's geographies. *Area*, 40: 393–400.

Vanderbeck, R., & Worth, N. (2015) *Intergenerational Space*. London: Routledge.

van Doorn, N. (2011) Digital spaces, material traces: How matter comes to matter in online performances of gender, sexuality and embodiment. *Media, Culture and Society*, 33(4): 531–47.

Van Hoven, B., & Horschelmann, K. (2005) *Spaces of Masculinities*. London: Routledge.

van Lanen, S. (2020) Encountering austerity in deprived urban neighbourhoods: Local geographies and the emergence of austerity in the lifeworld of urban youth. *Geoforum*, 110: 220–31.

Veal, C. (2016) A choreographic notebook: Methodological developments in qualitative geographical research. *Cultural Geographies*, 23(2): 221–45.

Vidal de la Blache, P. (1926) *Principles of Human Geography*. London: Constable.

VTO. (2003) Vindolanda Tablets Online website. http://vindolanda.csad.ox.ac.uk/index.shtml

Waitt, G., & Gorman-Murray, A. (2008) Camp in the country: Re-negotiating sexuality and gender through a rural lesbian and gay festival. *Journal of Tourism and Cultural Change*, 6(3): 185–207.

Walby, S. (1990) *Theorising Patriarchy*. London: John Wiley.

Walby, K., Spencer, D., & Hunt, A. (2012) Introduction. In D. Spencer, K. Walby & A. Hunt (eds.), *Emotions Matter*, pp. 3–8. Toronto: University of Toronto Press.

Walker, G. (2009) Globalizing environmental justice. *Global Social Policy: An Interdisciplinary Journal of Public Policy and Social Development*, 9(3): 355–82. https://doi.org/10.1177/1468018109343640

Walker, G. (2012) *Environmental Justice: Concepts, Evidence and Politics*. London: Routledge.

Walker, G. (2014) The dynamics of energy demand: Change, rhythm and synchronicity. *Energy Research & Social Science*, 1: 49–55. https://doi.org/10.1016/j.erss.2014.03.012

Walker, G., & Bulkeley, H. (2006) Geographies of environmental justice. *Geoforum*, 37(5): 655–59. https://doi.org/10.1016/J.GEOFORUM.2005.12.002

Walker, L. (1995) More than just skin-deep: Fem(me)ininity and the subversion of identity. *Gender, Place & Culture*, 2(1): 71–76.

Walton, H., Dajnak, D., Beevers, S., Williams, M., Watkiss, P., & Hunt, A. (2015) *Understanding the Health Impacts of Air Pollution in London*. London: Kings College.

Warlenius, R. (2018) Decolonizing the atmosphere: The climate justice movement on climate debt. *Journal of Environment & Development*, 27(2): 131–55. https://doi.org/10.1177/1070496517744593

Warner, M. (1993) *Fear of a Queer Planet: Queer Politics and Social Theory*. Minneapolis: University of Minnesota Press.

Warren, A. (2016) Crafting masculinities: Gender, culture and emotion at work in the surfboard industry. *Gender, Place & Culture*, 23(1): 36–54.

Warren, S. (2017) Pluralising the walking interview: Researching (im)mobilities with

Muslim women. *Social & Cultural Geography*, 18(6): 786–807.

Waters, J. L. (2006) Geographies of cultural capital: Education, international migration and family strategies between Hong Kong and Canada. *Transactions of the Institute of British Geographers*, 31(2): 179–92.

Waters, J. L. (2017) Education unbound? Enlivening debates with a mobilities perspective on learning. *Progress in Human Geography*, 41(3): 279–98.

Waters, J. L. (2018) Geographies of education. *Oxford Bibliographies*. http://www.oxfordbib liographies.com/view/document/obo-9780 199874002/obo-9780199874002-0182.xml

Watson, A., & Huntington, O. H. (2008) They're here – I can feel them: The epistemic spaces of Indigenous and Western knowledges. *Social & Cultural Geography*, 9: 257–81. https://doi.org/10.1080/14649360801990488

Watson, N., Roulstone, A., & Thomas, C. (eds.) (2012) *Routledge Handbook of Disability Studies*. London: Routledge.

Watson, S. (2005) Symbolic space of difference: Contesting the Eruv in Barnet, London and Tenafly, New Jersey. *Environment and Planning D: Society and Space*, 23(4): 597–613.

Watt, P. (1998) Going out of town: Youth, race, and place in the south east of England. *Environment and Planning D: Society and Space*, 16(6): 687–703.

Watt, P. (2009) Housing stock transfers, regeneration and state-led gentrification in London. *Urban Policy and Research*, 27(3): 229–42.

Webber, R., & Burrows, R. (2013) Life in an alpha territory: Discontinuity and conflict in an elite London 'village'. *Urban Studies*, 53(15): 3139–54.

Webber, R., & Burrows, R. (2018) *The Predictive Postcode: The Geodemographic Classification of British Society*. London: Sage.

Weber, C. (2011) I am an American. http:// iamanamericanproject.com

Weeks, J. (1995) *Invented Moralities: Sexual Values in an Age of Uncertainty*. Cambridge: Polity Press.

Weeks, J. (1998) The sexual citizen. *Theory, Culture and Society*, 15(3–4): 35–52.

Wharf, B. (2018) Digital technologies and reconfiguration of urban space. In B. Wharf (ed.), *Routledge Handbook on Spaces of Urban Politics*, pp. 96–106. London: Taylor & Francis.

Whatmore, S. (2002) *Hybrid Geographies: Natures, Cultures, Spaces*. London: Sage.

Wheeler, R. (2017) Local history as productive nostalgia? Change, continuity and sense of place in rural England. *Social & Cultural Geography*, 18(4): 466–86.

White, R. J. (2015) Animal geographies, anarchist praxis, and critical animal studies. In K. Gillespie & R. Collard (eds.), *Critical Animal Geographies*, pp. 31–47. London: Routledge.

Whitehead, M. (2014) *Environmental Transformations: A Geography of the Anthropocene*. London: Routledge.

Whitehead, M., Jones, R., Lilley, R., Howell, R., & Pykett, J. (2019) Neuroliberalism: Cognition, context, and the geographical bounding of rationality. *Progress in Human Geography*, 43(4): 632–49. https://doi .org/10.1177/0309132518777624

WHO. (2008) *Commission on the Social Determinants of Health: Closing the Gap in a Generation*. Geneva: World Health Organization.

Wiesel, I., & Bigby, C. (2016) Mainstream, inclusionary, and convivial places: Locating encounters between people with and without intellectual disabilities. *Geographical Review*, 106(2): 201–14.

Wilford, J. (2010) Sacred archipelagos: Geographies of secularization. *Progress in Human Geography*, 43(3): 328–48.

Wilkinson, E., & Ortega-Alcázar, I. (2019) The right to be weary? Endurance and exhaustion in austere times. *Transactions of the Institute of British Geographers*, 44: 155–67.

Wilkinson, R., & Pickett, K. (2009) *The Spirit Level: Why More Equal Societies Almost Always Do Better*. London: Allen Lane.

Williams, A. (ed.) (2017) *Therapeutic Landscapes*. London: Routledge.

Williams, G., & Mawdsley, E. (2006) Postcolonial environmental justice: Government and governance in India. *Geoforum*, 37(5): 660–70. https://doi .org/10.1016/J.GEOFORUM.2005.08.003

Williams, Z. (2019) Half-baked: What Greggs' vegan sausage roll says about Brexit Britain. *Guardian*, 7 January. https://www .theguardian.com/lifeandstyle/2019/jan/07/

greggs-vegan-sausage-roll-brexit-britain -culture-wars

Willis, P. (1977) *Learning to Labour: How Working-Class Kids Get Working-Class Jobs.* New York: Columbia University Press.

Wilson, H. (2011) Passing propinquities in the multicultural city: The everyday encounters of bus passengering. *Environment and Planning A: Economy and Space*, 43(3): 634–49.

Wilson, H. (2014) Multicultural learning: Parent encounters with difference in a Birmingham primary school. *Transactions of the Institute of British Geographers*, 39(1): 102–14.

Wilson, H. (2017) On geography and encounter: Bodies, borders, and difference. *Progress in Human Geography*, 41(4): 451–71.

Wilson, H., & Darling, J. (2016) The possibilities of encounter. In J. Darling & H. Wilson (eds.), *Encountering the City: Urban Encounters from Accra to New York*, pp. 1–24. Abingdon, UK: Routledge.

Wilton, R., Schormans, A. F., & Marquis, N. (2018) Shopping, social inclusion and the urban geographies of people with intellectual disability. *Social & Cultural Geography*, 19(2): 230–52.

Winders, J., & Smith, B. E. (2019) Social reproduction and capitalist production: A genealogy of dominant imaginaries. *Progress in Human Geography*, 43(5): 871–89. https:// doi.org/10.1177/0309132518791730

Wirth, L. (1938) Urbanism as a way of life. *American Journal of Sociology*, 44(1): 1–24.

Women and Geography Study Group. (1984) *Geography and Gender: An Introduction to Feminist Geography*. London: Hutchison.

Women and Geography Study Group. (1997/2014) *Feminist Geographies: Explorations in Diversity and Difference.* London: Routledge.

Wood, B. (2012) Crafted within liminal spaces: Young people's everyday politics. *Political Geography*, 31(6): 337–46.

Woods, M. (2007) Engaging the global countryside: Globalization, hybridity and the reconstitution of rural place. *Progress in Human Geography*, 31(4): 485–507.

Woods, M. (2018) Precarious rural cosmopolitanism: Negotiating globalization, migration and diversity in Irish small towns. *Journal of Rural Studies*, 64: 164–76.

World Inequality Lab. (2018) *World Inequality Report 2018.* https://wir2018.wid.world/files/ download/wir2018-full-report-english.pdf

Worth, N. (2011) Evaluating life maps as a versatile method for lifecourse geographies. *Area*, 43(4): 405–12.

Wright, M. (2008) Gender and geography: Knowledge and activism across the intimately global. *Progress in Human Geography*, 33(3): 379–86.

Wright, M. W. (2010) Geography and gender: Feminism and a feeling of justice. *Progress in Human Geography*, 34(6): 818–27. https://doi .org/10.1177/0309132510362931

Wylie, J. (2006) Depths and folds: On landscape and the gazing subject. *Environment and Planning D: Society and Space*, 24(4): 519–35.

Wyly, E., & Hammel, D. (2004) Gentrification, segregation, and discrimination in the American urban system. *Environment and Planning A: Economy and Space*, 36(7): 1215–41.

Yarker, S. (2017) Reconceptualising comfort as part of local belonging: The use of confidence, commitment and irony. *Social & Cultural Geography*, 20(4): 534–50. doi:10.10 80/14649365.2017.1373301

Young, I. M. (1990) *Justice and the Politics of Difference.* Princeton, NJ: Princeton University Press.

Young, L., & Barrett, H. (2001) Adapting visual methods: Action research with Kampala street children. *Area*, 33(2): 141–52.

Zedner, L. (2009) *Security*. Oxford: Routledge.

Zimmerer, K. S. (2015) Environmental governance through 'speaking like an Indigenous state' and respatializing resources: Ethical livelihood concepts in Bolivia as versatility or verisimilitude? *Geoforum*, 64: 314–24. https://doi.org/10.1016/j.geoforum .2013.07.004

Zook, M., Dodge, M., Aoyama, Y., & Townsend, A. (2004) New digital geographies: Information, communication, and place. In S. D. Brunn, S. L. Cutter & J. Harrington (eds.), *Geography and Technology*, pp. 155–76. Dordrecht: Springer.

Zukin, S. (1989) *Loft Living: Culture and Capital in Urban Change.* New Brunswick, NJ: Rutgers University Press.

INDEX

Page numbers of figures and tables are italicised.

Faria, C., 207

familism, 111

family: family-friendly work, employer provision of, 297; kinship networks, 291–92

farming. *See* agriculture

favela settlements, 266

fear, 10, 80, 125, 135, 160, 168, 170, 204, 253, 353

feeling: preindividual constitution of, 128–29. *See also* emotion/emotional geographies

femininity, 126, 166, 168, 171, 174

feminism/feminist geographies, *31*, 33, 163, 171, *249*; and everyday geographies, 122; feminist critiques, 28; feminist emotional geographies, 125–26; and intersectionality, 208. *See also* Black feminism/Black feminist thought; emotion/emotional geographies

Ferguson, Missouri, 74–75

'fictive kin', 254–55

fieldnotes, 76, 105

Filipino nurses, *273*

financial crash of 2008, 180, 216, 234

Finkelstein, Liz, 184

Finkelstein, Vic, 184

flesh: and digital focuses, 328–29. *See also* body/bodies

flooding, 337

flourishing, 26, 255, *293*, 333, 336, 347. *See also* well-being

flows: global, 112–13; global cities and, 269; knowledge, 264; spaces of, 68, *261*, 264

focus group transcripts, *46*

food, 27, 77, 277, 278, 351–62; 'alternative', 358; embodied food practices, 359; encounters with, *281*, 289; and everyday social, 356–59; food tastes and gut reactions of 'situated bodies', 355; framing value, 356–58; and more-than-human social, 360; researching food choices, 354–55; researching food production, 353–54; researching food systems, 353–56; situating value, 358; 'slow food' movement, 54–55; and strategic ignorance, 356

Fordism, 293, 298

fortress architecture, *261*

fossil fuel extraction, 340

Foucault, Michel, 29, 315

framing value, 356–58

France, 150, 164–65, 226, 229, 236, 317. *See also* Paris

freedom, 6, 99, *110*, 315

free market capitalism. *See* capitalism; neoliberalism

free speech, 137

Freire, Paulo, 37

friendship, 159, 188, 255, 296, 328

Fuglerud, O., 76

Fussey, P., 263

future: research in, 318–20; social geographies in, 77–78. *See also* Anthropocene era; sustainability

Fyfe, Nick, 260

G20 Summit 2010, *263*

Gale, R., 145, 149

Gallagher, Aisling, 295

Galton, Francis, 316

Gao, Q., 68

Garfinkel, Harold, 118, 303

Gaskell, Elizabeth, 109

gated communities, 75, *261*, 262

gay and lesbian geographies. *See* lesbian and gay (LGBTQ) geographies

Geiger, S., 15, 47

Gemeinschaft, 109–10, *110*

gender, 162–72; bias, 164–65; cis-gender, 168, 206; coloniality of, 167; defining, 165–67; differences, 171; within digital spaces, 181; divisions, 162–63, 171, 295, 297; equality, 16, 163–64, 170–71; gender-diverse geographies, 167–70, 172; identity, 170; inequality and, 163–65, 171; masculinities, 169–71; and migration, 273–74; migration recruitment practices, gendered, *275*; as nonbinary, 172; oppression and, 163–64, 167, 171, 172; pay gap, 164, *165*; social difference, intersection with other forms of, 172; welfare regimes, national gendered, 299–300. *See also* intersectionality; sex; sexuality/sexualities, geographies of

'gender-neutral' toilets, *169*, 170

generations: intergenerationality, 197–99; intergenerational justice, 234. *See also* age; sustainability

gentrification, 74, 156, 189, 213, 215, 220, 234, 261; 'super-gentrification', 227

geodemographics, 223, 230–32, *233*, 234; classification of localities, 223

geographical information systems (GISs), *40*, 250, 323

geopolitics, 62, 195, 305

Germany, 108, 109, 214, 226, 229, 277; Berlin, 178; Nazi, 139

Gesellschaft, 109–10, *110*

Gesler, Wil, 241

Ghana, *281*

Gibson, William, 324

Giddens, Anthony, 152

gig economies, 329

Gilmore, Ruth, 20

Glass, Ruth, 234

Gleeson, Brendan, 185

global cities, 82, 153, 235, 260, *261*; policing, 264–65, 269

global citizenship, 99, 159

global flows, 112–13

global inequalities, 87; changing shape of, 223–25. *See also* inequality/inequalities

global/intimate, 9, 28

globalisation, 54, 112, 117, 141, 175, 264, 280; antiglobalisation movements, 82; environmental justice and, 342–43; of HE, *249*; of knowledge, *249*; neoliberal, 75; scale and, 63, 66, 70–72; and social change, 70–72; sustainability and, 332, 335

All of the contributors to this book are part of the Newcastle Social Geographies Collective. The majority are based within or affiliated to the Geographies of Social Change Research Cluster in the Geography subject area of the School of Geography, Politics and Sociology at Newcastle University. Some are based in neighbouring disciplines or fields at Newcastle University but engage with social geographies in their research or identify with the subfield in different ways.

Rachel Pain is professor of human geography

Peter Hopkins is professor of social geography

Clare Bambra is professor of public health

Matthew C. Benwell is senior lecturer in human geography

Matej Blazek is senior lecturer in human geography

Carl Bonner-Thompson completed a PhD at Newcastle University and is lecturer in human geography at the University of Brighton

Alastair Bonnett is professor of social geography

Alessandro Boussalem is a doctoral student

Roger Burrows is professor of cities

Elaine Campbell is professor of criminology

Leah Chan is a doctoral student

Alison Copeland is lecturer in human geography

Niall Cunningham is lecturer in human geography

Robin Finlay is a postdoctoral research associate in geography

Quan Gao recently completed a PhD at Newcastle University and is a postdoctoral research fellow at Singapore Management University

Joe Herbert is a doctoral student

Julia Heslop is a postdoctoral research fellow in architecture

Suzanne Hocknell is a postdoctoral research associate in geography

Nathar Iqbal recently completed a PhD at Newcastle University

Al James is professor of economic geography

Helen Jarvis is professor of social geography engagement

Craig Jones is lecturer in human geography

Wen Lin is senior lecturer in human geography

Ruth McAreavey is reader in sociology

Janice McLaughlin is professor of sociology

Graeme Mearns is human geographer and lecturer in media, culture and heritage

Kawtar Najib is a visiting research fellow

Anoop Nayak is professor of social and cultural geography

Raksha Pande is senior lecturer in critical development studies

Gareth Powells is senior lecturer in human geography

Ruth Raynor is lecturer in urban planning

Lottie Rhodes is a doctoral student

Michael J. Richardson is lecturer in human geography

Ged Ridley is a doctoral student

Stefan Rzedzian recently completed a PhD at Newcastle University

Robert Shaw is senior lecturer in human geography

Katy Smith is a doctoral student

Alison Stenning is professor of social and economic geography

Simon Tate is professor of pedagogy in higher education

Maddy Thompson completed a PhD at Newcastle University and is now a postdoctoral research fellow at Keele University

Lightning Source UK Ltd.
Milton Keynes UK
UKHW051256240822
407769UK00017B/395